CW00751596

TUPE: Law and Practice

TUPE: Law and Practice

Robert Upex, MA, LLM(Cantab), ACIArb, FRSA, of
the Middle Temple, Barrister,
Professor of Law at the University of Surrey,
sometime Chairman of Employment Tribunals for
England and Wales (part-time).

Michael Ryley MA (Oxon), Solicitor,
Partner, Pinsent Masons.

JORDANS

2006

Published by
Jordan Publishing Limited
21 St Thomas Street
Bristol BS1 6JS

Whilst the publishers and the authors have taken every care in preparing the material included in this work, any statements made as to the legal or other implications of particular transactions are made in good faith purely for general guidance and cannot be regarded as a substitute for professional advice. Consequently, no liability can be accepted for loss or expense incurred as a result of relying in particular circumstances on statements made in this work.

© Jordan Publishing Limited 2006

Crown copyright material is reproduced under Class Licence Number C01W0000451 with the permission of the Controller of HMSO and the Queen's Printer for Scotland.

All rights reserved. No part of this publication may be reproduced, stored in a retrieval system, or transmitted in any way or by any means, including photocopying or recording, without the written permission of the copyright holder, application for which should be addressed to the publisher.

British Library Cataloguing-in-Publication Data

A catalogue record for this book is available from the British Library.

ISBN 978 0 85308 862 2

Typeset by Etica Press Limited
Printed in Great Britain by Antony Rowe Limited, Chippenham, Wilts

PREFACE

It is almost 25 years since the Transfer of Undertakings (Protection of Employment) Regulations (TUPE) first saw the light of day. The original Regulations were introduced on 7 December 1981 by the then Conservative administration with what it described as 'a remarkable lack of enthusiasm', to a chorus of concerns from MPs on both of sides of the House of Commons as to whether they went too far or not far enough. The Under-Secretary of State responsible for introducing them played down the drastic effect some feared they would have and expressed the view that they would have limited effect. The history of the ensuing 25 years suggests otherwise. Over that period the growing jurisprudence in the European Court of Justice has pointed to the wide scope of the Acquired Rights Directive (Council Directive 77/187/EEC, subsequently amended and now consolidated in Directive 2001/23/EC), against which TUPE falls to be interpreted. TUPE has given rise to a considerable number of important decisions of the Court of Appeal and the House of Lords.

From the start, however, this area of the law has been bedevilled with uncertainty, to the point where one judge commented latterly: 'The Law is in a state of critical uncertainty; it is almost impossible to give accurate advice to [those] involved in possible transfers with any degree of certainty.' Most practitioners would readily agree. In order to address a number of these concerns and in order to give effect to revisions to the Directive agreed in the summer of 1998, the Government embarked upon a lengthy process of consultation and consideration, finally resulting in a new set of TUPE Regulations, which came into effect on 6 April 2006.

The idea for this book was originally conceived in 2003 when the Government first put a draft of the new Regulations out for consultation but progress was halted as various iterations of the draft Regulations were released and further consultation took place. The delay in finalising the Regulations was largely due to concerns about the most appropriate way to deal with pensions in the context of TUPE. This was ultimately resolved in the Pensions Act 2004. Eventually, in early 2006, the final draft was published and the long-awaited introduction of the new TUPE Regulations happened.

This book sets the changes introduced by TUPE 2006 into the context of the Directives and the jurisprudence of the ECJ. It thus looks in detail at the opinions given by that Court on references from national courts. It also considers in detail many decisions of the Employment Appeal Tribunal, the Court of Appeal and the House of Lords relating to the 1981 Regulations. It thus aims to give a complete account of the law leading up to the 2006 Regulations. Bearing in mind that many of the provisions of the new Regulations arise from decisions of the ECJ or changes brought about by the revisions to the 1977 Directive, and that some of the changes are in response to decisions of the domestic courts, it is important to understand this background when approaching the new Regulations. We hope, therefore, that this book will give a compendious account both of the law which has given rise to the Regulations and of the changes brought about by the Regulations.

We are grateful to our publishers for their patience as we have struggled to meet deadlines; we are also grateful to them for compiling the Tables and Index. Nothing sparks debate amongst employment lawyers quite like TUPE and we would not want to omit acknowledgment of the many valuable contributions which colleagues have made to our thinking on this subject, many of which have found their way into these pages.

We have based our exposition of the law on our understanding of the materials available to us as at 15 September 2006.

Robert Upex
Old Square Chambers

Michael Ryley
Pinsent Masons

CONTENTS

Appendices

Legislation

Guidance notes, etc

Precedents, etc195

TABLE OF CASES

TABLE OF STATUTES

Paragraph references printed in **bold** type indicate where the Act is set out in part or in full.

TABLE OF
STATUTORY INSTRUMENTS

Paragraph references printed in **bold** type indicate where the instrument is set out in part or in full.

Chapter 1

INTRODUCTION

THE POSITION AT COMMON LAW

1.1   Although there has been legislation governing changes in the relationship between employer and employee for some considerable time now, it is important to remember that the basic principles of the employment relationship were established at a time when intervention by the legislature was peripheral. The first statutory intervention took the form of the Contracts of Employment Act 1963. That was followed by the Redundancy Payments Act 1965, which was the first statute to make any significant attempt to establish what Lord Wedderburn has called a 'floor of rights'. These acts have found their way, albeit in a modified form, into the current legislation, the Employment Rights Act 1996 (ERA 1996).

1.2   The emphasis of the common law has tended to be on the notion of personal service. If one looks at the test used to establish whether a person is an employee or not, the so-called 'multiple' test (and its variants), one can see the emphasis laid upon personal service. In *Ready Mixed Concrete (South East) Ltd v Minister of Pensions and National Insurance*,[1] McKenna J, in his classic formulation of the test, stated that one of the conditions that needed to be fulfilled for a contract of employment to exist was that:

> 'The servant [sic] agrees that in consideration of a wage or other remuneration he will provide his own work and skill in the performance of some service for his master.'

1.3   The idea that personal service is an essential part of the employment relationship remains important to this day and one can see it in recent decisions relating to employment status. So, for example, in *Express & Echo Publications v Tanton*,[2] the Court of Appeal said that the obligation to provide service personally is an 'irreducible minimum' of a contract of employment.

1.4   It is from the context of the judges' regard to the notion of personal service that the common law's attitude to changes of employer has arisen. This can be seen in the House of Lords decision in *Nokes v Doncaster Amalgamated Collieries Ltd*,[3] in the context of the dissolution of a company. The decision in

---

1   [1968] 2 QB 497. See at 515.
2   [1999] ICR 409, at 699–700. See also *Nethermere (St Neots) Ltd v Gardiner* [1984] ICR 612, at 623; *Clarke v Oxfordshire Health Authority* [1988] IRLR 125; *MacFarlane v Glasgow City Council* [2001] IRLR 7; and *Staffordshire Sentinel Newspapers Ltd v Potter* [2004] IRLR 752.
3   [1940] AC 1014.

that case was regarded as determinative of the common law position, until encroachments were made by the enactment of provisions relating to the preservation of an employee's continuity of employment where there was a 'change of employer'. The facts of the *Nokes* case, in brief, were that the colliery company which employed the employee was dissolved and an order was made under a provision of the Companies Act 1929 transferring its property, rights and liabilities to another company, Doncaster Amalgamated Collieries. The question was whether the effect of the court order was to transfer the employee to the company. The House of Lords, by a majority,[4] answered the question in the negative. In the speeches given by the majority one can see the importance attached by their Lordships to the importance of the idea that an employee should be free to choose his or her employer. Viscount Simon LC said:[5]

> '[A] free citizen, in the exercise of his freedom, is entitled to choose the employer whom he promises to serve, so that the right to his services cannot be transferred from the employer to another without his assent.'

Lord Atkin's language was more robust. He said:[6]

> '[I]t appears to me astonishing that ... power should be given to a court or to anyone else to transfer a man without his knowledge, and possibly against his will, from the service of one person to the service of another. I had fancied that ingrained in the personal status of a citizen under our laws was the right to choose for himself whom he would serve, and that this choice constituted the main difference between a servant and a serf ...'

1.5   Thus, until the advent of statutory provisions, the common law position was that an employee could not be transferred to a new employer without his or her express agreement and that a transfer without such agreement would be void. It is worth considering the extent to which the state of the present law can be said to reflect that position.

STATUTORY DEVELOPMENTS BEFORE 1981

1.6   The position at common law outlined in the previous section continued to obtain until, and even after, the enactment of legislation governing an employee's continuity of employment in the event of a change of ownership of a business. The first statutory provision to deal with the preservation of an employee's continuity of employment in such an event was Sch 1 to the Contracts of Employment Act 1963 (CEA 1963).[7] The Redundancy Payments Act 1965 provided[8] that computation of the period of continuous employment (including employment with a previous employer) was to be in accordance with Sch 1 to CEA 1963. This last provision was subsequently re-enacted in Sch 1 to the Contracts of Employment Act 1972[9] and consolidated into Sch 13,

---

4   Lord Romer dissenting.
5   [1940] AC 1014, at 1020.
6   [1940] AC 1014, at 1026.
7   Paragraph 10(2).
8   In s 8.
9   Paragraph 9(2).

para 17(2) to the Employment Protection (Consolidation) Act 1978 (EP(C)A 1978). The Redundancy Payments Act 1965 was also consolidated into EP(C)A 1978, becoming Part VI.[10] These provisions are now to be found in Part XI[11] of ERA 1996; the provisions of Sch 13, para17(2) to EP(C)A 1978 are in s 218(2) of the Act, which preserves the continuity of employment of an employee 'if a trade or business, or an undertaking ..., is transferred from one person to another ...'.

1.7 A look at the case-law to which the above statutory provisions have given rise shows that the judges and tribunals who were dealing with these provisions had difficulties similar to those encountered later in relation to the Transfer of Undertakings (Protection of Employment) Regulations (TUPE) 1981.[12] Section 153(1) of the 1978[13] Act stated that the word 'business' 'includes a trade or profession and ... any activity carried on by a body of persons, whether corporate or unincorporate'. The Court of Session said of this definition: 'If this obscure provision has any effect it seems to give the word business a wide connotation.'[14] In *Kenmir Ltd v Frizzell*,[15] Widgery J (as he then was) in the Divisional Court said:[16]

> 'In deciding whether a transaction amounted to the transfer of a business regard must be had to its substance rather than its form, and consideration must be given to the whole of the circumstances, weighing the factors which point in one direction against those which point in another. In the end the vital consideration is whether the effect of the transaction was to put the transferee in possession of a going concern the activities of which he could carry on without interruption. Many factors may be relevant to this decision though few will be conclusive in themselves. Thus, if the new employer carries on business in the same manner as before this will point to the existence of a transfer, but the converse is not necessarily true because a transfer may be complete even though the transferee does not choose to avail himself of all the rights which he acquires thereunder. Similarly, an express assignment of goodwill is strong evidence of a transfer of the business but the absence of such an assignment is not conclusive if the transferee has effectively deprived himself of the power to compete. The absence of an assignment of premises, stock-in-trade or outstanding contracts will likewise not be conclusive if the particular circumstances of the transferee nevertheless enable him to carry on substantially the same business as before.'

1.8 Statements of this kind seem to be a foretaste of things to come. One can see the courts wrestling with the same sorts of problems in relation to the statutory provisions on continuity as one sees when looking at the jurisprudence of the European Court of Justice (ECJ) and the domestic courts of the UK in relation to what amounts to a transfer of an undertaking.

---

10 Sections 81–120.

11 Sections 135–181.

12 SI 1981/1794.

13 See now s 235(1) of ERA 1996. The only difference is that the word 'unincorporate' has been changed to 'unincorporated'.

14 *HA Rencoule Joiners and Shopfitters Ltd v Hunt* (1967) 2 ITR 475, at 477.

15 [1968] 1 WLR 329. See also cases such as *Dallow Industrial Properties Ltd v Else* [1967] 2 QB 449; *Lloyd v Brassey* [1969] 2 QB 98; *Woodhouse v Peter Brotherhood Ltd* [1972] ICR 197; and *Hector Power Ltd v Melon* [1978] IRLR 258.

16 [1968] 1 WLR 329, at 335.

COUNCIL DIRECTIVE 77/187/EEC AND THE TRANSFER OF UNDERTAKINGS (PROTECTION OF EMPLOYMENT) REGULATIONS 1981

1.9   Until 1982, Sch 13, para 17(2) to EP(C)A 1978[17] was the only provision concerning the continuity of an employee's employment where a business was transferred from one employer to another. The position changed on 1 May 1982, however, when TUPE 1981 came into effect. These Regulations were introduced in response to Council Directive 187 of 14 February 1977, on the Approximation of the Laws of the Member States relating to the Safeguarding of Employees' Rights in the Event of Transfers of Undertakings, Businesses or Parts of Businesses.[18]

1.10   It is worth pausing here to consider the situation within the European Economic Community (as the European Union was then known) generally. The Community had rather fewer members than has the EU today; nevertheless, there was a variety of approaches within the Member States to the issue of what happens to an employee when the business of their employer transfers. A number of countries had laws similar to those described above in relation to the law in England and Wales. However, others had laws which were similar in effect to the Directive as it emerged.

1.11   A good example of the latter is France, which had laws governing this topic dating back to the 1920s. These laws were explicable on a macro-economic level in that they retained workers in employment rather than putting them back on the job market (as in the UK) and hence achieved a social and economic objective. At the same time, because the employment relationship was continued notwithstanding the transfer of assets, there was a skills transfer in relation to the exploitation of those assets.[19] Given that the philosophy of the Community at the time was to free employers to adapt and restructure their businesses to meet the changing needs of the market, whilst at the same time giving appropriate protection to the employees who would be affected by these changes, it is not surprising that the weight of opinion settled on promoting laws such as those described in France, rather than laws such as in England and Wales, which offered little or no protection to employees.

1.12   The Directive was part of the 1974–1976 Social Action Programme, which addressed the developing common market and the restructuring of businesses as a consequence. The Directive was enacted along with two other directives which were a part of the Programme, dealing with employee rights in the context of collective redundancies and insolvency. The common thinking behind these directives is clear – for example, the collective consultation

---

17   Now s 218(2) of ERA 1996.
18   77/187/EEC, [1973] OJ L61/26.
19   There is an interesting parallel between this aspect of the rationale behind one of the Directive's forefathers and the decision in *Süzen v Zehnacker Gebdudereinigung GmbH Krankenhausservice, Lefarth GmbH (Party joined)* [1997] ICR 662 (see **2.41**), in which assets assume a central role in the test of whether there is a transfer of an undertaking.

provisions in relation to the transfer of an undertaking and in relation to a collective redundancy exercise remain very similar to this day.

1.13 As has so often been the case in relation to the Directive and its revisions, the initial concept was more ambitious than was realised by the final form. What emerged was a piece of legislation which was designed to protect employee rights but which sought only to achieve a partial harmonisation amongst Member States. The particular significance of this for the employment lawyer is that the method of protection of the rights of employees can be set within the context of employment protection within each Member State. Take the issue of dismissal, for example. In England and Wales, the principal source of protection against unfair dismissal is an award of compensation. Hence the protection in respect of dismissals occurring in connection with a transfer of an undertaking in TUPE 1981 is couched in that language. By contrast, under German law an unfair dismissal results in the termination of the employment relationship being rendered a nullity. Accordingly, a dismissal in connection with a transfer will be null and void and the relationship persists with the transferee. In both Germany and England there is protection against dismissals effected by reason of a transfer of an undertaking, but the way in which this is achieved has not been harmonised.

1.14 It is clear from the preambles to the Directive that its primary purpose was the safeguarding of employees' rights. Thus, the second preamble speaks of the necessity 'to provide for the protection of employees in the event of a change of employer, in particular, to ensure that their rights are safeguarded'; and the third preamble speaks of the differences between the Member States in terms of the extent of the protection offered to employees. In view of the fact that, as will be seen, there has often appeared to be a tension between different views of the purposes of the Directive, it is as well to have in mind that the original objective appears to have been the social objective of safeguarding employees' rights in the event of a transfer of an undertaking.

1.15 The Directive gave Member States two years to bring in implementing legislation,[20] which should thus have been transposed into the domestic law of the UK by early 1979. The date for compliance coincided, however, with a general election which saw the overthrow of the Labour Government and the installation of the first of Margaret Thatcher's administrations. The new Government showed a marked lack of enthusiasm for the project of passing appropriate regulations to give effect to the Directive and it was not until late 1981 that the implementing Regulations came to be laid before Parliament, under s 2(2) of the European Communities Act 1972. The task of introducing the Regulations fell to David Waddington, the Under-Secretary of State for Employment. During the course of the debate in the House of Commons, he commented that he was recommending the adoption of the draft Regulations 'with a remarkable lack of enthusiasm'.[21] He also said that he did not believe that the Regulations would have 'the drastic effect on British business that some people believe' and expressed the view that they would have limited effect.[22] In the light of the history of the Regulations over the next 25 years, these views appear optimistic.

---

20 See Art 8(1).
21 HC Deb, vol 14, ser 6, cols 677–698 (7 December 1981). See col 680.
22 Ibid, at col 697.

1.16 One of the concepts introduced by TUPE 1981 was that of employee participation: the employer was required to consult trade union representatives so as to give them the opportunity to consider and comment on the consequences of business restructurings. This concept was not radical when introduced. There had been a requirement to consult collectively in the event of large-scale redundancies since the Employment Protection Act 1975.[23] However, the Conservative Government clearly underestimated the impact of the Regulations in the context of what would now be described as service provision changes. When the full relevance of the Directive in this area began to be made clear by the European Court in the early 1990s in such cases as *Dr Sophie Redmond Stichting v Bartol*[24] and *Rask and Christensen v ISS Kantineservice A/S*,[25] this struck at the heart of Conservative thinking in this area. The public sector was being encouraged to contract out the provision of services and one element of the reason behind this policy was to move what were perceived to be unduly restrictive employment terms, practices and industrial relations structures into the private sector, where they could be brought into line with the realities of the market and best practice. The Regulations, of course, have proved to be a serious hindrance to the realisation of this goal.

1.17 TUPE 1981 came into effect on 1 May 1982. One of the effects noted by commentators at the time was that they had the effect of reversing the House of Lords decision in *Nokes v Doncaster Amalgamated Collieries Ltd*,[26] since the effect of reg 5 of those Regulations was that an employee of the transferor automatically became an employee of the transferee, provided that there was a 'relevant transfer', as defined by reg 3. In the light of the ECJ's decision in *Katsikas v Konstantinidis*[27] (see below), it is tempting to suggest that little has changed. Under the *Nokes* principle the employee's express assent is required before he or she may become an employee of the transferee; reg 5 removes the need for express consent. On the other hand, an employee who actively *dissents* (by objecting) does not become an employee of the transferee under the Regulations. Thus, even under the statutory regime, it can be argued that the common law position is visible. What thus sometimes happens, to the detriment of the employees by contrast with the law prior to the introduction of the Regulations, is that the employee loses the right to collect a redundancy payment and then seek an employer of his or her choice.

1.18 As originally drafted, the definition of 'undertaking' in reg 2 of TUPE 1981 meant that the Regulations did not apply to undertakings or businesses which were 'not in the nature of a commercial venture'.[28] As a result of the decisions in *Dr Sophie Redmond Stichting v Bartol*[29] and *Rask and Christensen v ISS Kantineservice A/S*,[30] the definition was amended by the Trade Union

---

23   Section 99ff.
24   Case C-29/91, [1992] ECR I-3189. See **2.13**.
25   Case C-209/91, [1992] ECR I-5755. See also 2.14.
26   [1940] AC 1014. See **1.4**.
27   [1993] IRLR 179.
28   See *Woodcock v The Friends School, Wigton* [1987] IRLR 98.
29   [1992] IRLR 366.
30   [1993] IRLR 133.

Reform and Employment Rights Act 1993 (TURERA 1993),[31] with effect from 30 August 1993, so that it merely said: ' "undertaking" includes any trade or business'. Various other amendments were made to the Regulations to reflect developments in European law, usually interpretations by the ECJ of provisions of the Directive which appeared to put the Regulations at variance with the Directive. Thus TURERA 1993 also introduced new provisions[32] to TUPE 1981 covering employees' objections to a transfer, in response to the ECJ decision in *Katsikas v Konstantinidis*.[33] The 1981 Regulations were further amended by the Collective Redundancies and Transfer of Undertakings (Protection of Employment) (Amendment) Regulations 1995[34] and 1999.[35]

1.19   One final point should be noted here. In view of the fact that TUPE 1981 was introduced in order to transpose Directive 77/187/EEC into the domestic law of the UK, it is clear that, when interpreting the Regulations, courts and tribunals should do so in a way which enables them to give effect to the Directive. This is the effect of the House of Lords decision in *Litster v Forth Dry Dock & Engineering Co Ltd (in receivership)*.[36] In that case, following its earlier decision in *Pickstone v Freemans*,[37] the House of Lords held that TUPE 1981 should be given a purposive construction in a manner which would accord with the Directive itself and, where necessary, words should be implied to achieve that effect. This approach was in conformity with the principle set out by the ECJ in *Marleasing SA v LA Comercial Internacional de Alimentacion SA*:[38]

> '[I]n applying national law, whether the provisions in question were adopted before or after the Directive, the national court called upon to interpret it is required to do so, as far as possible, in the light of the wording and the purpose of the Directive in order to achieve the result pursued by the latter.'

1.20   The need to interpret the Regulations in this way had regularly been emphasised in decisions of the Court of Appeal and the Employment Appeal Tribunal, and it is clear from reported decisions that this approach is followed. Problems inevitably arise, of course, when a domestic court or tribunal is trying to interpret a decision of the ECJ which lacks the clarity to enable the court to make its decision with confidence. This problem is particularly apparent in the context of what constitutes a 'transfer' and what an 'undertaking', matters considered in **chapter 2**.

---

31   Section 33(1) and (2) and Sch 10.
32   Regulation 5(4A) and (4B), now reg 4(7) and (8) of the Transfer of Undertakings (Protection of Employment) Regulations (TUPE) 2006, SI 2006/246.
33   [1993] IRLR 179.
34   SI 1995/2587.
35   SI 1999/1925.
36   [1989] ICR 341. For a fuller discussion of this case, see **3.24**.
37   [1988] IRLR 357.
38   [1991] 1 CMLR 305.

THE JURISPRUDENCE OF THE EUROPEAN COURT OF JUSTICE

1.21   The ECJ is charged with the 'interpretation of acts of the institutions of the Community ...'.[39] It discharges this duty by giving 'preliminary rulings' in response to references made by national courts. The Court does not, however, render a definitive judgment. Its ruling gives an interpretation of the Directive as a step in proceedings before the national court and indicates to the national court what its decision on the point should be; but it is the national court which makes the decision. It must be stressed that it is not an appeal procedure. The preliminary reference procedure has certainly been of immense importance in the interpretation of the provisions of Directive 77/187/EEC, which have generated over 30 rulings since 1985.

1.22   The effect of the House of Lords decision in *Litster v Forth Dry Dock & Engineering Co Ltd (in receivership)*[40] and the ECJ decision in *Marleasing SA v LA Comercial Internacional de Alimentacion SA*[41] has already been noted. The purposive construction enjoined by the House of Lords means that courts and tribunals must approach the task of interpreting TUPE 1981 by having regard to the Directive and the way the ECJ has interpreted it. This will be evident from the chapters that follow.

DIRECTIVES 98/50/EC AND 2001/23/EC

1.23   Directive 77/187/EEC was subsequently amended by Directive 98/50/EC. The 1998 Directive came at the end of a period of debate within the EU concerning the effect of the 1977 Directive on the internal market. The debate had been underway for many years. The UK, with its strong services industry, had developed a concern from the mid-1990s that the Directive as interpreted by the ECJ was having a detrimental impact. There was an issue as to the proper scope of the Directive in relation to changes of service provider and a concern that the inconsistency shown by the courts in this area was playing havoc with those pricing contracts for the delivery of services.

1.24   As this debate continued, a number of other issues were considered, such as whether it was appropriate for pensions to remain outside the ambit of the Directive and the effects of the Directive in relation to the rescue of failing business. It proved extremely difficult to make the progress which had been hoped for and the European Court – in decisions such as *Süzen v Zehnacker Gebdudereinigung GmbH Krankenhausservice, Lefarth GmbH (Party joined)*[42] and *Beckmann v Dynamco Whicheloe MacFarlane Ltd*[43] – materially affected the impact of the Directive in certain areas whilst the politicians argued. The consensus reached at the Cardiff summit in the summer of 1998 was hailed as

---

39   See Art 234 EC.
40   [1989] ICR 341. For a fuller discussion of this case, see **3.24**.
41   [1991] 1 CMLR 305.
42   Case C-13/95, [1997] ICR 662.
43   Case C-164/00, [2003] ICR 50.

an achievement, but, in reality, the price of agreement was that a rather weak and unambitious revision to the Directive had been adopted.

1.25 Both the 1977 and the 1998 Directives were consolidated into Council Directive 2001/23/EC. The preamble to the 2001 Directive reiterates the necessity of providing 'for the protection of employees in the event of a change of employer, in particular, to ensure that their rights are safeguarded'.[44] Preamble (8) also states:

> 'Considerations of legal security and transparency required that the legal concept of transfer be clarified in the light of the case-law of the Court of Justice. Such clarification has not altered the scope of Directive 77/187/EEC as interpreted by the Court of Justice.'

1.26 Article 1(1)(a) states that the Directive is to apply to any transfer of an undertaking, business, or part of a business to another employer 'as a result of a legal transfer or merger'. This was the scope of the original Directive. To that has been added Art 1(1)(b), which deals with 'a transfer of an economic entity which retains its identity, meaning an organised grouping of resources which has the objective of pursuing an economic activity, whether or not that activity is central or ancillary'. Article 1(1)(c) applies the Directive to public and private undertakings 'engaged in economic activities whether or not they are operating for gain', but excludes administrative reorganisations. These matters are considered more fully in **chapter 2**.

1.27 There are other changes, for example, in relation to pension rights,[45] businesses subject to bankruptcy or insolvency proceedings,[46] and information and consultation obligations.[47] These are considered at **3.106**, **3.84** and **5.01**.

THE TRANSFER OF UNDERTAKINGS (PROTECTION OF EMPLOYMENT) REGULATIONS 2006[48]

1.28 The Transfer of Undertakings (Protection of Employment) Regulations (TUPE) 2006 were introduced to give effect to the reforms effected by the 1998 Directive, as consolidated into the 2001 Directive. They were essentially permissive and the UK Government was not under pressure to implement changes to the Regulations for them to conform to the Directive, although they had originally intended to implement reform of the Regulations swiftly. The debate over how to amend the Regulations lasted from the summer of 1998 until TUPE 2006 finally appeared. One issue which caused considerable difficulty was the issue of how to reform the Regulations so as to incorporate the protection of pension rights within the provisions of the Regulations. The

---

44 See preamble (3).
45 Article 3(4).
46 Article 5.
47 Article 7.
48 SI 2006/246. For a very helpful discussion of the new Regulations, see McMullen 'An Analysis of the Transfer of Undertakings (Protection of Employment) Regulations 2006' (2006) 35 ILJ 113.

issue was ultimately not resolved within the text of the Regulations but by the provisions of the Pensions Act 2004. The remaining issues continued to be discussed until the 2006 Regulations finally appeared. When they did so, there was an inevitable sense of anticlimax, in that a number of the issues which had caused so much difficulty in practice had not been tackled.

1.29   Although Art 8 of the Directive states that it does not affect the right of Member States to apply or introduce laws, regulations or administrative provisions which are more favourable to employees, it is arguable that s 2(2) of the European Communities Act 1972 only permits implementation of a 'Community' obligation and that a regulation which goes beyond the implementation of a community obligation would be ultra vires. To avoid the risk of this type of argument succeeding, s 38 of the Employment Relations Act 1999 was introduced to enable the Secretary of State to make regulations more favourable than Community law.[49] TUPE 2006 was laid using the powers given by both the above Acts.

1.30   McMullen[50] points to four main changes brought about by the TUPE 2006:

(1)   a wider definition of TUPE so that service provision changes are more likely to be covered by TUPE, in order to achieve greater certainty;
(2)   clarification of the effect of the Regulations in relation to transfer-related dismissals and as to when employers may change terms and conditions;
(3)   the introduction of a requirement on the old employer (transferor) to notify the new employer (transferee) of the identity of the employees and of various specified rights and liabilities that would pass on a transfer;
(4)   greater flexibility in the Regulations' application in certain cases where the transferor is insolvent.

As he points out, however, 'there are large areas of the law on business transfers and employee rights which are not fundamentally changed by the new TUPE Regulations 2006'.[51]

1.31   The changes brought about by TUPE 2006 are discussed, where appropriate, in the chapters which follow. It should be noted that the Regulations were accompanied by guidance published by the DTI.[52] This is also referred to and discussed where appropriate.

---

49   See s 38(2). For examples of regulations laid under this provision see the Transfer of Undertakings (Protection of Employment) (Rent Officer Service) Regulations 1999, SI 1999/2511 and the Transfer of Undertakings (Protection of Employment) (Transfer to OFFCOM) Regulations 2003, SI 2003/2715.
50   (2006) 35 ILJ 113, at p 115.
51   (2006) 35 ILJ 113, at p 116.
52   See http://www.dti.gov.uk/er/individual/tupeguide2006regs.pdf.

Chapter 2

WHEN DOES TUPE APPLY?

INTRODUCTION

2.1 This chapter considers the question of when Transfer of Undertakings (Protection of Employment) Regulations (TUPE) 2006[1] apply. This question requires a discussion of two main matters: (1) the nature and identity of the undertaking alleged to have been transferred; and (2) whether that undertaking has been transferred. Thus, the next two sections of this chapter deal with those two fundamental questions, looking first at the European context and then at the Regulations themselves. The fourth section looks at transfers of parts of undertakings. The fifth section looks at specific types of transfer, for example, bankruptcy, insolvency and similar proceedings and administrative re-organisations. The final section deals with exclusions from the Regulations, including offshoring.

2.2 So far as the two main issues considered in this chapter are concerned, it is clear from the way in which both Directive 2001/23/EC and TUPE 2006 are drafted that the issue of whether there has been a transfer of an undertaking requires to be dealt with in two stages. First, the court or tribunal must identify the undertaking which is alleged to have been transferred. Secondly, it must then establish whether that undertaking was in fact transferred. This is clear both from the way in which the European Court of Justice (ECJ) has approached the relevant provisions of the Directive and from the approach taken by the Employment Appeal Tribunal (EAT) and the Court of Appeal. A tribunal which fails to deal with the matter in this way is likely to commit an error of law. The text follows this approach.

THE POSITION UNDER EUROPEAN LAW

Identifying the business or undertaking

2.3 Article 1(1)(a) of Directive 2001/23/EC[2] states that it is to apply to 'any transfer of an undertaking, business or part of an undertaking or business to

---

1   SI 2006/246.
2   Article 1 of the original directive (77/187/EEC) was replaced by a new text, substituted by Council Directive 98/50/EC, Art 1, para 2 and consolidated by Council Directive 2001/23/EC.

another employer as a result of a legal transfer or merger'. This is the text which was in the original directive.[3] Paragraphs (b) and (c) of Art 1 were added by Directive 98/50/EC and state:

> '(b)   ... there is a transfer within the meaning of this Directive where there is a transfer of an economic entity which retains its identity, meaning an organised grouping of resources which has the objective of pursuing an economic activity, whether or not that activity is central or ancillary.
>
> (c)   This Directive shall apply to public and private undertakings engaged in economic activities whether or not they are operating for gain.' [The article then goes on to deal with administrative reorganisations; that part of the article is quoted below, at **2.141**.]

These new provisions are intended to clarify the legal concept of a transfer of an undertaking and to give effect to the case-law of the ECJ,[4] which is considered more fully below.

2.4   It is important to be able to decide whether a particular operation amounts to an undertaking within the terms of the Directive. This issue relates to the coverage of the Directive and the sorts of transfers which are embraced by it. In essence, the question is whether a wide or narrow construction should be given to Art 1(1). This in turn depends upon what objectives the court or tribunal perceives to be important. The case-law tends to show that if an economic objective is perceived to be important the court will give a more restrictive interpretation to the legislation; whereas if the social objectives of the legislation are regarded as paramount, the court will give a wider and more all-embracing construction. It is not always easy to reconcile those cases which follow these different objectives.

2.5   In some of its earlier decisions on this aspect of the Directive, the ECJ said that the Directive applied as soon as there was a change (resulting from a conventional sale or a merger) of the natural and legal person responsible for operating the undertaking. Thus, in *Foreningen af Arbejdsledere i Danmark v Daddy's Dance Hall A/S*,[5] the Court said:[6]

> '[T]he objective of Directive 77/187 is to ensure as far as possible the safeguarding of employees' rights in the event of a change of proprietor of the undertaking and to allow them to remain in the service of the new proprietor on the same condition as those agreed with the vendor. The Directive therefore applies as soon as there is a change, resulting from a conventional sale or a merger, of the natural or legal person responsible for operating the undertaking who, consequently, enters into obligations as an employer towards employees working in the undertaking, and it is of no importance to know whether the ownership of the undertaking has been transferred.'

2.6   The case involved the termination of a lease on restaurants and bars owned by Palads Teatret and the grant of a new lease by them to Daddy's Dance Hall A/S. The ECJ said that the Directive applied. It also made it clear that the applicability of the Directive is not excluded in a case where the

---

3   Directive 77/187/EEC.
4   See paras (7) and (8) of the preamble to Directive 98/50/EC.
5   [1988] IRLR 315.
6   [1988] IRLR 315, at 317.

transfer takes place in two phases, in the sense that as a first step the undertaking is transferred back from the original lessee to the owner who then transfers it to the new lessee. But it stressed that the economic unit must retain its identity. It added:[7]

> 'This is the case in particular where, as in the instant case, the business continues to be run without interruption by the new lessee with the same staff that was employed in the undertaking before the transfer.'

2.7   Thus, the ECJ was not concerned with whether the ownership of the undertaking had been transferred; it was concerned with whether the 'economic unit retains its identity', a phrase very similar to that which has found its way into the new Directive, though that talks of an economic entity rather than an economic unit. The other issue which was considered in *Daddy's Dance Hall* was whether employees who enter into a contract with the transferee of an undertaking may waive the rights conferred upon them by the Directive if this allows them to obtain such advantages that the change in their terms of employment does not place them overall in a less favourable position. This matter is considered in **chapter 4**: see **4.100**.

2.8   It should be noted that the factual scenario set out above is very similar to that which obtains in a situation where services are contracted out or 'outsourced'. The grantor of the right to operate the services grants a contract to A. That terminates and effectively reverts to the grantor. The grantor then re-grants the contract to B. So with a lease as above: the lessor grants a lease to A. The lease terminates or is forfeited and this reverts to the lessor who then re-grants it to B. Thus *Daddy's Dance Hall* (above) and *Ny Mølle Kro* (below) have the same sort of factual matrix as some of the later cases dealing with outsourcing, though in the latter case the lessor operated the business herself and did not re-grant the lease.

2.9   In *Landsorganisationen i Danmark v Ny Mølle Kro*,[8] which was decided a few months earlier, the facts of the case were that the owner of a tavern (which was only open during the summer months) granted a lease of premises to Inger Larsen, who gave an undertaking to an employees' association to abide by the terms of a collective agreement relating to employees who were members of the association. While the tavern was closed during the winter months the owner rescinded the lease and subsequently opened the tavern herself for the summer season and continued to run it each summer season herself. The case arose from a complaint by one of the waitresses that the wages paid by the owner of the tavern were less than those payable under the collective agreement, whose terms Ms Larsen had agreed to observe. The ECJ said that, on the forfeiture of

---

7   [1988] IRLR 315, at 317, para 10.

8   [1989] ICR 330. See also *Berg v Besselsen* [1990] ICR 396, whose facts are similar to *Ny Mølle Kro*. What was involved here was an agreement to sell a business but on terms that payment and transfer of the ownership of the business would be deferred. The purchasers took over the running of the business under the terms of the lease-purchase agreement, but the agreement was subsequently terminated. The ECJ held that the purchasers of the business were liable to one of the employees for arrears of salary during the time that they had run the business but that the original transferor after the termination of the lease-purchase agreement since there was in effect a transfer back to it.

the lease and the lessor becoming the employer, there was a transfer of an undertaking within Art 1(1)(a) of the Directive (as it now is). The Court made it clear that the transfer must be a transfer of a going concern and said that it was a question of fact whether there was such a transfer. The Court said:[9]

> 'The fact that the undertaking in question was temporarily closed at the time of the transfer and therefore had no employees certainly constitutes one factor to be taken into account in determining whether a business was transferred as a going concern. However, the temporary closure of an undertaking and the resulting absence of staff at the time of the transfer do not themselves preclude the possibility that there has been a transfer of an undertaking ...'

2.10   The more recent case of *Allen v Amalgamated Construction Co Ltd*[10] involved two subsidiaries of a mining company. The respondent employer (ACC) subcontracted driveage work at a colliery to another subsidiary, AM Mining Services Ltd (AMS). Both subsidiaries, though separate legal entities, had the same management and shared administrative and support functions. ACC made some employees redundant and they went to work for AMS. Later, ACC terminated the contract with AMS with a view to doing the driveage work itself. It therefore re-engaged the employees it had previously made redundant, but on terms less favourable than those they had originally enjoyed. The employees asked for the previous terms and conditions to be reinstated. The question referred to the ECJ was whether the Directive is capable of applying to two companies in the same corporate group. The Court held that the Directive could apply to a transfer between two subsidiary companies in the same group, even if the companies had the same ownership, management and premises and were engaged in the same work. The Court followed the approach of the two previous cases and said:[11]

> 'It is thus clear that the Directive is intended to cover any legal change in the person of the employer if the other conditions it lays down are also met and that it can, therefore, apply to a transfer between two subsidiary companies in the same group, which are distinct legal persons each with specific employment relationships with their employees. The fact that the companies in question not only have the same ownership but also the same management and the same premises and that they are engaged in the same works makes no difference in this regard.'

2.11   The Court pointed out that if transfers between companies in the same group were excluded from the Directive, that would be 'contrary to the Directive's aim, which is, according to the court, to ensure, so far as possible, that the rights of employees are safeguarded in the event of a change of employer by allowing them to remain in employment with the new employer on the terms and conditions agreed with the transferor ...'.[12]

2.12   The decision in this case also dealt with the question whether there had been a transfer: see **2.47**.

---

9   [1989] ICR 330, at 339.
10   [2000] ICR 436.
11   [2000] ICR 436 at 458.
12   [2000] ICR 436, at 459.

2.13 Decisions of the ECJ in the early 1990s suggested that the Court was prepared to take a broad view of activities which were to be treated as a business or part of a business. In *Dr Sophie Redmond Stichting v Bartol*,[13] the question of the applicability of the Directive arose when the local authority which funded the Redmond Foundation switched its grant to another foundation; the building leased to the Redmond Foundation was transferred to the new foundation, which took over the Redmond Foundation's clients and some of its employees. The question was whether the Directive applied in these circumstances. The ECJ held that it did. It said that 'activities of a special nature' may be regarded as comparable to a business or part of a business and continued:[14]

'In order to ascertain whether or not there is such a transfer in a case such as [the present], it is necessary to determine, having regard to all the circumstances surrounding the transaction in question, whether the functions performed are in fact carried out or resumed by the new legal person with the same activities or similar activities, it being understood that activities of a special nature which pursue independent aims may, if necessary, be treated as a business or part of a business within the meaning of the Directive.'

2.14 In *Rask and Christensen v ISS Kantineservice A/S*,[15] the ECJ took the matter a stage further. The facts of the case were that Phillips A/S decided to contract out the running of a staff canteen to ISS. Phillips agreed to pay ISS a fixed monthly fee to cover costs relating to management, wages, insurance and the provision of work clothing, and to provide premises, equipment, electricity and other services free of charge. ISS undertook to offer employment on the same pay to the staff employed by Phillips at the time the agreement came into force. The two employees complained about changes in their contracts. One of the questions submitted to the ECJ was whether the Directive can apply to a situation where the owner of an undertaking entrusts to the owner of another undertaking, by means of a contract, the responsibility of providing a service for employees, which it had previously operated directly, and which is ancillary to its economic activities. Here too the ECJ ruled that the Directive applied. The Court said:[16]

'The fact that ... the activity transferred is only an ancillary activity of the transferor undertaking not necessarily related to its objects cannot have the effect of excluding that transaction from the Directive. Similarly, the fact that the agreement between the transferor and the transferee relates to the provision of services provided exclusively for the benefit of the transferor in return for a fee ... does not prevent the directive from applying either ... [T]he decisive criterion for establishing whether there is a transfer ... is whether the business retains its identity, as would be indicated, in particular, by the fact that its operation was either continued or resumed ... [T]he Directive may apply to a situation in which the owner of an

---

13   [1992] IRLR 366.
14   [2000] ICR 436 at 370. The decision was applied by the High Court in *Porter v Queen's Medical Centre (Nottingham University Hospital)* [1993] IRLR 486, which held that the transfer of the supply of paediatric and neonatal services from two district hospitals to a NHS trust was a legal transfer of an undertaking within Art 1(1) of the Directive. It was conceded that the Directive was directly enforceable against a body such as an NHS trust.
15   [1993] IRLR 133.
16   [1993] IRLR 133, at 136.

undertaking entrusts to the owner of another undertaking by means of a contract the responsibility of providing a service for employees, previously operated directly, in return for a fee and other benefits the terms of which are determined by the agreement made between them.'

2.15 This approach to the interpretation of Art 1(1) was confirmed by the ECJ in *Commission of the European Communities v United Kingdom.*[17] It said: 'The Court has already accepted, at least implicitly, in the context of competition law ... or social law ... that a body might be engaged in economic activities and be regarded as an "undertaking" for the purposes of Community law even though it did not operate with a view to profit.'[18] It went on to hold that the UK had failed to fulfil its obligations under Art 1(1) of the Directive.

2.16 The ECJ developed this view further in *Schmidt v Spar- und Leihkasse der Früheren Ämter Bordesholm, Kiel und Cronshagen,*[19] when it decided that the Directive may apply to an ancillary activity where the transfer involves a single employee and does not involve the transfer of any tangible assets.[20] The employee was the sole cleaner employed by the bank at one of its branches. She was dismissed when the branch was renovated and enlarged; she was offered employment by the cleaning company which the bank wished to take over the cleaning but refused and challenged her dismissal. The ECJ said that the decisive criterion was whether the business retained its identity. It said that the application of the Directive was not precluded by the fact that the activity transferred was for the transferor an ancillary activity not necessarily connected with its objects. The Court also said:[21]

'Nor is the fact that the activity in question was performed, prior to the transfer, by a single employee sufficient to preclude the application of the Directive since its application does not depend upon the number of employees assigned to the part of the undertaking which is the subject of the transfer. It should be noted that one of the objectives of the Directive, as clearly stated in the second recital in the preamble[22] thereto, is to protect employees in the event of a change of employer, in particular to ensure that their rights are safeguarded. That protection extends to all staff and must therefore be guaranteed even when only one employee is affected by the transfer.'

2.17 These decisions undoubtedly had a significant effect upon the way in which domestic courts and tribunals in the UK interpreted the Transfer of Undertakings (Protection of Employment) Regulations (TUPE) 1981[23] during the 1990s, and, in turn, had a significant impact on market testing and compulsory competitive tendering.[24]

---

17   [1994] ICR 664.
18   [1994] ICR 664, at 717.
19   [1995] ICR 237.
20   See also *Merckx and Neuhuys v Ford Motors Co Belgium SA* [1997] ICR 352, in which the ECJ reiterated that the transfer of tangible assets is not conclusive of whether the entity in question retains its economic identity.
21   [1995] ICR 237, at 247, para 16.
22   Now the third preamble in the 2001 Directive.
23   SI 1981/1794.
24   See, for example, *Kenny v South Manchester College* [1993] ICR 934; and *Dines v Initial Healthcare Services* [1995] ICR 11.

2.18 Subsequent decisions of the ECJ have given rise to suggestions that the Court is taking a more cautious approach to interpretation of the Directive. Thus, for example, in *Ledernes Hovedorganisation (Acting on behalf of Rygaard) v Dansk Arbejdsgiverforening (Acting on behalf of StrøMølle Akustik A/S) (Rygaard's case)*,[25] the ECJ decided that the Directive did not apply to a situation where a subcontractor took over the completion of a building contract, together with the workers and materials assigned to it. The work lasted 3 months and, once it had been completed, StrøMølle (which had taken over the contract) gave the employee notice of dismissal. (When the agreement for StrøMølle to take over the work was entered into, the original contractor, Pedersen, gave the employee notice of dismissal but this appears to have been superseded by the later notice of dismissal.) The employee argued that there was an undertaking which was transferred; the ECJ rejected that, on the grounds that there was no undertaking to be transferred. After stating that the decisive criterion is whether the business in question retains its identity,[26] the Court went on to say:[27]

> 'The authorities cited above[28] presuppose that the transfer relates to a stable economic entity whose activity is not limited to performing one specific works contract ... That is not the case of an undertaking which transfers to another undertaking one of its building works with a view to the completion of that work. Such a transfer could come within the terms of the Directive ... only if it included the transfer of a body of assets enabling the activities or certain activities of the transferor undertaking to be carried on in a stable way ... That is not the case where, as in the case now referred, the transferor undertaking merely makes available to the new contractor certain workers and material for carrying out the works in question.'

The consequence of this decision was that Mr Rygaard could only pursue a claim against the original contractors and not against StrøMølle.

2.19 Whilst the decision in *Rygaard's case* arguably suggests a more cautious approach to interpretation of the Directive, it can also be argued that the decision merely shows that there are limits to what is to be considered a business or undertaking and that the view that the taking over of the completion of a contract does not amount to an undertaking is a view consistent with earlier decisions of the ECJ. It should be remembered that the duration of the contract was only 3 months and that the contract was to be completed rather than undertaken from the beginning. These factors should be borne in mind as part of the factual survey which needs to be made in all cases of alleged transfers of an undertaking.

2.20 The decision in *Rygaard's case* may be contrasted with the decision in *Merckx and Neuhuys v Ford Motors Co Belgium SA*,[29] decided some 6 months later. The case involved the transfer of a car dealership without a transfer of

---

25 [1996] ICR 333.
26 [1996] ICR 333, at 345, paras 15–17.
27 [1996] ICR 333, at 346, paras 20–22.
28 *Spijkers v Gebroeders Benedik Abattoir* [1968] ECR 1119 and *Schmidt v Spar-und Leihkasse der Früheren Ämter Bordesholm, Kiel und Cronshagen* [1995] ICR 237.
29 [1997] ICR 352. See also *Süzen v Zehnacker Gebaudereinigung GmbH Krankenhausservice, Lefarth GmbH (Party joined)* [1997] ICR 662.

tangible assets from Ford dealers, Anfo Motors (of which Ford were the main shareholders), to independent dealers, Novarobel. More than three-quarters of the Ford dealer's staff were dismissed but the employees in question were told that they would be transferred to the new dealers; after the transfer the Ford dealers discontinued their activities. Some of the employees transferred to the new dealer objected to being transferred and brought proceedings in the *Tribunal du Travail de Bruxelles* and then on appeal in the *Cour du Travail* in Brussels. They argued that there was a closure rather than a transfer of an undertaking; Ford argued to the contrary. The ECJ ruled that Art 1(1) of the Directive applied to the transfer of the dealership, emphasising, in common with the other cases, that the decisive criterion is whether the entity in question retains its economic identity.[30] The Court reiterated its view that the transfer of tangible assets is not conclusive of whether the entity in question retains its economic identity and said:[31]

> 'The purpose of an exclusive dealership for the sale of motor vehicles of a particular make in a certain sector remains the same even if it is carried on under a different name, from different premises and with different facilities. It is also irrelevant that the principal place of business is situated in a different area of the same conurbation, provided that the contract territory remains the same.'

2.21   The employees also contended, in support of their argument in favour of closure rather than transfer, that there could not be a transfer when an undertaking definitively ceased trading and was put into liquidation, as was the case with Anfo Motors, which had previously held the Ford dealership. They argued that the economic entity had ceased to exist and could not retain its identity. The Court dismissed this argument, saying:[32]

> 'In that regard, if the Directive's aim of protecting workers is not to be undermined, its application cannot be excluded merely because the transferor discontinues its activities when the transfer is made and is then put into liquidation. If the business of that undertaking is carried on by another undertaking, those facts tend to confirm, rather, that there has been a transfer for the purposes of the Directive.'

2.22   For a fuller discussion of transfers arising from situations of insolvency or liquidation, see **2.137**.

2.23   The difference between the decisions in the two cases resides in the nature of the transactions involved; both decisions may be seen as examples of the difficulty of deciding what amounts to the retention by an entity of its economic identity and tend to suggest that the issue is very much a question of fact in each case. The decision in *Merckx* is certainly consistent with a number of the earlier cases already discussed.

Has the undertaking been transferred?

2.24   Once it has been established that there is an undertaking which falls within the coverage of the Directive, it is then necessary to decide whether that

---

30   [1996] ICR 333, at 367.
31   [1996] ICR 333, at 367–368.
32   [1996] ICR 333, at 368.

undertaking has been transferred. This is the second main requirement for the application of the Directive, Art 1(1)(a) and (b) of which say:

'(a) This Directive shall apply to any transfer of an undertaking, business, or part of an undertaking or business to another employer as a result of a legal transfer or merger.

(b) [T]here is a transfer within the meaning of this Directive where there is a transfer of an economic entity which retains its identity, meaning an organised grouping of resources which has the objective of pursuing an economic activity, whether or not that activity is central or ancillary.'

2.25 This is the version now to be found in the 2001 Directive, which consolidates the amendments brought about by Directive 98/50/EC. That Directive in turn drew on the case-law of the ECJ for the re-formulation of the definition of transfer, as a reading of the text which follows will show. The definition in the original 1977 version was effectively confined to Art 1(1)(a).

2.26 The definition of 'transferor' and 'transferee' should also be noted. The definitions of these terms are to be found in Art 2(1) and are as follows:

'(a) "transferor" shall mean any natural or legal person who, by reason of a transfer within the meaning of Article 1(1), ceases to be the employer in respect of that undertaking, business or part of the undertaking or business;

(b) "transferee" shall mean any natural or legal person who, by reason of a transfer within the meaning of Article 1(1), becomes the employer in respect of the undertaking, business or part of the undertaking or business ...'

2.27 The starting-point for a consideration of the question of what amounts to a transfer is the case of *Spijkers v Gebroeders Benedik Abattoir*.[33] In that case, the ECJ emphasised that the aim of the Directive is to ensure 'the continuity of employment relationships existing within a business, irrespective of a change of owner' and said that the decisive criterion is 'whether the business in question retains its identity'. It went on to say:[34]

'[I]t is necessary to consider all the facts characterising the transaction in question, including the type of undertaking or business, whether or not the businesses tangible assets, such as buildings and movable property are transferred, the value of its intangible assets at the time of the transfer, whether or not the majority of its employees are taken over by the new employer, whether or not its customers are transferred and the degree of similarity between the activities carried on before and after the transfer and the period, if any, for which those activities were suspended. It should be noted, however, that all those circumstances are merely single factors in the overall assessment which must be made and cannot, therefore, be considered in isolation.'

2.28 What essentially the ECJ is saying is that a snapshot needs to be taken of the situation both before and after the transfer. It suggests a list of factors to be looked at in undertaking this exercise. In essence it is saying that it is a matter of comparison of the facts both before and after, and that provided there is a broad similarity between those two pictures there will be a transfer of an undertaking.

---

33   [1986] ECR 1119.
34   [1986] ECR 1119, at 1129.

2.29 The approach taken in *Spijkers* has been articulated in very similar language in the cases which have followed this decision and the emphasis of the ECJ has been on whether an undertaking retains its identity.[35] It may be said to be the starting-point in any discussion of whether there has been a transfer of an undertaking.

2.30 In *Landsorganisationen i Danmark v Ny Mølle Kro*,[36] the facts of which were set out at **2.9**, the ECJ said:[37]

> 'The Directive is ... applicable where, following a legal transfer or merger, there is a change in the legal or natural person who is responsible for carrying on the business and who by virtue of that fact incurs the obligations of the employer vis-à-vis employees of the undertaking, regardless of whether or not ownership of the undertaking is transferred. Employees of an undertaking whose employer changes without any change in ownership are in a situation comparable to that of employees of an undertaking which is sold, and require equivalent protection.'

2.31 This was applied in *Foreningen af Arbejdsledere i Danmark v Daddy's Dance Hall A/S*[38] to the case where the owner of premises revokes a lease granted to one lessee and grants it to a new lessee. The Court said:[39]

> 'The fact that in such a case the transfer takes place in two phases, in the sense that as a first step the undertaking is transferred back from the original lessee to the owner who then transfers it to the new lessee, does not exclude the applicability of the Directive as long as the economic unit retains its identity. This is the case in particular when, as in the instant case, the business continues to be run without interruption by the new lessee with the same staff that was employed in the undertaking before the transfer.'

2.32 As has already been pointed out, the factual scenario in the above two cases is very similar to that which obtains in a situation where services are contracted out or 'outsourced'. The grantor of the right to operate the services grants a contract to A. That terminates and effectively reverts to the grantor. The grantor then re-grants the contract to B. So with a lease as above: the lessor grants a lease to A. The lease terminates or is forfeited and this reverts to the lessor who then re-grants it to B. Thus *Daddy's Dance Hall* and *Ny Mølle Kro* have the same sort of factual matrix as some of the later cases dealing with outsourcing, though in the latter case the lessor operated the business herself and did not re-grant the lease. This should be borne in mind when the cases on outsourcing and contracting-in are considered. The point to note, however, is that in these cases the business was the same, though operated by different people. It is also worth noting that the legal arrangements under which the

---

35 The most recent examples are *Schmidt v Spar- und Leihkasse der Früheren Ämter Bordesholm, Kiel und Cronshagen* [1995] ICR 237; *Ledernes Hovedorganisation (Acting on behalf of Rygaard) v Dansk Arbejdsgiverforening (Acting on behalf of StrøMølle Akustik A/S) (Rygaard's case)* [1996] ICR 333; *Merckx and Neuhuys v Ford Motors Co Belgium SA* [1997] ICR 352; and *Süzen v Zehnacker Gebdudereinigung GmbH Krankenhausservice, Lefarth GmbH (Party joined)* [1997] IRLR 255. All these cases use the same language in identifying the test to be used.
36 [1989] ICR 330. See also *Berg v Besselsen* [1990] ICR 396.
37 [1989] ICR 330, at 338.
38 [1988] IRLR 315.
39 [1988] IRLR 315, at 317.

person running the business operates are not likely to be relevant. So, for example, the case of *Berg v Besselsen*,[40] whose facts are similar to *Ny Mølle Kro*, involved an agreement to sell a business but on terms that payment and transfer of the ownership of the business would be deferred. The purchasers took over the running of the business under the terms of the lease-purchase agreement, but the agreement was subsequently terminated. The ECJ held that the purchasers of the business were liable to one of the employees for arrears of salary during the time that they had run the business but that the original transferor was liable after the termination of the lease-purchase agreement since there was in effect a transfer back to it. The fact that the original transferor had not completed a sale to the transferee did not prevent there being the transfer of an undertaking; similarly, when the lease was terminated, liability reverted to the original transferor. In both parts of the transaction, *ownership* did not pass.

2.33   In *P Bork International A/S v Foreningen af Arbejdsledere i Danmark*,[41] the undertaking consisted of a factory which was leased. Notice of termination of the lease was given and the undertaking ceased operating; all the employees were dismissed. About a week later, the new owner bought it from the landlord and took possession, engaging more than half of the staff previously employed there, but taking on no new staff. Shortly after, the new owner bought from the old employer who was in liquidation the stock, spare parts, tools, auxiliary materials and furniture. The Court considered the question whether employees dismissed before the undertaking was transferred were protected by the Directive and concluded that they were. It emphasised that 'the undertaking must retain its identity, which is the case where there is an economic entity still in existence, the operation of which is in fact continued or resumed by the new employer carrying on the same or a similar business'.[42] It went on to say:[43]

> 'In order to determine whether these conditions all exist, it is appropriate to take account of all the factual circumstances surrounding the transaction, which may include in particular whether the tangible and intangible assets have been transferred, as well as the major part of the staff of the undertaking, the degree of similarity between its activities before and after the transfer and the duration of any period of stoppage connected with the transfer.'

2.34   It observed that the temporary closure of the undertaking and the absence of the staff at the time of the transfer were not in themselves sufficient to preclude the existence of a transfer of an undertaking. It went on to point out that the only workers who may invoke the Directive are those who have current employment relations or a contract of employment at the date of the transfer, saying that whether or not a contract of employment exists must be assessed under national law, 'subject, however, to the observance of the mandatory rules of the Directive concerning the protection of workers against dismissal by reason of the transfer'. The Court concluded by saying:[44]

---

40   [1990] ICR 396.
41   [1989] IRLR 41.
42   [1989] IRLR 41, at 43.
43   [1989] IRLR 41, at 43, para 15.
44   [1989] IRLR 41, at 44.

'[W]orkers employed by the undertaking whose contract of employment or employment relationship has been terminated with effect on a date before that of the transfer, in breach of Article 4(1) of the Directive,[45] must be considered as still employed by the undertaking on the date of the transfer with the consequence, in particular, that the obligations of the employer towards them are fully transferred from the transferor to the transferee, in accordance with Article 3(1) of the Directive. In order to determine whether the only reason for dismissal was the transfer itself, account must be taken of the objective circumstances in which the dismissal occurred and, in particular, ... the fact that it took place on a date close to that of the transfer and that the workers concerned were re-engaged by the transferee.'

2.35 The difference between the *Bork* case and the previous three cases – *Daddy's Dance Hall*, *Ny Mølle Kro* and *Berg v Besselsen* is that in *Bork* there was a gap of time between the dismissal by the transferor and the re-engagement by the transferee. That made no difference to the outcome, however.

2.36 The matter was taken a stage further in *Dr Sophie Redmond Stichting v Bartol*,[46] considered at **2.13**, when the ECJ ruled that a transfer within Art 1(1) of the Directive may take place where a public body decides to terminate a subsidy paid to one legal person, as a result of which the activities of that legal person are terminated, and to transfer it to another legal person with similar aims. The Court said that the decision by a public body to alter its policy on subsidies is as much a unilateral decision as the decision of an owner to change its lessee.[47] The Court pointed out that, in this respect, the nature of the subsidy cannot be taken into account. In some Member States, the grant of a subsidy is a unilateral act accompanied by certain conditions, whereas in others there are subsidy agreements. The Court said: 'In all cases, the change of the beneficiary of the subsidy takes place in the context of a contractual relationship within the meaning of the Directive and of the case law.'[48] In the final part of its judgment, the Court considered the relevant factors set out in the *Spijkers* judgment and applied them to the characteristics found by the referring judge in relation to the switch of subsidy, adding that those factors were essential if not determinative in characterising a transfer and could be relied upon in the interpretation and application of Art 1(1) of the Directive. The characteristics found by the judge were, amongst others, that the activities of the Redmond foundation were terminated, the transferee foundation (the Sigma foundation) partially absorbed the Redmond foundation, the two foundations collaborated to set up the transfer transaction, the two foundations pursued the same or a similar aim, the building leased by Redmond was subsequently leased to Sigma and Sigma offered new contracts of employment to some of the former employees of Redmond.

2.37 In the later case of *Ledernes Hovedorganisation (Acting on behalf of Rygaard) v Dansk Arbejdsgiverforening (Acting on behalf of StrøMølle Akustik*

---

45   This Article remains the same in the 2001 Directive and is considered more fully in **chapter 4**.
46   [1992] IRLR 366. See also *Schmidt v Spar-und Leihkasse der Früheren Ämter Bordesholm, Kielund Cronshagen* [1995] ICR 237.
47   [1992] IRLR 366, at 369, para 17.
48   [1992] IRLR 366, at 369.

A/S) *(Rygaard's case),*[49] the ECJ ruled that the taking over of the completion of a building contract by a subcontractor, together with the workers and materials assigned to it, did not fall within the Directive. That case is largely concerned, however, with the question whether there was an undertaking to be transferred, and is considered in more detail above: see **2.18**.

2.38 The issue of whether there has been a *transfer* of an undertaking has given rise subsequently to a number of significant cases. The first, *Merckx and Neuhuys v Ford Motors Co Belgium SA,*[50] involved the transfer of a car dealership without a transfer of tangible assets from Ford dealers (Anfo Motors, of which Ford was the main shareholder) to independent dealers, Novarobel. More than three-quarters of Anfo's staff were dismissed but the employees in question were told that they would be transferred to Novarobel; after the transfer Anfo discontinued its activities. The first question, considered at **2.20**, was whether there was an undertaking to be transferred. Having decided that there was, the ECJ noted that Ford transferred the dealership to Novarobel and 'so transferred the economic risk associated with that business to an undertaking outside its own group of companies, that Novarobel carried on the activity performed by Anfo Motors, without interruption, in the same sector and subject to similar conditions, that it took on part of its staff and that it was recommended to customers in order to ensure continuity in operation of the dealership'.[51] The employees advanced a number of arguments to the Court, saying that the transfer was outside the Directive:

(1)   because there had been no transfer of either tangible or intangible assets and no preservation of the undertaking's structure and organisation;

(2)   because the transferor dealer ceased trading and was put into liquidation after the transfer;

(3)   because the majority of the staff were dismissed upon the transfer; and

(4)   because the notion of a legal transfer within Art 1(1) of the Directive required the existence of a contractual link between the transferor and the transferee.

2.39 The Court rejected all these arguments. It said:[52]

'[T]he Court has given that concept [sc the concept of legal transfer] a sufficiently flexible interpretation in keeping with the objective of the Directive, which is to safeguard employees in the event of a transfer of their undertaking, and has held that the Directive is applicable wherever, in the context of contractual relations, there is a change in the natural or legal person who is responsible for carrying on the business and who incurs the obligations of an employer towards employees of the undertaking ... It is clear ... that, for the Directive to apply, it is not necessary for there to be a direct contractual relationship between the transferor and the transferee. Consequently, where a motor vehicle dealership concluded with one undertaking is terminated and a new dealership is awarded to another undertaking pursuing the same activities, the transfer of undertaking is the result of a legal transfer for the purposes of the Directive ...'

---

49   [1996] ICR 333.
50   [1997] ICR 352.
51   [1997] ICR 352, at 367.
52   [1997] ICR 352, at 368–369.

2.40 Two points should be noted here. First, in structural terms, the grant of a concession to one dealer and the subsequent withdrawal of that concession from that dealer and the re-grant to another dealer is similar to the grant of a lease to one person and the re-grant to another. That, of course, is not the end of the question since it is still necessary to undertake the factual survey required by *Spijkers*. Secondly, it is not necessary for there to be a contractual link between the transferor and the transferee, as pointed out by the ECJ in the quotation set out above.[53] In most cases there is no such contractual link, but that, in the light of the Court's views, is immaterial. In some cases there may be some kind of contractual link, as there appears to have been in *Sophie Redmond Stichting*, but that will be part of the factual survey undertaken by the national court or tribunal.

2.41 About a year after the decision in *Merckx and Neuhuys* the ECJ gave its decision in *Süzen v Zehnacker Gebdudereinigung GmbH Krankenhausservice, Lefarth GmbH (Party joined)*.[54] In that case the question was whether the termination of a cleaning contract with one contractor and the grant of the contract to another contractor may amount to a transfer within the Directive. As in the *Merckx* case, there was no transfer of tangible or intangible assets. The Court reiterated what it had said in previous cases, that the decisive question is whether the entity in question retains its identity, 'as indicated inter alia by the fact that its operation is actually continued or resumed'.[55] It said that, although the absence of a contractual link between the transferor and the transferee or (as here) the two undertakings successively granted the cleaning contract might point to the absence of a transfer, it was not conclusive. It added the transfer may take place in two stages, through the intermediary of a third party such as the owner or the person putting up the capital, and stressed that the transfer must relate to a stable economic entity whose activity is not limited to performing one specific works contract (as in *Rygaard's case*).[56] It said:[57]

> 'The term entity thus refers to an organised grouping of persons and assets facilitating the exercise of an economic activity which pursues a specific objective ... [T]he mere fact that the service provided by the old and the new awardees of a contract is similar does not therefore support the conclusion that an economic entity has been transferred. An entity cannot be reduced to the activity entrusted to it. Its identity also emerges from other factors, such as its workforce, its management staff, the way in which its work is organised, its operating methods or indeed, where appropriate, the operational resource available to it ... The mere loss of a service contract to a competitor cannot therefore by itself indicate the existence of a transfer ... In those circumstances, the service undertaking previously entrusted with the contract does not, on losing a customer, thereby cease fully to exist, and a business or part of a business belonging to it cannot be considered to have been transferred to the new awardee of the contract.'

---

53   [1997] ICR 352, at 369, para 30.
54   [1997] ICR 662.
55   [1997] ICR 662, at 670, para 10.
56   [1997] ICR 662, at 670, paras 10–12.
57   [1997] ICR 662, at 670–671, paras 13, 15 and 16.

2.42 The Court stressed[58] that, in order to determine whether the conditions for a transfer are met, all the facts characterising the transaction in question must be looked at, including the particular type of undertaking, thus in effect repeating what it had said in *Spijkers*.[59] It also pointed out that the absence of a transfer of assets does not necessarily preclude the existence of a transfer and that, in considering the various criteria which have identified as relevant to the question whether the business has retained its identity, the degree of importance to be attached to each criterion 'will necessarily vary according to the activity carried on, or indeed the production or operating methods employed in the relevant undertaking'. It said:[60]

> '[T]he degree of importance to be attached to each criterion for determining whether or not there has been a transfer within the meaning of the directive will necessarily vary according to the activity carried on, or indeed the production or operating methods employed in the relevant undertaking, business or part of a business. Where in particular an economic entity is able, in certain sectors, to function without any significant tangible or intangible assets, the maintenance of its identity following the transaction affecting it cannot, logically, depend on the transfer of such assets.'

2.43 In relation to the transferee taking over employees of the transferor, the UK Government and the Commission argued that it may be sufficient in certain circumstances for the new awardee of the contract to have voluntarily taken over the majority of the employees assigned by its predecessor to the performance of the contract. The ECJ pointed out in relation to that argument that the question whether or not a majority of the employees are taken over by the new employer is one of the factual circumstances to be taken into account in determining whether the conditions for a transfer are met.[61] It added that, in the case of labour-intensive sectors, a group of workers engaged in a joint activity on a permanent basis may constitute an economic entity, saying:[62]

> 'Since in certain labour-intensive sectors a group of workers engaged in a joint activity on a permanent basis may constitute an economic entity, it must be recognized that such an entity is capable of maintaining its identity after it has been transferred where the new employer does not merely pursue the activity in question but also takes over a major part, in terms of their numbers and skills, of the employees specially assigned by his predecessor to that task. In those circumstances ... the new employer takes over a body of assets enabling him to carry on the activities or certain activities of the transferor undertaking on a regular basis.'

It concluded by saying:[63]

> '[T]he Directive does not apply to a situation in which a person who had entrusted the cleaning of his premises to a first undertaking terminates his contract with the latter and, for the performance of similar work, enters into a new contract with a similar undertaking, if there is no concomitant transfer from one undertaking to the other of significant tangible or intangible assets or taking over by the new

---

58   [1997] ICR 662, at 670–671, para 14.
59   See **2.27**.
60   [1997] ICR 662, at 671, paras 17 and 18.
61   [1997] ICR 662, at 672 para 20.
62   [1997] ICR 662, at 672, para 21.
63   [1997] ICR 662, at 672, para 23.

employer of a major part of the workforce, in terms of their numbers and skills, assigned by his predecessor to the performance of the contract.'

2.44   The decision in *Süzen* has been thought to draw a distinction between so-called 'asset reliant' businesses and 'labour intensive' businesses and has been much criticised largely on the grounds that it appears to be taking a more restrictive view of the ambit of Art 1 of the Directive than had previously been thought to be the case. Nevertheless, it is arguable that it points to the limits of the ambit of the Article. It needs to be remembered that this was a case where there was no transfer of employees and no transfer of assets. Before the transfer one person or legal entity carried out the activity of cleaning; after it another carried out the same activity. Had the new legal entity used some of the assets or some of the employees it would have been arguable that there was a transfer of undertaking. The fact, however, that the new entity used none of the assets or employees used by the previous entity meant that there was no transfer of an undertaking. It is arguable, however, that the decisions in *Allen v Amalgamated Construction Co Ltd*[64] and *Abler v Sodexho MM Catering GmbH*[65] suggest a relaxation of the stance taken by the Court in *Süzen*. These are considered at **2.47** and **2.54**.

2.45   A similar approach may be detected in two groups of cases decided by the ECJ on the same day: *Francisco Hernández Vidal SA v Gomez Perez*[66] and *Sánchez Hidalgo v Asociacion de Servicios ASER*.[67] The first group of cases (two from Spain and one from Germany) involved contracting-in, where cleaning work was brought back in-house after being contracted out. Neither the cleaning company nor the company which took the cleaning back in-house wished to employ the employees concerned, all of whom complained of unlawful dismissal. The three references to the ECJ all effectively asked the same question, whether the Directive applies to contracting-in. The Court said that it did, with the proviso that the operation is accompanied by the transfer of an economic entity between the two undertakings. It said that such an entity refers to an organised grouping of persons and of assets enabling an economic activity which pursues a specific objective to be exercised. It pointed out that, whilst such an entity must be sufficiently structured and autonomous, it will not necessarily have significant assets, tangible or intangible and added:[68]

> 'Indeed, in certain sectors, such as cleaning, these assets are often reduced to their most basic and the activity is essentially based on manpower. Thus, an organised grouping of wage earners who are specifically and permanently assigned to a common task may, in the absence of other factors of production, amount to an economic entity ... It is for the national courts ... to determine ... whether the maintenance of the premises of the contract-awarding undertaking was organised in the form of an economic entity within the outside cleaning firm before the first undertaking decided to carry out the work itself.'

It concluded by saying:[69]

---

64   [2000] ICR 436, Case C-234/98.
65   [2004] IRLR 168, Case C-340/01.
66   [1999] IRLR 132, Cases C-127/96, C-229/96 and C-74/97.
67   [1999] IRLR 136, Cases C-173/96 and C-247/96.
68   [1999] IRLR 132, at 134, paras 27 and 28.
69   [1999] IRLR 132, at 135. It used identical words in the *Sánchez Hidalgo* case: see at 139.

'Since, in certain labour-intensive sectors, a group of workers engaged in a joint activity on a permanent basis may constitute an economic entity, it must be recognised that such an entity is capable of maintaining its identity after it has been transferred where the new employer does not merely pursue the activity in question but also takes over a major part, in terms of their numbers and skills, of the employees specially assigned by his predecessor to that task. In those circumstances, the new employer takes over a body of assets enabling him to carry on the activities or certain activities of the transferor undertaking on a regular basis (*Süzen*, cited above, paragraph 21) ... Article 1(1) of Directive 77/187 is to be interpreted as meaning that the Directive applies to a situation in which an undertaking which used to entrust the cleaning of its premises to another undertaking decides to terminate its contract with that other undertaking and in future to carry out that cleaning work itself, provided that the operation is accompanied by the transfer of an economic entity between the two undertakings. The term "economic entity" refers to an organised grouping of persons and assets enabling an economic activity which pursues a specific objective to be exercised. The mere fact that the maintenance work carried out first by the cleaning firm and then by the undertaking owning the premises is similar does not justify the conclusion that a transfer of such an entity has occurred.'

2.46   The second group of cases (one from Spain and one from Germany) involved a change of contractor. In the Spanish case, the employee was one of five employees employed by Minerva to provide home-help services in accordance with a contract granted to it by a municipality in Spain. When the contract expired, it was awarded to Aser, which took on Mrs Sánchez Hidalgo and her colleagues but refused to recognise their previous service with Minerva. In the German case, the employee was employed as a guard at a medical supplies depot of the German Federal Armed Forces by a succession of companies who had the contract for maintaining surveillance of the depot. His last employer, Ziemann, lost the contract after it was put out to tender. The new contractor employed all the watchmen of Ziemann except three, one of whom was Mr Ziemann, the applicant. The ECJ repeated much of what it had said in the *Sánchez Hidalgo* case,[70] which has been extensively quoted above. So, therefore, applying the principles stated by the Court, it would be safe to say that the likely outcome of both references in the *Sánchez Hidalgo* and *Ziemann* cases would be that the employees concerned became the employees of the transferee, so that in Mrs Sánchez Hidalgo's case, for example, her previous service with Minerva would count towards her service with Aser.

2.47   The approach taken in *Süzen* and followed in *Francisco Hernández Vidal* and *Sánchez Hidalgo* was followed in the later decision of *Allen v Amalgamated Construction Co Ltd*,[71] which involved the transfer of an employee between subsidiary companies in the same corporate group. Both companies shared the same management and premises and also shared administrative and support functions. The ECJ held that there was a transfer within Art 1 of the Directive. It should be noted here that the Court approached this case on the basis that it was one involving an activity based essentially on manpower. This was because, although the activity in question (the driving of underground tunnels) required

---

70   This was memorably castigated by the editor of the *Industrial Relations Law Reports* as 'jurisprudence by word processor': see [1999] IRLR 73.
71   [2000] ICR 436, Case C-234/98. See also **2.10**.

a significant amount of plant and equipment, the mine owner provided those assets and not the contractors. The ECJ pointed out that the fact that ownership of the assets required to run the undertaking do not pass to the new owner does not preclude a transfer.[72]

2.48 It is arguable that the significance of the *Allen* case has been underestimated. It is important to note, as has already been observed above, that the activity in question required a significant amount of plant and equipment and that neither of the contractors provided those assets; they were provided by the mine owner. This is important, since there may be analogous situations where different contractors carry out operations for a person who provides the main plant. For example, in the provision of catering services for a hospital or large company, the contractors will provide prepared food but they will need the kitchens, kitchen equipment and cookers on the premises of the organisation using their services. In such a case, following *Allen*, the fact that neither of the catering contractors provides the basic kitchen facilities will not preclude a transfer of undertaking taking place, provided that the other criteria are satisfied. The decision in *Allen*, interestingly enough, foreshadows the decision in *Abler v Sodexho MM Catering GmbH*,[73] which in fact involved a change in the provision of catering services, though it is not mentioned in that decision.

2.49 *Allen v Amalgamated Construction Co Ltd* was followed by *Oy Liikenne AB v Liskojärvi and Juntunen*.[74] The facts of the case were that the operation of seven bus routes was awarded to Oy Liikenne AB; they had previously been operated by Hakunilan Liikenne Oy. Hakunilan dismissed 45 drivers, of whom 33 were re-engaged by Oy Liikenne, but on less favourable terms and conditions. No vehicles or other assets connected with the operation of the bus routes were transferred, although Oy Liikenne bought uniforms from Hakunilan for some of the drivers who entered its service; it also leased two buses from Hakunilan while waiting for the 22 new buses it had ordered to be delivered. The applicants were amongst the 33 drivers who were taken on by Oy Liikenne. They claimed that there had been a transfer of an undertaking and that they were entitled to enjoy the terms and conditions applied by their previous employer. The Court reiterated the so-called 'multifactorial' approach and said:[75]

> '[T]o determine whether the conditions for the transfer of an economic entity are satisfied, it is also necessary to consider all the factual circumstances characterising the transaction in question, including in particular the type of undertaking or business involved, whether or not its tangible assets such as buildings and movable property are transferred, the value of its intangible assets at the time of the transfer, whether or not the core of its employees are taken over by the new employer, whether or not its customers are transferred, the degree of similarity between the activities carried on before and after the transfer, and the period, if any, for which

---

72 [2000] ICR 436, at 461, following *Landsorganisationen i Danmark v Ny Mølle Kro* [1989] ICR 330 and *Foreningen af Arbejdsledere i Danmark v Daddy's Dance Hall A/S* [1988] IRLR 315.
73 [2004] IRLR 168, Case C-340/01.
74 [2001] IRLR 171.
75 [2001] IRLR 171, at 174, para 33.

those activities were suspended. These are, however, merely single factors in the overall assessment which must be made, and cannot therefore be considered in isolation ...'

The Court also said:[76]

'[T]he national court, in assessing the facts characterising the transaction in question, must take into account among other things the type of undertaking or business concerned. It follows that the degree of importance to be attached to the various criteria for determining whether or not there has been a transfer within the meaning of the directive will necessarily vary according to the activity carried on, and indeed the production or operating methods employed in the relevant undertaking, business or part of a business.'

2.50   The Court went on to apply these principles to the facts of the case in front of it and said that, in the absence of a transfer of significant tangible assets from the old to the new contractor, the Directive does not apply. It said:[77]

'However, bus transport cannot be regarded as an activity based essentially on manpower, as it requires substantial plant and equipment (see, reaching the same conclusion with respect to driveage work in mines, *Allen*, paragraph 30[78]). The fact that the tangible assets used for operating the bus routes were not transferred from the old to the new contractor therefore constitutes a circumstance to be taken into account ... However, in a sector such as scheduled public transport by bus, where the tangible assets contribute significantly to the performance of the activity, the absence of a transfer to a significant extent from the old to the new contractor of such assets, which are necessary for the proper functioning of the entity, must lead to the conclusion that the entity does not retain its identity. Consequently, in a situation such as that in the main proceedings, Directive 77/187 does not apply in the absence of a transfer of significant tangible assets from the old to the new contractor.'

2.51   The following points should be noted about this case: (1) the ECJ reiterated its previous observation that there need be no direct contractual link between the transferor and the transferee for the Directive to be applicable; it did, however, go slightly further than in previous cases and suggest that the absence of a contractual link may point to the absence of a transfer within the meaning of the Directive;[79] (2) the transfer may take place in two stages, through the intermediary of a third party such as the owner or the person putting up the capital; (3) the fact that the operation of an activity, such as a bus route, is awarded following a public procurement procedure in accordance with Directive 92/50/EEC does not of itself rule out the application of Directive 2001/23/EC.

2.52   The approach taken in *Oy Liikenne* suggests that the decisive criterion in such cases is whether the tangible assets 'contribute significantly' to the activity and does not seem to take into account the possibility that there may be factors

---

76   [2001] IRLR 171, at 174–175, para 35.
77   [2001] IRLR 171, at 175, paras 39 and 42.
78   This statement would appear to be based on a misreading of *Allen*, since, as has already been observed, the heavy equipment for conducting the driveage operation was not transferred between transferor and transferee, but provided by the mine owner.
79   [2001] IRLR 171, at 174, paras 28–30.

pointing towards the conclusion that the entity retains its identity. It also seems to be at variance with the approach taken later in the *Abler* case: see **2.54**.

2.53   Subsequently, in *Temco Service Industries SA v Imzilyen*,[80] the ECJ held that there may be a transfer where the transferor is a subcontractor of the original contractor. The case involved the familiar scenario where a company contracts out an operation (again, a cleaning operation) to one contractor and then terminates that contract and grants the contract to another contractor. In this case, it was Volkswagen which contracted out the cleaning of a number of its production plants in Belgium to BMV. The difference between this case and other cases of the genre was that the first contractor, BMV, subcontracted the work to a subsidiary, GMC. Subsequently, Volkswagen terminated the contract with BMV and awarded the cleaning contract to Temco, which re-engaged some of GMC's staff who had been assigned to the cleaning contract granted to BMV. The question was whether there had been a transfer of an undertaking from GMC to Temco. The ECJ said that such an arrangement was capable of amounting to a transfer of an undertaking within Art 1 of the Directive, provided that: (1) the transfer must result in a change of employer; (2) it must concern an undertaking, business or part of a business; and (3) it must be the result of a contract. The Court pointed out, however, that the fact that the transferor undertaking is only the subcontractor of the original contractor has no effect upon the concept of legal transfer since it is sufficient for that transfer to be part of the web of contractual relations even if they are indirect. As has been noted, there have been many cases in which the Court has pointed out that there need be no contractual relation between the transferor and transferee. Temco tried to argue that there could be no transfer when there was no contract between the transferor and the original contractor (ie the person granting the contract). The Court said, however:[81]

> 'The fact that the transferor undertaking is not the one which concluded the first contract with the original contractor but only the subcontractor of the original co-contractor has no effect on the concept of legal transfer, since it is sufficient for that transfer to be part of a web of contractual relations even if they are indirect.'

2.54   The case of *Abler v Sodexho MM Catering GmbH*[82] develops the line of thought apparent in *Allen v Amalgamated Construction Co Ltd*,[83] though without mentioning it explicitly. The case involved a transfer of catering services, after a tendering process, to Sodexho. It refused to take over the materials, stock and employees of the previous contractor, Sanrest. The ECJ said that in a sector such as catering, where the activity is based essentially on equipment, the failure of a new contractor to take over an essential part of the staff which the predecessor contractor employed to perform the same activity is not sufficient to preclude the existence of a transfer of an entity which retains its identity within the meaning of the Directive, whose main objective is to ensure the continuity, even against the wishes of the transferee, of the employment contracts of the employees of the transferor. The Court said that catering cannot be regarded as an activity based essentially on manpower since

---

80   [2002] IRLR 214, Case C-51/00.
81   [2002] IRLR 214, at 217, para 28.
82   [2004] IRLR 168, Case C-340/01.
83   [2000] ICR 436, Case C-234/98.

it requires a significant amount of equipment. Thus, the transfer of the premises and the equipment provided by the hospital was sufficient to make this a transfer of an economic entity. The Court said:[84]

'Catering cannot be regarded as an activity based essentially on manpower since it requires a significant amount of equipment. In the main proceedings, ... the tangible assets needed for the activity in question – namely, the premises, water and energy and small and large equipment (inter alia the appliances needed for preparing the meals and the dishwashers) – were taken over by Sodexho. Moreover, a defining feature of the situation at issue in the main proceedings is the express and fundamental obligation to prepare the meals in the hospital kitchen and thus to take over those tangible assets. The transfer of the premises and the equipment provided by the hospital, which is indispensable for the preparation and distribution of meals to the hospital patients and staff is sufficient, in the circumstances, to make this a transfer of an economic entity. It is moreover clear that, given their captive status, the new contractor necessarily took on most of the customers of its predecessor.'

The Court went on:[85]

'It follows that the failure of the new contractor to take over, in terms of numbers and skills, an essential part of the staff which its predecessor employed to perform the same activity is not sufficient to preclude the existence of a transfer of an entity which retains its identity within the meaning of Directive 77/187 in a sector such as catering, where the activity is based essentially on equipment. As the United Kingdom and the Commission rightly point out, any other conclusion would run counter to the principal objective of Directive 77/187, which is to ensure the continuity, even against the wishes of the transferee, of the employment contracts of the employees of the transferor.'

2.55 Two other arguments advanced by Sodexho were that (1) there could be no transfer from the previous service provider (Sanrest) to it because it had no contractual relationship with Sanrest and (2) the fact that the contracting authority remained the owner of the premises and equipment necessary for the performance of the activity precluded a mere change of contractor from being regarded as a business transfer. In relation to the first argument the Court repeated the point it has made in many other cases, that there is no need for a direct contractual relationship between the transferor and the transferee.[86]

2.56 In relation to the second argument, the Court said that the fact that the tangible assets taken over by the new contractor did not belong to its predecessor but were provided by the contracting authority could not preclude the existence of a transfer, since it is clear that the Directive applies whenever there is a change in the legal or natural person who is responsible for carrying on the business.[87]

2.57 The most recent case to consider this question is *Güney-Görres v Securicor Aviation*.[88] The factual matrix of the case echoes that of the *Abler*

---

84   [2004] IRLR 168, at 171, para 36.
85   [2004] IRLR 168, at 171, para 37.
86   [2004] IRLR 168, at 171, para 39.
87   [2004] IRLR 168, at 171, paras 41–42.
88   [2006] IRLR 305, Cases C-232/04 and C-233/04.

case, except that the context was airport security rather than catering. There was a change in the provision of airport security from Securicor to Kötter Aviation Security. The security equipment was all provided by the German Government which also met the costs of maintaining it. Securicor employed 295 employees exclusively in airport security. When Kötter took over the contract it informed Securicor that it proposed to take on only a small proportion of Securicor's employees. Securicor therefore dismissed all the employees employed on the contract. In the event, Kötter took on 167 of the employees previously employed by Securicor. It also used the security equipment owned by the Government. Two of the dismissed employees brought actions claiming that their employment relationship had been transferred to Kötter. In the proceedings before the ECJ, the German Government argued that there cannot be a transfer of assets so as to amount to a transfer of an undertaking unless the assets are available for the independent commercial use of the new contractor. It should occasion little surprise that the ECJ rejected that argument, saying:[89]

> 'It does not appear that the fact that independent commercial use was made of the assets taken over by a contractor is decisive in establishing whether or not there has been a transfer of assets. That criterion is derived neither from the wording of Directive 2001/23 nor from its objectives, which are to ensure the protection of workers where there is a change of undertaking or business and to allow the completion of the internal market. Thus, the fact that the tangible assets are taken over by the new contractor without those assets having been transferred to him for independent commercial use does not preclude there being either a transfer of assets, or a transfer of an undertaking or business within the meaning of Directive 2001/23.'

2.58   Finally, it should be noted that the ECJ has held that the fact that an undertaking is temporarily closed and does not have any employees at the time of the transfer does not mean that a transfer of an undertaking within the Directive is precluded. It is a factor to be taken into account in deciding whether an economic entity still in existence has been transferred.[90] So, for example, in *Landsorganisationen I Danmark v Ny Mølle Kro*,[91] a question which fell to be considered by the ECJ was whether there could be a transfer if the transfer took place at a time when the undertaking was closed for the season and the staff were absent. The ECJ said:[92]

> 'In order to determine whether those conditions are satisfied it is necessary to take account of all the facts characterizing the transaction in question. The fact that the undertaking in question was temporarily closed at the time of the transfer and therefore had no employees certainly constitutes one factor to be taken into account in determining whether a business was transferred as a going concern. However, the temporary closure of an undertaking and the resulting absence of staff at the time of the transfer do not of themselves preclude the possibility that there has been a transfer of an undertaking within the meaning of article 1 (1) of the directive. That

---

89   [2006] IRLR 305, at 314, paras 39–41.
90   See, for example, *P Bork International A/S v Foreningen af Arbejdsledere i Danmark* [1989] IRLR 41, at 43; and *Landsorganisationen i Danmark v Ny Mølle Kro* [1989] ICR 330, at 339. See also **2.34**.
91   [1989] ICR 330, Case 287/86.
92   [1989] ICR 330, at 339, paras 19–21.

is true in particular in the case of a seasonal business, especially where, as in this case, the transfer takes place during the season when it is closed. As a general rule such closure does not mean that the undertaking has ceased to be a going concern. It is for the national court to make the necessary factual appraisal, in the light of the criteria for interpretation set out above, in order to establish whether or not there has been a transfer in the sense indicated.'

THE TRANSFER OF UNDERTAKINGS (PROTECTION OF EMPLOYMENT) REGULATIONS 2006

2.59 TUPE 2006 applies where there is a 'relevant transfer' of an 'undertaking'. It will be apparent from the preceding section that there has been a steady flow of decisions from the ECJ on the scope of the 1977 Directive which led to the drafting of the 2001 Directive and in the context of which these Regulations were made. The importance of these decisions lies in the fact that courts and tribunals in the UK are required to interpret the Regulations so that, as far as possible, they conform to the Directive.

2.60 The following matters are considered here:

(1) the meaning of 'undertaking'; and
(2) the meaning of 'relevant transfer'.

2.61 It should be noted that, as a general rule, a tribunal considering whether there has been a relevant transfer of an undertaking should consider as separate issues, first, whether the entity in question was an undertaking and, secondly, whether there was a relevant transfer. The EAT has made it clear that these two issues should be considered as separate questions and has said that, although it is not invariably an error of law not to raise the two questions as separate questions or to fail to deal with them in that order, a tribunal which fails in this way runs a real risk of error.[93]

The meaning of 'undertaking' and 'business'

2.62 TUPE 2006 contains no definition of the word 'undertaking', unlike its predecessor Regulations.[94] It should be noted, however, that reg 3 contains various phrases which clearly reflect the jurisprudence of the ECJ. In particular, reg 3(1)(a) refers to the transfer of an economic entity which retains its identity; reg 3(2) defines 'economic entity': see below. It should also be noted that, by virtue of reg 3(4)(a), the Regulations apply to public and private undertakings engaged in economic activities 'whether or not they are operating for gain'. Thus, although TUPE 2006 contains no express definition of the words 'undertaking' and 'business', it is clear that, when deciding whether a particular activity amounts to an undertaking, a tribunal or court cannot decide that question without having recourse to the substantial jurisprudence of the ECJ.

---

93 *Cheesman v R Brewer Contracts Ltd* [2001] IRLR 144. See also *Whitewater Leisure Management Ltd v Barnes* [2000] ICR 1049.
94 The definition was contained in reg 1(1) and was very brief: ' "undertaking" includes any trade or business.'

This process is underlined by the express references in reg 3(1)(a), (2) and (4) to phrases which are used in decisions of the ECJ. In addition, in the light of cases such as *Dr Sophie Redmond Stichting v Bartol*[95] and *Rask and Christensen v ISS Kantineservice A/S*,[96] it is suggested that the term 'undertaking' is to be given a wide meaning.

2.63 In this section of the chapter, the scope of TUPE 2006 will be considered first. Consideration will be given to the case-law on TUPE 1981, since that clearly will have an important effect on the way in which courts and tribunals look at the new Regulations.

The scope of TUPE 2006

2.64 Regulation 3(1)(a) states that the Regulations apply to the 'transfer of an economic entity which retains its identity'; reg 3(2) defines the term 'economic entity' as:

'... an organised grouping of resources which has the objective of pursing an economic activity, whether or not that activity is central or ancillary.'

2.65 A number of preliminary observations may be made here, all of which serve to emphasis that it is crucially important to read TUPE 2006 in the context of the ECJ's jurisprudence. First, the definition of 'economic entity' given above is clearly intended to give effect to cases decided by the ECJ on what is meant by an undertaking and to reflect the line of cases which has been considered earlier in this chapter. It will be recalled that in *Foreningen af Arbejdsledere I Danmark v Daddy's Dance Hall A/S*[97] the ECJ talked of the 'economic unit' retaining its identity. In later cases, such as *Francisco Hernández Vidal SA v Gomez Perez*,[98] the ECJ moved from talking of an 'economic unit' to the phrase 'economic entity' and said that the term 'refers to an organised grouping of persons and assets enabling an economic activity which pursues a specific objective to be exercised.' Clearly, reg 3(2) is following this line of jurisprudential thought when it speaks of 'an organised grouping of resources which has the objective of pursuing an economic activity'.

2.66 The third observation is that, when reg 3(2) states that economic activity pursued by the organised grouping of resources may be central or ancillary, it is clearly intended to reflect cases such as *Rask and Christensen v ISS Kantineservice A/S*,[99] in which the ECJ said that ancillary activities such as

---

95 [1992] IRLR 366. This case is considered at **2.13**.

96 [1993] IRLR 133. The *Sophie Redmond* and *Rask* cases were applied by the High Court in *Kenny v South Manchester College* [1993] IRLR 265. Cf *Wren v Eastbourne Borough Council* [1993] ICR 955, which involved the transfer of cleansing services from the local authority to a company as a result of compulsory competitive tendering. The EAT remitted the case to the tribunal for it to make a finding as to whether or not there was an undertaking capable of being transferred.

97 [1988] IRLR 315, at 317, para 10. See **2.5**.

98 [1999] IRLR 132, at 135, para 35. See **2.45**.

99 [1993] IRLR 133. The *Sophie Redmond* and *Rask* cases were applied by the High Court in *Kenny v South Manchester College* [1993] IRLR 265. Cf *Wren v Eastbourne Borough Council*

catering facilities were within the coverage of the 1977 Directive, and *Schmidt v Spar- und Leihkasse der Früheren Ämter Bordesholm, Kiel und Cronshagen*,[100] which involved a cleaning operation carried out by a single employee. The fourth preliminary observation is that the express extension of the Regulations to undertakings engaged in economic activities 'whether or not they are operating for gain' by reg 3(4)(a) is clearly intended to reflect cases such as *Dr Sophie Redmond Stichting v Bartol*.[101]

Interpretation of TUPE 1981

2.67   Cases decided in domestic courts and tribunals over the years have shown an increased preparedness on the part of the judges to look to ECJ cases when dealing with this issue and to follow the approach suggested by it in cases such as *Spijkers v Gebroeders Benedik Abattoir*,[102] considered above. Indeed, they have held to the principles of considering all the circumstances, as espoused by the *Spijkers* decision, even when it has been argued that a narrower view should be taken pursuant to such cases as *Süzen*. Bearing in mind that TUPE is intended to transpose the Directive into English law, deference to the ECJ's decisions is clearly the correct approach. So, for example, the *Sophie Redmond* and *Rask* cases were applied by the High Court in *Kenny v South Manchester College*,[103] in which employees sought a declaration that their contracts of employment would transfer to the College when it took over the provision of prison education services, which had previously been provided by the local education authority, Cheshire County Council being the employer of the plaintiff employees. The High Court granted the declaration that the prospective transfer from the local education authority to the College was a transfer within the meaning of Art 1 of the Directive. The judge reached this conclusion despite the fact that there was no direct relationship between the authority and the College, no transfer of assets, no transfer of clients and customers, no transfer of employees pursuant to the contract and the continuing function of providing education would be carried out in a different manner. The judge said that, taking into account all the relevant considerations in accordance with the ECJ decisions, after the transfer the education department at the prison would retain its identity and its operation would continue as a going concern.

2.68   In *Council of the Isles of Scilly v Brintel Helicopters Ltd*,[104] the EAT referred to the fact that the ECJ's decisions tend to speak of an 'economic entity' rather than a business and said:

[1993] ICR 955, which involved the transfer of cleansing services from the local authority to a company as a result of compulsory competitive tendering. The EAT remitted the case to the tribunal for it to make a finding as to whether or not there was an undertaking capable of being transferred.

100   [1995] ICR 237.
101   [1992] IRLR 366. This case is considered at **2.13**.
102   [1986] ECR 1119.
103   [1993] IRLR 265. Cf *Wren v Eastbourne Borough Council* [1993] ICR 955, which involved the transfer of cleansing services from the local authority to a company as a result of compulsory competitive tendering. The EAT remitted the case to the tribunal for it to make a finding as to whether or not there was an undertaking capable of being transferred.
104   [1995] ICR 249, at 255.

'A "business" implies an activity which is being carried on commercially for profit: that is not a requirement. The use of the word "business" may well lead a tribunal into error, simply because it is associated with the idea that there must be a transfer of a business "as a going concern" with an emphasis on an examination of whether there has been a transfer of outstanding orders and goodwill ... [W]e would respectfully suggest that by using the language of the Court of Justice, [employment] tribunals will find it easier to put aside some of the old case-law, ... which has now been overtaken by more recent cases.'

2.69 Decisions in the Court of Appeal and the EAT have drawn heavily on the case-law of the ECJ when considering whether a particular entity amounts to an undertaking. In *Whitewater Leisure Management Ltd v Barnes,*[105] the EAT said that there are two formulations which can be used to identify whether there is an economic entity. The first asks whether there is 'a stable and discrete economic entity'; the alternative version asks whether the entity is 'sufficiently structured and autonomous'. The EAT suggested that the expression 'distinct cost centre' might be helpful. The case itself involved a management contract by which a leisure centre was managed by Whitewater. Whitewater had a number of other operations and the six employees who formed the senior management of the leisure centre were also involved in those other operations. There was also a 'core' team of 14 employees, including a manager and two assistant managers, and a number of other employees, consisting of a mix of part-time, casual and seasonal employees. When the contract expired, Whitewater was unsuccessful in the ensuing tendering process. No tangible or intangible assets were transferred to the successor, nor did the six senior employees transfer. Of the 'core' team, seven transferred and seven (including the manager and assistant managers) did not. The EAT concluded that there was no economic entity capable of transfer. It said:[106]

'There is plainly a substantial argument that there was not a stable and discrete entity, or a sufficiently structured and autonomous entity, because of the fact that the Leisure Centre was so intricately bound up with the rest of the operations of Whitewater. The senior management was plainly not discrete, and on the face of it, at least without evidence, which was plainly not adduced, about the Leisure Centre as a cost centre, the Leisure Centre was, if its senior management is taken into account, not discrete, and if they are left out of account, then not stable, or for that matter autonomous.'

2.70 It is tempting to suggest that had the EAT considered the ECJ decision in *Allen v Amalgamated Construction Co Ltd.*[107] it might have reached a different conclusion. That case, it will be recalled, said that there may be a transfer of an economic entity even where there is no transfer of the plant and equipment necessary to carry out the activity because they are supplied by the person granting the contract.

2.71 The *Whitewater* decision also appears to be inconsistent with the later decision of another division of the EAT and of the Court of Appeal, in *RCO Support Services and Aintree Hospital Trust v UNISON and others.*[108] The case

---

105 [2000] ICR 1049.
106 [2000] ICR 1049, at 1061–1062.
107 [2000] ICR 436.
108 [2000] ICR 1502. See also *Argyll Training Ltd v Sinclair and Argyll & The Islands*

involved cleaners and caterers. The cleaners were employed by Initial Hospital Services Ltd at Walton Hospital, one of two hospitals run by the Aintree Hospitals NHS Trust. Initial tendered for the cleaning contract at Fazakerley, the other hospital run by the Trust, but it was won by RCO. None of the Walton cleaners applied for jobs with RCO and none was taken on. Subsequently, the employment of cleaners at Walton ended and a number of them brought unfair dismissal proceedings. The catering staff were employed at Walton by the Trust itself. Three of the support staff were dismissed for redundancy. Applications were invited by RCO, which held the catering contract at Fazakerley. One applicant was not offered a job and another declined the job offered to her. Thus, the significant facts about the cases were as follows:

(1)   In the case of the cleaning contract there were no assets to transfer; in the case of the catering contract only a few of the assets were transferred.

(2)   RCO offered to take on any cleaners who resigned from Initial, but none resigned and none were taken on. Most of the caterers were not taken on by RCO.

2.72   The employment tribunal held that there was a relevant transfer from Initial to RCO in respect of the cleaners and from the Trust to RCO in respect of the caterers. The EAT dismissed the appeals. It said that the absence of movement of significant assets or of a major part of the workforce does not necessarily deny the existence of a relevant transfer and expressed the view that *Süzen* can no longer safely be relied upon. It also favoured the approach taken by the Court of Appeal in *ECM*[109] over that taken by the earlier Court of Appeal in *Betts v Brintel*.[110] Lindsay J emphasised the safeguarding of employees' rights as being the crucial objective. He said:[111]

> '*Schmidt* still stands as a reminder of how very little is required to amount to something capable of being an undertaking ... once due regard is paid to the safeguarding of employees' rights, the subject-matter of the Directive.'

He also said:[112]

> '(iv) ... whilst it is wrong to look merely to see if a given activity continues in order to find whether there is either an undertaking or its transfer, both *Spijkers* (paragraphs 11 and 12) and *Schmidt* (paragraph 17) still stand for the propositions that the decisive criterion as to transfer is whether the business in question retains its identity and as to the importance in relation to that of whether its operation was continued by the new employer with the same or similar activities; (v) *Schmidt* still stands (paragraph 16) as a powerful reminder, when no assets are transferred, that the safeguarding of employees' rights, the very subject-matter of the Directive, cannot depend exclusively on such a factor, a factor which the European Court of Justice had in *Spijkers* held not to be decisive on its own; (vi) *Schmidt* still stands as

---

Enterprise Ltd [2000] IRLR 630, which held that a training contract and the arrangements made for its performance amounted to an undertaking. The case is considered more fully at **2.76**.
109   See **2.117**.
110   See **2.115**.
111   [2000] ICR 1502, at 1515.
112   [2000] ICR 1502, at 1515.

a reminder of how very little is required to amount to something capable of being an undertaking ... once due regard is paid to the safeguarding of employees' rights, the subject-matter of the Directive ...'

2.73   The Court of Appeal upheld the EAT's decision. The argument of RCO, based on the ECJ's decision in *Süzen*, was that, because no (or no significant) assets or employees were transferred from Walton to Fazakerley, there were two separate contracts and the Directive did not apply. Mummery LJ, with whom the other two members of the court agreed, expressed himself to be unable to agree with that argument. He said:[113]

'I do not read *Süzen* as singling out, to the exclusion of all other circumstances, the particular circumstance of none of the workforce being taken on and treating that as determinative of the transfer issue in every case ... Whether or not the majority of employees are taken on by the new employer is only one of all the facts which must be considered by the national court in making an overall assessment of the facts characterising the transaction. Single factors must not be considered in isolation ... [T]he employment tribunal was entitled to characterise the facts found by it as involving retention of the identity of the economic entities of cleaning and catering previously carried on at Walton Hospital. The finding of retention of identity was based on more than just a comparison of the similarity of the activities undertaken by the contractors before and after the move. It was reached by a consideration of all the circumstances.'

It should be noted that Mummery LJ's language is more cautious than Lindsay J's in avoiding mention of the social policy objectives of the Directive.

2.74   The Court of Appeal decision is consistent with other cases decided in UK courts which have taken the line that the decision in *Süzen* does not supersede *Spijkers*. Hence one is entitled to look at all the circumstances. It is not just a question of interpreting *Süzen* as stating a rule that one need only consider whether there is a transfer of assets or employees. The decision, in refusing to take a narrow interpretation of *Süzen*, will set the precedent for bringing a greater number of labour intensive transfers within the scope of the Regulations than would have been the case had they taken the narrow view. It would otherwise seem far too easy for an incoming contractor, where there are no significant transferring assets, to decline to employ any of the transferor's employees merely to avoid the prospect of a transfer. The motives of the transferee are something which the court or tribunal is entitled to consider when forming a decision.

2.75   Other aspects of this case are considered later in the chapter, at **2.121**.

2.76   There are other EAT decisions which need to be considered, some of them falling before and some after the Court of Appeal decision in *RCO*. In *Argyll Training Ltd v Sinclair and Argyll & The Islands Enterprise Ltd*[114] Lindsay J took a similar approach to that taken by him in *RCO* when deciding that a training contract and the arrangements made for its performance amounted to an undertaking. The facts were that Mrs Sinclair worked as a

---

113   [2000] ICR 1502, at 761–762.
114   [2000] IRLR 630. See also *Pinnacle AIC Ltd v Honeyman and Cape Industrial Services Ltd* (EAT/411/01).

training adviser for a company (BEST) which had a contract with Argyll and The Islands Training Enterprise Ltd (AIE) to provide training to local enterprise companies in the Argyll area. She had sole responsibility for the placement side of training. BEST lost its contract with AIE and so issued Mrs Sinclair with a redundancy notice. The contract was take over by Argyll Training Ltd (ATL), which took on 21 out of 32 placement trainees on BEST's books who remained with a training provider. The employment tribunal held that there had been a relevant transfer from BEST to ATL. On appeal ATL argued that there was no stable economic entity and that, even if there was, the entity's activity was limited to one specific contract and that, following *Rygaard's case*, Directive 77/187/EEC and so TUPE did not apply. It also argued that there can be no transfer of an undertaking where there is no transfer of significant assets or of the majority of the relevant employees.

2.77 The EAT held that the employment tribunal was entitled to find that the training contract made between BEST and AIE and the arrangements BEST made in connection with its performance amounted to an undertaking, in the sense of being a stable economic entity. It said that the training operation had an identifiable separate income and an employee; it consisted of more than activity, in the sense that it included an organised body of information. The EAT also held that the tribunal was entitled to find that there was a transfer of an undertaking when ATL took over the training contract, despite the fact that the activity concerned was limited to one specific contract. It said that *Rygaard's case* was not easy to comprehend and suggested that that decision should be confined to single specific contracts for building works. In fact, as the EAT pointed out, the two cases referred to in *Rygaard*[115] provide no basis for excluding all single-contract undertakings from the possibility of being covered by the Directive. It is suggested that the point about *Rygaard* is not that it dealt with a building contract as opposed to any other form of contract, but that it dealt with the *completion* of a contract; in other words, the contractor took over something which would otherwise have been incomplete. The fact that it was otherwise incomplete meant that it could not amount to a stable economic entity. It can be concluded, therefore, whatever one's views of *Rygaard*, that the decision in *Argyll Training Ltd* is consistent with the Court of Appeal decision in *RCO*.

2.78 The EAT considered this question again in *Cheesman v R Brewer Contracts Ltd*.[116] The case again involved the loss of a maintenance contract. The previous contractor, Onyx, took over the contract from a district council; it acquired as part of the contract use of the council's yard, its equipment and its office accommodation. It took on 14 employees who had previously been allocated by the council to the contract. When it lost the contract to Brewer, Onyx dismissed the 14 staff; none of them was taken on by Brewer and no tangible or intangible assets passed from Onyx to Brewer, either directly or

---

115 *Spijkers* and *Schmidt*: see **2.27** and **2.16**.
116 [2001] IRLR 144. See also *Perth and Kinross Council v Donaldson* [2004] IRLR 121, in which the EAT said that an operation which depends for its existence on a day-to-day handout of work to which it is not contractually entitled, and which could be terminated at any time, cannot be held to be a stable economic entity. The case also considered issues relating to insolvency: see **2.137**.

indirectly by way of the council. The dismissed employees claimed that there
had been a transfer of an undertaking to Brewer and brought claims against it.
The employment tribunal decided that there had been no transfer of an
undertaking. The employees' appeal was allowed by the EAT, which remitted
the case to the tribunal to decide whether there had been a transfer of an
undertaking. Lindsay J said:[117]

> '(i)   As to whether there is an undertaking, there needs to be found a stable
>   economic entity whose activity is not limited to performing one specific works
>   contract, an organised grouping of persons and of assets enabling (or
>   facilitating) the exercise of an economic activity which pursues a specific
>   objective ... It has been held that the reference to "one specific works
>   contract" is to be restricted to a contract for building works – see Argyll
>   Training,[118] ... EAT at paragraphs 14–19.
>
> (ii)   In order to be such an undertaking it must be sufficiently structured and
>   autonomous but will not necessarily have significant assets, tangible or
>   intangible ...
>
> (iii)   In certain sectors such as cleaning and surveillance the assets are often
>   reduced to their most basic and the activity is essentially based on manpower
>   ...
>
> (iv)   An organised grouping of wage-earners who are specifically and permanently
>   assigned to a common task may in the absence of other factors of
>   production, amount to an economic entity ...
>
> (v)   An activity of itself is not an entity; the identity of an entity emerges from
>   other factors such as its workforce, management staff, the way in which its
>   work is organised, its operating methods and, where appropriate, the
>   operational resources available to it ...'

2.79   The approach taken in the two cases mentioned above and when dealing
with the appeal in *RCO* lays emphasis on the social objectives of the Directive,
the safeguarding of employees' rights. That approach, if followed, would lead
to the conclusion that tribunals should be ready to find that an entity is an
undertaking and that that undertaking has been transferred. But it should be
noted that the Court of Appeal, whilst reaching the same result as the EAT in
RCO, did not emphasise the social objectives of the Directive and was rather
more confined in its approach.

2.80   There are subsequent decisions of the EAT worthy of note. In *Wynnwith
Engineering Co Ltd v Bennett*[119] the EAT held that TUPE did not apply to a
transaction where the employees involved enjoyed a common employment
status, in that they had all taken early retirement and then started work again
on short-term contracts. What happened was that British Aerospace took back
on short-term contracts some employees to whom they had given early
retirement under a special scheme. To avoid the risk of this group of workers
accumulating sufficient continuity of employment so as to be regarded as
permanent employees again, BAe arranged with Wynnwith that the employees
would be transferred to Wynnwith but would continue to provide services to
BAe as employees of Wynnwith. So BAe terminated the contracts of the
employees and invited them to register with Wynnwith, which they did. The

---

117   [2001] IRLR 144, at 147, para 10.
118   [2000] IRLR 630.
119   [2002] IRLR 170.

employees in question were all involved in different disciplines and had occupied different skilled positions whilst at British Aerospace. All that they had in common was their employment status. The employees argued that there was a transfer of an undertaking and the majority of the tribunal (the chairman dissenting) held that there had been a transfer. The EAT rejected this argument and said that an economic entity must be identified by reference to the function performed by a group of employees. In the present case, they all carried out different functions. The fact that they shared the same employment status was not sufficient to establish the existence of an economic entity which retained its identity after a transfer.

2.81 In *Dudley Bower Building Services Ltd v Lowe*[120] the EAT held that a 'package' of maintenance duties, which were almost exclusively performed by a single employee, amounted to a stable economic entity capable of being transferred under TUPE. The case involved an electrician who was employed at a military airbase on routine electrical maintenance duties by WS Atkins Facilities Management Ltd (which took over the building management duties of the Public Services Agency when they were privatised). In 1996 the Ministry of Defence invited tenders for a 3-year contract divided into nine packages of work. The employee's duties fell within package 6. A contract which included package 6 was awarded to Serco, which subcontracted the work to Williams Brothers (who were subsequently acquired by Dudley Bower). Atkins considered that the employee had been transferred to Williams Brothers but they denied that this was so. They appointed an electrician who spent some 90% of his time carrying out the work which the employee had carried out before ceasing work. Neither Atkins nor Serco nor Williams Brothers (later Dudley Bower) would accept the employee, who brought tribunal proceedings claiming breach of contract, unfair dismissal and redundancy. The employment tribunal decided that there was a relevant transfer of a stable economic entity of which the employee formed a part. The EAT upheld the tribunal's decision and held that the work performed by the employee was readily identifiable as the performance of package 6, which was transferred to the subcontractor as a distinct undertaking. The EAT considered the *Schmidt* case and concluded that, although as a general rule it might be loss common for one employee to constitute an economic entity, the fact that there was only one employee did not preclude the existence of an entity. The EAT said of *Schmidt*:[121]

> 'It [*Schmidt*] does not decide that the performance of contractual duties by a single person is in itself enough to constitute an economic entity; it decides that the fact that only one employee is within a particular sector does not preclude the application of the Directive. All the factors have to be considered, such as the workforce, management staff, the way in which the work is organised, the operating methods and where appropriate the operational resources. It must always be borne in mind that the activity in itself is not an entity.'

2.82 The EAT decision makes it clear,[122] following previous decisions, that whether a stable economic entity exists and whether that entity has been transferred are distinct questions with different factors to be considered and

---

120 [2003] ICR 843.
121 [2003] ICR 843, at 854, para 53.
122 [2003] ICR 843, at 854, paras 46 and 47.

sets out the five factors set out by Lindsay J in *Cheesman*[123] as to the existence of an economic entity. The EAT's discussion of the relevant case-law and its application to the facts of a particular case, in paras 47–54, contains a succinct and helpful summary of the relevant legal principles to be applied. It also makes clear that, although cases such as *Süzen* use the phrase 'grouping of persons', there is no requirement that there must be more than a single employee. It points out that the ECJ cited *Schmidt*'s case with approval in *Süzen*, which would not have been the case had the ECJ taken the view that the Directive 77/187/EEC should not apply to an operation performed by a single employee.[124] It said:[125]

> 'Whether a stable economic entity exists in any given case will always be a question of fact and degree but there is, in our judgment, no reason in principle why the work performed by a single employee should not amount to such an entity. Whether it does or not will depend upon the factors in the particular case. At one extreme, if the activity consists of no more than one cleaning lady and her mop, an economic entity may not exist, whereas if the task to be performed is complex and sophisticated and requires careful planning, specification and costings, it may be that an entity exists even though the work is performed by a single employee. There may well be some activities where the work of two or three employees is less complex and needs to be less structured and pre-planned than the work of a single employee. As a general rule it may be less common for one employee to constitute an entity but the fact there is only one employee cannot preclude the existence of such an entity.'

2.83   The EAT also held that TUPE applied in *McLeod v Ingram t/a Phoenix Taxis and Rainbow Cars Ltd t/a Rainbow Cars*,[126] a case in which neither assets nor employees were transferred. A written agreement between two employers involved one taxi company agreeing to buy the goodwill and telephone numbers of another; there was no transfer of employees or tangible assets. The EAT held that the money which had changed hands had clearly been payment for the identifiable business as defined in the agreement. There was therefore a transfer of an undertaking. In *Godrich v Public and Commercial Services Union and Another*[127] the EAT held that TUPE applies to the amalgamation of two trade unions. In this case, the Vice-Chancellor said:[128]

> 'TUPE was enacted to give effect to Council Directive 79/7/EEC and its successor Council Directive 2001/23/EC ... By Article 1(a) the Directive is applied "to any transfer ... to another employer as a result of a ... merger". By Article 1(c) the Directive is applied "to public and private undertakings engaged in economic activities whether or not they are operating for gain." In my view it is clear from these provisions of the Directive that TUPE should, if possible, be interpreted to embrace amalgamations of trade unions so that contracts of employment which would otherwise have terminated are transferred to the union created by the amalgamation.'

---

123   See **2.78**.
124   [2003] ICR 843, at 854, para 49.
125   [2003] ICR 843, at 854, para 48.
126   EAT/1344/01.
127   [2002] EWHC 1642 (Ch).
128   [2002] EWHC 1642 (Ch), at [11].

2.84 In *Computacentre Ltd v Specialist Computer Centres and others*,[129] on the other hand, the EAT held that TUPE did not apply, saying that there was no undertaking to be transferred because the identity of the economic entity had not been retained. Although the service provided by the new contractor remained identical, the new contractor's allocation of staff to the new contract differed so significantly that it could not be said that the economic entity retained its identity in the new contractor's hands.

2.85 A question which has become vexed, particularly since the ECJ decision in *Oy Liikenne AB v Liskojärvi and Juntunen*,[130] relates to changes of contractor in asset-intensive sectors. In *P&O Trans European Ltd v Initial Transport Services Ltd*,[131] the relevant facts were that, as part of the transfer to P&O from Shell of its delivery function, P&O took over from Initial (which had previously provided a back-up delivery service to Shell) its delivery drivers, but not the four administrators who had worked for Initial or any of Initial's vehicles. The question was whether the contract between Initial and Shell could be said to amount to an undertaking. The employment tribunal found that there was a discrete economic entity capable of being transferred. Despite the fact that the assets were not transferred from Initial to P&O, the tribunal concluded that there had been a transfer of an undertaking. It took into account the fact that there had been no transfer of assets but, whilst noting that this was an important factor, nevertheless held that Initial's activity of providing a back-up delivery service had retained its identity. The EAT upheld the tribunal's decision. The EAT said that all relevant factors have to be weighed in assessing whether or not a transfer has taken place and that the weight to be given to the various factors will vary in accordance with the facts of the case. It emphasised that the approach to this issue remains the 'multifactorial' approach set out in the *Spijkers* case:[132]

> 'In our opinion the Court of Justice was not laying down a principle that in all cases of asset intensive industries the absence of a transfer, to a significant extent, of such assets would always lead to the conclusion that no transfer had taken place. When the judgment is read as a whole it is apparent that the Court of Justice was reaffirming the principle that all relevant factors had to be weighed in assessing whether a transfer had taken place or not, and that the weight to be given to particular factors would vary in accordance with the facts of the case. Thus, in an asset intensive industry the fact that assets were not transferred will be "a circumstance to be taken into account." In some cases of this type the absence of a transfer will be decisive in some it will not. On the facts of the case before them relating to "scheduled public transport by bus" they concluded that the absence of a transfer of assets was such an important circumstance that it must lead to the conclusion that no transfer had taken place.

> The relative significance of assets in relation to manpower and how each contributes to the performance of the particular activity will vary according to the

---

129 EAT/0256/04.
130 [2001] IRLR 171. See also *Balfour Beatty Power Networks Ltd v Wilcox* [2006] IRLR 258. Leave has been given in this case to appeal to the Court of Appeal.
131 [2003] IRLR 128.
132 [2003] IRLR 128, at 131, para 39.

facts of the particular case. The whole of the transaction has to be looked at in order to see whether one particular factor is decisive; that includes all the circumstances of the transaction.'

2.86   There are two other cases to note in relation to asset-intensive activities: the EAT decision in *NUMAST v P&O Scottish Ferries Ltd*[133] and the Court of Session decision in *Scottish Coal Co Ltd v McCormack*.[134] In the *NUMAST* case the EAT held that the employment tribunal was entitled to conclude that a ferry service provided for a number of years is a stable economic entity. The EAT said that, although the major tangible assets used in the service, the ships, were not handed over to Northlink Orkney and Shetland Ferries Ltd (which took over the service from P&O Scottish Ferries), the new service provider took over numerous premises and piers integral to the operation of the ferry service and the government subsidy, a high percentage of seafarers were taken on by the new provider, the service continued to be used by the same passengers and there was a high degree of similarity in the activities carried on. The EAT upheld the tribunal's decision that there was a stable economic entity which constituted an undertaking and that that undertaking had been transferred. See also **2.90**, where the question whether there had been a *transfer* is considered.

2.87   The facts of the *Scottish Coal* case were that C Ltd carried out mining activities at an opencast mining site; it possessed the necessary heavy excavating plant, dumper trucks and ancillary equipment to carry out the activities. When S Ltd took over C Ltd's activities at the site it did not acquire the plant or equipment, as C Ltd did not wish to sell it. The majority of C Ltd's former employees returned to the site to work for S Ltd. The tribunal decided that C Ltd's activities before the transfer amounted to a stable economic entity and that the economic entity had retained its identity after the transfer. The EAT upheld the tribunal's decision. The Court of Session, however, said that the factual findings of the tribunal did not provide a proper basis on which to apply the ECJ's guidance and remitted the case to the tribunal for further fact-finding. Lord Penrose said:[135]

> 'In assessing the degree of importance to be given to plant, and the transfer or non-transfer of it as part of the transaction, the national court must have regard to all the circumstances and must take into account the type of undertaking or business transferred, having regard in particular to the sector of activity in which it operates. That requires a close examination of the wider industry context, and the activities of the predecessor entity within that context. It is in the light of that inquiry that the national court must determine what are the essential and indispensable elements required in order for the economic entity to carry on operating and establish whether these elements have been taken over by the transferee.'

He went on to say:[136]

> '[W]e doubt whether the recent decisions of the Court of Justice in *Oy Liikenne* and *Abler* represent the shift away from previous authorities for which counsel for the appellants contended. In both cases, the Court reaffirmed the guidance previously

133 [2005] ICR 1270.
134 [2005] CSIH 68. See also *Balfour Beatty Power Networks Ltd v Wilcox* [2006] IRLR 258.
135 [2005] CSIH 68, at para 32.
136 [2005] CSIH 68, at para 35.

given in *Spijkers* and other cases to the effect that all relevant facts and circumstances must be identified, and weighed in the balance, to determine whether an undertaking has or has not been transferred. *Oy Liikenne* and *Abler* were decided on the facts found in them. We do not read either case as laying down an invariable requirement that, in the context of a claimed TUPE transfer, a given business must necessarily be characterised as either "asset-reliant" or "labour-intensive", as if those were mutually exclusive categories that defined exhaustively the range of possibilities that could arise. The range of intermediate possibilities appears, a priori, to be unlimited.'

2.88   This decision is consistent with the approach taken in others of the cases discussed in this section, that tribunals must continue to weigh all the factors when considering whether an undertaking has been transferred, but that appropriate weight must be given to the factors depending on the nature of the case. It is also, with respect, correct in rejecting the view that a business must of necessity be classified as 'asset-reliant' or 'labour-intensive'.

2.89   Many of the cases cited above deal with the difficult issues surrounding whether the provision of a service is an economic entity in a given set of facts and whether that entity has transferred. In the context of mergers and acquisitions, these difficulties generally do not arise, for the very purpose of the acquisition will usually be to acquire the economic entity which is capable of delivering a return for the purchaser. Where the difficulties do arise is in distinguishing between a business, on the one hand, and a collection of assets, on the other, where the latter do not constitute an economic entity.

The meaning of 'relevant transfer'

Introduction

2.90   As was indicated at the start of this chapter, the decision whether there has been a transfer of an undertaking has two separate components, both of which need to be considered: (1) the undertaking alleged to have been transferred must be identified; and (2) it must then be established whether that undertaking was *transferred*, the key issue being whether there is an identifiable entity following the transfer. The matter must be approached in these two stages. Indeed, the EAT has made it clear that an employment tribunal which fails to do so will commit an error of law. In *Whitewater Leisure Management Ltd v Barnes*[137] Burton J said:[138]

'It seems to us quite clear that a tribunal should consider these questions separately and in turn, for different considerations relate to each. It will normally be best and clearest for an employment tribunal to deal first with the question of whether there was a relevant and sufficiently identifiable economic entity, and then proceed, whatever be the answer to that question, to ask and answer whether there was (or would have been, if such hypothetical question can be answered, in the event of a conclusion that there was no such entity) a relevant transfer of any such entity.'

---

137 [2000] ICR 1049. See also *Betts v Brintel Helicopters Ltd* [1997] ICR 792, at 798.
138 [2000] ICR 1049, at 1053.

2.91   In *NUMAST v P & O Scottish Ferries Ltd*,[139] Bean J suggested that the question whether the economic entity has been transferred contains two elements: (1) whether the entity has retained its identity and (2) whether it has been transferred as a going concern.

2.92   As will be seen from the text that follows, the original definition of 'transfer of an undertaking' has been considerably altered so as to reflect the considerable accretion of case-law that there has been over the last 20 or so years. One is tempted to wonder whether any useful purpose has been served by attempting to codify, in effect, the case-law of the ECJ and whether the state of the law has been improved by the process.

The new definition – service provision changes

2.93   In reg 3 of TUPE 2006 two situations are treated as relevant transfers. The first is similar to the one found in TUPE 1981 and states that the Regulations apply to 'a transfer of an undertaking, business or part of a business or part of an undertaking or business situated immediately before the transfer in the United Kingdom to another person where there is a transfer of an economic entity which retains its identity'.[140] The meaning of the words 'undertaking', 'business' and 'economic entity' has been considered above at **2.62**; transfers of a part of an undertaking or business are considered at **2.131**.

2.94   It will be appreciated from the discussion above that many of the difficulties in determining when there is a relevant transfer have arisen in relation to service provision transfers. In some ways this is not surprising. The Directive was conceived with mergers and acquisitions in mind. In the mid-1970s, when it was introduced into European law, there was no developed outsourcing industry and support services companies were much less active then they are today. The Directive was not designed with service provision changes in mind and does not address the circumstances which arise in such cases. It has been left to the courts to describe how the Directive applies in these cases.

2.95   In the world of mergers and acquisitions, it is much less frequent that one encounters difficulties over whether the Regulations apply. The purchaser of a business is ordinarily seeking to acquire an economic entity, for that is the very thing of value within the target which he seeks to purchase. In the area of service provision changes, there has been a great deal of difficulty in understanding the extent to which the Directive and the Regulations can properly be applied to practical situations. The struggle for certainty began following the decisions of the ECJ in such cases as *Sophie Redmond* and *Rask* in the early 1990s, when the full implications of the Directive in cases of service provision changes began to become clear. The decision in *Süzen* can be seen in this context as an attempt to achieve a degree of certainty, by adopting a position at the narrow end of the spectrum, favouring a limited view of the Directive's application. In fact, this decision did not achieve the desired

---

139   [2005] ICR 1270, at 1278, para 25.
140   See reg 3(1)(9a).

certainty and the English courts were reluctant to interpret it so as to exclude from the protection of the Regulations large numbers of employees, particularly where the transferor was deliberately trying to avoid the application of the Regulations. Hence the continued reference by the English courts to the decision in *Spijkers* and the need to consider all the factors. The solution found by TUPE 2006 is to provide that most service provision changes will now be caught by the Regulations. This is a significant departure from the position taken by the ECJ in *Süzen* and it puts the situation in England and Wales out of line with the position in Europe generally.

2.96 To achieve this, TUPE 2006 introduced a second type of relevant transfer, labelled 'a service provision change'; it is defined in reg 3(1)(b) as a situation in which:

'(i)   activities cease to be carried out by a person ("a client") on his own behalf and are carried out instead by another person on the client's behalf ("a contractor");

(ii)   activities cease to be carried out by a contractor on a client's behalf (whether or not those activities had previously been carried out by the client on his own behalf) and are carried out instead by another person ("a subsequent contractor") on the client's behalf; or

(iii) activities cease to be carried out by a contractor or a subsequent contractor on a client's behalf (whether or not those activities had previously been carried out by the client on his own behalf) and are carried out instead by the client on his own behalf.'

2.97 In relation to a service provision change, reg 2(1) defines the transferor as 'the person who carried out the activities prior to the service provision change' and the transferee as 'the person who carries out the activities as a result of the service provision change'.

2.98 The conditions set out in reg 3(3) must also be satisfied. These are:

'(a)   immediately before the service provision change—
(i)   there is an organised grouping of employees situated in Great Britain which has as its principal purpose the carrying out of the activities concerned on behalf of the client;
(ii)   the client intends that the activities will, following the service provision change, be carried out by the transferee other than in connection with a single specific event or task of short-term duration; and
(b)   the activities concerned do not consist wholly or mainly of the supply of goods for the client's use.'

2.99 A number of preliminary observations are worth making here. First, there must be 'an organised grouping of employees' and that grouping must have as its principal purpose 'the carrying out of the activities concerned on behalf of the client'. The phrase 'organised grouping of employees' clearly refers back to the jurisprudence of the ECJ which talks of an 'organised grouping of persons and assets facilitating the exercise of an economic activity which pursues a specific objective' (*Süzen*'s case) or an 'organised grouping of persons and assets enabling an economic activity which pursues a specific objective to be exercised' (*Francisco Hernández*).[141] The DTI Guidance[142] says that this is intended to confine the coverage of the Regulations to cases where the transferor has in place a team of employees dedicated to carrying out the activities that are to transfer and would exclude cases where there was no identifiable grouping of employees. The Guidance gives as an example the provision by a contractor of a courier service where the collections and deliveries are carried out each day by different couriers on an ad hoc basis rather than by an identifiable team of employees.

2.100 There may, of course, be a temptation on the part of the transferor to configure the service provision employees into an arrangement that comes within the reg 3(1)(b) test. A typical situation where this might be an issue would be a call centre servicing a number of customers. To maximise operational efficiency, the call centre operatives may handle calls from all of the customers. If the call centre operator was to lose a contract, the employees would not be organised in such a way that there would be an identifiable group which had as its principal purpose the handling of calls in relation to the contract which has been lost. The call centre operator will be overstaffed following the transfer as a consequence. Hence it may wish to reconfigure the workforce so that there is a dedicated team handling the calls in relation to the contract which has been lost. Given that the test is applied 'immediately before the service provision change' the service provider will ordinarily have the opportunity to reconfigure in this way.

2.101 Equally, the converse may be true. A team may be servicing a number of customers but there may be one dominant customer, so that the 'principal purpose' test is satisfied. The group which transfers will be correspondingly overstaffed by reason of the fact that there will no longer be any need to service the minor customers.

2.102 The second observation is that the organised grouping of employees may consist of one person only.[143] This reflects the decision of the ECJ in *Schmidt*'s case. This aspect of the definition has already been considered at **2.16**, in the context of what constitutes an undertaking. As the EAT pointed out in *Dudley Bower Building Services Ltd v Lowe*,[144] although cases such as *Süzen* use the phrase 'grouping of persons', there is no requirement that there must be more than a single employee.

2.103 The third observation is that TUPE 2006 does not apply to situations where a contractor is engaged to organise a single specific event or task and the event or task is of short-term duration. Regulation 3(3)(a)(ii) specifically refers to the activities being carried out by the transferee 'other than in connection with a single specific event or task of short-term duration'. This provision was clearly drafted with *Rygaard's case*[145] in mind. The DTI Guidance says that the Regulations should not be expected to apply where a client engages a

---

141 See **2.41** and **2.45**.
142 See http://www.dti.gov.uk/er/individual/tupeguide2006regs.pdf.
143 See reg 2(1).
144 [2003] ICR 843.
145 [1996] ICR 333, Case C-48/94. See **2.18**.

contractor to organise a single conference on its behalf, even though the contractor establishes an organised grouping of staff, for example, a project team, to carry out the activities involved in fulfilling the task. So if the client later held a second conference using a different contractor, the members of the first project team would not transfer to the second contractor. Another example given by the Guidance relates to the 2012 Olympic Games. The Guidance draws a distinction between a contract relating to the provision of security advice to the event organisers over a period of years leading up to the event and a contract for the hiring of security staff to protect athletes during the event itself. Although both hypothetical contracts concern the holding of a specific event, the first would run for a significantly longer period than the second. The second would thus have more of the character of a 'one-off contract' of the type seen in *Rygaard's* case.

2.104 The fourth observation is that reg 3(3)(b) states that the Regulations exclude activities which 'do not consist wholly or mainly of the supply of goods for the client's use'. The DTI Guidance gives as an example the situation where a client engages a contractor to supply sandwiches and drinks to its canteen every day for the client to sell on to its staff. On the other hand, it would be likely that a contract for a contractor to run the client's staff canteen would be covered by the Regulations.

2.105 The Guidance published by the DTI states that the provisions of reg 3(1)(b), applying the Regulations to service provision changes, are intended to apply to three main types of service provision change:

(1) contracting out or 'out-sourcing';[146]
(2) assignment of a contract to a new contractor on subsequent re-tendering;[147] and
(3) contracting in or 'in-sourcing', ie where a contract with an outside contractor ends and the service is brought back 'in house' by the former client.[148]

But this provision is subject to the overriding requirement, as mentioned above, that immediately before the service provision change there is 'an organised grouping of employees ... which has as its principal purpose the carrying out of the activities concerned on behalf of the client'.

2.106 It would appear that TUPE 2006 has cleared up one problem which arose under the TUPE 1981, where a transfer of services occurred indirectly to a third party. Take, for example, a situation where a client terminates a contract with contractor A and immediately contracts with contractor B for the service to be continued by contractor B. Is the transfer of employees a transfer from contractor A to contractor B or is there a transfer from contractor A to the client for a scintilla of time, followed by a transfer on to contractor B? The issue is of importance as it determines whether the client may bear any direct liability under the Regulations. Moreover, liabilities that pass pursuant to the rule in the *Litster* case are not capable of passing along a chain of contracts.

---

146 Regulation 3(1)(b)(i).
147 Regulation 3(1)(b)(ii).
148 Regulation 3(1)(b)(iii).

They can only transfer once. Hence there is a risk of such liabilities lodging with the client. The same issues would arise where a contractor contracts to provide a service but immediately subcontracts responsibility for providing the service.

2.107 The wording of reg 3(3)(a)(ii) talks of the activities, following the service provision change, being 'carried out' by the transferor. In the example set out above, there is no way in which it can be said that the 'middle man' in any way 'carries out' any services, and the correct reading of the new regulation would appear to be that there is a transfer direct from the outgoing contractor to the incoming contractor without any intermediate transfer.

2.108 The new regulation will not be without its problems. For example, where a service is re-tendered on the basis that part of the service will be re-tendered and part taken in house, there is no clear fit with the test in reg 3(3)(a)(ii). Assuming that this difficulty can be overcome by a purposive interpretation, there are no clear guidelines in TUPE 2006 as to who transfers in each direction. The allocation of employees as between two incoming contractors could be an area of considerable contention.

2.109 During the consultation period running up to the introduction of the new Regulations, there was discussion of an exception for professional services, such as services provided by lawyers and accountants. This was dropped; hence the Regulations are capable of applying to professional services as much as to any other form of services. Another debate surrounded the possibility of a carve out for 'innovative bids'. Prior to the introduction of TUPE 2006, if a service was undertaken post transfer in a materially different way, this could break the necessary continuity for a transfer of an undertaking. Again, this proposed carve out was not adopted. Hence the incoming service provider may inherit a workforce which is not capable of retraining to cope with the demands of a service which is to be delivered in a radically different way. Nevertheless, the burden of the severance costs will fall on the incoming contractor.

2.110 By virtue of reg 3(4)(a), TUPE 2006 applies to public and private undertakings engaged in economic activities 'whether or not they are operating for gain'. The Regulations also apply to transfers or service provision changes 'howsoever effected' despite the fact that the transfer or service provision change is governed or effected by the law of a country or territory outside the UK or that the employment of persons employed in the undertaking or (in the case of a service provision change) persons employed in the organised grouping of employees is governed by any such law.[149] They also apply to transfers of undertakings (including service provisions changes) where persons employed in the undertaking ordinarily work outside the UK.[150] Regulation 3(5) excludes from the ambit of the Regulations administrative reorganisations of public administrative authorities and transfers of administrative functions between public administrative authorities is not a relevant transfer. This provision is considered more fully at **2.141**.

---

149 Regulation 3(4)(b).
150 Regulation 3(4)(c).

2.111 Regulation 3(6)[151] provides that a transfer may be effected by a series of two or more transactions and that it may take place whether or not any property is transferred to the transferee by the transferor.[152] This would appear to give effect to some of the ECJ decisions considered earlier in this chapter, particularly *Landsorganisationen i Danmark v Ny Mølle Kro*[153] and *Foreningen af Arbejdsledere i Danmark v Daddy's Dance Hall A/S*.[154]

General approach of the UK courts and tribunals

2.112 The problem in the context of the meaning of the phrase 'relevant transfer' consists in trying to identify whether there has been a *transfer* of an undertaking. In the context of Directive 2001/23/EC, the approach of the ECJ has already been looked at. What falls to be considered here is how the courts and tribunals in the UK have approached the ECJ's decisions, since it is clear that they are bound to interpret the Regulations in such a way as to bring them into conformity, if possible, with European law. This means that the starting-point of any discussion of whether there has been a transfer of an undertaking is the ECJ decisions discussed in the preceding section.

2.113 The earliest case in the series is the *Spijkers* case,[155] but after that the most recent run of cases starts with the trio of cases *Süzen v Zehnacker Gebdudereinigung GmbH Krankenhausservice, Lefarth GmbH (Party joined)*,[156] *Francisco Hernández Vidal SA v Gomez Perez*[157] and *Sánchez Hidalgo v Asociacion de Servicios ASER*.[158] These were considered above at **2.41**, **2.45** and **2.46**.

2.114 The ECJ decision in *Süzen* is really the starting-point for a discussion of the case-law of the domestic courts and tribunals of the UK. It was preceded, however, by the Court of Appeal decision in *Dines v Initial Healthcare Services Ltd*,[159] a case which involved labour-intensive undertakings. In that case, the facts were that the employees involved were employees of a private company which provided cleaning services at an NHS hospital. As a result of the compulsory competitive tendering process, the contract was awarded to a different company. The employees were dismissed for redundancy but were offered employment at the hospital with the new company, but on less favourable terms and with no continuity of employment. They brought complaints of unfair dismissal under what is now reg 7,[160] on the grounds that they had been dismissed because of a relevant transfer. The EAT

---

151 Previously reg 3(4) of TUPE 1981.
152 In *Longden v Ferrari Ltd* [1994] ICR 443, the EAT said that a succession of events causally linked to each other do not constitute a series of transactions by which a transfer of the undertaking is effected.
153 [1989] ICR 330. See also *Berg v Besselsen* [1990] ICR 396.
154 [1988] IRLR 315.
155 [1986] ECR 1119; see **2.27**.
156 [1997] ICR 662.
157 [1999] IRLR 132.
158 [1999] IRLR 136.
159 [1995] ICR 11.
160 Regulation 8 of TUPE 1981.

refused to interfere with the employment tribunal's decision that, although the provision of cleaning services was a separate economic entity, there had been no transfer of that entity. It took the view that the correct analysis was that one business had ceased and another had begun. The Court of Appeal allowed the employees' appeal, stressing that the correct approach to the interpretation of the Regulations is that they should be interpreted in line with the Directive as interpreted by the ECJ. Following the *Rask* and *Schmidt* cases, it held that, when a company takes over the provision of certain services as a result of competitive tendering, that does not mean that the business or undertaking of the first company did not come to an end. There had therefore been a transfer of an undertaking.

2.115 Very soon after the decision in *Süzen*, the Court of Appeal heard the appeal from the High Court in *Betts v Brintel Helicopters Ltd*.[161] It re-examined *Dines* and *Süzen* and attempted to reconcile the approaches taken in the two cases. The case involved the loss by one company (Brintel) of a contract to provide helicopter services and its transfer to another (KLM). KLM did not take over most of the assets (apart from rights associated with the contract) and engaged none of Brintel's employees. Some of Brintel's employees sought a declaration that there had been a relevant transfer and, therefore, that as from 1 July 1995 (when KLM took over the service) they were employed by KLM. The High Court granted the declaration and said that there had been a relevant transfer. The main issue in the Court of Appeal was whether there was a transfer of an undertaking, in other words, whether the undertaking had retained its identity in the hands of the transferee.

2.116 Kennedy LJ reviewed the relevant case-law of the ECJ, which emphasised that the decisive question is whether the business in question retains its identity as an economic entity. He said that the *Süzen* decision represented a change of emphasis and meant that the reasoning of some of the previous decisions might have to be reconsidered. He added that, in the case in question, however, the limited transfer of assets (the right to land on oil rigs and use oil rig facilities) could not lead to the conclusion that the undertaking had retained its identity. He said:[162]

> 'The real distinction ... is between (1) labour-intensive undertakings, of which *Dines*[163] is an example, in which if the staff combine to engage in a particular activity which continues or is resumed with substantially the same staff after the alleged transfer the court may well conclude that the undertaking has been transferred so that it has retained its identity in the hands of the transferee; and (2) other types of undertaking in relation to which the application of the *Spijkers* test involves a more wide-ranging inquiry. Consequently I have no difficulty in accepting as appropriate to its facts the approach adopted by this court in *Dines*.'

2.117 This decision may be contrasted with the decision of another division of the Court of Appeal, about a year later, in *ECM (Vehicle Delivery*

---

161 The High Court's decision is reported at [1996] IRLR 45 and the Court of Appeal's at [1997] ICR 792.

162 [1997] ICR 792, at 806.

163 *Dines v Initial Healthcare Services* [1995] ICR 11.

Service) Ltd v Cox.[164] A contract to distribute cars ('the VAG contract') was
lost by one contractor and awarded to ECM. ECM chose to organise the
contracted service in a different way; it dispensed with the previous contractor's
base and refused to engage any of the staff employed on the vehicle delivery
contract because they had asserted that their employment was protected by
TUPE. The Court of Appeal upheld the decision of the tribunal and the EAT
that there had been a relevant transfer. The argument of ECM in the Court of
Appeal was that there was no transfer of an undertaking, although it accepted
that there was an undertaking carried on by the previous contractor. The basis
of its argument was that *Süzen* signalled a change of emphasis in the ECJ and
that the position on transfers of undertakings following that decision was that,
where the only continuing feature is the nature of the activity itself and all that
continues is the service itself, it is impossible to find that an undertaking has
been transferred. So in the case in question, it was argued, all that continued
was the activity of delivering cars under the VAG contract. Mummery LJ, with
whom the other Lords Justices agreed, rejected that argument and held that the
employment tribunal had applied the correct test, as laid down in *Spijkers* and
subsequent cases. He also observed that the tribunal was entitled to have
regard, as a relevant circumstance, to the reason why the employees were not
taken on by ECM.[165] He suggested that the importance of *Süzen* had been
overstated and pointed out that the ECJ had not overruled its previous
interpretative rulings. He also observed that the criteria laid down by the ECJ
still involve consideration of 'all the facts characterising the transaction in
question' as identified in *Spijkers*. He said, however:[166]

> '(4) The importance of *Süzen* is that the Court of Justice identified limits to the
> application of the Directive. On the one hand, it affirmed that: (a) "The decisive
> criterion for establishing the existence of a transfer within the meaning of the
> Directive is whether the entity in question retains its identity, as indicated *inter alia*
> by the fact that its operation is actually continued ..." (paragraph 10); (b) a direct
> contractual link or relationship between the transferor and the transferee is not
> conclusive against a transfer (paragraphs 12 and 13); (c) consideration of all the
> facts characterising the transaction in question is necessary (paragraph 14). (5) On
> the other hand, it set limits by indicating that: (a) "... the mere fact that the service
> provided by the old and the new awardees of a contract is similar does not therefore
> support the conclusion that an economic entity has been transferred." Other factors
> are important – the workforce, the management staff, its operating methods and its
> operational resources (paragraph 15): (b) "The mere loss of a service contract to a
> competitor cannot therefore by itself indicate the existence of a transfer within the
> meaning of the Directive ... In those circumstances, the service undertaking
> previously entrusted with the contract does not, on losing a customer, thereby cease
> fully to exist, and a business or part of a business belonging to it cannot be
> considered to have been transferred to the new awardee of the contract"
> (paragraph 16); (c) The question whether the majority of the employees are taken
> over by the new employer to enable him to carry on the activities of the undertaking
> on a regular basis is a factual circumstance to be taken into account, as well as the

---

164 [1999] ICR 1162. See also *Lightways (Contractors) Ltd v Associated Holdings Ltd* [2000]
   IRLR 247, in which the Court of Session said that it was open to the tribunal to take into
   account a declaration by the transferee before the transfer that TUPE would apply.
165 [1999] ICR 1162, at 1169.
166 [1999] ICR 1162, at 1168–1169.

similarity of the pre- and post-transfer activities and the type of undertaking concerned e g in labour-intensive sectors (paragraphs 20 and 21).'

He said that the case was unaffected by the limits indicated in *Süzen*.

2.118 In *ADI (UK) Ltd v Willer*,[167] a different division of the Court of Appeal returned to this issue. The case involved the provision of security services and thus involved a labour-intensive undertaking. The company which took over the contract from ADI took on none of its staff, two of whom made claims against ADI and the putative transferee. The employment tribunal decided that there had been no transfer of an undertaking. On appeal, the EAT held that there was no transfer of an undertaking when a contract to provide security services was awarded to a new contractor but none of the workforce transferred. The EAT said that this was a conclusion which was open to the tribunal. The Court of Appeal allowed the transferor's appeal and remitted the case to a tribunal to consider whether the reason for the transferees not taking on the employees was in order to avoid TUPE. The court said that if the circumstances of an alleged transfer of an undertaking are such that an actual transfer of labour would be a relevant factor to be taken into account in deciding whether there has been a TUPE transfer, an employment tribunal is obliged to consider the reason why the labour was not transferred, in accordance with the Court of Appeal's decision in *ECM (Vehicle Delivery) Service Ltd v Cox* (above). If the economic entity is labour intensive such that, applying *Süzen*, there is no transfer if the workforce is not taken on, but there would be if they were, the tribunal is obliged to treat the case as if the labour had transferred if it is established that the reason or principal reason for this was in order to avoid the application of TUPE. May LJ said:[168]

> 'In my judgment, Mr Randall [counsel for the employees] was correct to accept that there would have been a transfer in the present case for the purpose of the 1981 Regulations if the nine security officers had been taken on by Firm Security Group, and that there would also be a transfer if the reason why they were not taken on was in order to avoid the application of the Regulations. More generally, it seems to me that if, as in the present case, the economic entity is labour intensive such that, applying *Süzen*, there is no transfer if the workforce is not taken on, but there would be if they were, there will be a transfer if, although the workforce is not taken on, it is established that the reason or principal reason for this was in order to avoid the application of the Regulations.'

Dyson LJ said:[169]

> 'It seems to me that, if the circumstances of an alleged transfer of undertaking are such that an actual transfer of labour would be a relevant factor to be taken into account in deciding whether there has been a transfer of undertaking, then the tribunal will not only be entitled, but will be obliged, to consider the reason why the labour was not transferred, if that has been raised as an issue.'

2.119 In the subsequent case of *Astle v Cheshire County Council*[170] the EAT upheld the tribunal's decision that there was no transfer, in circumstances where

---

167 [2001] IRLR 542, [2001] EWCA Civ 971.
168 [2001] IRLR 542, [2001] EWCA Civ 971, at [36].
169 [2001] IRLR 542, [2001] EWCA Civ 971, at [52].
170 [2005] IRLR 12.

it had found that the employer's reason for not taking on staff was not to thwart the application of TUPE. The case involved the outsourcing by the Council of its architectural services to a contractor. All the relevant staff transferred. The Council later became unhappy with the contractor's performance and, in late 2001, decided to engage a panel of consultants to provide the services rather than a single contractor. This was called a 'market economy' approach. The contractor's contract ended with effect from 31 March 2002. Between the end of the contract and the panel taking up the projects, there was an interim period during which the Council carried out some minor activities of an architectural nature. None of the contractor's staff were taken on by the Council. The employment tribunal found that the reason for the Council's decision not to take on any of the contractor's workforce was not to 'thwart' TUPE (as the tribunal put it); it accepted the Council's argument that it had genuinely decided that the 'market economy' was the best method of delivering the architectural services. The tribunal concluded that there had been no relevant transfer. The EAT upheld the decision. The EAT said:[171]

> 'The tribunal thus correctly approached the issues, first by deciding whether there was (and in the event deciding there was not) an *ECM reason*, and then, given that there was no *ECM reason* in their judgment, applying the *Spijkers* test without it. Had there been in its conclusion an *ECM reason*, the Tribunal would plainly have injected the *ECM reason* as a relevant factor into the *Spijkers* test ...'

2.120   Subsequent to the decisions of the Court of Appeal in *ECM* and *ADI*, there have been a number of decisions of the EAT which are not easy to reconcile with each other. They represent a difference of approach between different divisions of that tribunal. The first is *Whitewater Leisure Management Ltd v Barnes*,[172] the facts of which were set out at **2.69**. The EAT, presided over by Burton J, concluded that when Whitewater lost the contract to manage the leisure centre there was no transfer of an undertaking, on the basis that no tangible or intangible assets were transferred and none of the senior managers transferred, with only half of the 'core' team of 14 employees transferring. As was pointed out earlier, the decision in this case appears to ignore the ECJ's decision in *Allen v Amalgamated Construction Co Ltd*,[173] consideration of which might have led it to a different conclusion. It is also inconsistent with the subsequent decisions of other divisions of the EAT and the Court of Appeal.

2.121   The first of these is *RCO Support Services and Aintree Hospital Trust v UNISON*,[174] the facts of which were set out at **2.71**. The EAT said that the absence of movement of significant assets or of a major part of the workforce does not necessarily deny the existence of a relevant transfer and expressed the view that *Süzen* can no longer safely be relied upon. It also favoured the approach taken by the Court of Appeal in *ECM* over that taken by the earlier Court of Appeal in *Betts v Brintel*. Lindsay J emphasised the safeguarding of employees' rights as being the crucial objective. He said:[175]

---

171   [2005] IRLR 12, at para 25.
172   [2000] IRLR 456.
173   [2000] ICR 436.
174   [2000] ICR 1502.
175   [2000] ICR 1502, at 1515.

'*Schmidt* still stands as a reminder of how very little is required to amount to something capable of being an undertaking ... once due regard is paid to the safeguarding of employees' rights, the subject-matter of the Directive.'

The Court of Appeal upheld the EAT's decision. Its decision is considered after the EAT decision in *Cheesman* (**2.123**).

2.122   *Argyll Training Ltd v Sinclair*[176] involved the loss of a training contract by one company to another. Mrs Sinclair was employed as a training adviser but lost her job when the training contract was lost by her employers. Despite the decision in *Rygaard's case*, the EAT concluded that there had been a transfer of an undertaking, following the same line of thought as in the previous case. Again, Lindsay J relied upon the ECJ's decision in *Schmidt* and said that it stands for the proposition that the decisive criterion for establishing whether there is a transfer is whether the business in question retains its identity and that that is indicated by the actual continuation or resumption of the same or similar activities.

2.123   The later decision in *Cheesman v R Brewer Contracts Ltd*[177] again involved the loss of a maintenance contract. The previous contractor, Onyx, took over the contract from a district council; it acquired as part of the contract use of the council's yard, its equipment and its office accommodation. It took on 14 employees who had previously been allocated by the council to the contract. When it lost the contract to Brewer, Onyx dismissed the 14 staff; none of them was taken on by Brewer and no tangible or intangible assets passed from Onyx to Brewer, either directly or indirectly by way of the council. The dismissed employees claimed that there had been a transfer of an undertaking to Brewer and brought claims against it. After considering the question of what amounts to an undertaking, Lindsay J addressed the question of what constitutes a transfer. He said:[178]

'As for whether there has been a transfer:

(i)   As to whether there is any relevant sense a transfer, the decisive criterion for establishing the existence of a transfer is whether the entity in question retains its identity, as indicated, inter alia, by the fact that its operation is actually continued or resumed ...

(ii)   In a labour-intensive sector it is to be recognised that an entity is capable of maintaining its identity after it has been transferred where the new employer does not merely pursue the activity in question but also takes over a major part, in terms of their numbers and skills, of the employees specially assigned by his predecessors to that task. That follows from the fact that in certain labour-intensive sectors a group of workers engaged in the joint activity on a permanent basis may constitute an economic entity ...

(iii)   In considering whether the conditions for existence of a transfer are met it is necessary to consider all the factors characterising the transaction in question but each is a single factor and none is to be considered in isolation ... However, whilst no authority so holds, it may, presumably, not be an error of law to consider "the decisive criterion" in (i) above in isolation; that, surely, is

176   [2001] IRLR 630.
177   [2001] IRLR 144.
178   [2001] IRLR 144, at 147–148.

an aspect of its being "decisive", although, as one sees from the "inter alia" in (i) above, "the decisive criterion" is not itself said to depend on a single factor.

(iv) Amongst the matters thus falling for consideration are the type of undertaking, whether or not its tangible assets are transferred, the value of its intangible assets at the time of transfer, whether or not the majority of its employees are taken over by the new company, whether or not its customers are transferred, the degree of similarity between the activities carried on before and after the transfer, and the period, if any, in which they are suspended …

(v) In determining whether or not there has been a transfer, account has to be taken, inter alia, of the type of undertaking or business in issue, and the degree of importance to be attached to the several criteria will necessarily vary according to the activity carried on …

(vi) Where an economic entity is able to function without any significant tangible or intangible assets, the maintenance of its identity following the transaction being examined cannot logically depend on the transfer of such assets …

(vii) Even where assets are owned and are required to run the undertaking, the fact that they do not pass does not preclude a transfer …

(viii) Where maintenance work is carried out by a cleaning firm and then next by the owner of the premises concerned, that mere fact does not justify the conclusion that there has been a transfer …

(ix) More broadly, the mere fact that the service provided by the old and new undertaking providing a contracted-out service or the old and new contract-holder are similar does not justify the conclusion that there has been a transfer of an economic entity between predecessor and successor …

(x) The absence of any contractual link between transferor and transferee may be evidence that there has been no relevant transfer but it is certainly not conclusive as there is no need for any such direct contractual relationship …

(xi) When no employees are transferred, the reasons why that is the case can be relevant as to whether or not there was a transfer …

(xii) The fact that the work is performed continuously with no interruption or change in the manner or performance is a normal feature of transfers of undertakings but there is no particular importance to be attached to a gap between the end of the work by one subcontractor and the start by the successor …

More generally the cases also show:

(i) The necessary factual appraisal is to be made by the national court …

(ii) The Directive applies where, following the transfer, there is a change in the natural person responsible for the carrying on of the business who, by virtue of that fact, incurs the obligation of an employer vis-à-vis the employees of the undertaking, regardless of whether or not ownership of the undertaking is transferred …

(iii) The aim of the Directive is to ensure continuity of employment relationships within the economic entity irrespective of any change of ownership … and our domestic law illustrates how readily the courts will adopt a purposive construction to counter avoidance …'

2.124 Lindsay J's remarks are set out at length because of light it sheds on questions of transfer. In view of the emphasis on the social purposes of the Directive, the continuing validity of cases such as *Betts v Brintel* and *Whitewater Leisure Management v Barnes* will need to be reconsidered.

2.125   As was mentioned earlier, the EAT's decision in *RCO Support Services and Aintree Hospital Trust v UNISON*[179] was appealed to the Court of Appeal, which upheld the decision.[180] (The *Cheesman* case was referred to in counsels' skeleton arguments but not in the court's decision.) The Court of Appeal's decision signals a preference for the *Spijkers* approach. Mummery LJ, with whom the other two members of the court agreed, said that the mere fact that a putative transferee carries on the same activities or supplies the same services as the putative transferor is not by itself determinative in favour of a transfer, nor does it by itself support a conclusion that an entity retains its identity. Similarly, the fact that none of the workforce is taken on is not necessarily conclusive on the issue of retention of identity. He said that these matters are all factors to be considered in making an overall assessment of all the facts characterising the transaction, with no single factor being considered in isolation. He said:[181]

> 'I am inclined to accept the submissions of RCO that a subjective motive of the putative transferee to avoid the application of the Directive and the 1981 Regulations is not the real point. The relevant exercise is that in *Spijkers* ... ie objective consideration and assessment of all the facts, including the circumstances of the decision not to take on the workforce.'

2.126   Many of the case considered in the preceding paragraphs relate to labour-intensive undertakings and the problems posed when the transferee does not take on the workforce of the transferor. The cases of *P & O Trans European Ltd v Initial Transport Services Ltd*[182] and *NUMAST v P & O Scottish Ferries Ltd*[183] are both cases which involved asset-intensive undertakings. They have been considered in detail in the preceding section,[184] and reference should be made to the quotation from the judgment of Nelson J in the *P & O* case. In the *NUMAST* case, the company which took over the ferry services did not take over the four ships used by the previous company to provide the services. Apart from the ships, the tribunal found that significant tangible assets were transferred, as well as a significant intangible asset, in the form of a government subsidy. It concluded that there was a relevant transfer. The EAT said:[185]

> 'The Tribunal's conclusion on this issue was that an observer would conclude that the ferry service to the Northern Isles had continued just as it had done before – no doubt with a number of changes and improvements, but basically continuing the same service. They found that there was retention of identity with the business being continued as a going concern, and accordingly that the undertaking was transferred to Northlink within the meaning of TUPE. These are unimpeachable conclusions ...'

2.127   In the context of mergers and acquisitions, the key issue will be whether there is a mere asset purchase, following which there is no economic

---

179 [2000] ICR 1502.
180 [2002] ICR 751, [2002] EWCA Civ 464.
181 [2002] ICR 751, [2002] EWCA Civ 464, at [36].
182 [2003] IRLR 128.
183 [2005] ICR 1270.
184 See **2.85** and **2.86**.
185 [2005] ICR 1270, at para 33.

entity identifiable, or whether the collection of assets makes up an economic entity which retains the identity of the entity which operated pre transfer. One might imagine a piece of equipment, an asset which could be bought without any suggestion that it constitutes, by itself, an economic entity. However, various other assets may interact with that piece of equipment – it may be situated in a building and the purchaser of the equipment might seek real estate rights so as to be able to leave the equipment in situ and to operate from that location. The equipment might be used to make distinctive products to which the vendor may have intellectual property rights. There may be a group of employees who are trained to operate the equipment, who the purchaser might like to employ. A vendor might ask the purchaser to finish off work on some manufacturing contract work in progress following the sale. Clearly, the more of these assets that are acquired, the greater the likelihood of there being a transfer of an undertaking. The *Spijkers* test is useful in this respect, but it is still difficult to determine when the boundary has been passed from the transfer of a collection of assets to the transfer of an economic entity. What one is looking for is whether there is sufficient to suggest that breath has been given to the dry bones of the assets, so that instead of merely acquiring a collection of assets, they together make up something which is greater than the sum of the parts. The key element is often goodwill. The issue will be determined by a tribunal in each case as a question of fact.

2.128   In *Woodhouse v Peter Brotherhood Ltd*[186] the Court of Appeal was considering the sale of a factory, plant and equipment by a company which manufactured diesel engines to a company which manufactured spinning machines, compressors and turbines. The case concerns the entitlement to a redundancy payment but the case is directly relevant to the issue which arises under TUPE. Lord Denning commented as follows:

> 'So the question is this: was there a "transfer" or the "business" of only a transfer of the "physical assets".'

2.129   Applying this principle he concluded that there had not been a transfer of a business. The business had, in fact, moved elsewhere, and certain assets had been used by the purchaser in a different business. In *Lloyd v Brassey*[187] Lord Denning had used the test of whether post transfer 'the business remains the same business but in different hands'. In *Melon v Hector Powe*[188] a suit-making factory in Scotland was closed. The purchaser was able to offer jobs to almost all of the employees. However, the conclusion of the House of Lords was that there had been a transfer of assets but not a transfer of a business as a going concern. The purchaser was utilising the assets in the same way, namely to manufacture suits. However, it was a different business from that carried on by the seller of the assets. The greater the difference between the activities carried on prior to the transfer from those carried on after the transfer, the less is the likelihood that a transfer of an undertaking will be identified. This may be a marginal decision. In *Mathiesen v United News*[189] a

---

186   [1972] 3 All ER 91.
187   [1969] 2 QB 98.
188   [1981] IR 43.
189   EAT 554/95.

hospital foyer was redeveloped. As part of the development, space was provided for a shop. Prior to the redevelopment, a portakabin adjacent to the foyer had housed a shop selling flowers, chocolates and the like which were bought by patients and visitors. Following the development's completion, the portakabin closed and a shop opened in the foyer selling similar goods together with a wider range of items. The employees claimed that this had been a transfer, but the EAT held that the differences in the range of goods were sufficient to justify the conclusion that this had not been a transfer of an undertaking. It is clear from the judgment, however, that the EAT would not have overturned a tribunal decision to the contrary, such was the marginal nature of the differences.

2.130 Time can also be a distinguishing factor. What happens when the undertaking closes and then subsequently starts up in a similar guise? The classic case would be the business of a shop which is sold, closed by the purchaser for refurbishment/refitting and is then re-opened. There appears to be no authority on the point of how much time must elapse to breach the necessary continuity. The point was acknowledged as having the capability to prevent a transfer of an undertaking in *Gaines v Picturehouse Theatres*[190] but was taken no further.

TRANSFERS OF PART OF AN UNDERTAKING

The position under European law

2.131   Article 1(1) of the 2001 Directive refers to the transfer of 'part of an undertaking or business'. In *Botzen v Rotterdamische Droogdok Maatschappij BV*[191] the ECJ ruled on the interpretation of the Directive in the context of the transfer of part of a business and its application to employees assigned to that part. The two questions asked of the Court which are relevant for present purposes were: first, whether the Directive extends to employees whose duties are not performed exclusively with the aid of assets belonging to the transferred part of the undertaking; and, secondly, whether the Directive extends to employees employed in a staff department of the undertaking (for example, general management services, personnel matters and the like), where the staff department carries on duties for the benefit of the transferred part of the undertaking but has not itself been transferred. In the case in question certain departments such as marine, general engineering, heavy machinery and turbines were transferred, but not the general administrative and personnel department. The ECJ ruled that the Directive does not protect employees who, although not employed in the transferred part of the undertaking, perform duties involved with the use of assets assigned to the part transferred or who, whilst being in an administrative department of the undertaking which has not itself been transferred, carried out certain duties for the benefit of the part transferred.[192] The Court said:[193]

---

190   EAT/661/95.
191   [1985] ECR 519, Case No 186/83.
192   [1985] ECR 519, at 528, para 16.

'[T]he only decisive criterion regarding the transfer of employees' rights and obligations is whether or not a transfer takes place of the department to which they were assigned and which formed the organisational framework within which their employment relationship took effect … In order to decide whether the rights and obligations under an employment relationship are transferred under [the Directive] … it is therefore sufficient to establish to which part of the undertaking or business the employee was assigned.'

Application in the UK

2.132 TUPE 2006 applies both to the transfer of an undertaking and the transfer of part of an undertaking or business. In a case involving the transfer of a part of an undertaking or business, the same question will arise as with the transfer of an undertaking: whether the part transferred in itself amounts to an economic entity. In *Michael Peters Ltd v Farnfield and Michael Peters Group plc*[194] the EAT said that the appropriate test to apply when dealing with the transfer of part of an undertaking is the test enunciated by the ECJ in *Botzen v Rotterdamische Droogdok Maatschappij BV*,[195] considered at **2.131**, whether the employee was assigned to the part transferred. The case involved the chief executive of a holding company responsible for overseeing the financial management and operations of 25 subsidiary companies; four of them were sold by receivers but the holding company was not a party to the sale agreement. The employment tribunal held that the four subsidiary companies, together with that part of the holding company's assets belonging to those companies, formed a single economic unit and that part of the holding company was transferred, so that the chief executive was protected on the transfer. The EAT reversed this decision, on the grounds that he could not be said to have been assigned or allocated to the part of the company transferred, ie the four subsidiary companies.

2.133 In *Northern General Hospital National Health Service Trust v Gale*[196] the Court of Appeal suggested, obiter, that the issue is whether the employee in question is 'part of the human stock' of the part transferred. In *Duncan Webb Offset (Maidstone) Ltd v Cooper*,[197] however, the EAT said that that was the same as the *Botzen* test put another way. In that case, the EAT held that three employees who worked for one company ('Maidstone') in a group but spent some of their time working for other companies in the group were employed by Maidstone, even though some of their time was spent looking after other parts of the group. The EAT upheld the employment tribunal's decision that when Maidstone was sold, the employees were employed in the undertaking transferred and therefore were protected by reg 5. This approach was confirmed by the later decision of the EAT in *Buchanan-Smith v Schleicher & Co International Ltd*.[198] The EAT said that for an employee to be employed in part

---

193 [1985] ECR 519, at 528, paras 14 and 15.
194 [1995] IRLR 190.
195 [1985] ECR 519, Case No 186/83.
196 [1994] ICR 426, at 432H. See also *Securicor Guarding Ltd v Fraser Security Services Ltd* [1996] IRLR 552 and *CPL Distribution Ltd v Todd* [2003] IRLR 28, [2002] EWCA Civ 1481.
197 [1995] IRLR 633, at 635. See also *Sunley Turriff Holdings Ltd v Thomson* [1995] IRLR 184.
198 [1996] ICR 613.

of an undertaking he or she does not have to work exclusively in the part of the undertaking transferred. The question is one of fact to be determined by considering all the relevant circumstances. In that case, the EAT held that an employee who organised and ran the service side of the business, which was sold to a transferee, as well as other parts of the business, was employed in the service side and therefore transferred.

2.134 The most recent case to consider this question is *Fairhurst Ward Abbotts Ltd v Botes Building Ltd.*[199] The court held that where there is a transfer of something less than an entire undertaking, it is sufficient for the purposes of TUPE if a part of an economic entity becomes identified for the first time as a separate economic entity when the transfer separates the part from the whole; it is not necessary for the particular part transferred itself to exist as a discrete and identifiable entity before the date of the transfer. Mummery LJ said:[200]

> 'This case is concerned with the effect of partitioning the borough into two separate areas ... A part of an undertaking is simply something less than the whole of an undertaking. Neither the legislation nor the case law expressly requires that the particular part transferred should itself, before the date of the transfer, exist as a discrete and identifiable stable economic entity. Nor do I think that such a requirement is implicit in the need to identify a pre-existing stable economic entity. In my judgment, it is sufficient if a part of the larger stable economic entity becomes identified for the first time as a separate economic entity on the occasion of the transfer separating a part from the whole.

> I agree that, if it is possible to identify part of an undertaking as a discrete economic entity before the transfer takes place, the applicant will find it easier to satisfy both the "transfer" test that the part transferred retains its identity in the hands of the transferee, and the requirement that the applicant was employed, immediately before the transfer, in the part transferred. But I do not agree that, in the absence of a part which is identifiable as a discrete economic entity before the transfer takes place, there can be no transfer of a part or that it will be impossible for the applicant to establish that there was a transfer of the part of the undertaking in which he was employed. It all depends on the evidence available in the particular case. In contending for transfer of a part it may be more difficult to make the required "before" and "after" comparison where the part becomes a discrete economic entity for the first time on the making of the transfer, but it is not necessarily an impossibility.'

2.135 A majority of the Court of Appeal also held that an employee may be employed in the part transferred even though he or she is not actually at work at the time of the transfer, but away on sick leave. Mummery LJ said of this issue:[201]

> 'A person on sick leave, like a person on holiday, on study leave or on maternity leave, remains a person employed in the undertaking, even though he is not actually at his place of work. The question is whether he was employed in the part transferred. That is a factual matter.'

---

199 [2004] ICR 919, [2004] EWCA Civ 83. See also *Astle v Cheshire County Council* [2005] IRLR 12, in which a help desk manned by two employees was held to have been validly transferred to another organisation.
200 [2004] ICR 919, [2004] EWCA Civ 83, at [32]–[33].
201 [2004] ICR 919, [2004] EWCA Civ 83, at para 40.

2.136   In *Balfour Beatty Power Networks v Wilcox*[202] the EAT had to consider the situation where the contract won by a successor service provider contained no guarantee of work. If TUPE applies in such circumstances, there may be a transfer of a workforce but no work for them to do post transfer. The court held that such matters should be decided by reference to questions of what happens in practice rather than by legal constraints.

SPECIFIC TYPES OF TRANSFER

Bankruptcy, insolvency and similar proceedings

2.137   Separate considerations arise in cases where the employer is an undertaking which is in liquidation. In *Jules Dethier Équipement SA v Dassy*[203] the ECJ said that the 1977 Directive applied to a transfer of an undertaking subject to an administrative or judicial procedure if the purpose of the procedure is to keep the undertaking in business with a view to its recovery in the future. The Court said that Art 1(1) accordingly applied to the transfer of an undertaking which was being wound up by the court if it continued to trade while it was being wound up so that continuity of the business was assured when the undertaking was transferred. It also said, however, that the Directive did not apply to an undertaking which was in the course of insolvency proceedings or to transfers of undertakings or businesses made in the context of procedures comparable to bankruptcy proceedings.[204] It stressed that the determining factor to be taken into account was the purpose of the procedure in question.

2.138   There is now a specific provision in the 2001 Directive[205] dealing with bankruptcy and insolvency proceedings. This is Art 5(1), which provides that, unless Member States provide otherwise, Arts 3 and 4 are not to apply to a transfer of an undertaking or business:

> '… where the transferor is the subject of bankruptcy proceedings or any analogous insolvency proceedings which have been instituted withy a view to liquidation of the assets of the transferor and are under the supervision of a competent public authority (which may be an insolvency practitioner authorised by a competent public authority).'

2.139   This provision effectively states the position set out by the ECJ in *Jules Dethier Équipement* above. Article 5(2)(a), however, enables the Member States to provide that the transferor's debts arising from any contract of employment or employment relationships and payable before the transfer or before the opening of the insolvency proceedings are not to be transferred to the transferee, provided that the proceedings give rise, under the law of the Member State, to protection at least equivalent to that provided for by Council

---

202   [2006] IRLR 258
203   [1998] ICR 541.
204   See also *Abels v Administrative Board of the Bedrijfsvereniging voor de Metaalindustrie en de Electrotechnische Industrie* Case 135/83 [1985] ECR 469 and *d'Urso v Ercole Marelli Elettromecanica Generale SpA* [1991] ECR I-4105.
205   Introduced by Council Directive 98/50/EC, Art 1, para 2.

Directive 80/987/EC.[206] It also enables 'the transferee, transferor, or person or persons exercising the transferor's functions, on the one hand, and the representatives of the employees, on the other hand, to agree alterations to the employees' terms and conditions of employment designed to safeguard employment opportunities by ensuring the survival of the undertaking or business'.[207] Article 5(2) applies where Arts 3 and 4 apply to a transfer during insolvency proceedings which have been opened in relation to a transferor (whether or not the proceedings have been instituted with a view to the liquidation of the assets of the transferor) and provided that the proceedings are under the supervision of a competent public authority (which may be an insolvency practitioner determined by national law). The provisions of Art 6(1), third paragraph, should also be noted here. Their effect is that where the transferor is the subject of bankruptcy proceedings within Art 5(1), Member States may take the necessary measures to ensure that the transferred employees are properly represented until the new election or designation of representatives of the employees.

2.140   TUPE 2006 contains a specific regulation relating to insolvency, reg 8. This is considered in **chapter 3**, at **3.84**.

Administrative re-organisations

2.141   The issue of administrative reorganisations arises from the case of *Henke v Gemeinde Schierke and Verwaltungs-gemeinschaft 'Brocken'*, considered in more detail below, in which the ECJ ruled that the 1977 Directive did not apply to a transfer of administrative functions as part of a local government reorganisation. As a result of this decision Directive 98/90/EC introduced a new Art 1(1)(c), which says:

> '(c)   … An administrative reorganisation of public administrative authorities, or the transfer of administrative functions between public administrative authorities, is not a transfer within the meaning of this Directive.'

The amendment serves to confirm the *Henke* decision, but does not affect the subsequent cases.

2.142   Article 1(1)(c) has been given effect to by reg 3(5), which provides that an administrative reorganisation of public administrative authorities or the transfer of administrative functions between public administrative authorities is not a relevant transfer. The DTI Guidance on TUPE 2006 points out that such transfers are covered by the Cabinet Office's Statement of Practice 'Staff Transfers in the Public Sector' (see Appendix 11). This is considered at **3.127**.

2.143   The provisions of the Directive and of reg 3(5) are intended to give effect to the ECJ decision in *Henke   v   Gemeinde   Schierke   and*

---

206   As amended by Directive 87/164/EEC.

207   Article 5(2)(b). Note also Art 5(3) which enables a Member State to apply para 2(b) to any transfers where the transferor is in a situation of serious economic crisis, as defined by national law, provided that the situation is declared by a competent public authority and open to judicial supervision, on condition that such provisions already exist in national law by 17 July 1998.

Verwaltungs-gemeinschaft 'Brocken',[208] where the issue was whether the Directive applies to a transfer of administrative functions as part of a local government reorganisation. Mrs Henke lost her job as secretary to the mayor of the municipality of Schierke when the municipal administration was dissolved and its functions transferred to a regional authority. She brought proceedings claiming that the termination of her contract was null and void and, in the alternative, that she had been dismissed contrary to the relevant German legislation. The decision of the ECJ was that Art 1(1) of the Directive 'does not apply to the transfer of administrative functions from a municipality to an administrative collectivity ...'.

2.144   The Court's judgment is extremely brief and terse. At para 13, it refers to the first recital in the preamble to the Directive and points out that the Directive 'sets out to protect workers against the potentially unfavourable consequences for them of changes in the structure of undertakings resulting from economic trends at national and Community level, through, inter alia, transfers of undertakings ...'. It goes on to say, in para 14:

> 'Consequently, the reorganisation of structures of the public administration or the transfer of administrative functions between public administrative authorities does not constitute a "transfer of an undertaking" within the meaning of the [1977] Directive.'

2.145   The judgment makes no mention of the cases considered earlier in the chapter,[209] particularly the *Sophie Redmond Stichting* and *Rask* cases. The ECJ's stress in *Henke* on whether a business has been transferred is incompatible with the language it used in the *Sophie Redmond Stichting* case. It is also surprising, in view of the fact that the Court held the exclusion of non-commercial ventures to be incompatible with the Directive. Comparison of the Court's decision with the Opinion of the Advocate General in the same case merely serves to highlight the inadequacies of the decision and make its conclusions the more surprising. At the end of a carefully reasoned Opinion, which considered the preceding case-law in considerable depth, he proposed that the Court should answer the question whether there was an undertaking in these terms:[210]

> 'A transfer of an undertaking ... is involved where – in the case of a voluntary amalgamation of two or more independent municipalities into an independent collectivity – the municipalities employ persons who are protected as employees under domestic legislation and the operations of the municipalities are actually continued. In this connection, all the facts characterising the transaction in question (the formation of an administrative collectivity) must be taken into consideration, namely the type and extent of the powers transferred, the activities carried out, the area of territorial responsibility, the right to have disposal over records and other administrative materials and whether the workforce is taken over. It is for the national court to make these findings of fact.'

2.146   It is arguable that the decision – and thus Art 1(1)(c) of the Directive and reg 3(5) of TUPE 2006 – should be given a narrow reading and that its

---

208   [1996] IRLR 701.
209   See **2.13–2.17**.
210   [1996] IRLR 701, at 708.

effect is to exclude from the scope of the Directive administrative functions which relate purely to the exercise of public powers and which do not involve any economic activity.[211]

2.147 Two subsequent cases in the ECJ suggest indeed that the Court is giving a narrow interpretation to *Henke*. In *Mayeur v Association Promotion de L'Information Messine (APIM)*[212] the facts were that the employee was employed as a publicity manager by APIM, a non-profit making organisation which aimed to promote opportunities offered by the City of Metz. In 1997 these activities were taken over by the municipality and APIM was dissolved. Mr Mayeur was dismissed on the grounds that APIM had ceased its activities. The ECJ held that the 1977 Directive applied where the activities of a private undertaking are transferred to a public undertaking, even if the private undertaking was a non-profit making organisation. The ECJ rejected the French Government's argument that APIM was in reality a public service so that what had happened was an administrative reorganisation and outside the scope of the Directive.

2.148 The second case, *Collino and Chiappero v Telecom Italia SpA*,[213] involved the reorganisation of the Italian telephone services and the transfer of employees from a state body to a state-owned company. The ECJ held that the Directive applied and that Art 3(1)[214] requires a transferee to take into account the entire length of service of the employees transferred when calculating rights of a financial nature such as a termination payment. It also pointed out that the persons concerned must be workers subject to national employment law in order to be within the Directive. Thus self-employed contractors or office-holders would be outside the scope of the Directive.

2.149 The provisions of s 38 of the Employment Relations Act 1999 should also be noted. These empower the Secretary of State to provide TUPE-equivalent protections to cases or classes of cases falling outside the scope of the Directive. At the time of going to press, the Secretary of State had made two sets of Regulations using this power.[215] In addition, legislation dealing with particular transfers within public administrations sometimes contains provisions equivalent to TUPE in relation to the specific transfer.

EXCLUSIONS FROM TUPE

2.150 Article 1(3) of the Directive states that it is not to apply to sea-going vessels. Transfers of ships were excluded by reg 2(2) of TUPE 1981,[216] but there

---

211 See [1996] IRLR 653, where this suggestion is advanced by the editor of the Reports.
212 [2000] IRLR 783.
213 [2000] IRLR 788.
214 The Article number is the same in both the 1977 and the 2001 Directives.
215 The Transfer of Undertakings (Protection of Employment) (Rent Officer Service) Regulations 1999, SI 1999/2511 and the Transfer of Undertakings (Protection of Employment) (Transfer of OFCOM) Regulations 2003, SI 2003/2715.
216 In *Addison v Denholm Ship Management (UK) Ltd* [1997] IRLR 389 the EAT held that 'Flotels' used in connection with offshore oil and gas installations are ships.

is no equivalent provision in TUPE 2006. For a consideration of the classes of employees excluded from the Regulations, reference should be made to **4.10**.

2.151 Regulation 18 provides that the parties to what would be a transfer under TUPE cannot contract out of their rights. However, the position is not entirely clear. Under TUPE 1981 there was a clear statement that any provision of an agreement which purported to exclude or limit the operation of the transfer principle, the provisions relating to dismissal or those relating to informing and consulting with employee representatives, was void. Likewise any attempt to preclude any person from bringing a claim in respect of an alleged failure to inform and consult in an employment tribunal was void.[217]

2.152 The provisions in TUPE 2006 are less clear. Regulation 18 refers to the Employment Rights Act 1996, s 203, the general provision that prohibits contracting out of employment rights, and states that it shall apply as if those restrictions were contained within TUPE itself. What has caused controversy is how the regulation was intended to apply in relation to the contracting out of rights through a compromise agreement. The view is generally held that claims arising out of TUPE, whether under its own provisions (for example, arising out of a failure to inform and to consult), or under some other provision (for example, an unfair dismissal) can be compromised. However, there is a need for authority on the point before anyone can be certain that a compromise agreement will have its intended effect.

2.153 Whilst the parties may be precluded from contracting out, it is open to them to arrange their affairs so as to circumvent the application of TUPE. In *Brookes v Borough Care Services*,[218] Wigan Metropolitan Borough Council had decided to transfer a number of care homes to the private sector. During the course of the deal, the proposed purchaser's lawyers explained to the purchaser the implications of TUPE and certain issues arose which caused concern. In particular, the purchaser felt that it would be essential to renegotiate the terms and conditions of employment of the employees, in order to put the finances of the homes on a firmer financial footing. When it became clear that TUPE would be a major impediment to a change of this nature, the transaction was restructured as an acquisition of the company limited by guarantee in which the operation and ownership of the care homes was vested. The employees complained that this was, in effect, contracting out of TUPE and that their rights had been violated as a consequence.

2.154 The court disagreed. It was held that the provisions of TUPE do not apply to a share sale and that the parties to a transaction are free to choose how they structure the transaction, even if in doing so they have as a deliberate objective the avoidance of the consequences were TUPE to apply.

2.155 It is interesting to note that a deliberate strategy to avoid the consequences of TUPE was upheld in *Brookes* whereas the TUPE avoidance motive was a significant factor in bringing the transfer in *ECM v Cox*[219] within

---

217 TUPE 1981, reg 12.
218 [1998] IRLR 636.
219 See **2.117**.

the scope of TUPE. Having said that, the structure of the transaction in *Brookes* was quite clearly outside TUPE, whereas the circumstances of *Cox* have always been acknowledged to be in an area of uncertainty.

2.156 Although TUPE applies generally across the UK, there are variations in respect of Northern Ireland. Schedule 1 to TUPE 2006 specifically provides that the Regulations apply to Northern Ireland subject to the modifications set out in that Schedule. In essence, there are no differences of substance, merely mechanics designed to apply the principles of the Regulations to the differing legislative background in the province. In particular, the Employment Relations Act 1999, s 38, under which the service provision changes were enacted, does not apply in Northern Ireland and hence there was a need to take a separate legal route to implement these provisions in Northern Ireland.

Offshoring

2.157 One increasingly important area, in which it is unclear to what extent the Regulations apply, concerns transfers where the undertaking moves from the UK to another jurisdiction.[220] Neither the Directive[221] nor TUPE deals with the issue of whether they apply in these circumstances. This uncertainty has always been an issue in relation to cross-border mergers and acquisitions, but it has become much more of an issue in recent years as developments in technology have opened up the possibility of international outsourcing, particularly to Eastern Europe and to the Indian subcontinent. At first sight, there is no difficulty in applying the Regulations, because the only factor which matters so far as the Regulations are concerned is whether, immediately before the transfer, the undertaking or the supply of services is situated in the UK. The Directive takes a similar line – it applies where the undertaking is situated within the territorial scope of the EU Treaty.[222] No mention is made of where the undertaking or services will be situated following the transfer, so this would not appear to be a relevant criterion when considering whether the Regulations or the Directive apply in a cross-border context.

2.158 However, two problems emerge with certain aspects of TUPE when one tries to understand the consequences. First, there will generally be no provision which obliges the transferee, situated in another jurisdiction, to recognise the transferred rights. If a job moves from the UK to another Member State of the EU, it would have been possible for the Directive to have provided that the recipient must honour the transferring UK terms and conditions in respect of the employment relationship. However, the Directive does not do so and indeed

---

220 The most comprehensive review of the law in this area is the paper prepared by Professor Bob Hepple for the European Commission in 1998: 'The Legal Consequences of Cross Border Transfer of Undertakings within the European Union'.

221 Earlier drafts of the Directive did provide that it should apply in the case of cross-border transfers, whether within the EEA or involving third party countries. The fact that these provisions were removed from the Directive in its final form suggests that there was an unwillingness to legislate for the Directive to have a wide application in such circumstances. If this inference is correct, it would suggest that the Directive does not apply to cross-border outsourcing.

222 2001 Directive, Art 1(2).

to do so could be argued to be countercultural. To compound the problem, the Directive has no provisions relating to the conflict of laws. Under ordinary conflict of laws principles, an employment relationship will usually be governed by the law of the state where the employment relationship subsists. To suggest that a transferring employee should continue his or her employment in another Member State but subject to a contract of employment governed by UK law and not local laws would seem inappropriate. Some countries within the EU have nevertheless provided that the transferee is bound to honour the rights transferring from abroad in certain circumstances, but many jurisdictions will not have any such law. Moreover, there is no basis for the Directive or the Regulations to have extra-territorial effect where the transferee is not governed by the laws of an EEA state.

2.159 It may be argued that the rights of employees in relation to information and consultation are adequately protected by TUPE, and so this problem is not of general effect. This is correct to a point – the transferor can be required to comply with its ordinary obligations and a remedy lies against the transferor if it defaults. However, on further examination the process is materially impaired by virtue of the fact that there is no basis for the transferee in another jurisdiction to be compelled to disclose information concerning the 'measures' which are proposed in relation to the transfer.

2.160 Another concern is the apparent conflict between the object of the Directive and TUPE, on the one hand, that is to protect the acquired rights of employees, and, on the other, the consequences of the Regulations if applied to offshoring. For example, if a call centre worker in Cardiff is employed in the provision of a service which is offshored to India, that employee will in all probability not wish to take up employment in India, preferring to find another job locally. However, if the employee did wish to transfer, he or she would be faced with the difficulty of persuading an Indian court to recognise the burden which the Regulations seek to place onto the shoulders of the Indian transferee. Hence the objective of preserving the employment relationship in most cases will either not be of interest or will be unachievable; the only issue then would be the preservation of the employee's outstanding rights under the contract of employment, in particular the claim to a redundancy payment and the prospect of an unfair dismissal claim. If the Regulations apply, the claims are transferred to an entity which may have neither a presence nor assets in the UK, thereby seriously undermining the ability of the employee to enforce those rights. The position is probably not so bleak as it may appear, because if the Regulations do apply and it is clear that the transferee is going to take the position that it is not bound by them, there is likely to be a claim for constructive dismissal which could be brought against the transferor.[223]

2.161 There is an interesting issue as to whether TUPE 2006 has increased the likelihood that the Regulations apply to an offshoring, when contrasted with TUPE 1981. Under the latter, as under the former, one can run the argument that if the Regulations apply to an offshoring they will detract from rather than protect the rights of the employees. However, under the 1981 Regulations there was also an argument that the Regulations did not apply to offshoring, based

---

223 See *University of Oxford v Humphreys* [2000] ICR 405.

upon the very concept of a transfer of an undertaking. Whereas the 2006 Regulations, in the provisions relating to service provision changes, do not require any consideration of how the service is to be delivered post transfer (other than that there is still a service being delivered),[224] under TUPE 1981 it was necessary to consider how the service was being delivered post transfer. Given that offshorings generally involve a mix of changes – geographical, technical and cultural – there was often a reasonable case for arguing that there was no identifiable entity post transfer which could be said to have sufficient in common with the way in which the services were delivered pre transfer to amount to a relevant transfer. That argument has certainly been taken away by TUPE 2006, increasing the likelihood that the Regulations will be held to apply to a transfer offshore, though other objections remain.

2.162   Under TUPE 1981, when applying a *Süzen* test to an offshoring, there may have been little or nothing in the way of a transfer of assets and, if there was no employee transfer either, there was a strong argument that there was no relevant transfer. These difficulties do not arise under the new service provision changes of TUPE 2006, so again there is an argument that the 2006 Regulations are more likely to apply to an offshoring then their 1981 counterparts.

2.163   There is no evidence, bearing in mind the consultation exercises which surrounded the implementation of TUPE 2006, that the 2006 Regulations are intended to modify the law in relation to outsourcing.

2.164   Hence there is a debate – which as yet has no clear answer[225] – about the applicability of TUPE 2006 in these circumstances. The issue has come to the attention of the European Commission and is to be reviewed in the context of whether there is a need to amend the Directive to deal with this issue expressly.

2.165   In practice, it is rare for UK-based employees to wish to 'follow' their jobs overseas on an offshoring. Consequently, the very fact of offshoring is likely to give rise to a significant cost in terms of severance payments. The only real significance of TUPE is to determine as a matter of law where that cost lies. In practice, the cost will invariably fall on the transferor, either because the Regulations do not apply and therefore the cost remains with the transferor as a matter of law, or because the Regulations move the liability to the transferee, who will wish to pass that cost back to the transferor as a matter of contract by reason of the fact that it is an inevitable cost incurred in changing the method of delivery of the service. Hence many offshorings will be handled by the transferor by negotiation with the workforce and the Regulations will have limited significance. The duties to inform and consult are perhaps the most significant – those duties will fall largely on the transferor, as will the legal burden of non-compliance in most cases, pursuant to reg 13(9). The application of the Regulations to an offshoring in the context of information and consultation obligations are not open to the same objections as a matter of law, as discussed above.

---

224   See **2.93**.
225   The problem is compounded by a lack of helpful case-law on the point.

2.166   There are other areas within the EEA where the impact of a cross-border undertaking would be of much less impact than in the UK, where it requires a sea crossing at the very least. The Dutch-Belgian border, for example, experiences a regular throughflow of commuters. If a Dutch undertaking was to transfer just 10 miles down the road, but across the border into Belgium, the Directive might be expected to have a relevance far beyond its relevance in the case of a UK offshoring. The employees are likely to want to retain their jobs and to commute 10 miles is unlikely to be an inconvenience such as to lead to their resignation. It is surprising, therefore, that there are not a number of cases in the courts of EEA states which have dealt with this issue over the past 30 years. The reason why there are so few contested transfers, it is suggested, is that even where the possibility of keeping the employment relationship alive is a real one, it makes little sense to attempt to apply the employment contract of one jurisdiction in relation to an employment relationship in another jurisdiction. If the employees wish to transfer and the transferee is willing to employ them, it makes sense to enter into a new contract of employment in the jurisdiction of the transferee, recognising the altered balance of local laws, taxes and social security rights. It will need to be of broadly equivalent value, otherwise the employee will not accept it and there will be a severance cost, as there will be in circumstances where the employee is otherwise not transferred. The severance costs are likely to be factored into the economics of the transfer. Hence pragmatism has taken the place of a largely unattainable objective were the Directive to apply in such circumstances. There is no doubt that, in view of the complexity of the arguments, many political transferors and transferees will turn a Nelsonian eye to the issue and simply apply a pragmatic solution that is likely to be conducive to employers and employers' wishes.

2.167   The fact that TUPE 2006 focuses on the situation of the target means that employees overseas could be caught by a transfer of a 'business situated immediately before the transfer in the United Kingdom'. An employee based overseas but whose role is an integral part of the UK-situated business will transfer. Regulation 3(4) provides that 'these Regulations apply to—(c) a transfer of an undertaking ... where persons employed in the undertaking ... ordinarily work outside the United Kingdom'. The issue in practice is the extent to which an overseas-based employee is an integral part of the UK-situated business.

2.168   The provisions relating to service provision changes refer to 'an organised grouping of employees situated in Great Britain'.[226] Hence there is no latitude for overseas employees to be caught within the ambit of this type of transfer. In this respect, the provisions relating to a relevant transfer via the service provision change route would appear to be narrower than those provisions relating to a transfer of an undertaking or business.

2.169   The fact that a transaction is governed by the laws of another country is immaterial[227] as is the law which governs the contract of employment.[228] It is

---

226   Regulation 3(3)(a)(i).
227   Regulation 3(4)(b)(i).
228   Regulation 3(4)(6)(ii).

quite usual, for example, for a sale of a global business to be conducted between US lawyers in the US, but for the UK aspects of the transaction to be governed by TUPE.

Chapter 3

THE EFFECT OF A TRANSFER OF AN UNDERTAKING

3.1   When a relevant transfer takes place, what is often called a 'statutory novation' occurs. The effect of this, put briefly, is to place the transferee into the shoes of the transferor. This means that the transferee takes over the contracts of employment of all employees who were employed in the 'organised grouping of resources or employees' immediately before the transfer or who would have been so employed had they not been unfairly dismissed by reason of the transfer. The transferee cannot choose which employees to take on without incurring liability for unfair dismissal; nor can it dismiss employees merely because the transfer has occurred. The transferee takes over all the rights and obligations arising from the contracts of employment it has taken over, except for criminal liabilities and some benefits under an occupational pension scheme. The transferee will also take over any collective agreements made by or on behalf of the transferor in respect of any transferring employees and may also be required to take over the recognition of an independent trade union. This chapter considers all these matters. It also considers the provisions relating to insolvency and pensions.

3.2   The regulation of the Transfer of Undertakings (Protection of Employment) Regulations (TUPE) 2006[1] which deals generally with the 'statutory novation' is reg 4, whose provisions are considered in detail below. Regulation 5 deals specifically with the effect of a relevant transfer on collective agreements; reg 6 deals with the effect of a relevant transfer on trade union recognition: see **3.78** and **3.99**. Regulation 8 contains provisions relating to the transfer of liability in an insolvency and reg 10 contains provisions in relation to pensions: see **3.84** and **3.106**.

3.3   Regulation 4 should be seen in the context of the provisions of Directive 2001/23/EC, together with the case-law of the European Court of Justice (ECJ). The relevant provisions for the purposes of the regulations considered in this chapter are Arts 3, 4(2) and 5. The general provisions are considered here; those relating to insolvency (Art 5) and pensions (Art 3(4)) are considered in the appropriate context. It should be borne in mind that, when interpreting TUPE 2006, a tribunal or court will give it a purposive construction so as to enable them to accord, where possible, with the Directive,[2] bearing in mind that the objective of the Directive is 'to protect workers and, more particularly, to

---

1   SI 2006/246.
2   See *Litster v Forth Dry Dock & Engineering Company Ltd* [1989] ICR 341.

safeguard their rights upon a change of employer', as was stated by the ECJ in *Abels v Administrative Board of the Bedrijfsvereniging voor de Metaalindustrie en de Electrotechnische Industrie*.[3]

3.4 Article 3(1) starts with the general provision that the transferor's rights and obligations arising from a contract of employment 'or from an employment relationship' existing on the date of a transfer are to be transferred to the transferee. It also provides for the possibility of joint and several liability as between transferor and transferee, though this option has only been taken up by TUPE 2006 in relation to personal injury claims. In *Celtec Ltd v Astley*[4] the ECJ said that 'the date of a transfer' in Art 3(1) is a particular point in time which cannot be postponed to another date at the will of the transferor or transferee. It went on to say that the date is the date on which responsibility as employer for carrying on the business of the unit transferred moves from the transferor to the transferee. Thus, contracts of employment or employment relationships existing on the date of the transfer, as so defined, between the transferor and the workers assigned to the undertaking transferred are deemed to be handed over, on that date, irrespective of what was agreed between the parties. This case is considered more fully at **3.13**, where the decision of the House of Lords in relation to the application of the ECJ's opinion is discussed.

3.5 Article 3(3) provides that, following the transfer, the transferee is to continue to observe the terms and conditions contained in any collective agreement.

3.6 Article 4(2) provides that, if the contract of employment or employment relationship is terminated 'because the transfer involves a substantial change in working conditions to the detriment of the employee', the employer is to be regarded as having been responsible for the termination of the contractual relationship.[5] Article 4(2) is given effect to by reg 4(9) and (11) of TUPE 2006. Whilst reg 4(9) is fuller than Art 4(2), in one respect it would appear to have a narrower application than was perhaps intended: it requires the substantial change in working condition to be to the '*material* detriment' of the employee whereas Art 4(2) speaks merely of 'detriment'.

---

3   Case 135/83 [1985] ECR 469.
4   Case C-478/03 [2005] ICR 1409.
5   In *Boor v Ministre de la Fonction Publique et de la Réforme Administrative* Case C-425/02 [2005] IRLR 61, the ECJ said that Directive 77/187/EEC does not in principle preclude a public employer, when taking over employees on a transfer from a private employer, from reducing the amount of the remuneration of the employee(s) concerned for the purpose of complying with the national rules in force for public employees. It also said that if the calculation involved leads to a substantial reduction in the employee's remuneration, it will constitute a substantial change in working conditions to the detriment of the employees concerned within Art 4(2).

GENERAL EFFECT OF REG 4

3.7   The effect of reg 4(1) of TUPE 2006[6] is that a relevant transfer does not of itself terminate the employee's contract, so there is no dismissal, no obligation to give notice of termination or to make a payment in lieu and no liability to make a redundancy payment; the contract will be treated as if it had always been made between the employee and the transferee (ie the new employer). This is what is sometimes called a 'statutory novation'. It applies to the transfer of an undertaking or a part of an undertaking.[7] It should be noted that reg 4 will only apply if the employee was employed by the transferor; if not, reg 4 will not apply. This issue is considered more fully at **3.9**.

3.8   The general position set out in reg 4(1) is subject to two qualifications. First, reg 4(7) provides that reg 4(1) and (2) will not operate to transfer employees' contracts of employment and the rights, powers, duties and liabilities under or in connection with them, if they inform the transferor or the transferee that they object to becoming employed by the transferee. This is considered more fully at **3.33**. Secondly, reg 4(9) gives the employee the right to resign and (subject to the ordinary qualifications) to bring a claim for unfair dismissal where a substantial change is made in the working conditions to his or her 'material' detriment: see **3.41**. In relation to both these provisions, reg 4(11) states that they are without prejudice to any right of the employee arising apart from TUPE 2006 to terminate the contract of employment without notice in acceptance of a repudiatiory breach of contract by the employer: see **3.35**.

EMPLOYEES COVERED BY THE TRANSFER

3.9   Regulation 4(1) applies to an employee who was 'employed by the transferor and assigned to the organised grouping of resources or employees that is subject to the relevant transfer'. Regulation 4(3) amplifies this provision by including persons who would have been employed immediately before the transfer had they not been dismissed 'in the circumstances described in regulation 7(1)': see **3.14**.

3.10   A corollary of the application of reg 4(1) to employees employed by the transferor is that reg 4 will not apply to employees not employed by the transferor. This may seem an obvious proposition, but an examination of the Court of Appeal decision in *Askew v Governing Body of Clifton Middle School*[8] shows the problems that may lurk. The facts of the case were that the employee was employed as a teacher by a local education authority. He worked at a school which was closed down, as a result of a decision by the local authority to reorganise its schools. The dismissal of the school's staff was in accordance with the relevant statutory procedures which required the governing body of a

---

6   Formerly reg 5(1) of the Transfer of Undertakings (Protection of Employment) Regulations (TUPE) 1981, SI 1981/1794.
7   For a discussion of the cases which consider whether an employee is employed in part of an undertaking, see **2.131** ff.
8   [1999] IRLR 708.

school to notify the local education authority once it had determined that any person employed to work at the school should cease to work there. In accordance with this procedure, the governors notified the authority which gave the employee notice of termination of his contract. The employee applied to work at the new school but was not appointed to a post there. In proceedings which ended up in the Court of Appeal he argued that his rights when employed by the old governing body should be automatically transferred to the new governing body by the operation of the either the Directive (which was conceded to be directly applicable) or TUPE. The Court of Appeal rejected this argument. It said that for either provision to apply there must be a contract between the person concerned and the transferor, which in this case was the governing body of the old school. The employee was employed by the local education authority and did not therefore have an employment relationship with the transferor. Neither the Directive nor TUPE could be held to apply.

3.11 A similar issue arises not infrequently in relation to the employment arrangements of groups of companies. It is not unusual for the employees of a group to be employed through a single service company. Apart from anything else, this makes personnel management more straightforward. However, if the group sells off a part of its business, it is unlikely that the employees will be employed by the transferor. The transferor in such circumstances will usually be an operating company. The issue was addressed by Morison J in *Duncan Web Offset (Maidstone) v Cooper*[9] when he asserted:

> 'Industrial tribunals will be astute to ensure that the provisions of the Regulations are not evaded by devices such as service companies, or by complicated group structures which conceal the true position.'

3.12 One of the ways in which it appears that the judge might have had it in mind to solve this problem is by implying an agency relationship so that the company in receipt of services is seen as an agent for the employer and hence the employer acts as a transferor through its agent, which is itself a transferor; alternatively, the employer could be considered to be a transferor by being named in the sale and purchase agreement for this purpose only.

3.13 The impact of the House of Lords decision in *North Wales Training and Enterprise Council Ltd (t/a Celtec) v Astley*[10] (reported under the name *Celtec Ltd v Astley* in its earlier stages, including a reference to the ECJ) in the present context should be noted. The facts of the case were that, on the creation in the early 1990s of Training and Enterprise Councils (TECs), civil servants were seconded to the TECs to help them in the initial stages of their operations. The civil servants concerned enjoyed their normal pay and conditions of employment. It was later announced by the Government that secondments would be phased out at the end of each TEC's fifth year of operation, when the civil servants could either return to the civil service or accept an offer of employment from a TEC. The issue which gave rise to the litigation was whether the continuity of employment of a civil servant who entered the employment of a TEC would count towards the length of their employment with a TEC. When the case reached the House of Lords it referred

---

9   [1995] IRLR 633. See also **3.4** where the ECJ decision is considered.
10   [2006] UKHL 29.

questions to the ECJ relating to the time at which the transfer of an undertaking is deemed to be complete. The ECJ's ruling was twofold.[11] It said that 'the date of a transfer' in Art 3(1) is a particular point in time which cannot be postponed to another date at the will of the transferor or transferee. It went on to say that the date is the date on which responsibility as employer for carrying on the business of the unit transferred moves from the transferor to the transferee. It also said that contracts of employment or employment relationships existing on the date of the transfer, as so defined, between the transferor and the workers assigned to the undertaking transferred are deemed to be handed over, on that date, irrespective of what was agreed between the parties. The effect of the House of Lords decision, in its application of the ECJ's ruling, is that, irrespective of any agreement between the individual civil servants and the Department of Employment (as it then was) or between the Department and the TECs, on the transfer of the Department's functions to the TECs the civil servants involved became employees of the TECs. The agreement that they should be seconded but remain civil servants was thus overridden and they became employees of the TECs at the time of the transfer, in September 1990. The other issue considered by the House of Lords was whether the employees who chose to remain civil servants could be said to have refused to have their contracts transferred to Celtec Ltd, as it then was. This issue is considered in the next section at **3.34**.

3.14 Regulation 4(3) applies reg 4(1) so as to include persons employed 'immediately before the transfer, or who would have been so employed if he had not been dismissed in the circumstances described in regulation 7(1)...'. Dismissals in the context of transfers of undertakings and the effect of reg 7 are considered more fully in **chapter 4**.

3.15 Interpreted literally, TUPE 2006 would only appear to catch employees who are within the scope of the transfer at the last moment. A literal interpretation of the phrase 'immediately before' gives rise to the possibility of moving employees in and out of scope during the period leading up to the transfer, so as to manipulate the consequences of the Regulations.

3.16 In one direction, this can involve the removal by the transferor of employees who are highly regarded by the transferor and who the transferor wishes to retain. If the terms and conditions of the employee are sufficiently wide to allow the employer to move an employee out of scope, there is little that a transferee can do to stop this. If the move out of scope requires a variation in the contract of employment, one might object on the basis that the change necessary to move the employee out of scope is void as it arises directly out of the transfer. In fact, the discussion is academic for an employee always has the right to opt out of the transfer and the employer can always re-employ the employee elsewhere in its retained organisation. In public sector outsourcing, it is quite common for this to be done in an organised and widespread manner: the public sector employer asks employees if they want to transfer to the private sector and, if they do not, may seek to redeploy them elsewhere in the public sector.

---

11 See [2005] ICR 1409, Case C-478/03.

3.17   In the other direction, the practice has grown up in some quarters of 'dumping' employees or 'lemon-dropping'. The transferor moves into scope employees who the transferor wishes to remove from its employment, particularly poor performers and problem employees. On a strict interpretation of the concept of 'immediately before', there is little that can be done about this practice. However, tribunals will try to stop such abuses, perhaps by taking an expansive view of the term 'immediately before'.

3.18   One example of an employment tribunal finding a way of dealing with dumping is *Carisway Cleaning Consultants v Richards and Cooper Cleaning Services*.[12] In that case, an employee was employed on a contract to clean a Sainsburys store. Sainsburys was unhappy with the service which was being offered and there were a number of issues surrounding the employee. The employer offered the employee an internal transfer, in circumstances where – although the employee was unaware of this fact – the contract on which the employee was newly deployed was about to come to an end. The Court held that the employee had been 'gulled'; the way in which the employer had behaved in order to try to entice the employee into a situation where the Regulations would then migrate his employment was fraudulent. Hence it found that there had been no transfer.

3.19   It is often left to the tribunals to ascertain exactly what has happened and to try to stop such abuses. There is plenty of evidence to suggest that, when they do so, the appellate courts will not intervene.[13] In a situation where warranties are available from the transferor of an undertaking, it is prudent to seek a warranty to the effect that all the transferring employees have been in post for a given amount of time, so as to flush out cases where employees have been moved and possibly 'dumped'.

3.20   Not only must employees be employed 'immediately before' the transfer, they must be 'assigned' to the undertaking. 'Assigned' is defined – not particularly helpfully – in reg 2(1) as meaning 'assigned other than on a temporary basis'. In the case of a transfer of a part of a wider undertaking, this can cause problems. Very often, employees who perform a number of services will not be formally 'assigned' to one part of the business or another. For example, assume that an enterprise has two lines of business. These are supported by head office functions such as legal, treasury and human resources. One business is sold – does a proportionate part of the head office function transfer with the business being sold? Those working in the various head office functions will work for both businesses but generally without a formal assignment to one or the other.

3.21   In circumstances where an employee is assigned to the part of the business which transfers, it is clear that the employee will transfer notwithstanding that not all their time is spent in that part of the business. Assume, for example, that the head office function contains four lawyers, three of whom are assigned to the part of the business which will transfer, though

---

12   EAT 629/97/1906.
13   See *Carisway Cleaning v Richards* (ibid) and *Jones v Darlows Estate Agency* [1998] EWCA Civ 1157.

they only spend two-thirds of their time on work related to that part of the business. Three lawyers will transfer and the transferred legal function will have the equivalent of one person surplus. The retained legal function will be a man short, just one lawyer remaining. Where there is no formal assignment – which is generally the case – the tribunal has to establish, as a matter of fact, whether an employee can be considered to be assigned. This is ordinarily done by an analysis of how much time the employee devotes to the undertaking which is transferring and how much time is spent on other activities. However, it is important to note that this is only one factor to be taken into account and, when it is, there is no threshold beyond which an employee will be considered to be assigned.

3.22   The classic test of who is assigned was set out by Morison J in *Duncan Web Offset (Maidstone) Ltd v Cooper*:[14]

'There will often be difficult questions of fact for industrial tribunals to consider when deciding who was "assigned" and who was not. We were invited to give guidance to industrial tribunals about such a decision, but declined to do so because the facts will vary so markedly from case to case. In the course of argument a number were suggested, such as the amount of time spent on one part of the business or the other; the amount of value given to each part by the employee; the terms of the contract of employment showing what the employee could be required to do; how the cost to the employer of the employee's services had been allocated between different parts of the business. This is, plainly, not an exhaustive list; we are quite prepared to accept that these or some of these matters may well fall for consideration by an industrial tribunal which is seeking to determine to which part of his employers' business the employee had been assigned.'

3.23   In *Mowlem Technical Services v King*,[15] Lord Osborne pointed out, when giving the judgment of the Inner House of the Court of Session, that: 'It is evident [from Morison J's judgment] that a range of circumstances require to be considered in reaching a decision on the question of assignment.' Accordingly, even though two employees spent 80% of their time in the scope of the transfer, the court nevertheless refused to overturn the decision of the employment tribunal that only one of the employees transferred.

3.24   The wording of reg 4(3) expands on the wording of reg 5(3) of TUPE 1981 and is clearly intended to give effect to the interpretation of that provision by the House of Lords in *Litster v Forth Dry Dock & Engineering Co Ltd (in receivership)*.[16] In that case, the facts were that the transferor agreed to transfer the undertaking to the transferee and, as part of the agreement, agreed to dismiss the workforce before the completion of the transfer. One hour before the completion of the transfer, the workforce was dismissed. The House of Lords held that the Regulations should be given a purposive construction in a manner which would accord with the decisions of the ECJ on the Directive 1977/187/EEC and, where necessary, words should be implied to achieve that effect. There should be implied into reg 5(3) (as it then was) after the words 'immediately before the transfer' the words 'or would have been so employed if

---

14   [1995] IRLR 633, at 635.
15   [2005] CSIH 46.
16   [1989] ICR 341. See also *Re Maxwell Fleet and Facilities Management Ltd (in Administration)* [2000] ICR 717.

he had not been unfairly dismissed in the circumstances described by regulation 8(1)' (now reg 7(1)). As a consequence, the dismissals took effect but the liabilities relating to such employees (including in relation to the dismissals) transferred. The *Litster* ruling has been incorporated into the new regulation.

3.25 In cases of this kind, the starting-point for considering the position of employees dismissed before the transfer of an undertaking is the reason for the dismissal. The tribunal should start, therefore, by considering reg 7(1). If the reason for the dismissal is the transfer or is connected with the transfer, the employee will be treated as an employee of the transferee, against whom any action in connection with the dismissal will lie. If the reason for the dismissal is not the transfer and is not connected with the transfer, the law as stated by the Court of Appeal in *Secretary of State for Employment v Spence*[17] will apply. This means that reg 4(1) will not operate and liability will remain with the transferor. This will also be the case if the dismissal of an employee or group of employees takes place at a time when no transfer was in prospect, since it cannot then be said either that they were employed immediately before the transfer or that their dismissals were connected with it.[18]

3.26 The application of these principles in practice can cause problems, as is shown by two differing decisions of the Employment Appeal Tribunal (EAT). In *Harrison Bowden Ltd v Bowden*,[19] the EAT applied the decision in *Litster* to the dismissal of an employee by a receiver at a time when a potential buyer was interested in buying the company by which he had been employed, but was not formally committed to buying it. He was later engaged by the transferee but dismissed after a month. The EAT upheld the tribunal's decision that he had sufficient accrued continuity to make a claim against the transferee. Tuckey J said:[20]

> 'We think that the reference to "the transfer" is a reference to a transfer which actually takes place which these regulations contemplate by the definition of "the relevant transfer". Regulation 8(1)[21] is directed to the situation both before and after such a transfer. We cannot see that it is of importance that the transferee has been identified at or before the moment of dismissal. *P Bork International A/S v Foreningen of Arbejdsleddene i Danmark*[22] which is the decision of the European Court of Justice which prompted and informed the decision of the House of Lords in *Litster* suggests that the approach in considering cases such as these is to look

---

17   [1986] ICR 651.
18   An example of this situation is *Tsangancos v Amalgamated Chemicals Ltd* [1997] ICR 154, in which the employee was dismissed 2 months before the employers ceased trading and staff then employed by them were transferred to an associated company. The employee made complaints of unfair dismissal and race discrimination against the employers and tried to join the associated company as a second respondent, arguing that the employers' liabilities had transferred to the by virtue of what is now reg 4(2). The EAT upheld the tribunal's decision to reject the application. On the facts of that case it seems reasonably clear that the dismissal and the subsequent transfer were unconnected and the decision therefore stands as a good example of the proposition stated in the text. No mention was made in that decision of the *Spence* case.
19   [1994] ICR 186.
20   [1994] ICR 186, at 191.
21   Now reg 7(1).
22   [1989] IRLR 41.

back in time to see what actually happened. In that case there was no question of the transferee being identified at the moment of dismissal and yet it was a case in which the workers concerned were protected by the directive.'

3.27 In *Ibex Trading Co Ltd (in administration) v Walton*,[23] on the other hand, the facts were that employees were sent letters of dismissal by the administrators to take effect on 4 November 1991. On 11 November an offer to purchase the business was made and it was sold to the transferee on 13 February 1992. The EAT held that, because of the lapse of time between the dismissals and the sale of the business, they were not employed in the transferred undertaking immediately before the transfer within the meaning of what is now reg 4(3). It did not follow the decision in *Harrison Bowden*. Morison J said:[24]

'Contrary to what was said in the *Harrison Bowden* case, we attach significance to the definite article in Regulation 8(1) "that employee shall be treated ... as unfairly dismissed if *the* transfer or a reason connected with it is the reason or the principal reason for the dismissal". The link, in terms of time, between the dismissals and the transfers will vary considerably. In *Litster* the time difference was one hour; often it will be more. A transfer is not just a single event: it extends over a period of time culminating in a completion. However, here, the employees were dismissed before any offer had been made for the business. Whilst it could properly be said that they were dismissed for a reason connected with a possible transfer of the business, on the facts here we are not satisfied that they were dismissed by reason of *the* transfer or for a reason connected with *the* transfer. A transfer was, at the stage of the dismissal, a mere twinkle in the eye and might well never have occurred. We do not say that in every case it is necessary for the prospective transferee to be identified; because sometimes one purchaser drops out at the last minute and another purchaser replaces him.'

3.28 Subsequently, the EAT found itself having to choose between the two decisions discussed in the preceding paragraph, in *Morris v John Grose Group Ltd*.[25] The facts of the case were similar to those of the preceding cases. Receivers were appointed in September 1996 and sought to reduce the workforce before selling the business. On 27 September they decided to dismiss the employee as redundant as from 30 September; on that day they entered into negotiations with the company which culminated in an agreement on 5 November. The employee complained of unfair dismissal. The tribunal decided that, although on 30 September the receivers had in mind the possibility of a transfer to the company, on 27 September they did not have in mind any specific purchaser. It held that, giving significance to the phrase 'the transfer' in what is now reg 7(1),[26] his dismissal was not by reason of the transfer, since he had been dismissed before any offer to purchase the business had been made. The EAT said that the phrase did not by necessary construction refer only to the transfer which actually took place and that the tribunal had erred in attaching significance to the definite article in the phrase 'the transfer'. It said that the correct question for the tribunal to address was whether a transfer to any transferee who might appear, or a reason connected

---

23   [1994] ICR 907.
24   [1994] ICR 907, at 914.
25   [1998] ICR 655.
26   Regulation 8(1) of TUPE 1981.

with such a transfer, was the reason or principal reason for the dismissal; it remitted the case to another tribunal to consider this question. The EAT said that the views expressed in the *Harrison Bowden* case were to be preferred to those in the *Ibex* case. Bell J said:[27]

> 'In our view, however, the words "the transfer" towards the end of regulation 8(1) do not by necessary construction have to refer to the relevant particular transfer which has actually taken place. If that was the necessary meaning of regulation 8(1) it could have been made quite clear by the use of words such as "that transfer" or "the particular transfer". Although "the" is described as a definite article, it is not always used as such in ordinary English, and in our view the words "the transfer", as they are used in regulation 8(1), could perfectly well mean "transfer" or "a transfer". In our judgment this view of the meaning of regulation 8(1) is more consistent with the broad scope of the Directive.
>
> Moreover, to decide otherwise would lead to quite unfair anomalies, as the Appeal Tribunal in *Harrison Bowden* pointed out. Why, for instance, should employees who are dismissed by reason of a particular anticipated transfer which does not go through but which is promptly replaced by another comparable transfer in circumstances where a transfer to someone was inevitable, not have the benefit of regulation 8(1), subject to regulation 8(2), when they would have had that protection if the original transfer had gone through? Yet this would be the result of a restrictive construction of "the transfer" in regulation 8(1).'

3.29 One explanation of the divergence of approach between the EAT and the employment tribunal (and, indeed, between the different divisions of the EAT in the cases considered) is that the tribunal was looking at the matter prospectively, whereas the EAT was looking at the matter retrospectively. In other words, the tribunal appears to have been looking at the matter as at the date of dismissal, whereas the EAT was saying that, looking at the whole episode with hindsight, it can be said that the dismissal *was* connected with the transfer despite the fact that at the time of the dismissal the receivers did not know if there would be a transfer to the transferee or, indeed, any transfer at all. The notion that the matter should be looked at retrospectively is supported by the dicta in *Harrison Bowden* and the approach of the ECJ, as expressed in *Bork*.[28]

3.30 More recently the EAT was faced with unusual circumstances in *G4S Justice Services Ltd v Anstey*,[29] where two employees were dismissed prior to transfer. They appealed against their decision and their appeals were heard by the transferor after the transfer had taken place. In each case the appeal was successful and the employees reinstated. The EAT found that the consequence of the successful appeals was that they should be treated as if they had been employed at the time of the transfer. Hence the two employees transferred to the transferee. The transferee not only became the employer of two employees who he had not expected to transfer, but it became liable for arrears of remuneration back to the date of the original dismissals.

---

27 [1998] ICR 655, at 666.
28 [1989] IRLR 41.
29 [2006] IRLR 588.

3.31 Regulation 4(3)[30] applies reg 4(1) where the transfer 'is effected by a series of transactions' so that it applies to a person employed by the transferor and assigned to the organised grouping of resources or employees subject to the transfer 'or who would have been so employed and assigned immediately before any of those transactions'. In *Longden v Ferrari Ltd*,[31] the EAT said that what it called 'a succession of events' does not amount to 'a series of transactions'. The 'succession of events' in that case consisted of the receivers sending the prospective purchaser a draft contract of sale, the payment by the purchaser of a sum of money on account to enable the company to continue trading for another week and the subsequent negotiations which preceded the agreement for sale. These events did not amount to a series of transactions by which the transfer was 'effected'. The 'succession of events' took place from 26 March 1991, with the employees being dismissed on 28 March. The sale was completed on 10 April. The EAT held that the transfer was effected by the single agreement on that date, so that the employees were not employed immediately before the transfer. The EAT described what happened on 26 and 27 March as 'a succession of events which can be loosely described as causally linked to one another and to the ultimate conclusion of the Receivership Sale of Assets Agreement'.[32] It said that it was sufficient for the purposes of what is now reg 4(3) that there existed a series of two or more transactions linked in a chain of events. 'The language of the Regulations requires that the transfer of the undertaking is "*effected*" by a series of two or more transactions.' It said that the transactions of 26 and 27 March did not have that effect and that the transfer was effected by the single agreement of 10 April. The EAT also upheld the tribunal's decision that the reason for the dismissals was, on the evidence, not connected with the transfer, but was connected with the financial pressures bearing upon the transferor and pressure from its bank. In the course of his judgement Mummery J said:

> 'We wish to add some preliminary observations relevant to the construction of Regulations 3(4)[33] and 5(3)[34] which cannot be seriously disputed.
>
> (1) Those particular regulations have an evident anti-avoidance purpose. They should, where the words allow, be construed in a purposive manner in order to defeat ingenious devices and schemes designed to deprive employees in an undertaking of the protection which it is intended they should have in the context of a transfer.
>
> (2) The obvious case at which Regulations 3(4) and 5(3) are aimed is that of an attempt to disguise the fact that there is a transfer of an undertaking within the meaning of the Regulations and the Directive. The parties to the proposed transfer of an undertaking may ... arrange for the transfer to be effected in a series of two or more transactions dealing with separate assets, none of which, taken individually, could be regarded as the transfer of an undertaking. A composite plan of sub-division or fragmentation of a transfer may be adopted for no sensible commercial purpose, other than to avoid the consequence of the application of Regulations enacted for the protection of employees. These Regulations direct the

---

30   Note also reg 3(6), which states that a transfer may be 'effected by a series of two or more transactions'.
31   [1994] ICR 443.
32   [1994] ICR 443, at 452.
33   Now reg 3(6)(a), which is briefer than its predecessor.
34   Now reg 4(3).

Tribunal to treat as a single transfer of an undertaking a transfer which is effected by such a series of transactions. Although these Regulations do not define a transfer, they direct a Tribunal to treat what might in form be a series of separate transactions as, in substance, a single transfer ...

(3) A similar approach is required in dealing with the related question in Regulation 5(3) whether a person is employed in an undertaking or part of one *immediately before* the transfer. In such cases the Tribunal must ask itself: (a) was the transfer effected by a series of two or more transactions? and, if so, (b) was the person employed in the undertaking *immediately before any* of those transactions?'

3.32 The decision in *Longden v Ferrari Ltd* may be contrasted with the decision in *Re Maxwell Fleet and Facilities Management Ltd (in Administration)*,[35] in which the Companies Court held that the transactions in that case were engaged upon to circumvent the Regulations. Applying the dicta of Mummery J (above), the judge held that the employees were employed immediately before the transfer and liability in respect of them was thus transferred to the transferee.

EMPLOYEES' OBJECTIONS TO THE TRANSFER

3.33 The general position set out in reg 4(1) is subject to two qualifications. The first, considered here, arises where the employee objects to the transfer. This is essentially a right to opt out of the transfer without cause. The predecessors to the present provisions[36] were introduced in response to the ECJ decision in *Katsikas v Konstantinidis*,[37] in which the Court held that the wording of Art 3(1) did not prevent an employee objecting to the transfer of his contract of employment and that to hold otherwise would jeopardise the fundamental rights of the employee 'who must be free to choose his employer and cannot be obliged to work for an employer whom he has not freely chosen'.[38] The reasoning is in line with the longstanding principle of English law in *Nokes v Doncaster Amalgamated Collieries*.[39] In that case Lord Atkin famously noted that the distinction between a slave and a servant (to use the contemporary terminology for what we would now describe as the employer-employee relationship) is that a slave may be sold in the marketplace and has no say over the identity of his master; a servant, by contrast, is free to make this choice. The Court in *Katsikas* also held that Art 3 did not oblige a Member State in such circumstances to legislate for automatic termination or transfer of the employment relationship: 'It is for the Member States to decide the fate of the contract of employment or of the employment relationship with the transferor.'[40] Accordingly, a number of Member States have not legislated

---

35   [2000] ICR 717.
36   Regulation 5(4A) and (4B) of TUPE 1981. The wording of these provisions is identical to that of the new provisions.
37   Cases C-132, 138 and 139/91 [1992] ECR I-6577, [1993] IRLR 179. See also *Foreningen af Arbejdsledere I Danmark v Daddy's Dance Hall A/S* [1988] IRLR 315.
38   [1993] IRLR 179, at para 32.
39   [1940] AC 1014
40   [1993] IRLR 179, at para 37.

on the point; where they have done so, the consequences of exercising the right vary from Member State to Member State.

3.34   The provision in TUPE 2006 dealing with employees' objections is reg 4(7), which provides that reg 4(1) and (2) will not operate to transfer employees' contracts of employment and the rights, powers, duties and liabilities under or in connection with them, if they inform the transferor or the transferee that they object to becoming employed by the transferee. There is no provision within the Regulations for scrutinising the validity of the objection to becoming employed by the transferee. A mere statement of objection on the part of the employee would appear to be enough, provided that the employee does not act in a manner which is inconsistent with this assertion.[41] Regulation 4(8) follows on by stating that the effect of an objection will be that the employees' contracts of employment will be terminated by the transfer, but they will not be treated as having been dismissed by the transferor. The effect will be the same, therefore, as if they had resigned before the transfer. In certain circumstances, reg 4(7) may fall to be read with reg 4(9), considered at **3.41**, but reg 4(9) only operates in the circumstances specified in that subsection. The Court of Appeal considered the relationship between the two sets of provisions in *Humphreys v University of Oxford*,[42] considered at **3.49**.

3.35   The other qualification to consider in respect of the general position as set out in reg 4(1) relates to the right to opt out of the transfer for cause, which can arise under reg 4(9) and (11). Regulation 4(11) amplifies the position set out in reg 4(7) and (8) by stating that reg 4(7) is without prejudice to any right of the employee arising apart from the Regulations to terminate the contract of employment without notice in acceptance of a repudiatory breach of contract by the employer. It would appear that this last provision has been introduced to give effect to the Court of Appeal's decision in *Rossiter v Pendragon plc*,[43] in which the Court of Appeal held that the differently worded predecessor of what is now reg 4(9)[44] requires a repudiatory breach on the part of the employer before the employee can resign under this provision and claim constructive dismissal. As discussed below, the wording of reg 4(9) in TUPE 2006 provides an alternative right to opt out for cause, even though the cause may not amount to grounds for successfully claiming that there has been a constructive dismissal.

3.36   The first question which arises here concerns what form the reg 4(7) objection should take. In *Hay v George Hanson (Building Contractors) Ltd*,[45] the EAT said that the question whether the employee has objected to the transfer is a question of fact for the employment tribunal to decide. It also said that an objection for the purposes of the regulation may be defined as 'the

---

41   The decision of the House of Lords in *North Wales Training and Enterprise Council Ltd (t/a Celtec) v Astley* [2006] UKHL 29 in this respect should be noted. The House of Lords held that an employee's voluntary agreement to be seconded to a transferee cannot be said to amount to an implicit refusal to have his or her contract transferred.

42   [2000] ICR 405.

43   [2002] EWCA Civ 745, [2002] ICR 1063.

44   Regulation 4(5) of TUPE 1981.

45   [1996] IRLR 427. See also *Hope v PGS Engineering Ltd (in administration)* EAT/0267/04.

withholding of consent' and said that it should not be difficult to distinguish between that and mere expressions of concern or unwillingness. The EAT said:[46]

> 'Having said that, it seems to us that the scheme of [the] ... legislation is clear, and does not require to be approached in any artificial or so-called purposive way. What is intended is to protect the right of an employee not to be transferred to another employer against his will, and it is "against his will" that is the executive part of the process. We, therefore, construe the word "object" as effectively meaning a refusal to accept the transfer, and it is equally clear from reg. [4(9)] that that state of mind must be conveyed to either the transferor or transferee. But we do not consider it necessary to lay down any particular method whereby such a conveyance could be effected. In our opinion, it could be by either word or deed, or both, and each case must be looked at on its own facts to determine whether there was a sufficient state of mind to amount to a refusal on the part of the employee to consent to the transfer, and that that state of mind was in fact brought to the attention of either the transferor or the transferee. Furthermore, it must be so brought to their attention before the date of the transfer because, under reg. [4(9)], the transfer itself automatically terminates the contract. Accordingly, if the terms of reg. [4(9)] are not satisfied in fact, there is an automatic transfer on the appropriate date.'

3.37   In *Senior Heat Treatment Ltd v Bell,*[47] the facts were that when Lucas Bryce contracted out its heat treatment department it offered a number of options to its employees, including the option of opting out of TUPE by notifying Lucas Bryce of their intention to do so. Employees who took this option would receive a severance package, including a statutory redundancy payment or its equivalent, a further ex gratia redundancy payment and a sum equivalent to pay in lieu of notice. The employee chose this option and signed a form saying that he did not wish to transfer. Subsequently, however, he took a job with SHT Ltd, to whom the department was transferred. When he was later dismissed by SHT Ltd, the issue arose as to whether he had sufficient continuity of service with the company, since he did not have the requisite qualifying period of employment with that company and could only make a complaint of unfair dismissal if his period of employment with Lucas Bryce could be counted. The EAT held that the effect of his action in taking the option of a severance package was that, despite his agreement to 'opt out of' the transfer, he had not objected to the transfer within the meaning of reg 4(7). This meant that reg 4 was not disapplied and, therefore, operated to carry forward the continuity he had accumulated with Lucas Bryce, thus giving him sufficient continuity of employment to make a claim against SHT.

3.38   These provisions can cause significant practical difficulties for the transferee. For example, at the moment of transfer the transferee may come under an obligation to deliver a service to an agreed specification. At that very moment, the workforce it was expecting to transfer and on whom it was intending to rely to deliver that service may suddenly become unavailable by reason of the exercise of opt outs. Transferees are well advised to plan with this in mind. Likewise, a purchaser of a business may regard the knowledge, skills or experience of the employees of the target as central to realising the value in the target. However, at the moment of acquisition it may find that the very

---

46   [1996] IRLR 427, at para 10.
47   [1997] IRLR 614.

asset it seeks to acquire becomes unavailable. Some form of condition or price adjustment mechanism should be built into the sale and purchase agreement to deal with this eventuality.

3.39 The potential for an organised opt out has always been apparent since the decision in *Katsikas*. A trade union may wish to consider threatening a collective opt out in relation to a transfer which it wishes to oppose, where the effect of the opt out would be to deprive the business of the workforce which it needs to make the transfer viable. Another application of the organised opt out is in the Retention of Employment Model,[48] where it is the key to retaining the workforce within the public sector by preventing the transfer of employees into the private sector.

3.40 The timing of the opt out varies from Member State to Member State, where this principle has been adopted. Under TUPE the weakness of the principle is that it is dependent upon the employee being aware of the imminent transfer. In Germany, by contrast, where the right operates to take the employee out of the scope of the transfer rather than terminating the employment as in the UK, the right to opt out can be exercised well after the transfer if the employee has relied on inaccurate information disclosed by the employer.

EFFECT OF SUBSTANTIAL CHANGES TO EMPLOYEES' WORKING CONDITIONS

3.41 A new basis of opting out of the transfer was introduced by TUPE 2006 in the form of reg 4(9),[49] which gives effect to Art 4(2) of the Directive.[50] This provision comes into play where the relevant transfer involves (or would involve) a substantial change in working conditions to the employee's 'material' detriment. In that case, he or she may treat the contract as having been terminated and will be treated as having been dismissed by the employer.[51] As has already been noted, the requirement that the change should be to the employee's *material* detriment appears to confine the operation of Art 4(2) which refers merely to 'detriment'.

3.42 This provision is differently worded from its predecessor which did not use the term 'material' and which also excluded a change in the identity of the employer unless the employee could show that the change was 'significant' and 'to his detriment'. It also preserved the right of the employee to terminate the contract of employment without notice, but did not give the right to claim constructive dismissal, as the Court of Appeal made clear in *Rossiter v*

---

48   See **3.139**.
49   Formerly reg 5(5) of TUPE 1981.
50   See *Merckx v Ford Motors Co (Belgium) SA* Case C-171/94 [1997] ICR 352.
51   This provision replaces reg 5(5) of TUPE 1981, but with some differences. The part of reg 5(5) relating to changes in the employer's identity has been dropped, i e in effect the second half of the old reg 5(5). What has been added is that the change in working conditions must be to the material detriment of the employee. It is not entirely clear what the difference is between a detriment and a material detriment.

Pendragon plc.[52] In that case the Court of Appeal said that reg 5(5) of TUPE 1981 did not create a new right for an employee on a transfer of an undertaking to claim that he or she had been constructively dismissed by reason only of a substantial detrimental change in his or her working conditions, in the absence of any repudiatory breach of contract by the employer. It also said that reg 5(5) preserved rights which arose apart from TUPE 1981 and the only such right to claim constructive dismissal was the employee's right at common law to resign when faced with a repudiatory breach by the employer. On the facts of the case in question, the Court of Appeal upheld the tribunal's decision that an employee who had resigned in response to changes in his working conditions which did not amount to a repudiatory breach on the part of the employer had resigned voluntarily.

3.43   The new reg 4(9) appears to have the effect of reversing the *Rossiter* decision, since it states that in the circumstances where a relevant transfer involves (or would involve) a substantial change in working conditions to the employee's material detriment, the employee may not only treat the contract as having been terminated but may also treat himself or herself as having been dismissed by the employer. Provided, therefore, that the employee in *Rossiter* had been able to establish that (1) the transfer involved a substantial change in working conditions *and* (2) the change was to his *material* detriment, he or she would have been able to claim to have been dismissed. However, it should be noted that *Rossiter* applies the language of a breach of contract. The right to claim constructive dismissal subsists under reg 4(11). What reg 4(9) offers is the prospect of a claim for unfair dismissal but there is no requirement that there must have been a breach of contract before this right can be exercised. Hence, for example, an employee walking away from an employment relationship under the provisions of reg 4(9) might expect those provisions of his or her contract of employment which subsist beyond termination (notably restrictive covenants) to remain in place whereas the employee who walks away pursuant to reg 4(11) may argue that the provisions cease to have effect as a consequence of the breach.[53]

3.44   Regulation 4(9) therefore occupies the space between opting out of the transfer without cause and opting out in circumstances where there is a claim for constructive dismissal. In the former, there is no right to any further payment. In the latter, there would be a claim for notice money plus (if the employee has the necessary qualifying service) unfair dismissal compensation. Where the employee leaves by reason of reg 4(9) there is no entitlement to notice pay. However, if successful in a claim for unfair dismissal, the compensatory award would inevitably take this into account. It remains to be seen how the tribunals will apply this new provision. The DTI Guidance to TUPE 2006[54] offers as an example of what might constitute a substantial change to working conditions, the situation where the place of work is moved so that the employee incurs much greater expense in travelling to work. It is likely that a cumulative approach will be taken by the tribunals – changes such as a move to an open plan office, the unavailability of a parking space or

---

52   [2002] EWCA Civ 745, [2002] ICR 1063.
53   See *General Billposting v Atkinson* [1909] AC 118.
54   See http://www.dti.gov.uk/er/individual/tupeguide2006regs.pdf.

withdrawal of a staff canteen may all in themselves or when taken together amount to a substantial change. Accordingly, the transferee which makes changes within the bounds of the contract of employment – and is ordinarily not exposed to a claim for constructive dismissal claim – may nevertheless be exposed to similar consequences by reason of the operation of reg 4(9). The boundaries of what is permissible are frustratingly unclear.

3.45　Should an employee elect to treat the contract of employment as being at an end pursuant to reg 4(9), 'the employee shall be treated for any purpose as having been dismissed'. Given that reg 4(9) applies 'where a relevant transfer involves or would involve a substantial change ...', the dismissal will clearly be in connection with a transfer and hence automatically unfair. It would not be open to the employer to raise a defence based on organisational, technical or organisational reason entailing changes in the workforce.[55] The Guidance, by contrast, seems to suggest that the dismissal would not be automatically unfair and envisages a tribunal determining whether the dismissal was unfair. If there is an automatic dismissal in these circumstances, the purpose behind the bigger picture is difficult to discern. A change to terms and conditions arising from the transfer would not be permissible; is the purpose of reg 4(9) to make a substantial change in working conditions similarly unlawful? It seems unlikely, but the sentiments in the Guidance do not appear to have been reflected in the regulation.

3.46　Quite how a tribunal will determine whether a dismissal is unfair is not explained. The Guidance mentions that there will be no presumption that it is unreasonable for an employer to make changes. It is conceivable that they will approach the issue along similar lines to the approach that would be taken to a change in terms and conditions in a situation where there was not a TUPE transfer. In such circumstances the key issues would be whether the employer had sound business reasons for wishing to make the change and an examination of the procedures followed by the employer in seeking to action a consensual change and in implementing changes.[56]

3.47　One area that has sparked some debate is whether there is a right to use reg 4(9) to claim unfair dismissal resulting from a material change in the pension benefits receivable by an employee. The claim does not appear to be ruled out by reg 10(3), which specifically excludes certain claims in respect of the non-transfer of pension rights under TUPE. However, for this route to be open to employees would be extraordinary given that Parliament has legislated to describe the obligations of the transferee in these circumstances; it is very difficult to imagine that this was intended by the legislators. It would appear that 'working conditions' for the purposes of reg 4(9) are intended to mean something outside the terms and conditions of the contract of employment. A substantial change in the latter would invariably give rise to the right to claim constructive dismissal, which would fall within reg 4(11) and reg 4(9) would not be necessary. The issues surrounding a change in pension terms are clearly dealt with in reg 10(3). It is likely that pension rights were not intended to be seen as a 'working condition' for these purposes.

55　See further at **4.87**.
56　See *Hollister v NFU* [1979] ICR 542.

3.48 The Guidance tells us that the statutory disciplinary procedures do not apply to a reg 4(9) dismissal.[57] If this is correct, it means that the employer will not necessarily have any prior warning that the employee is going to walk out or the opportunity to attempt to deal with the grievance.

3.49 The relationship between what is now reg 4(9) and 4(7) was considered by the Court of Appeal in *Humphreys v University of Oxford*.[58] The facts were that the employee was employed for a number of years by the university, working for its delegacy of local examinations. In 1995, the university indicated that it intended to transfer the business of the delegacy to an examinations board. Before the transfer took place the employee notified the university that he objected to becoming an employee of the board. When the transfer took place he brought an action against the university claiming damages for wrongful dismissal on the grounds that the transfer constituted wrongful dismissal. On an application to strike out the action, the judge rejected the university's argument that under reg 5 liability had been transferred to the board. The university appealed. At the hearing of the appeal it was conceded for the purposes of the appeal that the transfer would have involved a substantial and detrimental change to the employee's working conditions. The Court of Appeal held that the effect of an objection under reg 4(7)[59] was to prevent the operation of reg 4(1) so that no transfer would take place. In those circumstances, reg 4(9) preserved the objecting employee's right at common law to terminate his contract in respect of the detrimental change in his working conditions and to sue the transferor for wrongful dismissal. The court rejected the argument advanced on behalf of the university that, if an objection is made by an employee on the ground of detriment, reg 4(7) operates to prevent a transfer and reg 4(8) operates to deprive the aggrieved employee of the right to sue both the transferor and the transferee for constructive dismissal because reg 4(9) must be read as subject to it. Potter LJ observed that acceptance of the argument would effectively involve disenfranchising the employee and would be contrary to the overall purpose of the Directive.[60] Thus the position is that, where an employee objects to a transfer, reg 4(8) operates to prevent the statutory novation under reg 4(1) from taking effect. This means that any liability will not pass to the transferee. Regulation 4(9), however, preserves the employee's right to take action against the transferor, *provided that* the conditions for its operation (which were set out above) are met.[61]

3.50 The case raises particular issues for the transferor, who may become liable to an employee who elects not to transfer by reason of the anticipatory acts or omissions of the transferee.

---

57 Presumably, the Guidance takes the view that the dismissal falls within s 95(1)(a) of the Employment Rights Act 1996 (ERA 1996) and hence the statutory procedures do not apply by reason of reg 6(5) of the Employment Act 2002 (Dispute Resolution) Regulations 2004, SI 2004/752. To do so, the contract must have been terminated by the employer, which is consistent with reg 4(9).

58 [2000] ICR 405.

59 Regulation 5(4A) of TUPE 1981.

60 [2000] ICR 405, at 419.

61 It should be noted that in the *Humphreys* case it was conceded for the purposes of the appeal that the transfer would involve a substantial and detrimental change in the employee's terms and conditions of employment. Had that not been so, what is now reg 4(9) would not be capable of application.

RIGHTS AND OBLIGATIONS WHICH TRANSFER

Introductory questions

3.51　Regulation 4(2)[62] provides that, on the completion of the transfer, all the transferor's (ie old employer's) rights, powers, duties and liabilities 'under or in connection with' the employee's contract of employment, or the contract of employment of any person assigned to the organised grouping of resources, are transferred to the transferee;[63] 'any act or omission before the transfer is completed, of or in relation to the transferor in respect of that contract or a person assigned to that organised grouping of resources or employees' is treated as an act or omission of or in relation to the transferee.[64] It should be noted that criminal liabilities do not pass.[65] This section considers the question of what rights and obligations transfer; the next section examines those rights which do not. Both issues are two sides of the same coin. It should be noted that TUPE 2006 makes specific provision in respect of employers' liability compulsory insurance; there was no specific provision in TUPE 1981. This matter is considered at **3.67**.

3.52　Although it has been held that a transfer under reg 4 will be effective irrespective of whether the employees knew of the transfer and the identity of the transferee,[66] it should be borne in mind that in practice employees are likely to know of the transfer because of the employer's obligation to inform and consult employee representatives under reg 13: see **chapter 5**. Having said that, it happens from time to time that an undertaking will transfer without an employee being aware that there has been a transfer or without the transferee knowing that an employee has transferred. Employees absent on long-term sickness leave are a classic example of this situation. However, the absence of knowledge on either side does not prevent the transfer taking full effect.

3.53　The effect of reg 4(2) is, therefore, that when a relevant transfer takes place, liability passes to the transferee and the transferor drops out of the picture.[67] An early example of the operation of the predecessor of this

---

62　Formerly reg 5(2) of TUPE 1981.

63　Regulation 4(2)(a).

64　Regulation 4(2)(b). In TUPE 1981, reg 5(2) spoke of 'anything done before the transfer is completed by or in relation to the transferor …'. The change of wording does not appear to effect any change of substance.

65　By virtue of reg 4(6).

66　In *Photostatic Copiers (Southern) Ltd v Okuda and Japan Office Equipment Ltd (in liquidation)* [1995] IRLR 11 the EAT suggested that reg 5 (now reg 4) does not take effect unless and until the employee is given notice of the fact of the transfer and the identity of the transferee and said that the employee would be unable to exercise the right to object without such knowledge. In the later case of *Secretary of State for Trade and Industry v Cook* [1997] ICR 288, however, another division of the EAT, presided over by Morrison J, the President, said that the *Okuda* decision should not be followed by employment tribunals.

67　See *Allan v Stirling District Council* [1995] ICR 1082. In that case the Court of Session suggested that a provision for joint and several liability after the transfer of an undertaking would be a sensible and desirable measure for the protection of employees: see at 1088–1089. The only regulation in TUPE 2006 to provide for joint liability is reg 15(9), which expressly

provision is to be found in *Secretary of State for Employment v Anchor Hotel (Kipford) Ltd.*[68] In that case, the facts were that the terms of the sale of a hotel stipulated that the vendors should maintain the hotel as a going concern but should also ensure that that there were no full-time employees engaged by the business at the time it was transferred. The vendors therefore gave their employees notice of dismissal to expire on the transfer date. They subsequently made statutory redundancy payments to the employees and claimed a redundancy rebate from the Secretary of State (as was then possible). The EAT held that, when the relevant events occurred on the same day, the effect of the Regulations was to pass liability to the transferee, irrespective of the order in which the two events – the expiration of the dismissal notices and the completion of the transfer – occurred. The EAT stressed that the Regulations should be broadly construed in the spirit of the Directive.[69] Thus, in the light of this conclusion, the vendor/employers should not have paid a redundancy payment since liability passed under reg 4(2) to the purchasers of the business.

3.54 Bearing in mind the obligation of the courts and tribunals to give a purposive interpretation to the Regulations so as to bring them into conformity, if at all possible, with the Directive and the decisions of the ECJ, it seems clear that reg 4(2) should be given a broad construction wherever possible. It seems reasonable to suggest, therefore, that reg 4(2)(a), which uses the phrase 'under or in connection with' the contract, should be interpreted so as to embrace both contractual and non-contractual rights and liabilities on the part of the transferor. So, for example, it has been hold to cover post-termination restraints[70] and a contractual right to an appeal.[71]

Contractual liabilities

Employee liability insurance

3.55 In *Bernadone v Pall Mall Services,*[72] the Court of Appeal held that the transferor's rights under an employer's liability insurance policy transferred to the transferee. In that case, the facts were that while the claimant was employed by Pall Mall Services (the first defendant), which had employer's liability insurance in place, she suffered an accident at her place of work. She brought proceedings against the first defendant and the National Health Service Trust (the second defendant) which subsequently took over the first defendant's undertaking. The NHS Trust claimed that the first defendant's rights under the insurance policy had transferred to it. The Court of Appeal held that, before the transfer, the first defendant had a vested or contingent right to recover from

---

states that both the transferor and transferee are to be jointly and severally liable for a failure to consult or inform under reg 15. See also **5.83**.

68   [1985] IRLR 452. This approach was followed in the later case of *Fenton v Stablegold Ltd (t/a Chiswick Court Hotel)* [1986] IRLR 64, whose facts were similar to those of *Secretary of State for Employment v Anchor Hotel (Kipford) Ltd.*

69   Then Directive 77/187/EEC.

70   *Morris Angel & Son Ltd v Hollande* [1993] ICR 71. See also 3.60.

71   *G4S Justice Service (UK) Ltd v Anstey* [2006] IRLR 588.

72   [2001] ICR 197.

its insurers under the policy in respect of its liability to the claimant. Since that liability, being 'in connection with' the claimant's contract of employment, transferred to the transferee, the transferor's right was a right to recover from the insurers an indemnity in respect of a liability arising in connection with the contract and, as such, a right arising in connection with the contract of employment which transferred under reg 4(2) (as it now is). Thus the transferees of the undertaking were able to sue on the transferor's insurance policy. The case also considered the question of the transfer of an employer's *tortious* liability: see **3.66**.

Incentive schemes

3.56   Rights relating to share option schemes, profit sharing schemes, bonus schemes and the like are capable of transferring under TUPE, but careful regard must be had to the detail of the scheme. Where the scheme cannot transfer, the transferee may be obliged to provide an equivalent benefit to avoid liability for breach of contract.

3.57   In *Unicorn Consultancy Services Ltd v Westbrook*,[73] the EAT held that the payment of sums due to employees under the transferor's profit-related pay scheme was a liability which passed to the transferee on the transfer of the undertaking. The EAT made it clear that it was deciding the case on a narrow basis, based on its construction of the rules of the scheme.[74] It did point out, however, that, in appropriate circumstances, a transferee company might be under an obligation to provide a replacement scheme or make payments equivalent to those earned under the transferor's scheme. It said:[75]

> 'In reaching this conclusion we have not forgotten that in other situations ... practical problems would arise that do not arise on the facts of this case ... [I]n our judgment the correct approach to the application of TUPE in respect of transferred contracts of employment is to construe and apply the relevant package of rights and obligations of the employees and employer ... in the circumstances that exist and the result is not simply a matter of construction of the original contract and related documents ... [I]t follows that we should concentrate on the facts of this case ... [I]n a different factual situation which gave rise to practical problems and although we express no view on it, the alternative argument of the employees that the [transferee] company was under an obligation to provide a replacement scheme or make payments equivalent to those "earned" under the [transferor company's] Scheme could be relevant and provide a solution that accords with the underlying purpose of TUPE.'

3.58   Subsequently, in *MITIE Management Service Ltd v French*,[76] the question arose whether the benefits of a profit-sharing scheme, provided by the transferor, passed to the transferee. The EAT said that, since the transferee had no control of the transferor's scheme, it was impossible for it to provide any of the benefits to the transferred employees. It held that the entitlement of the employees under reg 4(2) was to participation in a scheme of substantial

---

73   [2000] IRLR 80.
74   See [2000] IRLR 80, at 86, para 50.
75   [2000] IRLR 80, at 86, para 50.
76   [2002] ICR 1395.

equivalence to the transferor's scheme. The EAT accepted the submissions made on behalf of the transferee that what was transferred under reg 4(2)[77] was 'eligibility for company profit-sharing' and that the natural construction of reg 4(2) was one which did not give rise to absurdities and injustices and, when applied to the case in question, produced an entitlement on transfer to an equivalent or comparable scheme rather than, literally, the transferor's scheme. It said:[78]

> 'It would make it difficult if not impossible to contend that a profit-related pay entitlement could not be the subject of transfer but it is not conclusive as to precisely what has transferred by way of contractual entitlement in relation to a particular scheme. So far as that is concerned it is our view that the entitlement of the transferred employees in a case such as this, which has complications absent from, say *Unicorn*, is to participation in a scheme of substantial equivalence but one which is free from unjust, absurd or impossible features.'

3.59 The case establishes a principle which can be applied in a variety of circumstances where benefits cannot be replicated by the transferee – participation in a scheme related to the shares of a listed public company employer or a discount scheme related to the employer's products being good examples. Sight should not be lost of the fact that it is the contractual right which transfers and that contractual right may only exist for so long as the employee is employed by the employer in question. Hence the right may not be transferable on its terms.[79]

3.60 As regards the transferability of the right to enforce post-termination restraints, the Court of Appeal has held that reg 4(2)(a) applies to the transferor's right to enforce a restrictive covenant in an employment contract against a departed employee. In *Morris Angel & Son Ltd v Hollande*[80] the court said that, by virtue of the predecessor of that regulation,[81] the transferor's right to enforce transferred to the transferee. The enforceability of the covenant is, of course, a separate issue.

Enhanced severance schemes

3.61 The transferee will frequently be planning some degree of reorganisation post transfer and hence the existence of some sort of enhanced severance entitlement will be of concern. Typically, for example, an employer may have committed to making payments on a basis which is more generous than the formula for a statutory redundancy payment. In *Jefferies v Powerhouse Retail Ltd*[82] the EAT confirmed that contractual enhanced severance schemes will transfer under TUPE. Given the wide wording of reg 4(2), which clearly goes beyond contractual rights, there is every reason to believe that a non-contractual scheme of this nature will transfer under TUPE. If it does, its

---

77   At that time, reg 5(2) of TUPE 1981.
78   [2002] ICR 1395, at para 16.
79   See, for example, *Chapman and Elkin v CPS Computer Group Plc* [1987] IRLR 462.
80   [1993] ICR 71.
81   Regulation 5(2).
82   [1996] UKEAT 1328.

status post transfer will remain the same as prior to the transfer – that is to say that it will not be contractually binding and will not therefore be a liability for the transferee.

Variation of contract

3.62 The final point to consider, in this discussion of the transfer of contractual liabilities, is variations of contract. Until TUPE 2006, these were dealt with by the courts' interpretation of reg 5(1) of TUPE 1981.[83] The matter has now been expressly dealt with by TUPE 2006. Regulation 4(4) and (5) now expressly protects rights which the employee has against the transferor so that they cannot be varied on a transfer to the transferee. Regulation 4(4) provides that any purported variation of the employee's contract will be void if the sole or principal reason is the transfer itself or a reason connected with the transfer that is not an economic, technical or organisational reason entailing changes in the workforce. Regulation 4(5), however, permits the employer and employee to agree a variation if the sole or principal reason for the variation is a reason connected with the transfer that is an economic, technical or organisational reason entailing changes in the workforce or is a reason unconnected with the transfer. These provisions effectively encapsulate the case-law that had grown up in this area. For a fuller discussion of these provisions, reference should be made to **4.100**.

Non-contractual liabilities

3.63 So far as *non-contractual matters* are concerned, the predecessor of reg 4(2)[84] has been widely interpreted. So, for example, in *BSG Property Services v Tuck*[85] the EAT held that liability in connection with a dismissal transfers to the transferee. It also held that the transferor's reason for the dismissal is the relevant reason even though the transferor's liability passes to the transferee. Linked with the transfer of an employee's accrued unfair dismissal right is the transfer of continuity of employment. In *Green-Wheeler v Onyx (UK) Ltd*[86] the employee's right to bring an unfair dismissal claim against the transferee (Onyx) depended upon whether he could rely on his previous service with the transferor, since his period of employment with the transferee was insufficient to qualify him to bring a claim. The EAT held that his accrued continuity of employment could be carried forward. In arriving at this conclusion it observed that an employee who has been employed sufficiently long to have accrued the right not to be unfairly dismissed is protected by what is now reg 4(2)(a), since the statutory right comes within the phrase 'liabilities ... in connection with any such contract'. The later case of

---

83 Regulation 5 was construed by the courts so as to make void any variation of the employee's contract by the transferee, unless the variation was not in any way connected with transfer. See *Crédit Suisse First Boston (Europe) Ltd v Lister* [1999] ICR 795; *Crédit Suisse First Boston (Europe) Ltd v Padiachy* [1999] ICR 569; and *Solectron Scotland Ltd v Roper* [2004] IRLR 4.

84 Regulation 5(2) of TUPE 1981.

85 [1996] IRLR 134.

86 EAT/925/92.

Euro-Die (UK) Ltd v Skidmore[87] takes the matter a stage further by linking the employer's behaviour in relation to the employee's accrued continuity with the implied duty of mutual trust and confidence. In that case, the EAT upheld the employment tribunal's decision that the transferor's failure to assure an employee that his continuity of employment would be protected following a transfer of the business amounted to a breach of the implied term of trust and confidence, so that the employee's resignation amounted to a constructive unfair dismissal, liability for which passed to the transferee. The President of the EAT, Lindsay J, said:[88]

> 'Where an employer, in answer to a concerned employee, fails at a crucial juncture to give an assurance which asks no more than for the true employment position to be recognised on a subject as essential to the employee's ease of mind as continuity of employment it cannot be said, in our view, that that failure cannot represent so fundamental a breach of the implied terms as to trust and confidence as to entitle the employee to treat himself as constructively dismissed. If, accordingly, such a failure *could* be such a breach, it was open to the Tribunal as masters of fact, to hold, as they did, that it was such a breach.'

3.64   Another statutory right which has been held to transfer to the transferee is an employee's right to claim sex discrimination. In *DJM International Ltd v Nicholas*[89] the EAT held that the effect of what is now reg 4(2)(b)[90] is to transfer liability for an act of sex discrimination allegedly committed by the transferor before the transfer. As another division of the EAT pointed out in the later case of *Tsangacos v Amalgamated Chemicals Ltd*,[91] the decision in the *DJM* case turns on the fact that there was in existence an employment relationship between the transferor and the employee at the date of the transfer. As the EAT pointed out, if reg 5 were held to apply to an employee who had been dismissed well before the date of the transfer, an employee with a contingent claim arising from his or her dismissal years before the transfer, at a time when a transfer was 'not even a twinkle in the employers' eye', would have a claim against the transferee. The EAT dismissed this, saying:[92]

> 'If the contract of employment or the employment relationship was not existing at the date of the transfer then there will be no transfer of the contract of employment nor of any contingent rights and liabilities.'

3.65   It should be noted that in both cases the EAT was mindful of the views of the House of Lords in relation to employees dismissed in anticipation of a transfer, expressed in *Litster v Forth Dry Dock & Engineering Co Ltd*.[93] The House of Lords' view of the interpretation of reg 5(3) of TUPE 1981 has been given statutory form in reg 4(3) of TUPE 2006. Needless to say, what holds good for the transfer of liability for an alleged act of sex discrimination committed by the transferor holds good, mutatis mutandis, for all the other types of unlawful discrimination.

---

87   EAT/1158/98.
88   At para 16.
89   [1996] ICR 214.
90   Formerly reg 5(2)(b).
91   [1997] ICR 154, at 163.
92   [1997] ICR 154, at 163.
93   [1989] ICR 341.

3.66 In *Bernadone v Pall Mall Services, Martin v Lancashire County Council*,[94] the facts of which were set out at **3.55**, the Court of Appeal held that what is now reg 4(2) is wide enough to transfer to the transferee the transferor's tortious liability towards an employee injured at work and thus liability in negligence may pass to the transferee. Peter Gibson LJ observed[95] that it would be 'surprising' if the rights and obligations which transferred were to be limited to contractual claims and to exclude claims in tort. The court also held that the transferor's liability under s 2 of the Occupiers' Liability Act 1957 transferred to the transferee, though Peter Gibson LJ pointed out, in deference to the argument advanced by counsel that the duty under the 1957 Act is imposed on occupiers not employers, that in such cases the particular circumstances of the alleged liability must be examined to see whether it did arise from or was in connection with the contract of employment in question.[96]

Employers' liability compulsory insurance

3.67 TUPE 2006 now contains a specific provision dealing with employers' liability compulsory insurance. The decision in *Bernadone* means that, in many cases, the concern of the transferee about the risk of transferring personal injury claims will be allayed by the ability to claim against the transferor's insurance policy. There is a wide-ranging duty on employers to insure against injury to their employees at work under the Employers' Liability (Compulsory Insurance) Act 1969 so in the majority of cases appropriate insurance cover will be in place. However, the *Bernadone* case is of no value in circumstances where no such insurance cover is in place, particularly in the case of public sector employers who fall outside the scope of the 1969 Act.

3.68 Regulation 17 applies in two sets of circumstances: (1) where the transferor is not required by the Employers' Liability (Compulsory Insurance) Act 1969[97] to take out any compulsory insurance; or (2) where the transferor is exempted from the requirement of the Act to take out compulsory insurance.[98] In either of those cases, on the completion of a relevant transfer both the transferor and transferee will be jointly and severally liable in respect of any liability covered by s 1(1) of the Act, but only insofar as liability relates to the employee's employment with the transferor. The very fact of joint and several liability as between transferor and transferee gives rise to some degree of responsibility on the part of the transferor and allows the court to adjudicate on the allocation of liability, having regard to general principles of law attaching to the concept of joint and several liability.

3.69 Regulation 17 does not provide the transferee with complete protection – it is vulnerable under the decision in *Bernadone* where the transferor has

---

94   [2001] ICR 197.
95   [2001] ICR 197, at para 34.
96   [2001] ICR 197, at para 39.
97   Section 3(1)(a) or (b).
98   By virtue of s 3(1)(c) of the 1969 Act.

failed to meet its duty to insure or has done something to void the policy. Equally, under the provisions of reg 17, it is dependent upon the ability of the transferor to pay.

RIGHTS AND OBLIGATIONS WHICH DO NOT TRANSFER

3.70   Regulation 4(6) expressly provides that criminal liabilities are not to pass under reg 4(2). In addition, reg 10 provides that some benefits under occupational pension schemes are not to pass under reg 4: see **3.106**.

3.71   In the early days of its dealings with TUPE, the EAT refused to extend the scope of what is now reg 4 to non-contractual liabilities. Thus, in *Angus Jowett Ltd v National Union of Tailors and Garment Workers*,[99] it refused to hold that a transferor employer's liability for a protective award under s 189 of the Trade Union and Labour Relations (Consolidation) Act 1992 (TULR(C)A 1992)[100] passed to the transferee. The EAT said:[101]

> 'Even if all the other requirements of the regulations were in a given case fulfilled, we would not think it right to describe the employers' duties and liabilities under [s 189] as a duty or liability under or in connection with any such contract as is referred to in Regulation 5. It is true that the words "in connection with" are extremely wide; but it seems to us that the employers' duties or liabilities which lead to the making of a declaration and protective award arise under the Act and arise in connection not with any contract with an individual employee but by reason of a failure to consult recognised trade unions, which is a duty imposed by [s 189]; and it arises from a proposal to dismiss certain employees as redundant.'

3.72   In the later case of *Kerry Foods Ltd v Kreber*,[102] on the other hand, the EAT held that liability for a failure to consult under s 188 was a liability arising 'in connection with' an individual worker's contract and so fell within reg 4(2). It is clear from the judgment[103] that the tribunal would have preferred to follow the *Angus Jowett* decision, but it accepted the argument advanced by counsel for the employees that, in the light of the decision of the ECJ in *Commission of the European Communities v United Kingdom*,[104] the distinction between liabilities arising in connection with individual contracts of employment and liabilities arising in connection with a failure to consult on a collective basis cannot stand. Morison J said:[105]

> '[I]t is not possible to say that a liability for failure to consult does not arise in connection with an individual worker's contract of employment ... [T]he duty to consult, whether or not there is a recognised trade union, is a right which arises from the individual contracts between each worker and his employer. This is emphasised by the nature of the remedy which belongs to the individual and is

---

99   [1985] ICR 646.
100   Formerly s 99 of the Employment Protection Act 1975.
101   [1985] ICR 646, at 658.
102   [2000] ICR 556.
103   See para 24.
104   [1994] ICR 664.
105   [1994] ICR 664, at para 24.

regarded as part of his contractual entitlement. We would say that this was a liability in connection with a contract of employment within regulation [4](2)(a).[106] But we also agree with Miss Tether that it would be apt to fall within [4](2)(b)[107] as well.'

3.73 In the later case of *TGWU v McKinnon*,[108] the Scottish EAT said that liability for a failure to consult *under reg 13* of TUPE 2006[109] does not pass to the transferee. This was on the basis that the construction of the words 'liabilities under or in connection with ...' in what is now reg 4(2)(a) should ensure that the employer has an incentive to comply with the obligations imposed on it in the transfer process. 'Such a construction ... requires that the conclusion that the transferor will retain responsibility to pay compensation for his own failure to consult with his employees ...'[110] The EAT in England, however, has not followed this decision and has held, in *Alamo Group (Europe) Ltd v Tucker*,[111] that liability under reg 13 may pass to the transferee. The EAT pointed out that the Scottish EAT in *McKinnon* had overlooked the words 'in connection with' in reg 4.[112] The EAT also said:[113]

> '[I]t seems to us that whether the origin of the right under examination is contractual or from statute or regulations, and whether it is within or without the regime of TUPE itself, the question is the same, namely whether the right being examined arises "under or in connection with the contract of employment or arises from the employment relationship". Had regulation [4] dealt only with rights "under" the contract of employment, then it may indeed have been necessary to determine the origin of the right in the contract of employment, but as Peter Gibson LJ pointed out in the passage quoted from *Martin and Bernadone*,[114] in which both tort and statutory liability under the Occupiers Liability Act transferred:
>
> > "... the width of the language used in subparagraph (a) of Regulation [4](2) ... does not suggest that the rights etc need to be contractual ..."
>
> [T]he modern relationship of employer and employee is not confined to the terms of the contract between employer and employer for there are not only terms that have been implied by statute, but statute has created a number of rights and liabilities that are imposed on the parties and which they cannot exclude by agreement. The very purpose of such provisions is, very often, to give added protection to employees. It seems to us that it would be wholly artificial to distinguish liabilities that are contained in the actual contract from those imposed by statute in determining whether they are subject to regulation [4]. Once the legislator has determined that the best way to protect employees on transfer is under

---

106 Regulation 5(2)(a) of TUPE 1981.
107 Regulation 5(2)(b) of TUPE 1981. It should be noted that the new reg 4(2)(b) is differently worded from the previous provision but that the difference is not one of substance and does not render Morison J's observations any less valid in relation to the new regulation.
108 [2001] ICR 1281.
109 Formerly reg 10 of TUPE 1981.
110 [2001] ICR 1281, at para 5.
111 [2003] ICR 829.
112 [2003] ICR 829, at para 31. It should be noted that the paragraph numbers are those used in the ICR report of the case. There is a discrepancy between the paragraph numbering used in the ICR and in the report of the case to be found at http://www.bailii.org.
113 [2003] ICR 829, at paras 30 and 31.
114 [2001] ICR 197 at para 35.

regulation [4] it seems to us that it would be curious if the legislator were then to intend to exclude statutory or regulatory rights that the legislator had introduced for the very purpose of protecting employees.'

3.74   Pending any clarification of this issue by the Court of Appeal or the Court of Session, the best course of action is to follow the latest decision. If that is correct, then the position is that liability for failure to consult will pass to the transferee. That approach would certainly be consistent with the approach taken by the ECJ.

It should be noted that the issue in relation to a failure to consult under reg 13 has been superseded by reg 15(9) which provides for joint and several liability in relation to the award of compensation for failure to consult (see **5.83**). However, the cases discussed above remain of interest in relation to a failure on the part of the transferor to consult under s 188.

3.75   Another matter which the EAT has held not to be covered by what is now reg 4(1) is an order under ss 163 and 164 of TULR(C)A 1992 granted to an employee seeking interim relief. The facts of *Dowling v ME Ilic Haulage and Berkeley Logistics Ltd*[115] were that the employee obtained an order under s 163 and 164 of TULR(C)A 1992 against the first respondent. Meanwhile the business was acquired by the second respondent. The employee argued that the first respondent's liability in respect of the orders transferred to the second respondent. The tribunal rejected that argument, and the EAT dismissed the employee's appeal. Burton J pointed out that when an order is made under s 163 of TULR(C)A 1992 it continues only in force for the purposes set out in s 164(1)(a) and (b) and that what is effected by the continuation order is not a contract of employment, as no service is provided to the employer. He said that at the time the orders were made the employee was an ex-employee whose contract had terminated so that there was no subsisting contract of employment between him and the first respondent. There was therefore no subsisting contract on which reg 4(1)[116] could have any effect.

3.76   In *Cross and Gibson v British Airways Plc*[117] the Court of Appeal held that the normal retirement age of an employee does not transfer under TUPE. A number of employees transferred from British Caledonian (where the contractual retirement age was 60) to British Airways (where it was 55). Hence, when the employees were retired at 55 they claimed unfair dismissal.[118] The court held that they were not entitled to claim unfair dismissal because they had not retained a contractual right to retire at 60 and had become subject to the normal retirement age of 55. However, it is important to note the conceptual distinction drawn in the decision of the Court of Appeal between a contractual retirement age – which will transfer – and normal retirement age for the purposes of unfair dismissal legislation, which is a statutory concept determined by reference to what is normal for a group of employees holding

---

115   [2004] ICR 1176.
116   Regulation 5(1) of TUPE 1981.
117   [2006] EWCA Civ 549, [2006] ICR 1239.
118   Under ERA 1996, s 109(1), the right to claim unfair dismissal is lost where the employee has reached normal retirement age.

the same position. This is determined by reference to the facts at the time of dismissal and not by reference to the facts at the date of the transfer.

3.77 Finally, the EAT has refused to hold that the benefit of a compromise agreement entered into between the transferor and a group of employees passed to the transferee.[119]

COLLECTIVE AGREEMENTS

3.78 Regulation 5 of TUPE 2006 provides for the transfer of collective agreements in respect of transferring employees. It covers collective agreements made by the employer itself and agreements made on behalf of the employer – for example, through an employer's association. The agreement will be binding on the transferee in so far as it applies to the transferring employee. Its legal status post transfer will mirror its status prior to the transfer, having regard in particular to the fact that collective agreements are subject to a presumption that they are not legally binding.[120]

3.79 The EAT held, in *Whent v T Cartledge Ltd*,[121] that an employer's contractual obligations arising from a collective agreement incorporated into employees' individual contracts will transfer under reg 4. The employees involved in the case were employed by a local authority in the street lighting department. Their contracts provided that their pay and conditions would be in accordance with the local authority's NJC[122] agreement 'as amended from time to time'. The street lighting contract was taken over by the respondent transferees, who wrote to the GMB union (which had been a party to the collective agreement) withdrawing recognition and stating that any collective agreements affecting employees transferred from the local authority would no longer have any effect. Subsequently, the transferees argued that the employees' pay was frozen at the level last fixed before they withdrew from the NJC agreement. The EAT rejected this argument and held that the transferees were still bound by the collective agreement so far as it was incorporated in individual contracts of employment, despite their withdrawal from the collective agreement. The EAT also rejected the transferees' argument that a term should be implied to the effect that if the employer/transferee ceased to be a party to the NJC process neither party would continue to be bound by the results of any subsequent NJC negotiations.

3.80 The Court of Appeal took a similar line in *Glendale Managed Services v Graham*.[123] In that case, the contract of employment provided that pay and conditions would 'normally be in accordance' with the NJC agreed rates 'as

---

119 In *Thompson v Walon Car Delivery and BRS Automotive Ltd* [1997] IRLR 343.
120 See TULR(C)A 1992, ss 179 and 180.
121 [1997] IRLR 153.
122 The National Joint Council for Local Authorities' Administrative, Professional, Technical and Clerical Services.
123 [2003] IRLR 465.

adapted from time to time'. The court held that the employer could depart from these terms, but only where prior notice had been given of an intention to depart from the normal situation.

3.81   The above decisions should be contrasted with the later EAT decision in *Ackinclose v Gateshead Metropolitan Borough Council*,[124] which also involved the NJC collective agreement. The factual difference between the two cases above and *Ackinclose* was that, in the *Ackinclose* case, the local authority employees were transferred to the private sector (in 1995) and later, on 1 January 2000, were transferred back to the local authority. In the intervening time, the relevant national agreements in local government were combined in a single status agreement for local authority employees, which reduced the working week for full-time staff and gave them an increase in the standard hourly rate, with effect from 1 April 1999. The employees who transferred back to the local authority claimed that they should have been paid the increased hourly rate for the period 1 April to 31 December 1999. The EAT said that the terms of the employees' contracts, as at the date of the transfer, provided for their terms and conditions to be in accordance with the national agreement for local government manual workers, but did not allow for any subsequent collective agreement which might be adopted by the successor body to the NJC for manual workers. The contracts only made reference to the NJC for manual workers as a negotiating body and their handbook (the 'White Book') as the relevant collective agreement. It said that no successor body or successor agreement could be held to be part of the contract of employment without any further reference or incorporation. The difference between the two groups of cases is that in *Whent and Glendale* the issue was whether an agreement in existence at the time of the transfer continued to bind the transferee. The position in *Ackinclose* is at one remove from that, since that case concerns the successor to the NJC and the White book.

3.82   These cases must now be read in the light of the ECJ's decision in *Werhof v Freeway Traffic Services GmbH*.[125] In that case, Mr Werhof's contract of employment incorporated an industry-wide collective agreement, which determined the level of his pay. The business in which he worked was transferred subject to the German equivalent of TUPE. Following the transfer his new employer negotiated a pay increase locally with its own works council, rather than increasing pay by reference to the industry-wide collective agreement. The industry-wide collective bargain settled on a higher wage increase than the one agreed locally by Mr Werhof's new employer. Mr Werhof therefore claimed a pay increase to the level of the industry-wide collective agreement, on the basis that a contractual term setting his pay by reference to the industry-wide collective bargaining had transferred. The ECJ did not find in his favour. It held that where the transferee is not a party to the collective bargaining machinery, it is not bound by future changes to the collective agreement.

---

124 [2005] IRLR 79. See also *Ralton v Havering College of Further and Higher Education* [2001] IRLR 738.
125 [2006] IRLR 400.

3.83   A key issue emerging from the judgment is the way in which the contract is phrased. Does it have a 'dynamic' element which envisages changes governed by the collective bargaining forum in future or is it 'static', whereby the contract term simply refers to a current collective bargain which will inevitably become outdated in due course, revision being an issue for further agreement between the parties? However, the impact of the decision may be broader than that, for an essential element in the ECJ's reasoning was that it offends the right to freedom of association for an employer to be bound to a collective agreement determined by a forum in which the employer does not participate. Followed through, that reasoning suggests that *Werhof* is authority for the proposition that changes in an industry-wide collective agreement post transfer do not bind a transferee which does not participate in that collective bargain.

INSOLVENCY

3.84   The transfer of an insolvent undertaking gives rise to particular concerns for the transferee. The risk of liabilities transferring to the transferee from the pre-transfer activities of the transferor is particularly high, given the financial state of the transferor. At the same time, the contractual protection which a transferee might typically seek from the transferor is unlikely to be available. For example, a receiver selling a distressed business is unlikely to be willing to give the warranties and indemnities in the sale and purchase agreement which would ordinarily be available in an arm's length sale of a solvent business.

3.85   Consequently, the prospect for the transferee of a transfer governed by TUPE is extremely unattractive and many potential rescues of insolvent businesses have foundered on this point, particularly where the potential transferee has been unable to do any detailed due diligence so as to be able to assess the extent of the liability which is likely to transfer.

3.86   The 2006 revision of TUPE has sought to address this by putting a part of the burden of liability in these circumstances onto the state. Furthermore, acknowledging that the maintenance of pre-transfer terms and conditions may be unrealistic in the circumstances, some latitude is given in the rules relating to the variation of terms and conditions.

What circumstances fall within the scope of regs 8 and 9?

3.87   The provisions of regs 8 and 9 apply where at the time of the transfer, the transferor 'is subject to relevant insolvency proceedings'. This is defined by reg 8(6) as:

> '... insolvency proceedings which have been opened in relation to the transferor not with a view to the liquidation of the assets of the transferor and which are under the supervision of an insolvency practitioner.'

Whilst this wording reflects the wording of the Directive[126] it has caused a degree of confusion as to which types of insolvency procedures are within the

---

126   See Art 5(1) of the Directive.

scope of the regulations and which are not. An administration would be covered; however, the position as regards other types of insolvency proceedings is unclear.

3.88   The Guidance sets out the DTI's position:

> 'It is the Department's view that "relevant insolvency proceedings" mean any collective insolvency proceedings in which the whole or part of the business or undertaking is transferred to another entity as a going concern. That is to say, it covers an insolvency proceeding in which all creditors of the debtor may participate, and in relation to which the insolvency office – holder owes a duty to all creditors. The Department considers that "relevant insolvency proceedings" does *not* cover winding-up by either creditors or members where there is no such transfer.'

3.89   However, there was a clear need for a statement of those types of insolvency proceedings which fall within the scope of this area of the law and those which are excluded. Perhaps mindful of this, the Redundancy Payments Office stepped in and issued its own guidance (see **appendix 10**). Its view is that any compulsory winding-up is clearly outside the scope of TUPE. Given that the position remained unclear, the DTI has issued a paper which expands on the Guidance.[127] This sets out – in relation to each type of insolvency procedure – how the DTI understands that the regulations should be applied. Whilst the paper is of limited value in terms of pure law, it is valuable in practice as it sets out the approach which the DTI will take in terms of making payments.

3.90   Regulation 8(7) disapplies the employee protections in regs 4 and 7 in relation to dismissals and changes in terms and conditions in respect of a transfer when the transferor is the subject of bankruptcy proceedings or any analogous insolvency proceedings instituted with a view to the liquidation of the transferor's assets under the supervision of an insolvency practitioner.

Transfer of liabilities

3.91   The 2006 revisions to TUPE reflect the fact that if a distressed business is not saved by reason of concerns over TUPE, the state will be liable for payments in respect of certain protected rights in any event. Hence the rules have been relaxed to provide for transfers to take place with the state accepting responsibility for liabilities to which it would otherwise be liable in any event.

3.92   The mechanism in reg 8 is that liability in relation to certain sums payable under the 'relevant statutory schemes' does not transfer to the transferee. These debts are instead borne by the National Insurance Fund. They are payments of statutory redundancy pay or sums representing debts to the employee covered by the insolvency provisions of ERA 1996: arrears of pay; payment in lieu of notice; holiday pay; and the basic award in relation to unfair dismissal.

---

127 See **appendix 8**.

3.93 Alas, this is another area which is unclear, largely due to an apparent conflict between reg 8(3) and the Guidance. Both are agreed that the National Insurance Fund will meet the payments due to employees under the insolvency provisions of ERA 1996 as if there had been a dismissal at the date of transfer. However, the Guidance suggests that payments due under the redundancy provisions of ERA 1996 will be paid, whereas reg 8(3) suggests that they will not.

3.94 Accordingly, the statement by the Redundancy Payments Office as to the practice it will adopt is extremely welcome.[128] It has stated that it will adopt the following approach:

(1) The National Insurance Fund will meet unpaid wages and holiday pay for transferring employees. It will not meet redundancy pay, pay in lieu of accrued holiday not taken or notice pay, as there has been no dismissal. Payment will be made up to the statutory limits in respect of the period prior to the insolvency.

(2) Employees who are unfairly dismissed because of the transfer will also receive pay and holiday pay.

(3) Employees dismissed for an economic, technical or organisational reason entailing a change in the workforce will be considered redundant – hence they will receive redundancy pay, wages and holiday pay (both taken and accrued).

(4) Employees who refuse to transfer will be paid wages and holiday pay.

3.95 It should be borne in mind against the background of all these provisions that the payments borne by the state may be only a small part of the total bill. The transferor may still be left with a considerable liability.

Variation of terms and conditions

3.96 The rules regarding variations to terms and conditions of employment (see **chapter 4**) are relaxed in the case of employees transferring from insolvent businesses. To make a change reg 9 requires the following steps to be taken:

(1) the variation must be designed to safeguard employment opportunities by ensuring the survival of the undertaking or business that is the subject of the transfer;

(2) the changes need to be approved by the appropriate representatives;

(3) if the changes are approved by appropriate representatives who are not trade union representatives, the agreement must be made in writing and be signed by each representative (or, where impractical, by his or her authorised agent);

(4) if the changes are approved by non-union representatives, the employer must give each employee whose terms will be changed a copy of the agreement before it is available for signature, together with 'such guidance as those employees might reasonably require in order to understand [the agreement] fully'.

---

128 See **appendix 10**.

Note that there is no need for the employees themselves to consent to the change.

3.97 The appropriate representatives for these purposes must be trade union representatives where the employees are of a description in respect of which a union is recognised. In the absence of union representatives, the employer may choose as for the selection of representatives for the purpose of reg 14 (see **5.52**).

3.98 The provisions of reg 4 of TUPE 1981 have not found their way into TUPE 2006. Regulation 4 dealt with hiving down. It was arguably neither consistent with the Directive nor necessary.

TRADE UNION RECOGNITION

3.99 Maintenance of trade union recognition is seen by TUPE as an important element of protecting employee rights. Unfortunately, these provisions have had a chequered history in that they are difficult to apply in practice.

3.100 Regulation 6 applies where an independent trade union is recognised 'to any extent' by the transferor in respect of a group of employees who will transfer by reason of TUPE. Recognition is defined by reference to s 178(3) of TULR(C)A 1992:

'(3) In this Act "recognition", in relation to a trade union, means the recognition of the union by an employer, or two or more associated employers, to any extent, for the purpose of collective bargaining; and 'recognised' and other related expressions shall be construed accordingly.'

This section must be read with s 178(1) and (2):

'**178 Collective agreements and collective bargaining**

(1) In this Act "collective agreement" means any agreement or arrangement made by or on behalf of one or more trade unions and one or more employers or employers' associations and relating to one or more of the matters specified below; and "collective bargaining" means negotiations relating to or connected with one or more of those matters.

(2) The matters referred to above are—

(a)   terms and conditions of employment, or the physical conditions in which any workers are required to work;

(b)   engagement or non-engagement, or termination or suspension of employment or the duties of employment, of one or more workers;

(c)   allocation of work or the duties of employment between workers or groups of workers;

(d)   matters of discipline;

(e)   a worker's membership or non-membership of a trade union;

(f)   facilities for officials of trade unions; and

(g)   machinery for negotiation or consultation, and other procedures, relating to any of the above matters, including the recognition by employers or employers' associations of the right of a trade union to represent workers in such negotiation or consultation or in the carrying out of such procedures.'

3.101 In these circumstances, the key determinant is whether, post transfer, the organised grouping of resources or employees maintains an identity distinct from the remainder of the transferor's undertaking. Hence in many cases the prospect of the transfer of recognition will be snuffed out by the integration of the transferring entity into the transferee entity. In such cases whether the transferee recognises a trade union in relation to (inter alia) the transferring employees is a matter for the transferee, without regard to the arrangements which were in place pre transfer. One can see the logic of these provisions, for it is difficult to envisage any meaningful recognition arrangements subsisting within the enlarged entity in those circumstances. However, it would appear to be all too easy for the transferee simply to integrate the transferring employees into its existing operations, at which time existing recognition arrangements are brought to an end.

3.102 Where the entity does retain a discrete identity, recognition may transfer. The recognised union will be deemed to have been recognised by the transferee to the same extent as prior to the transfer. Likewise, recognition agreements are deemed to have been varied or rescinded accordingly.[129]

3.103 In practice, these provisions are rather toothless. The provisions of reg 6 only apply to voluntary union recognition. In such circumstances, recognition persists as a matter of consensus between the employer and the union. Recognition can be withdrawn by the employer unilaterally without penalty, so the transfer of this fragile right is of limited value. A failure on the part of the transferee to maintain recognition is an industrial relations issue rather than a legal issue. As far as recognition agreements are concerned, these often do not travel well in any event. It is quite possible that, other than in respect of the bare fact of recognition, a recognition agreement will be inapplicable in many respects to the revised circumstances following the transfer.

3.104 Whilst the ability of the employer to derecognise in the case of voluntary recognition makes the provisions of reg 6 rather weak, a transfer of mandatory recognition[130] would be of rather greater significance. At the time of writing it is understood that the Government is proposing to change the law to include mandatory recognition within the scope of reg 6.

3.105 The importance of recognition goes well beyond the narrow issue of giving the union the right to be heard, of course. Recognition brings with it certain rights and benefits which enhance the capability of the union to represent the workforce, such as the right to information in connection with collective bargaining, the right to be consulted on certain issues and the right for the union representatives to benefit from paid time off.

PENSIONS

3.106 In certain circumstances relating to pension rights, reg 10 of TUPE 2006 disapplies the general principle of the transfer of contract terms. In many

---

129 Regulation 6(2)(b).
130 Pursuant to the provisions of the Employment Rights Act 1999.

cases, the pension benefits received by an employee may be expected to form an important and valuable element of the remuneration package, so the failure of these rights to transfer will be a matter of some concern to the transferring employees. Not only does the entitlement not transfer, but the employee has no right to complain about the reduced value of the remuneration package.[131]

3.107 However, the exception in respect of pension rights from the transfer principle is limited in scope and indeed has become narrower over time. Regulation 10(1) provides that a contract term or a collective agreement shall not transfer to the extent that it relates to an 'occupational pension scheme', that term being defined as in the Pension Schemes Act 1993.[132] Rights which form a part of the contract of employment and which relate to individual pension benefits will transfer. For example, if an employee is contractually entitled to receive a sum equivalent to a given percentage of his or her salary paid into a personal pension plan each month, this right would not fall within the pensions exception and would transfer. Of course, if an employee is a member of a group personal pension plan, he or she will be in much the same position save that the pension 'pot' will have the mantle of the group scheme wrapped around it. Whether that makes it an 'occupational pension scheme' is open to doubt. The issue is unclear, but the balance of the divided opinion leans towards the view that a group personal pension plan is not an 'occupational pension scheme' and hence falls outside the exception.

3.108 Such is the significance of the exception in relation to occupational pension scheme rights that it has come under challenge in a number of cases. In *Adams v Lancashire County Council*[133] a school meals service run by Lancashire County Council was put out to tender and the contract was won by a private sector contractor. There was a transfer to which TUPE applied. The employees argued that the exception should be read as relating to accrued rights in an occupational pension scheme but not to future rights. Hence, they argued, there remained a contractual obligation upon the transferee to provide an equivalent level of benefits. However, the Court of Appeal disagreed and this put an end to a series of cases which had sought to go behind the apparently clear wording of TUPE on this point.[134]

3.109 In the case of transfers out of the public sector, a public authority will ordinarily require a private sector transferee to provide broadly comparable pension benefits.[135] The basis of this policy was originally the advice given by the Attorney-General and the Lord Advocate to the effect that an employee who was not offered broadly comparable pension rights has an entitlement to

---

131 The right to claim that there has been a breach of contract or a constructive unfair dismissal is specifically excluded by reg 10(3) and assuming that reg 4(9) cannot be used for this purpose.

132 Pension Schemes Act 1993, s 1, as amended by the Pensions Act 2004.

133 [1996] IRLR 154.

134 See also *Walden Engineering v Warrener* [1993] ICR 967; and *Eidesund v Stavanger Catering A/S* [1996] IRLR 684.

135 See Cabinet Office 'Statement of Practice – Staff Transfers in the Public Sector and its Annex A: HM Treasury's Statement of Practice on Staff Transfers from Central Government "A Fair Deal for Staff Pensions" ' (January 2000); and 'Code of Practice on Workforce Matters in Public Sector Service Contracts' (March 2005) (reproduced at **appendices 11 and 12**).

resign and to claim constructive dismissal. That was seen by many at the time as legally suspect; there seemed to be a certain political expediency to the advice. Certainly, it is difficult to see how the advice can stand up in the light of the decision in *Adams* which was subsequently handed down by the Court of Appeal or to the provisions of reg 10(3), which did not have a similar forerunner in TUPE 1981. However, government policy in respect of pension rights in public sector transfers is now so well established that there is unlikely to be any change regardless of the law in this area.

3.110 A further limitation on the scope of the pensions exception is set out in reg 10(2). It is only the provisions of an occupational pension scheme which relate to 'old age, invalidity or survivors' which fall within the exception. It is not unusual for pension schemes to include benefits which do not fall within the category of an old age pension – such as, for example, an enhanced redundancy payment entitlement – and the transferor's pension scheme will need to be scrutinised carefully by the transferee to establish whether there are pensions benefits within the rules of the transferor's occupational pension scheme which are capable of transferring to the transferee under TUPE.

3.111 The most spectacular example of this point is the case of *Beckmann v Dynamco Whicheloe Macfarlane*.[136] Mrs Beckmann's terms and conditions derived from her employment within the National Health Service prior to transfer. She had been a member of the NHS Pension Scheme, which contains an entitlement in the event of dismissal prior to normal retirement in the form of an immediate pension and compensation. Mrs Beckmann was made redundant by the transferee. The ECJ held that early retirement benefits cannot be described as 'old age benefits' for the purposes of the pensions exception:

> 'It is only benefits paid from the time when an employee reaches the end of his normal working life as laid down by the general structure of the pension scheme in question, and not benefits such as those in point in the main proceedings (dismissal for redundancy) that can be classified as old age benefits, even if they are calculated by reference to the rules for calculating normal pension benefits.'

3.112 The passage quoted above suggests that any benefits payable prior to the normal retirement date will fall outside the exception, not just those arising on redundancy. This was confirmed when the *Beckmann* decision was considered and followed in *Martin v South Bank University*.[137] Given that a large proportion of pension schemes provide members with the right to an early retirement pension,[138] these decisions caused widespread alarm, bearing in mind that a transferee could now be held responsible to provide an early retirement pension but without any corresponding right to receive a transfer of the assets that would have been built up in the transferor's pension scheme to meet this liability.[139] Just what entitlements employees have in the circumstances and what obligations lie upon the parties to the transfer and on

---

136 [2002] 2 CMLR 45.

137 [2004] IRLR 74

138 The problem is likely to be similar where the employer has a discretion as to whether to allow the employee to retire early, as the courts are likely to imply an obligation on the part of the employer to exercise the discretion reasonably: see *Clarke v BET plc* [1997] IRLR 348.

139 It has been suggested that the courts may be able to solve this problem by using a solution

the trustees of the schemes of which the employees were formerly active members remains unclear following these two decisions of the ECJ. However, the basic principles are set out clearly in the decision of the Court in *Martin*:

'Rights contingent upon dismissal or the grant of early retirement by agreement with the employer fall within the "rights and obligations" referred to in Article 3(1) of Business Transfers Directive 77/187. It is clear from the wording of Article 3 that all the transferor's rights and obligations arising from the contract of employment, except in the cases mentioned in Article 3(3), are transferred to the transferee, regardless of whether or not their implementation is contingent upon the happening of a particular event, which may depend on the will of the employer.

Early retirement benefits arising by agreement between the employer and the employee to employees who have reached a certain age are not old-age, invalidity or survivors' benefits under supplementary company or inter-company pension schemes falling within the exception provided for by Article 3(3) of the Business Transfers Directive and therefore obligations arising upon early retirement are transferred to the transferee.

In light of the decision in the Beckmann case that only benefits paid from the time when an employee reaches the end of his or her working life can be classified as old-age benefits, there was no reason to treat benefits applied for upon dismissal by reason of redundancy, as in Beckmann, any differently from those applied for upon early retirement which does not correspond to the departure of an employee at the end of his or her normal working life, as in the present case.

Article 3 of the Business Transfers Directive precludes the transferee from offering the employees of a transferred entity less favourable terms than those offered to them by the transferor in respect of early retirement, and those employees from accepting those terms, where those terms are merely brought into line with the terms offered to the transferee's other employees at the time of the transfer, unless the more favourable terms previously offered by the transferor arose from a collective agreement which is no longer legally binding on the employees of the entity transferred.

Where, contrary to Article 3 of the Business Transfers Directive, employees have accepted early retirement on terms less favourable than that to which they were entitled under their employment relationship with the transferor, it is for the transferee to ensure that those employees are accorded early retirement on the terms to which they were entitled under their employment relationship with the transferor.'

3.113 After *Beckmann* and *Martin*, the pensions exception is a wounded animal. Old age pensions remain within the exception, as do ill health early retirement benefits (they fall within the 'invalidity' category) and benefits payable to dependents (survivor provisions), but a shroud of uncertainty hangs over the implications of these decisions in respect of other pension scheme benefits.

3.114 There are no answers to some of these problems, which leads the cautious to avoid a TUPE transfer where the transferring employees have participated in an occupational pension scheme which contains such rights. It is unclear whether the obligation to pay an early retirement pension only relates

---

similar to that applied in relation to insurance policies in *Bernadone* (see **3.55**). However, the point has not been considered by the courts as yet.

to the period leading up to the normal retirement date, at which point the old age pension obligation (which will not have transferred) kicks in.

3.115 A further limitation on the now much reduced scope of the pensions exception was introduced by the Pensions Act 2004. As a consequence of the agreed revisions to the Directive brokered at the Cardiff Summit in the summer of 1998 and embodied in the amended Directive,[140] Art 3(4)(a) now provides an option which Member States may take up to include pensions within the scope of their transfer of undertakings legislation. This option has been taken up in the UK, but the provisions are to be found not in the 2006 revision of TUPE but in the Pensions Act 2004, ss 257 and 258 and in the Transfer of Employment (Pension Protection) Regulations 2005.[141] With effect from 6 April 2005, the transferee now has a modified obligation to provide pension benefits following a TUPE transfer. The obligation is triggered by the answer to the question of whether the transferor provided access to an occupational pension scheme (or would have done so but for a deliberate attempt to avoid these provisions). If it did, then those transferring employees who were members of the scheme, were eligible to be members or were in a waiting period to become eligible to become a member will have a right to be provided with certain pension benefits post transfer. These will not be an entitlement to participate in a broadly comparable pension scheme, the benchmark for public to private sector transfers. Instead, the transferee will be obliged to provide a certain minimum standard of pension benefits, subject to the right of the transferee and the employee to agree whatever pension terms they wish (including the right to opt out of the right to any pension benefits at all) at any time post transfer, pursuant to s 258(6) of the Pensions Act 2004. There is (unlike the general principle elsewhere within TUPE) no attempt to replicate the level of benefit received pre transfer. Hence the employee may be better off or worse off following the transfer; the level of benefits enjoyed prior to the transfer is of no consequence in relation to his rights following the transfer.

3.116 Once the obligation is triggered the transferee may choose either to provide membership of a defined benefits scheme (which must meet certain minimum standards) or of a money purchase scheme, which could be a stakeholder scheme. In the case of the latter, the employer contribution will be a matching contribution of up to 6% of the employee's basic pay.

3.117 If the transferee opts for the defined benefit route, the minimum standard with which that scheme must comply is either:

(1) the statutory reference scheme test for contracting out purposes; or
(2) the test set out in the Transfer of Employment (Pension Protection) Regulations 2005, whereby the value of the benefits accruing under the scheme each year must be at least 6% of the employee's pensionable pay, excluding the value of the employee contributions. If employees are required to make contributions, these must not exceed 6% of pensionable salary. Alternatively, the employer must make matching contributions of up to 6% of the employee's basic pay.

---

140 See **appendix 4.**
141 SI 2005/649.

3.118 The date on which the obligations arise will either be the date of the relevant transfer for the purposes of TUPE or the date on which the employee reaches the end of the waiting period.

3.119 In the case of transfers out of the public sector, Government guidance to public authorities is to require the transferee to commit, as a matter of contract, to provide a higher level of pension benefits as compared with those which would otherwise be provided pursuant to the ordinary principles under TUPE.[142] Hence the common label 'TUPE Plus' which attaches to these enhanced obligations.

3.120 Assuming that the public authority places TUPE Plus pension obligations on the transferee as a contractual burden, the two key principles in 'A Fair Deal for Staff Pensions' are:

(1)   that staff should continue to have access post transfer to a good quality occupational pension scheme in respect of future service; and

(2)   that staff should be given options for handling the accrued benefits which they have already earned.

3.121 The benchmark for the provision of pension benefits going forward is a pension scheme which is 'broadly comparable' to the public sector pension scheme in which the employees participated pre transfer. Before the public authority will be prepared to enter into a contract which will result in a TUPE transfer, it will ordinarily want to see a 'pensions passport' – that is to say a certificate of broad comparability from the Government Actuary's Department, following scrutiny of the transferee's scheme.[143]

3.122 As regards accrued benefits, Government guidance provides that:[144]

> '... when transferred staff have to become early leavers of a public sector pension scheme it is essential to provide them not only with a "broadly comparable" private sector scheme for their future service, but also with the cover of a "bulk transfer agreement" to allow them, if they wish, to maintain a link between their future earnings growth and their past service pension benefits.'

3.123 It is intended that the bulk transfer terms will be made available early in the bidding process. Tenders can then be submitted taking into account these terms, although bidders are expected to indicate what element of the price is attributable to this factor. In practice, there is often a wide disparity between the assumptions made by public sector actuaries and by private sector actuaries in relation to the appropriate terms of a bulk transfer and the disparity can become a significant commercial issue. The guidance provides for the regulation of second generation transfers in certain circumstances – that is to

---

142   See **3.137**.

143   See 'Passport System for Pensions – Notice by The Government Actuary's Department' (July 2002), available at http://www.gad.gov.uk/Publications/docs/Passport_system_for_pensions_July_2002.pdf.

144   See HM Treasury Guidance Note 'Fair Deal for Staff Pensions: Procurement of Bulk Transfer Agreements and Related Issues' (June 2004), at p 2, available at http://hm-treasury.gov.uk/media/66D/D5/pensions_bta_guidance_290604.pdf.

say a transfer between private sector contractors where the original outsourcing was from the public sector. Hence a pensions passport is still likely to be required and the incoming contractor will have to be prepared to accept a bulk transfer.

3.124 In respect of new recruits into a workforce which has been the subject of a TUPE transfer out of the public sector, the Code of Practice on Workforce Matters in Local Authority Service Contracts[145] requires contractors to provide 'reasonable pension arrangements'. This means either including the new recruits in the scheme into which the transferred staff have moved, or offering an alternative which could be another contracted-out defined benefits scheme or a defined contribution scheme whereby the employer matches employee contributions up to 6% of pay.

3.125 So far as the Local Government Pension Scheme is concerned, since 2000 private sector employers have been entitled to apply for 'admitted body status' whereby they participate as an employer in the scheme and the employees who transfer to their employment are permitted to remain in the scheme. This has a number of attractions. The employees remain in the scheme without any changes being necessary and hence their remuneration position is preserved in the best possible way. The employer does not have to worry about the issue of a pensions passport and the cost of setting up a broadly comparable scheme. However, there are dangers. The contribution rate is fixed by the scheme actuary, so is outside the employer's control. The requirement to post a bond to guarantee the employer's liabilities will add expense. The contractor could be responsible, at the end of the contract, for a deficit not attributable to its period as employer. Accordingly, although there is a standard form of admission agreement for participation, it is usual for employers to seek to negotiate further provisions elsewhere in the documentation so as to protect their position.

PUBLIC POLICY AND TRANSFERS FROM THE PUBLIC SECTOR

3.126 With the advent of the widespread contracting out of public services from the early 1980s and the development of procurement models such as the Private Finance Initiative (PFI), some of the largest transfers of staff have taken place on the outsourcing of responsibility for the provision of services from the public to the private sector. Although TUPE applies in this context as much as in private sector transactions,[146] there are certain transactions which arise out of the administrative reorganisation of public authorities or the transfer of administrative functions between public authorities which do not constitute a relevant transfer for the purposes of the Regulations.[147] However, when considering public sector transfers in England and Wales it is necessary to have regard to public policy in tandem with TUPE. Such transfers are usually

---

145 2005. See **Appendix 12**.
146 Regulation 3(4)(a) provides that TUPE applies to 'public and private undertakings engaged in economic activities whether or not they are operating for gain'.
147 Regulation 3(5).

governed by contract terms which modify the orthodox situation under the Regulations. Contractual provisions which enhance the rights of the transferring employee, commonly known as 'TUPE Plus', are frequently implemented pursuant to government policy, which is set out in a number of guidance documents. In many ways, in such transactions the dictates of government policy is the dominant factor rather than the underlying law.

Cabinet Office Statement of Practice – Staff Transfers in the Public Sector (COSOP)

3.127   This document, published in January 2000, contains a set of instructions to public bodies as to how they should approach staff transfers. It dictates the terms on which public authorities should contract for the transfer of staff. It serves both a political and a practical function. In the political context it safeguards the rights of public sector employees at a higher level than is normal in a conventional transfer subject to TUPE. In so doing it has helped to overcome political concerns in some quarters about the contracting out of public sector services. In the practical context it introduced some clarity and certainty to the obligations of the parties at a time when there was considerable uncertainty as to when the Regulations applied and what their implications were.

3.128   COSOP is conceived as a set of instructions to central government departments and agencies and the NHS, but it is clear that it is intended that other public sector organisations should follow suit. Local government bodies are expected to apply COSOP to the extent possible having regard to their best value duties.

3.129   The central principle of COSOP is that where the public sector contracts out the provision of services to the private sector and voluntary organisations or where there is a transfer between different parts of the public sector, these will be conducted on the basis that staff transfer and that TUPE should apply, 'unless there are genuinely exceptional reasons not to do so'. The concept of 'genuine exceptional reasons' is narrowly interpreted. It includes contracts ancillary to the supply of goods, one-off projects and projects where there is a significant change in the way in which the functions are carried out.[148]

3.130   The mechanics for putting the policies of COSOP into effect are contract clauses whereby the transferee agrees to act to all intents and purposes as if TUPE applies, regardless of whether it does actually apply.[149] There are two legal limitations to the contractual route if the Regulations do not apply. The first is that there will not be a transfer if the employee does not want to transfer, leaving the public body with a redundancy liability. The most that the transferee can do in the circumstances is to make an offer of employment on the terms that would have applied had the Regulations applied; the employee

---

148   It may be that the Cabinet Office will wish to revisit this aspect of the Guidance in the light of the new law in relation to service provision changes.

149   The very fact of the transferee employing all the employees may, of itself, ensure that the Regulations apply, having regard to the rules set out in the *Süzen* case.

cannot be transferred automatically unless the Regulations actually apply. Secondly, continuity of employment is a statutory concept and cannot be transferred by contract.[150] The best that can be achieved is a commitment on the part of the transferee to act in all respects towards the employee as if his or her continuity of employment was continuous with his or her service up to the point of transfer.

3.131 COSOP applies not only on the initial transfer out of the public sector but also to subsequent changes of contractor, regardless of whether TUPE applied to the initial transfer out of the public sector. Hence the 'TUPE Plus' commitments imposed on employers under COSOP can continue for many years.

3.132 Pensions, redundancy and severance terms are singled out for protection. Redundancy and severance terms will be the subject of specific contractual commitments on the part of contractors. Pensions are dealt with in a separate document annexed to COSOP, a Statement of Practice issued by the Treasury entitled 'A Fair Deal for Staff Pensions'.

3.133 One implication of COSOP is that the information and consultation provisions of TUPE are extended. Staff (not merely representatives, as in the Regulations) and recognised unions (or, where there are none, other independent staff representatives) are to be provided with written notification of the intention that staff will transfer. The notification is to be given 'at the earliest appropriate stage'. Indeed, the information and consultation exercise in such transfers is habitually far more extensive than the minimum required by the Regulations. The exercise will often span several months and be supported by extensive communication such as newsletters to staff and the use of intranet sites.

3.134 As COSOP points out, s 38 of the Employment Relations Act 1999 contains a power to apply the Regulations in circumstances where they would not otherwise apply. One example where this power has been used is the Transfer of Undertakings (Protection of Employment) (Rent Officer Services) Regulations 1999.[151]

Two Tier Code

3.135 The Code of Practice on Workforce Matters in Public Sector Service Contracts was introduced in March 2003 for the purposes of local government outsourcing. In March 2005 the Code was extended across the public sector. It applies generally, subject to certain specified cases including where the Retention of Employment Model applies.[152] It has as its primary purpose the object of eliminating the 'two tier workforce'. The concern which had arisen was that where a workforce to which COSOP applies had transferred on the basis of 'TUPE Plus', over a period of time the proportion of ex-public sector

150 *Secretary of State for Employment v Globe Elastic Thread* [1979] IRLR 327.
151 SI 1999/2511.
152 See **3.139**.

transferees would diminish as new recruits took the place of those moving on. The latter would be recruited on market terms – generally rather less than 'TUPE Plus'. Contractors would naturally seek to drive down the terms and conditions of the new employees. Hence the emergence of two tiers within the workforce – those recruited on market terms and those on the more lucrative TUPE Plus terms. Somewhat surprisingly, given the initial thinking behind the move to the widespread contracting out of public sector services, the Code states:

'Service providers who intend to cut costs by driving down the terms and conditions for staff, whether for transferees or for new joiners taken on to work beside them, will not be selected to provide services for the public sector organisation.'

3.136 Much of the rhetoric of the Two Tier Code follows the language of COSOP, but the key point is the obligation on the transferee to offer new employees who work on public sector contracts (not just replacement staff) 'fair and reasonable terms and conditions which are, overall, no less favourable than those of transferred employees'. It will be noted that there is some latitude here, for the benchmark is the overall value of the remuneration package. In determining what terms and conditions to offer, the transferee is bound to consult the representatives of a recognised trade union (if there is one) or 'other elected representatives of the employees'. The consultation must involve a 'genuine dialogue' with a view to reaching agreement on the terms to be offered.

3.137 The pension terms to be offered foreshadow what is now required pursuant to the Pensions Act 2004 in respect of a transfer pursuant to TUPE. The employer must provide:

● membership of a good quality pension scheme, being a contracted out defined benefit scheme or a defined contribution scheme with matched contributions up to 6%; or

● a stakeholder pension scheme with matched contributions up to 6%.

3.138 The Code provides for information to be collected for monitoring purposes. The contractor will be responsible not only for compliance with the Code itself but will also be under an obligation to ensure compliance with the Code by its subcontractors.

Retention of employment

3.139 As described above, COSOP and the Two Tier Code apply to transfers of staff out of the NHS. However, these rules must be read subject to the Retention of Employment Model (ROE) which significantly modifies a conventional transfer under the Regulations by taking out of scope of the transfer a large number of employees.

3.140 ROE embodies an agreement reached between the public sector union, UNISON, and the Department of Health. It arises from a reluctance on the part of many employees and unions to be 'privatised' and hence describes a way in which PFI schemes involving NHS trusts in England can go ahead without large numbers of employees transferring to the private sector, as would ordinarily be the case.[153]

3.141   ROE works as follows. Staff in five ancillary roles – portering, catering, cleaning, laundry and security services (the 'five trades') – are offered the opportunity to remain employed by the NHS Trust, notwithstanding that the service in which they work will be transferred to a private sector contractor and that there will be a relevant transfer for the purpose of TUPE. This is achieved by the employee opting out of the transfer by serving a notice pursuant to reg 4(7). However, upon serving such a notice the NHS Trust offers to employ the employee in question on like terms and conditions with effect from the date of the transfer and the employee is then seconded to the private sector contractor. A mass opt out is organised so that the private sector contractor will undertake the provision of services with a public sector workforce. ROE only affects those employees in the five trades who exercise the right to opt out. However, in practice this means that approximately 85% of the employees will have a right to opt out. Those who do not do so and those who work in other functions outside the scope of ROE transfer under the Regulations in the ordinary way. Staff in the five trades whose trade has already been contracted out are to be brought back within the NHS.[154]

3.142   ROE is a pragmatic solution to a political problem. It works by reason of contractual duties on the private sector contractor which modify the effects of TUPE. There are many legal concerns about the model, given that it is contrary to the whole purpose of the Regulations and is tantamount to contracting out of the application of the Regulations.

3.143   In addition, there are many operational issues. For example, the service provider is contracting to provide a service but without the workforce to do so. It relies upon a workforce made available to it which is not subject to its control in a way that its own employees would be. Disciplinary issues are outside its control, beyond a certain level. The initial stages of the disciplinary process are the subject of delegated responsibility to the contractor's management. Recruitment is outside the contractor's control in the sense that the new recruits are recruited into the NHS and then seconded. Documentation has been developed to deal with these various risks and to allocate responsibility between the NHS trust and the contractor in accordance with a risk matrix.

3.144   Although conceived for the specific purpose of PFI schemes involving NHS trusts, the ROE model has begun to find favour in other areas. It is

---

153   The PFI was conceived as a procurement method whereby public sector facilities such as hospitals and schools may be built, operated and financed by the private sector. Because the scheme will involve the provision of a range of services to the facility which is the subject of the procurement, TUPE will ordinarily apply in respect of the transfer of responsibility for those services. PFI schemes have been the subject of objection in principle in some quarters, including from the trade union movement, since they were first introduced in 1992. ROE was pioneered by UNISON against a background of continuing opposition to PFI in principle. ROE may be expected to apply in any PPP scheme (that is to say any form of public-private partnership) within the NHS, though designed originally only to apply to PFI schemes.

154   For a more detailed treatment of this subject, see Davies (2004) ILJ 95.

effective where there is strong employee/union opposition to the prospect of a service being contracted out by the public sector. Hence variants on ROE, not limited to the five trades and not applying in the context of either a PFI scheme or an NHS Trust, have been seen in a number of different environments. For example, in July 2005 a ROE variant was used in the contracting out of a local authority's IT services. Faced with the threat of widespread strike action over its outsourcing proposals, Bradford City Council signed a 10-year outsourcing contract with IBM and Serco Solutions which allows employees to remain in the employment of the Council or to transfer to Serco. The employees were given the right to transfer to Serco at a later stage.

Chapter 4

DISMISSALS AND ISSUES ARISING IN CONNECTION WITH THE TRANSFER

4.1   This chapter considers issues which arise in connection with the transfer of an undertaking: dismissals and variations of employees' contracts. The first is covered by reg 7 of the Transfer of Undertakings (Protection of Employment) Regulations (TUPE) 2006;[1] the second by regs 4(4) and (5) and 9. This last regulation comes into play where a proposed variation arises when the transferor is subject to insolvency proceedings.

4.2   The relevant provisions of Directive 2001/23/EC in relation to the matters covered by this chapter are Arts 3(1), 4 and 5. As will be seen, Art 3(1) does not expressly deal with variations of contract. The fact that it embraces variations is the consequence of the way the European Court of Justice (ECJ) has interpreted it. Article 3(1) has also been subject to considerable scrutiny in relation to cases dealing with dismissal; but it is Art 4 which expressly deals with dismissals. As will be seen, the issue has been whether a dismissal in breach of its provisions is a nullity. Essentially, the applicability of the appropriate Article of the Directive (and, thus, of the relevant regulation of TUPE 2006) depends on the facts of the particular case. If the employee was transferred to the transferee without a dismissal being involved, Art 3(1) and reg 4(4) and (5) are involved; if there was a dismissal, then Art 4 and reg 8 will be engaged.

4.3   Article 5 of the Directive applies where the transferor is the subject of bankruptcy proceedings or analogous insolvency proceedings. In that case, Art 5(1) specifies that, unless the Member States provide otherwise, Arts 3 and 4 will not apply to the transfer of an undertaking. This Article is considered at **3.84** together with reg 9 of TUPE 2006.

4.4   It should be noted that Art 4(2) and reg 4(9) make express provision for the situation where the employment is terminated 'because the transfer involves a substantial change in working conditions to the detriment of the employee'. Finally, there is a specific provision in TUPE 2006 (reg 4(7)–(9) and (11)), reflecting the case-law of the ECJ, which deals with an employee's objections to a transfer. These last two matters are considered in **chapter 3**, at **3.41** and **3.33**.

---

1   SI 2006/246.

DISMISSALS

Article 4 of the Directive

4.5　Article 4(1) provides that the transfer 'shall not in itself constitute grounds for dismissal by the transferor or the transferee', but goes on to state that that provision is not to 'stand in the way of dismissals ... for economic, technical or organisational reasons entailing changes in the workforce'. (This is reflected in reg 7(1) and (2) of TUPE 2006.) Article 4(1) goes on to provide that the Member States may exclude specific categories of employees who are not covered by their laws or practice in respect of protection against dismissal. This provision has been transposed into domestic law by reg 7(6).[2] Thus, those who are excluded from the right to complain of unfair dismissal by a relevant provision of the Employment Rights Act 1996 (ERA 1996), the Employment Tribunals Act 1996 or the Trade Union and Labour Relations (Consolidation) Act 1992 are also excluded from TUPE 2006. The main exclusions are considered at **4.39–49**. Article 4(2) of the Directive[3] provides that if the contract of employment or employment relationship is terminated because the transfer involves 'a substantial change in working conditions to the detriment of the employee', the employer is to be regarded as having been responsible for the termination. This provision has been given effect to by reg 4(9), which is considered at **3.41**.

4.6　As was mentioned above, Art 4(1) states that a transfer 'shall not in itself constitute grounds for dismissal'. The question is what effect these words are to be interpreted as having. An early straw in the wind is to be found in the opinion of the Advocate General in *Wendelboe v LJ Music ApS*:[4]

> 'Whether the remedy for such unlawful dismissal consists in a court order declaring that dismissal to be a nullity or the award of damages or some other effective remedy is for the member states to determine.'

4.7　Two other decisions of the ECJ are relevant here. In the first, *P Bork International A/S v Foreningen af Arbejdsledere I Danmark*,[5] the question arose as to whether the close-down of a factory with dismissal of staff followed by a takeover of the factory some 2 weeks later constituted the transfer of an undertaking so that the transferee was required to safeguard the rights and obligations arising under the contract of employment in existence at the date of the transfer. It is clear from the judgment of the ECJ that the Court did not regard Art 4(1) as invalidating the dismissals. It said[6] that employees who were dismissed by the transferor contrary to Art 4(1) must be regarded as still in the

---

2　This provision is the successor of reg 8(5) of the Transfer of Undertakings (Protection of Employment) Regulations (TUPE) 1981, SI 1981/1794, which was itself inserted by the Collective Redundancies and Transfers of Undertakings (Protection of Employment) (Amendment) Regulations 1995, SI 1995/2587, and subsequently amended by ERA 1996.

3　Article 4(2) of Council Directive 77/187/EEC had identical wording.

4　Case 19/83 [1985] ECR 457, at 460–461. See also *Foreningen af Arbejdsledere I Danmark v A/S Danmols Inventar* Case 105/84 [1985] ECR 2639, at 2650–2651, paras 15 and 16.

5　[1988] ECR 3057.

6　[1988] ECR 3057, at 3077–3078, para 18.

employment of the undertaking on the date of the transfer, with the result that the transferor's obligations towards them were automatically transferred to the transferee in accordance with Art 3(1). Had the Court taken the view that the effect of Art 4(1) was to invalidate the dismissals, one would have thought that the consequence would have been that the employees would have remained employed by the transferor, though in fact the conclusion of the Court of Appeal in *Wilson v St Helens Borough Council, Meade v British Fuels Ltd* [7] was to the contrary. Such a conclusion would have negated the purpose of the Directive, as reiterated in numerous cases by the ECJ, which is 'to ensure that the rights of employees are safeguarded in the event of a change of employer by enabling them to remain in employment with the new employer on the terms and conditions agreed with the transferor'.[8]

4.8   The second ECJ decision, *Foreningen af Arbejdsledere I Danmark v Daddy's Dance Hall A/S*,[9] develops the *Bork* line of thought further. The facts of the case were that the employee was dismissed when the company employing him had to give up its lease; he was taken on by the new lessee of the premises. The Court said:[10]

> '16. However, as the Court held in its judgments of 11 July 1985 in (case 105/84) *Foreningen af Arbejsdsledere i Danmark v. Danmols Inventar*,[11] ... Directive 77/187/EEC is intended to achieve only partial harmonization, essentially by extending the protection guaranteed to workers independently by the laws of the individual Member States to cover the case where an undertaking is transferred. It is not intended to establish a uniform level of protection throughout the Community on the basis of common criteria. Thus the directive can be relied on only to ensure that the employee is protected in his relations with the transferee to the same extent as he was in his relations with the transferor under the legal rules of the Member State concerned.
>
> 17. Consequently, in so far as national law allows the employment relationship to be altered in a manner unfavourable to employees in situations other than the transfer of an undertaking, in particular as regards their protection against dismissal, such an alternative is not precluded merely because the undertaking has been transferred in the meantime and the agreement has therefore been made with the new employer. Since by virtue of Article 3(1) of the directive the transferee is subrogated to the transferor's rights and obligations under the employment relationship, that relationship may be altered with regard to the transferee to the same extent as it could have been with regard to the transferor, provided that the transfer of the undertaking itself may never constitute the reason for that amendment.'

4.9   When the House of Lords came to consider this issue, in *British Fuels Ltd v Baxendale and Wilson v St Helens Borough Council*,[12] the question was whether the relevant regulation of TUPE 1981[13] should be interpreted as

---

7   [1998] ICR 387. See **4.9**.
8   [1988] ECR 3057, at 3076, para 13. Similar observations can be found in many of the case mentioned, particularly those discussed in **chapter 2**.
9   [1988] ECR 739.
10   [1988] ECR 739, at 754–755, paras 16 and 17. See also *Rask v Kantineservice A/S* Case C-209/91 [1992] ECR I-5755, at 5782–5783, paras 28 and 31.
11   [1985] ECR 2639.
12   [1998] ICR 1141.
13   Regulation 8(1), now reg 7(1) of TUPE 2006.

meaning that a dismissal which contravened the regulation should be regarded as a nullity, as had been held by the Court of Appeal.[14] The effect of the Court of Appeal's decision was that dismissed employees continued to be employed by the transferee on the terms of their former employment, so that their subsequent agreement with the transferee employer to different terms and conditions was void. The House of Lords rejected that view and said that an actual dismissal before, on or after the transfer was effective and not a nullity and that the employee could not compel the transferee to employ him on the same terms and condition as he had previously enjoyed. Lord Slynn of Hadley, who gave the sole speech in the House of Lords, said:[15]

> 'In my opinion, the overriding emphasis in the European Court's judgments is that the existing rights of employees are to be safeguarded if there is a transfer. That means no more and no less than that the employee can look to the transferee to perform those obligations which the employee could have enforced against the transferor. The employer, be he transferor or transferee, cannot use the transfer as a justification for dismissal, but if he does dismiss it is a question for national law as to what those rights are. As I have already said, in English law there would as a general rule be no order for specific performance. The claim would be for damages for wrongful dismissal or for statutory rights including, it is true, reinstatement or re-engagement where applicable. It may be in other countries that an order for specific performance could be obtained under the appropriate domestic law and that on this approach different results would be achieved in different Member States. That I do not find surprising or shocking. The Directive is to "approximate" the laws of the Member States. Its purpose is to "safeguard" rights on a transfer. The "rights" of an employee must depend on national rules of the law of contract or of legislation. There is no Community law of contract common to Member States, nor is there a common system or remedies. The object and purpose of the Directive is to ensure in all member states that on a transfer an employee has against the transferee the rights and remedies which he would have had against the original employer. To that extent it reduces the differences which may exist in the event of a change of employers as to the enforcement by employees of existing rights. They must all provide for enforcement against the transferee of rights existing against the transferor at the time of transfer. It seems to me that the Court has clearly recognised that the precise rights to be transferred depend on national law. But neither the Regulations nor the Directive nor the jurisprudence of the Court create a community law right to continue in employment which does not exist under national law.'

Exclusions from the right to make an unfair dismissal claim under TUPE 2006

4.10   TUPE 2006, like its predecessor Regulations, links the specific regulation to the general law of unfair dismissal. Before looking in detail at reg 7 and the relevant case-law, it is necessary to consider two preliminary matters: (1) exclusions from the general provisions; and (2) the meaning of 'dismissal'. If an employee is excluded from the general unfair dismissal provisions, he or she will not be in any better position by dint of the fact that there was a relevant transfer and that TUPE 2006 came into play. Similarly, if he or she was not

---

14   See [1998] ICR 387.
15   [1998] ICR 1141, at 1159–1160.

dismissed, then again, subject to the provisions of reg 4(9), he or she will be in no better position because the situation took place against the background of a relevant transfer.

4.11   Regulation 7(6) of TUPE 2006 provides that reg 7(1) is not to apply in relation to the dismissal of an employee if any of the exclusion provisions apply. Thus, those who are excluded from the right to complain of unfair dismissal by a relevant provision of ERA 1996, the Employment Tribunals Act 1996 or the Trade Union and Labour Relations (Consolidation) Act 1992 are also excluded from the 2006 Regulations.

4.12   In this section the following matters are considered:

(1)   the definition of 'employee';
(2)   homeworkers and casual workers;
(3)   part-time workers;
(4)   agency and 'temporary' workers;
(5)   employees over retirement age;
(6)   short-term and casual employees; and
(7)   employees working outside the UK.

4.13   In the present context it is only possible to give a general indication of the main problems that arise in each of the above categories. For a full discussion of the problems relating to those entitled to the statutory rights and those excluded from them, reference should be made to Upex, *The Law of Termination of Employment*,[16] chapter 1.

The definition of 'employee'

4.14   The right to claim unfair dismissal is only available only to 'employees', as defined by s 230(1) of ERA 1996.[17] Those who are not employed under a contract of employment (or service) are likely to be employed under a contract for services. Such people are variously called 'self-employed', 'independent contractors' or 'consultants', but there is no definition of any of these terms in the Act.

4.15   The courts have laid down tests to enable a distinction to be made between employees and self-employed and contracts of service and contracts for services. The test currently used is the 'multiple' test, which was formulated in *Ready Mixed Concrete (South East) Ltd v Minister of Pensions and National Insurance*,[18] where MacKenna J said:

'A contract of service exists if the following three conditions are fulfilled:[19]

(i)   The servant agrees that in consideration of a wage or other remuneration he will provide his own work and skill in the performance of some service for his master.

---

16   7th edn, Jordans, 2006.
17   See s 230(2) for the definition of 'contract of employment'.
18   [1968] 2 QB 497.
19   [1968] 2 QB 497, at 515.

(ii)   He agrees expressly or impliedly that in the performance of that service he will be subject to the other's control in sufficient degree to make that other master.

(iii)   The other provisions of the contract are consistent with its being a contract of service.'

4.16   The judge formulated his conclusion in terms of whether the person in question was in business on his own account, a formulation which has been recurrent ever since. Despite the fact that a number of factors in the case suggested the conclusion that the person concerned was an employee, the judge based his conclusion that he was self-employed on what he called 'the ownership of the instrumentalities', ie the tools of the trade.

4.17   This case was followed soon after by *Market Investigations Ltd v Minister of Social Security*.[20] Cooke J's approach was similar to that of MacKenna J, but he refined the third part of that judge's test. He said that the fundamental test was: 'Is the person who has engaged himself to perform these services performing them as a person in business on his own account?' He went on:[21]

> 'No exhaustive list has been compiled and perhaps no exhaustive list can be compiled of considerations which are relevant in determining that question, nor can strict rules be laid down as to the relative weight which the various considerations should carry in particular cases. The most that can be said is that control will no doubt always have to be considered, although it can no longer be regarded as the sole determining factor; and that factors, which may be of importance, are such matters as whether the man performing the services provides his own equipment, whether he hires his own helpers, what degree of financial risk he takes, what degree of responsibility for investment and management he has, and whether and how far he has an opportunity of profiting from sound management in the performance of his task.'

4.18   The most recent case in which the Court of Appeal has considered this issue is *Express & Echo Publications Ltd v Tanton*.[22] The facts of the case are reminiscent of those of *Ready Mixed Concrete*. They involved a driver who was made redundant from his employment and who was later re-engaged under a contract which the company intended, and the driver agreed, should be a contract for services. Clause 3.3 of the agreement provided that should the driver be 'unable or unwilling to perform the services personally he shall arrange at his own expense entirely for another suitable person to perform the services'. The driver applied to the employment tribunal for a declaration that his status was that of employee and an order that he should be supplied with a written contract of employment in similar terms to those enjoyed by the

---

20   [1969] 2 QB 173. See also *Lee Ting Sang v Chung Chi-Keung* [1990] ICR 409, a decision of the Privy Council.

21   [1969] 2 QB 173, at 184–185.

22   [1999] ICR 693. See also *Staffordshire Sentinel Newspapers Ltd v Potter* [2004] IRLR 752. Cf *MacFarlane v Glasgow City Council* [2001] IRLR 7, which involved qualified gymnastic instructors working at sports centres operated by the Council. If an instructor could not take a class, she would arrange for a replacement from a register of coaches maintained by the Council. The replacements were paid by the Council, not by the applicant. She was held to be an employee.

company's employees. The tribunal determined that he was an employee and the Employment Appeal Tribunal (EAT) dismissed the company's appeal. The Court of Appeal, however, allowed the company's appeal, saying that as a matter of law where a person is not required to perform the contract personally the relationship is not one of employee and employer. Thus, clause 3.3 was wholly inconsistent with the contract being one of service. Peter Gibson LJ, with whom the other members of the court agreed, said:[23]

> '[I]t is necessary for a contract of employment to contain an obligation on the part of the employee to provide his services personally. Without such an irreducible minimum of obligation, it cannot be said that the contract is one of service ... [I]t is established on the authorities that, where, as here, a person who works for another is not required to perform his services personally, then as a matter of law the relationship between the worker and the person for whom he works is not that of employee and employer.'

4.19   From the cases so far considered it can be seen that the main elements which are necessary for there to be a contract of employment are: personal service; mutuality of obligation; and control. Of the three, mutuality of obligation is of particular importance in cases which involve casual workers and is considered in more detail at **4.22**. The element of control has proved to be of particular significance in cases involving agency (or temporary workers) and is considered at **4.30**.

4.20   The process of deciding whether a person is an employee or whether he or she is carrying on business on his or her own account has been described by Mummery J in *Hall v Lorimer*,[24] in the following terms:

> '[I]t is necessary to consider many different aspects of that person's work activity. This is not a mechanical exercise of running through items on a checklist to see whether they are present in, or absent from, a given situation. The object of the exercise is to paint a picture from the accumulation of detail. The overall effect can only be appreciated by standing back from the detailed picture which has been painted, by viewing it from a distance and by making an informed, considered, qualitative appreciation of the whole. It is a matter of evaluation of the overall effect of the detail, which is not necessarily the same as the sum total of the individual details. Not all details are of equal weight or importance in any given situation. The details may also vary in importance from one situation to another ... The process involves painting a picture in each individual case.'

4.21   The following factors are the most important to evaluate in painting a picture of a person's work activity:

(1)   the contractual provisions;
(2)   the degree of control exercised by the 'employer';
(3)   the obligation of the 'employer' to provide work;
(4)   the obligation on the person to do the work;

---

23   [1999] ICR 693, at 699–700. See also *Nethermere (St Neots) Ltd v Gardiner* [1984] ICR 612, at 623, per Stephenson LJ; and *Clarke v Oxfordshire Health Authority* [1998] IRLR 125, per Sir Christopher Slade.

24   [1992] ICR 739, at 744–745. The Court of Appeal upheld his decision that the taxpayer was not an employee: see [1994] ICR 218. See also *Lee Ting Sang v Chung Chi-Keung* [1990] ICR 409, at 414, where the Privy Council used similar language.

(5) the provision of tools, equipment, instruments and the like;
(6) the arrangements made for tax, National Insurance contributions, sick pay and VAT;
(7) the opportunity to work for other employers;
(8) other contractual provisions, such as fees, expenses, and holiday pay; and
(9) whether the relationship by which the person is a self-employed independent contractor is genuine or whether it is designed to avoid the employment protection legislation.

Homeworkers and casual workers

4.22 Those who work for a person but do the work away from the premises are outworkers, and, if they do the work in their own domestic environment, are called homeworkers. Whether such persons are employees will depend upon the facts of any given case, as the cases have stressed. In *Airfix Footwear Ltd v Cope*,[25] for example, the decision that the homeworker in question was an employee was due to the fact that she had been working for Airfix Footwear 5 days a week for 7 years. In *Nethermere (St Neots) Ltd v Taverna and Gardiner*[26] both the homeworkers involved worked under flexible arrangements; they took as much work as they wanted and did not work when they wanted. They were held to be employees.

4.23 In this area the element of mutuality of obligation comes to the fore. This is usually expressed as an obligation on the part of the employer to provide work and a corresponding obligation of the employee to accept and perform any work offered. In cases of the kind discussed in this section, the individual carries out work on a casual or irregular basis over a period of time. The question which then arises is whether mutuality of obligation continues to subsist when the individual is not working. If there is, this will give rise to what is called a 'global' contract of employment spanning the separate engagements. If it does not, then the first question will be whether in relation to each individual assignment there was a contract of employment. If there was, then a further question will arise as to whether there is 'continuity of employment' between each period of work. In each case, the tribunal will look at the working periods themselves, and take into account their frequency and duration. Where there has been a regular pattern of work over a period, the tribunal is more likely to find the existence of a continuing overriding arrangement amounting to a contract of employment, as was found to be the case in *Nethermere (St Neots) Ltd v Gardiner*.[27]

4.24 In that case Dillon LJ said that a contract of employment could arise where a course of dealing between the parties continued over several years by which the individual's obligation to accept work implied an obligation on the employer to provide work.[28] He also said that the fact that the individuals concerned could fix their own hours of work, take holidays and time off when

---

25 [1978] ICR 1210.
26 [1984] ICR 612.
27 [1984] ICR 612.
28 [1984] ICR 612, at 634.

they wished and could vary how much work they were willing to take on in any day did not negative a contract of employment. Stephenson LJ quoted from MacKenna J's judgment in the *Ready Mixed Concrete* case:

'There must be a wage or other remuneration. Otherwise there will be no consideration, and without consideration no contract of any kind. The servant must be obliged to provide his own work and skill.'

The judge went on to say:[29]

'There must, in my judgement, be an irreducible minimum of obligation on each side to create a contract of service. I doubt if it can be reduced any lower than in the sentences I have just quoted ...' [these being set out in the preceding quotation].

4.25   In *O'Kelly v Trusthouse Forte plc*,[30] which involved the question whether 'regular casuals' called in to work at banquets were employees, the decision of the employment tribunal was that they were not. The determinant factor was that there was no mutuality of obligation as they were effectively on 'standby' unless and until they were asked to come in and assist with a particular banquet. The Court of Appeal said that, as the tribunal had correctly weighed up all the factors involved in the case, there were no grounds for interfering with its decision.

4.26   The status of casual employee has received attention from both the Court of Appeal and House of Lords in recent years. In *Clark v Oxfordshire Health Authority*,[31] the issue was whether a nurse retained by a health authority on a casual basis to fill temporary vacancies in hospitals was an employee. She worked for the authority's 'nurse bank'; she had no fixed or regular hours of work but was offered work as and when a vacancy occurred at one of the authority's hospitals. When she did not work, she had no entitlement to pay, or to holiday pay or sick leave. She worked on this basis for some 3 years, from January 1991 to January 1994; during that period, however, there were various gaps, during 1992 and 1993. The only issue decided by the employment tribunal, and thus the subject of appeal, was whether there was a 'global contract of employment' between the parties. This was described by Sir Christopher Slade in the case under discussion as 'a continuing overriding arrangement which governed the whole of [the parties'] relationship and itself amounted to a contract of employment ...'.[32] If a global contract of employment existed, the gaps in employment during the time she was on the nurse bank would have counted towards her length of employment and she would have had sufficient continuity; if there was not, each gap would have

---

29   [1984] ICR 612, at 623.
30   [1983] ICR 728. See also *Mailway (Southern) Ltd v Willsher* [1978] ICR 511, in which the EAT held that a person who registered as a part-time packer with the employers was not an employee. The employers called upon her to work as and when they needed her and she was not obliged to work, when asked, if she did not want to. The EAT took the view that the arrangements in question did not amount to a contract of employment in accordance with which she was normally required to work. It should be noted, however, that this case arose under the guarantee payments provisions of the legislation.
31   [1998] IRLR 125. See also *Stevedoring & Haulage Services Ltd v Fuller* [2001] IRLR 627.
32   [1998] IRLR 125, at 127, para 15.

broken continuity and she would not accumulate sufficient continuity.[33] The Court of Appeal said that a contract of employment cannot exist in the absence of mutual obligations subsisting over the entire duration of the relevant period. It said that, although the mutual obligations required to found a global contract of employment need not necessarily consist of obligations to provide and perform work, some mutuality of obligation is required. In the present case, there was no mutuality of obligation: the authority was under no obligation to offer work nor was Ms Clark under any obligation to accept it. She had no entitlement to any pay when she did not work and no entitlement to holiday pay or sick leave. There was thus no global contract of employment.

4.27   The issue of casual staff was again considered by the House of Lords in *Carmichael v National Power plc*.[34] The case involved tour guides who were taken on by means of an exchange of letters on a 'casual as required basis' to act as guides taking parties on tours of power stations operated by the predecessor of the respondent company. As in the *Clark* case, they were not obliged to take work and the company did not guarantee that work would be available. They were paid only for the hours they worked. The House of Lords held that they were not employees. Lord Irvine of Lairg LC said that it was clear that the parties did not intend the letters to 'constitute an exclusive memorial of their relationship' and that, in looking at the documents, the surrounding circumstances and how the parties conducted themselves, the tribunal was correct to conclude that they did not intend that their relationship should be regulated by contract.[35]

4.28   It should be noted that in the cases considered above the courts were dealing with the question whether mutuality of obligation could be inferred from the previous course of dealing between the parties. In none of the cases, however, was there an express agreement. These cases may be contrasted with the Court of Appeal decision in *Stevedoring & Haulage Services Ltd v Fuller*.[36] In that case, the Court of Appeal decided that a person who worked for an employer expressly on the basis that no mutual obligations as to the provision and acceptance of work existed was not an employee. The important point about this case, however, is that the express agreement between the parties negatived mutuality of obligation; in other words the conduct of the parties could not override the express agreement between them.

Part-time workers

4.29   Similar questions arise when considering whether part-time workers are employees. It may be that a person may work for five different employers on

---

33   It should be remembered that this case arose at a time when the qualifying period of employment for employees claiming the right not to be unfairly dismissed was 2 years.

34   [1999] ICR 1226. See also *Cornwall County Council v Prater* [2006] ICR 731, which involved a home tutor who was assigned individual pupils over a period of years. The EAT upheld the tribunal's decision that this arrangement gave rise to a separate contract of employment for each assignment of a pupil. See also *Thomson v Fife Council* (IDS Brief 792); and *Cotswold Developments Construction Ltd v Williams* [2006] IRLR 181.

35   See at 1230G–1231F.

36   [2001] IRLR 627. Cf *Wilson v Circular Distributors Ltd* [2001] IRLR 627.

five different days of the week, doing a full day's work for each employer. If that is so, then, if the factors set out above point to employment, such a person's status is properly to be regarded as that of an employee. Equally, however, the very fact that such a person does work for five different 'employers' on five different days of the week must also raise the question whether he or she is more properly to be regarded as self-employed.

Agency/temporary workers

4.30 Those covered here are workers whose services are supplied by an intermediary (the labour supplier[37]) for the benefit of a third party (the hirer) for a period of time, which may be limited or, in some cases, of longer duration. Two relationships are involved – that between the worker and the agency and that between the worker and the hirer. Both types of relationship have been the subject of judicial scrutiny in recent years. It is in this area that the element of control has tended to be of significance, but the requirement of mutuality of obligation, mentioned earlier, may also lead to the conclusion in particular cases that no contract of employment existed. If it is shown that the agency or the hirer has control over the person whose status is in question, that will tend to lead to the conclusion that that person has become an employee. One other point to note here is that it is immaterial whether the individual supplying the services supplies them directly, or indirectly through a personal service (or other) company. The task of the tribunal is to ascertain whether there was a contractual relationship between the individual and the end user.[38]

4.31 The traditional view of the relationship between worker and agency is to be found in *Construction Industry Training Board v Labour Force Ltd.*[39] In that case, the Divisional Court expressed the view that the contractual relationship between the supplier/agency and the worker was not one of service, but one *sui generis*. As with the relationship between the worker and the hirer, there must be found in the relationship between worker and agency the irreducible minimum of mutuality of obligation to enable the tribunal to reach the conclusion that there was a contract of employment between them. This was emphasised by the Court of Appeal in *Montgomery v Johnson Underwood Ltd,*[40] which said that, in determining whether a contract of employment exists, the guidance given by MacKenna J in the *Ready Mixed*

---

37   The activities of fee-charging labour suppliers are now regulated by the Conduct of Employment Agencies and Employment Businesses Regulations 2003, SI 2003/3319.

38   *Hewlett Packard Ltd v Murphy* [2002] IRLR 4. In fact, the EAT held that there was no contractual relationship between the worker and the end user, but the principle stated in the text was stated by the EAT in its judgment and remains valid irrespective of the outcome.

39   [1970] 3 All ER 220. See also *Wickens v Champion Employment* [1984] ICR 365; *Ironmonger v Movefield Ltd t/a Deering Appointments* [1988] IRLR 461; and *Pertemps Group Ltd v Nixon* EAT/496/91.

40   [2001] IRLR 269. The judgment of the Court of Appeal throws doubt upon the judgment of an earlier Court of Appeal in *McMeechan v Secretary of State for Employment* [1997] ICR 549, which in any event should be regarded as turning on its own facts. In that case, the Court of Appeal had treated a worker as employed by an agency in respect of one single engagement with a particular client in respect of which the money he was claiming on the agency's insolvency had been earned.

Concrete case[41] should be followed. The factor which caused the Court of Appeal to say that the tribunal had erred was the absence of control. The court said that a contractual relationship concerning work to be carried out in which there is no control cannot sensibly be called a contract of employment. They said that it is not essential that there is control of how the work is done, but there must be some sufficient framework of control. They added that an offer of work by an agency could, in appropriate circumstances, satisfy the requirement of mutuality of obligation.

4.32   This area has received the attention of the Court of Appeal in three further decisions – *Dacas v Brook Street Bureau (UK) Ltd*;[42] *Bunce v Postworth Ltd t/a Skyblue*;[43] and *Muscat v Cable & Wireless plc*.[44] The first case involved a worker who was supplied by the Brook Street Bureau to a local authority. She had a 'temporary worker agreement' with the agency which was expressly stated to be a contract for services and specifically excluded any contract of employment between them. The local authority exercised day-to-day control over her and supplied her with cleaning materials, equipment and an overall. She was paid by the agency on the basis of time sheets supplied by the local authority. After an allegation that she had been rude, the local authority asked the agency not to send her to work there in the future. The agency told her that no further work would be found for her. She brought a complaint of unfair dismissal against both the agency and the local authority. The tribunal decided that she was employed by neither, but her appeal to the EAT was only against that part of the decision that she was not employed by the agency. This effectively precluded both the EAT and the Court of Appeal from dealing with that aspect of the tribunal's decision relating to her relationship with the local authority. The Court of Appeal upheld the tribunal's decision. It said that the agency was under no obligation to provide the applicant with work, nor was she under any obligation to accept work offered by the agency; nor did the agency exercise any relevant day-to-day control over her work for the local authority. In effect, therefore, both the necessary elements for a contract of employment were missing from the arrangements between Mrs Dacas and the agency. The judgment of the Court of Appeal in this case contains an extensive analysis of the relevant authorities and principles to be applied and used in such cases. Mummery LJ concluded his judgment by saying that, when dealing with cases of this kind, tribunals should not determine the status of the applicant without also considering the possibility of an implied contract of employment.[45]

4.33   It is clear that the same requirements of mutuality of obligation and a sufficient degree of control apply in the case of the relationship between the

---

41   [1968] 2 QB 497.
42   [2004] ICR 1437.
43   [2005] IRLR 557. The facts of this case are similar to those of *Dacas*. The Court of Appeal held that the employee was not employed by the agency.
44   [2006] EWCA Civ 220.
45   [2004] ICR 1437, at 1456.

worker and the hirer or 'end user', as this person has come to be called. In *Stephenson v Delphi Diesel Systems Ltd*[46] Elias J said:

> 'The significance of mutuality is that it determines whether there is a contract in existence at all. The significance of control is that it determines whether, if there is a contract in place, it can properly be classified as a contract of service, rather than some other kind of contract.'

4.34 In general, in view of these requirements, it is unlikely that a worker placed by an agency will become an employee of the hirer, although application of the tests already considered may lead to the conclusion that an employment relationship has arisen. In this context, as in the other considered, it is important to emphasise that each case depends on its own facts.

4.35 Recent examples of this general proposition are *Serco Ltd v Blair*[47] and *Costain Building & Civil Engineering Ltd v Smith and Chanton Group plc.*[48] In both cases, employees were supplied by an employment agency to a customer of the agency in circumstances such that the EAT held that no employment relationship arose. In the second case, an engineer was supplied by an agency to Costain. There was an agreement between the agency and Costain for the supply of services by the engineer and the agreement stated that he would be under the strict supervision of Costain. There was no agreement between him and Costain, however, and he did not receive any disciplinary or grievance documentation, nor did he expect to receive sick pay or holiday pay, and there was no clause providing for notice of termination. The EAT held that he did not become an employee of Costain and that therefore he could not complain of unfair dismissal.

4.36 This case may be contrasted with the decision in *Motorola Ltd v Davidson and Melville Craig Group Ltd*,[49] where the worker was held to have become an employee of the end user. The agency was Melville Craig, the end user Motorola. Mr Davidson was taken on; under the terms of his contract he was bound to comply with all reasonable instructions and requests made by Motorola. He was later suspended by Motorola's regional service manager, following a disciplinary hearing. The manager then decided to terminate his assignment with Motorola. He presented a complaint of unfair dismissal and the tribunal decided that he was an employee of Motorola. His appeal to the EAT was confined to the issue whether as between Motorola and Mr Davidson there existed a right of control sufficient to make Motorola his employer. The EAT held that there was. It said that in determining whether there is a sufficient degree of control to establish an employment relationship, there is no good reason to ignore practical aspects of control. In the present case, once he was at Motorola's site, Mr Davidson became largely subject to control as he would have been had he been a full-time employee.

---

46 [2003] ICR 471, at 474. See also *Hewlett Packard Ltd v Murphy* [2002] IRLR 4, in which the EAT held that there was no evidence to suggest a contractual nexus between the worker and the end user.

47 (Unreported) 31 August 1998, EAT.

48 [2000] ICR 215.

49 [2001] IRLR 4. See also *Stephenson v Delphi Diesel System Ltd* [2003] ICR 471.

4.37 In the present context, the significance of the Court of Appeal decision in *Dacas v Brook Street Bureau (UK) Ltd*[50] should not be overlooked. Although that case was confined to a consideration of the relationship between the worker and the agency, the observations of the Court of Appeal make it clear that in dealing with these kinds of cases tribunals should examine the facts very carefully to ascertain whether an employment relationship between the worker and the end user can be inferred. It is clear, at least from the judgment of Mummery LJ, that he regarded it as likely that there might have been an implied contract between Mrs Dacas and the authority, but that the case would have had to be remitted to the tribunal for it to determine the issue.

4.38 There seems to be a clear tendency to treat the decision of the Court of Appeal in *Dacas* as giving tribunals encouragement to decide that, in the kinds of cases considered in the preceding paragraphs, the agency worker has become the employee of the end user. In *Muscat v Cable & Wireless plc*,[51] its most recent decision on this issue, the Court of Appeal has said that the view of the majority in *Dacas* was correct. Smith LJ said that it was right for tribunals to follow the guidance given in that case, but pointed out that the guidance does not direct tribunals to reach any particular conclusion, only to consider the possibility that an implied contract may exist between the person performing the work and the end user.

Employees over retirement age

4.39 The provision governing the exclusion from the statutory right not to be unfairly dismissed of employees over retirement age is s 109 of the Employment Rights Act 1996. The exclusion does not apply to employees dismissed, or selected for dismissal for redundancy, for the various reasons provided for by the Trade Union and Labour Relations (Consolidation) Act 1992, s 154(2) and Sch A1, para 164 and ERA 1996, s 109(2), as amended.

4.40 In *Nothman v Barnet London Borough Council*,[52] the House of Lords held, by a majority, that s 109(1):

'... sets up only one barrier to be overcome by the class of employee whose conditions of employment specify a normal retiring age, and another and entirely different barrier to be overcome by the class of employee whose conditions of employment specify no retiring age.'

So it is necessary to determine first whether there is a normal retiring age; if there is, the second barrier will not apply; if, on the other hand, there is no normal retiring age, the second barrier will then operate.[53]

---

50   [2004] ICR 1437. See also *Royal National Lifeboat Institution v Bushaway* [2005] IRLR 674.

51   [2006] EWCA Civ 220.

52   [1979] ICR 111. See at 116, per Lord Salmon, at 118–119, per Lord Edmund-Davies, and at 121, per Lord Russell of Killowen.

53   For an example of this type of case, see *Patel v Nagesan* [1995] ICR 988. In that case, the Court of Appeal said that there was no evidence that there was a normal retiring age for an employee holding the employee's position, since all that the evidence showed was an employer trying to impose a contract with a term that the employee should retire at 60, which she resisted.

4.41   The House of Lords, however, did not specifically discuss what is meant by the phrase 'normal retiring age', although Lord Salmon indicated that it will be necessary to look at the conditions of employment to see if they specify a normal retiring age.[54] The House of Lords subsequently decided, in *Waite v Government Communications HQ*,[55] that it means the retiring age laid down in the terms and conditions upon which the employee was employed ('the contractual retiring age'). The presumption that the contractual retiring age is the normal retiring age may be displaced by evidence that there is in practice some higher age at which employees holding the position are regularly retired, and which they have reasonably come to regard as their normal retiring age. Lord Fraser of Tullybelton said:[56]

> 'The proper test is … not merely statistical. It is to ascertain what would be the reasonable expectation or understanding of the employees holding that position at the relevant time. The contractual retiring age will prima facie be displaced by evidence that it is regularly departed from in practice. The evidence may show that the contractual retirement age has been superseded by some definite higher age, and, if so, that will have become the normal retiring age. Or the evidence may show merely that the contractual retirement age has been abandoned and that employees retire at a variety of higher ages. In that case there will be no normal retiring age and the statutory alternatives of 65 for a man and 60 for a woman will apply.'

4.42   In the later case of *Brooks v British Telecommunications plc*[57] the Court of Appeal emphasised that the employment tribunal has to consider what, at the effective date of termination of the employee's employment, and on the basis of the facts known at that time, was the age at which employees of all age groups in the employee's position could reasonably regard as the normal age of retirement applicable to that group. It said that the employment tribunal was right to reject the inclusion into the test of the reasonable expectations of members of the group of what would happen to those approaching 60 at the dates of the dismissed employees' dismissals. The authorities in this area have subsequently been reviewed by the Court of Appeal in *Barclays Bank plc v O'Brien*.[58]

4.43   A further question is whether the normal retiring age may be below the contractual retiring age. In *Bratko v Beloit Walmsley Ltd*,[59] the EAT said that the employer cannot reduce the normal retiring age below the contractual age of retirement, without going through the normal steps necessary to change a contractual term. It said that the decision of the House of Lords in the *Waite* case contemplates only the possibility of a normal retiring age higher than the contractual retiring age, and not lower.

---

54   [1979] ICR 111, at 116.

55   [1983] ICR 653. See also *Swaine v Health and Safety Executive* [1986] IRLR 205.

56   [1983] ICR 653, at 662–663. This test was applied in *Hughes and Coy v DHSS* [1985] ICR 419, in the context of retirement policy in the civil service. See also *Whittle v Manpower Services Commission* [1987] IRLR 441; and *Mauldon v British Telecommunications plc* [1987] ICR 450.

57   [1992] ICR 414.

58   [1994] ICR 865.

59   [1996] ICR 76. For a recent decision on this issue, see *Royal and Sun Alliance Group plc v Payne* [2005] IRLR 848.

Short-term and casual employees

4.44   Section 108(1) of the Employment Rights Act 1996, as amended,[60] sets out the general rule that an employee must have been continuously employed[61] for one year before qualifying for the right not to be unfairly dismissed. This means that short-term, seasonal and casual workers are likely to be excluded, as are employees taken on as temporary replacements for employees absent on maternity leave (or for other reasons).

4.45   The one-year qualifying period does not apply, however, to employees dismissed, or selected for dismissal for redundancy, for various reasons provided for by the Trade Union and Labour Relations (Consolidation) Act 1992, s 154(2) and Sch A1, para 164 and ERA 1996, s 109(2), as amended.

Employees working outside the UK

4.46   Until 25 October 1999, the effect of s 196(3) of ERA 1996 was to exclude an employee who 'under his contract of employment ... ordinarily works outside Great Britain' from the right not to be unfairly dismissed. The whole of s 196 was repealed with effect from that date, however. The question which has perplexed the tribunals and courts ever since is: what is the correct test to apply to a case in which the employee claims the jurisdiction of the UK employment tribunals?

4.47   The decision of the Court of Appeal in *Lawson v Serco Ltd* was preceded by a number of decisions of the EAT,[62] but they should be read in the light of the House of Lords' decision in *Lawson* and *Crofts v Veta Ltd*.[63] The appeals in these two cases, together with the appeal in *Botham v Ministry of Defence*, were all heard in a consolidated appeal by the House of Lords towards the end of 2005; the opinions of the Lords of Appeal were given in late January 2006. *Lawson* and *Botham* involved 'expatriate employees' and *Crofts* involved 'peripatetic employees' (to use Lord Hoffman's terminology).

4.48   The case of *Lawson v Serco Ltd* involved an employee of British nationality, and domiciled in England, who worked for Serco on Ascension Island. When he was dismissed by the company he made a complaint of unfair dismissal to an employment tribunal in England. The case of *Crofts v Veta Ltd* involved international airline pilots. Five of them were based in London, six in

---

60   By the Unfair Dismissal and Statement of Reasons for Dismissal (Variation of Qualifying Period) Order 1999, SI 1999/1436. The Order affects employees whose effective date of termination falls on or after 1 June 1999.

61   Continuity of employment is discussed later in this chapter.

62   See, for example, *Bryant v Foreign and Commonwealth Office* EAT 0018/02, in which the EAT upheld the employment tribunal's decision that it had no jurisdiction to hear the unfair dismissal claim of an employee employed by the Foreign and Commonwealth Office at the British Embassy in Rome. See also *Financial Times Ltd v Bishop* EAT/0147/03; and *Jackson v Ghost Ltd* [2003] IRLR 824. In both these cases, different divisions of the EAT suggested that the employee must have a 'substantial connection' with this country. This test was rejected by the Court of Appeal in *Lawson v Serco Ltd.*

63   [2006] UKHL 3.

Hong Kong and one was based in North America but lived in London. Their contracts were governed by Hong Kong law and their salaries were paid in Hong Kong but reflected the cost of living of their base area. The third of the cases to be heard by the House of Lords in the consolidated appeals was *Botham v Ministry of Defence*, the facts of which were that the employee worked at various Ministry of Defence establishments in Germany, but was treated as resident in the UK for various purposes including taxation.

4.49   In the House of Lords, Lord Hoffman gave the sole judgment. He observed that interpretations of s 196 of ERA 1996 had looked to the position between the parties at the time of the making of the contract, but went on to say that the application of s 94(1) should now depend upon whether the employee was working in Great Britain at the time of the dismissal.[64] He went on to make a distinction between what he called 'peripatetic employees' and 'expatriate employees'. In the case of the former, he said that he could think of no sensible alternative to asking where they are based.[65] In view of the tribunal's findings of fact, he therefore concluded that the airline pilots in *Crofts v Veta Ltd* were based in London. In the case of expatriate employees, he said that the concept of a base provides no help. He went on to say that the circumstances would have to be unusual for an employee who works and is based abroad to come within the scope of UK employment legislation. He then identified the characteristics which such cases would have. He said that it would be unlikely that someone working abroad would be within the scope of s 94(1) unless he or she was working for an employer based in Great Britain. He gave two examples of situations in which s 94(1) may apply to expatriate employees: (1) employees posted abroad to work for a business conducted in Great Britain;[66] and (2) employees working 'in a political or social British enclave' abroad.[67] He added that there might be others, but that he had not been able to think of any examples. He concluded that 'they would have to have equally strong connections with Great Britain and British employment law'.[68] He therefore concluded that the employees expatriate employees in *Lawson v Serco Ltd* and *Botham v Ministry of Defence* were not excluded from the unfair dismissal provisions.

The meaning of 'dismissal'

4.50   It is fundamental to any complaint of unfair dismissal that the employee should have been dismissed. Unless the tribunal is satisfied that there has been a dismissal, the case will fail. Section 95 of ERA 1996 contains the definition of dismissal, which is exhaustive. Considerations of space preclude an examination in detail of this area. For a full examination of it, reference should be made to Upex *The Law of Termination of Employment*.[69] See also para 3.41

---

64   [2006] UKHL 3, at [27].
65   [2006] UKHL 3, at [31].
66   [2006] UKHL 3, at [38].
67   [2006] UKHL 3, at [39] and [40].
68   [2006] UKHL 3, at [40].
69   7th edn, Jordans, 2006.

where the right to claim constructive dismissal in the context of substantial changes to an employee's working conditions is discussed.

4.51　　The statutory definition of dismissal is as follows:[70]

'... an employee is dismissed by his employer if (and ... only if)—

(a)　　the contract under which he is employed is terminated by the employer (whether with or without notice),

(b)　　he is employed under a contract for a fixed term and that term expires without being renewed under the same contract, or

(c)　　the employee terminates the contract under which he is employed (with or without notice) in circumstances such that he is entitled to terminate it without notice by reason of the employer's conduct.'

Termination with or without notice

4.52　　As a general rule, termination occurs when either party informs the other clearly and unequivocally that the contract is to end, or the circumstances are such that it is clear that termination was intended or that it can be inferred that termination was intended. The words used to terminate the contract must be capable of being construed as words of termination. The principles are the same whether the termination consists of a dismissal by the employer or a resignation by the employee. Once a notice of termination has been given, it cannot be withdrawn by the party giving it without the agreement of the other party.[71]

4.53　　In the case of a dismissal by the employer, phrases such as 'I hereby give you notice of dismissal' are clear. Problems arise, however, where there is a row between the employer and the employee and words are used in the heat of the moment. If the words used by the employer are not ambiguous or could only be interpreted as amounting to words of dismissal, then the conclusion is clear. If, on the other hand, the words used are ambiguous and it is not clear whether they do amount to words of dismissal (for example, 'You're finished with me'), it is necessary to look at all the circumstances of the case, particularly the intention with which the words were spoken, and consider how a reasonable employee would, in all the circumstances, have understood them.[72]

4.54　　An example of the kind of problem which can occur is *Martin v Yeoman Aggregates Ltd*.[73] The employee obtained the wrong spare part for a broken-down car. There was an angry exchange between a director and the employee. He refused to collect the correct part and was dismissed by the director. A few minutes later, the director realised that he had acted in anger and that he was in breach of the correct disciplinary procedure. So he told the employee he was suspended without pay for 2 days. The employee treated what

---

70　　ERA 1996, s 95(1).

71　　*Riordan v War Office* [1961] 1 WLR 210; and *Harris and Russell Ltd v Slingsby* [1973] ICR 454.

72　　*BG Gale Ltd v Gilbert* [1978] ICR 1149; *Tanner v DT Kean Ltd* [1978] IRLR 110; *Sothern v Franks Charlesley & Co* [1981] IRLR 278; and *J & J Stern v Simpson* [1983] IRLR 52.

73　　[1983] ICR 314. See also *Norrie v Munro's Transport (Aberdeen) Ltd* (EAT 437/88).

had happened as instant dismissal. The EAT held that there had been no dismissal, saying that it was a matter of common sense, vital to industrial relations, that either an employer or an employee should be given an opportunity of recanting from words spoken in the heat of the moment.

4.55 The requirement in the case of dismissals with notice is that the notice must be explicit and unequivocal. This means, first, that a notice which enables an employer to terminate an employee's contract only if the employee does or does not perform a particular act specified in the notice which only the employee can choose whether or not to perform will not be an unequivocal notice to terminate the contract.[74] Secondly, for a notice to be valid it must specify the date of termination or contain material from which the date is ascertainable. It follows, therefore, that if the employer utters a warning that the employee will be made redundant at some unspecified date in the future or that, if the employee does not resign, he or she will have to be dismissed at some future date, and the employee acts on that warning, finds another job and resigns, that action will be treated as a resignation only; he or she will not be treated as having been dismissed.[75] In *Morton Sundour Fabrics Ltd v Shaw*,[76] for example, the employers told the employee that his employment would cease when the department in which he worked was closed down, but they did not specify when that would occur. The employee made arrangements to find another job, and duly gave notice. He later applied for a redundancy payment, but his claim was rejected. Widgery J said:

> 'As a matter of law an employer cannot dismiss his employee by saying "I intend to dispense with your services at some time in the coming months." In order to terminate the contract of employment the notice must either specify the date or contain material from which that date is positively ascertainable.'

Employee repudiation

4.56 In the case of an employee whose actions amount to a repudiation of his or her contract of employment, the employer's acceptance of that repudiation will be treated as a dismissal for the purposes of the statutory definition of dismissal.[77] If an employee's actions amount to a repudiation of his or her contractual obligations, the contract will not be terminated until the repudiation is accepted by the employer.

What amounts to a resignation?

4.57 The requirements in the case of a resignation by an employee are very similar to those for a dismissal. It is important for employers to know whether

---

74 See *Rai v Somerfield Stores Ltd* [2004] ICR 656. The employers notified the employee that if he did not return by a given date his employment would be regarded as terminated. The EAT held that the employers' letter and subsequent termination did not amount to a dismissal.

75 *Morton Sundour Fabrics Ltd v Shaw* (1967) 2 ITR 84; and *Haseltine Lake & Co v Dowler* [1981] ICR 222. See also *Pritchard-Rhodes Ltd v Boon* [1979] IRLR 19; and *International Computers Ltd v Kennedy* [1981] IRLR 28.

76 (1967) 2 ITR 84. Cf *Wadham Stringer Motor Group t/a Wadham Stringer v Avery* (EAT 405/91) (IDS Brief 498).

77 *London Transport Executive v Clarke* [1981] ICR 355; *Rasool v Hepworth Pipe Co Ltd* [1980] ICR 494; and *Pendlebury v Christian Schools North West Ltd* [1985] ICR 174.

an employee has resigned, since if they treat the employee as having resigned when that is not in fact the case, they may be held to have dismissed the employee. If the employee's resignation is prompted by a repudiatory act or breach of contract by the employer, that may be treated as a constructive dismissal by the employer (see **4.63**). A resignation does not require acceptance by the employer and, if the employee wishes to change his or her mind and withdraw the resignation, the withdrawal requires the employer's agreement. Failure to give it does not amount to a constructive dismissal.[78]

4.58   As with dismissal, similar questions have arisen as to what amounts to a resignation, particularly where there has been a row between the employer and the employee and it is not clear from the language used whether the employee was in fact intending to resign. If the employee's words are not ambiguous (for example, 'I am resigning') or, when construed, have a clear meaning, he or she will be treated as having resigned, irrespective of whether they were intended to bear that meaning, unless the words of resignation were uttered in the heat of the moment or as a result of pressure exerted by the employer. In *Sovereign House Security Services Ltd v Savage*[79] May LJ said:

> '[G]enerally speaking, where unambiguous words of resignation are used by an employee to the employer direct or by an intermediary, and are so understood by the employer, the proper conclusion of fact is that the employee has in truth resigned ... However, in some cases there may be something in the context of the exchange between the employer and the employee or, in the circumstances of the employee himself, to entitle the tribunal of fact to conclude that notwithstanding the appearances there was no real resignation despite what it might appear at first sight.'

4.59   If the words used are ambiguous, it becomes necessary to look at all the circumstances of the case, and, in particular, the intention with which the words were spoken, and to consider how a reasonable employer would, in all the circumstances, have understood the employee's words.[80] The approach is the same as that in used in relation to dismissals: see **4.53**.

4.60   A resignation will be treated as a dismissal if the employee is invited to resign and it is made clear that, unless he or she does so, he or she will be dismissed.[81] In *Martin v Glynwed Distribution Ltd*,[82] Sir John Donaldson MR said of these kinds of cases:

---

78   *Denham v United Glass Ltd* EAT/581/98.
79   [1989] IRLR 115, at 116. See also *Sothern v Franks Charlesly & Co* [1981] IRLR 278. In *Kwik-Fit (GB) Ltd v Lineham* [1992] ICR 183 the EAT gave examples of the sort of circumstances which may make it unreasonable for an employer to assume a resignation on the part of the employee.
80   *Sothern v Franks Charlesly & Co* [1981] IRLR 278; and *J & J Stern v Simpson* [1983] IRLR 52. See also *Tanner v DT Kean* [1978] IRLR 110; *Barclay v City of Glasgow District Council* [1983] IRLR 313 (employee said he wanted his books next day; words held not to be words of termination as he was mentally defective); and *Sovereign House Security Services Ltd v Savage* [1989] IRLR 115.
81   *East Sussex County Council v Walker* (1972) 7 ITR 280. See also *Jones v Mid Glamorgan County Council* [1997] ICR 815; and *Lassman v De Vere University Arms Hotel* [2003] ICR 44.
82   [1983] ICR 511, at 519. Cf *Caledonian Mining Co Ltd v Bassett* [1987] ICR 425.

'Whatever the respective actions of the employer and the employee at the time when the contract of employment is terminated, at the end of the day the question always remains the same, "Who really terminated the contract of employment?" If the answer is the employer, there was a dismissal within [s 95(2)(a) of ERA 1996] ... If the answer is the employee, a further question may then arise, namely, "Did he do so in circumstances such that he was entitled to do so without notice by reason of the employer's conduct?" '

4.61   In that case, the employee was caught driving the employer's vehicle under the influence of excess alcohol. He was threatened with a disciplinary inquiry and was told that it would be in his best interests to resign. He did so. The Court of Appeal held that there was not a dismissal.

Expiry of limited-term contract

4.62   Section 95(1)(b) of ERA 1996[83] treats the expiry of what is now called a 'limited-term' contract as a dismissal. A confirmation to an employee of the date of expiry of a fixed- (or limited-) term contract is a dismissal falling within s 95(1)(b), not s 95(1)(a). A distinction is to be drawn between telling an employee that his or her contract will end by effluxion of time and exercising a power to bring the contract to an end by notice.[84] If an employee is employed under a succession of fixed- or limited-term contracts, there can be a dismissal each time a contract expires. If, after the expiry of one contract, the employer offers the employee a new contract on less favourable terms than previously, there will be no breach of contract, since the employee's previous contract has expired and, at the time of the offer, he or she has no employment with the employer. That means also that the employee cannot claim to have been constructively dismissed.[85]

Constructive dismissal

4.63   Constructive dismissal is the term commonly applied to a resignation by the employee in circumstances such that he or she is entitled to terminate the contract without notice because of the employer's conduct, although it is not a term to be found in the legislation. In *Western Excavating (ECC) Ltd v Sharp*,[86] the Court of Appeal affirmed that the question whether an employee is entitled to terminate without notice should be answered according to the rules of the law of contract. Lord Denning MR said:[87]

'If the employer is guilty of conduct which is a significant breach going to the root of the contract of employment, or which shows that the employer no longer intends to be bound by one or more of the essential terms of contract, then the employee is

---

83   As amended by the Fixed-term Employees (Protection of Less Favourable Treatment) Regulations 2002, SI 2002/2034, reg 11 and Sch 2, para 3(1), (7) and (13). For the definition of 'limited-term contract', see ERA 1996, s 235(2A) and (2B), inserted by the same Regulations, reg 11 and Sch 2, Pt 1, para 3(1) and (18).

84   *London Underground Ltd v Fitzgerald* [1997] ICR 271.

85   *Pfaffinger v City of Liverpool Community College* [1997] ICR 142.

86   [1978] ICR 221.

87   [1978] ICR 221, at 226.

entitled to treat himself as discharged from any further performance ... [T]he conduct must ... be sufficiently serious to entitle him to leave at once ...'

4.64   The correct approach, therefore, is to ask whether the employer was in breach of contract, not whether the employer acted unreasonably. There may be circumstances, however, where the employer's conduct is so seriously unreasonable that it provides sufficient evidence that there has been a repudiatory breach of contract.[88]

4.65   It is important to note that the evaluation of whether the employer's conduct is repudiatory depends upon whether the conduct, viewed objectively, showed an intention no longer to be bound by the contract. It does not depend upon whether the employer intended the conduct to be repudiatory or could reasonably have believed that it would be accepted as such;[89] nor is the fact that the employer acted on a genuine, though mistaken, belief of fact, enough to prevent its conduct amounting to a repudiation.[90]

4.66   In cases of constructive dismissal, the employment tribunal must first consider whether the employer's action is in breach of its contractual obligations or is a repudiation of them.[91] That will involve ascertaining the express terms of the contract and considering whether any terms should be implied. If the tribunal finds that there was no contractual term covering the matter in question, then it follows that there can have been no breach of contract.[92]

4.67   Once the breach or repudiation has been established, it must be serious enough to entitle the employee to leave without notice.[93] This is a mixed question of fact and law.[94] In addition, the tribunal must be satisfied that the employee's resignation was caused by the breach and that the employee did not waive the right to terminate the contract and claim constructive dismissal.

---

88   *Brown v Merchant Ferries Ltd* [1998] IRLR 682.
89   *Lewis v Motorwold Garages Ltd* [1986] ICR 157. See also *Post Office v Roberts* [1980] IRLR 347; *Millbrook Furnishing Industries Ltd v McIntosh* [1981] IRLR 309; and *BBC v Beckett* [1983] IRLR 43.
90   *Bridgen v Lancashire County Council* [1987] IRLR 58; and *Brown v JBD Engineering Ltd* [1993] IRLR 568.
91   So, for example, if the employer makes a vague promise which is insufficient to amount to a binding contractual obligation, the failure to honour the promise will not amount to a repudiatory act entitling the employee to resign and claim constructive dismissal: see *Judge v Crown Leisure Ltd* [2005] EWCA Civ 571, [2005] IRLR 823.
92   *France v Westminster City Council* EAT 0214/02. The employer ended an agreement by which the employee could work at home in certain circumstances. The EAT upheld the tribunal's decision that the agreement between the employer and employee did not constitute a contractual term.
93   *Gillies v Richard Daniels & Co Ltd* [1979] IRLR 457; and *White v London Transport Executive* [1981] IRLR 261.
94   *Pedersen v Camden London Borough Council* [1981] ICR 674; *Millbrook Furnishing Industries Ltd v McIntosh* [1981] IRLR 309; and *Woods v WM Car Services (Peterborough) Ltd* [1982] ICR 693, CA.

4.68 A failure to pay an employee's wages will amount prima facie to a breach of contract,[95] although there may be circumstances in which a breach of contract will be held not to have occurred or that, although what happened amounted to a breach, the breach was not fundamental. In *RF Hill Ltd v Mooney*,[96] Browne-Wilkinson J said:[97]

> 'The obligation on the employer to pay remuneration is one of the fundamental terms of a contract ... [I]f an employer seeks to alter that contractual obligation in a fundamental way, such attempt is a breach going to the very root of the contract and is necessarily repudiation.'

4.69 These issues were considered by the Court of Appeal in *Cantor Fitzgerald International v Callaghan*.[98] What happened there was that the employer refused to honour an agreement relating to the employees' salary packages. The employees resigned in consequence. The issue was whether the failure to honour the agreement was a significant breach going to the root of the contract (although clearly it was a breach). Judge LJ, with whom Nourse and Tuckey LJJ agreed, analysed the issues arising from a failure to honour a salary package and said:[99]

> '[I]t is difficult to exaggerate the crucial importance of pay in any contract of employment ... In my judgment the question whether non-payment of agreed wages, or interference by an employer with an agreed salary package, is or is not fundamental to the continued existence of the contract depends on the critical distinction to be drawn between an employer's failure to pay, or delay in paying, agreed remuneration and his deliberate refusal to do so. Where the failure or delay constitutes a breach of contract, depending on the circumstances, this may represent no more than a temporary fault in the employer's technology, an accounting error or simple mistake, or illness, or accident, or unexpected events ... On the other hand, if the failure or delay in payment were repeated and persistent, perhaps also unexplained, the court might be driven to conclude that the breach or breaches were indeed repudiatory. Where, however, an employer unilaterally reduces his employee's pay, or diminishes the value of his salary package, the entire foundation of the contract of employment is undermined. Therefore, an emphatic denial by the employer of his obligation to pay the agreed salary or wage, or a determined resolution not to comply with his contractual obligations in relation to pay and remuneration, will normally be regarded as repudiatory.'

He concluded that the employer's refusal to pay was deliberate and determined and constituted a repudiatory breach. Issues may also arise relating to the payment of bonuses and whether a refusal to pay a bonus amounts to a breach of contract.[100]

---

95 But cf *Adams v Charles Zub Associates Ltd* [1978] IRLR 551. See also *Reid v Camphill Engravers* [1990] ICR 435.

96 [1981] IRLR 258.

97 [1981] IRLR 258, at 260.

98 [1999] ICR 639.

99 [1999] ICR 639, at 648–649.

100 See, for example, *Clark v Nomura International plc* [2000] IRLR 766; and *Manor House Healthcare v Hayes and Skinner* (EAT 1196/99) (2000) (IDS Brief B674/6).

4.70   Other examples of a breach of an express term are a refusal of holiday entitlement,[101] the withdrawal of an employee's company car[102] and unilateral alterations in the employee's pay, status, place of work or hours, even on a temporary basis.[103] In a case involving alterations in the employee's place of work, the tribunal will need to consider whether the employee was subject to an express or implied mobility obligation: see **4.74**.

4.71   An employer whose conduct is alleged to have been repudiatory may seek to rely on the terms of a flexibility clause to rebut that allegation. Thus, if an employer seeks to impose a unilateral change on the employee, it may argue that the change was covered by the terms of an express flexibility clause in the employee's contract. In *Land Securities Trillium Ltd v Thornley*[104] the facts were that the employers imposed a new job description on the employee which fundamentally changed her duties. The employers sought to rely on the terms of a flexibility clause and argued that its terms gave them a wide discretion to require her to carry out a wide range of duties. The employment tribunal decided that the terms of the clause did not entitle the employers to make the substantial changes which they had sought to make and they concluded that she had been constructively dismissed. The EAT upheld their decision.

4.72   Examples of terms *implied* into employees' contracts are terms obliging the employer to maintain the relationship of trust between employer and employee, or not to treat the employees arbitrarily, capriciously or inequitably, or not to behave intolerably and not in accordance with good industrial practice.[105] An example of the application of the duty of trust and confidence is to be found in *TSB Bank plc v Harris*,[106] in which the EAT upheld the tribunal's decision that the employers were in fundamental breach of the implied term of trust and confidence by revealing in a reference to a prospective employer complaints against the employee of which she was unaware, thereby blocking her progress in the financial services sector. In *Euro-Die (UK) Ltd v Skidmore*,[107] the EAT held that an employer's failure to assure an employee that his continuity of employment would be protected following a transfer of the business amounted to a fundamental breach of the term of trust and confidence. The consequence was that the employee was treated as constructively dismissed and the transferee was liable for the unfair dismissal.

---

101   *Lytlarch Ltd v Reid* [1991] ICR 216.

102   *Triton Oliver (Special Products) Ltd v Bromage* (EAT 709/91) (IDS Brief 511).

103   See, for example, *Wadham Stringer Commercials (London) Ltd and Wadham Stringer Vehicles Ltd v Brown* [1983] IRLR 46; *Lytlarch Ltd v Reid* [1991] ICR 216; and *Greenaway Harrison Ltd v Wiles* [1994] IRLR 380. *Millbrook Furnishing Industries Ltd v McIntosh* [1981] IRLR 309 and *McNeil v Charles Crimin (Electrical Contractors) Ltd* [1984] IRLR 179 both involved temporary alterations.

104   [2005] IRLR 765.

105   *Woods v WM Car Services (Peterborough) Ltd* [1981] ICR 666 and [1982] ICR 693, CA; *Courtaulds Northern Textiles Ltd v Andrew* [1979] IRLR 84; *Wigan Borough Council v Davies* [1979] ICR 411; and *White v London Transport Executive* [1981] IRLR 261. See also *Bliss v South East Thames Regional Health Authority* [1987] ICR 700.

106   [2000] IRLR 157.

107   EAT 1158/98. Cf *Sita (GB) Ltd v Burton* [1998] ICR 17.

4.73   In *Horkaluk v Cantor Fitzgerald International*[108] the High Court held that an employee who was subjected to a campaign of bullying and intimidation, accompanied by foul and abusive language, had been constructively dismissed. The judgment of Newman J contains a useful and helpful discussion of the recent cases in which the implied term of trust and confidence has been developed.[109]

4.74   The question of mobility arose in *Courtaulds Northern Spinning Ltd v Sibson*.[110] The facts were that the employee worked as a lorry driver at the same depot from the start of his employment in 1973. His contract had no express mobility term. All the drivers belonged to the same union, but in 1985 he resigned from the union. To avert strike action, the employer required him to rejoin the union or transfer to another depot. He resigned and claimed that he had been constructively dismissed. The Court of Appeal held that a term should to be implied into the contract that the employer could, for any reason, direct the employee to work at any place within reasonable daily reach of the employee's home. The employers had therefore acted within their contractual rights and the employee had not been constructively dismissed. The court accepted that the employee could reasonably have demanded that the mobility requirement should be reasonable daily travelling distance.[111]

4.75   The EAT has applied the implied term not to behave in a manner calculated or likely to destroy or seriously damage the relationship of trust and confidence between employer and employee to the employer's conduct in the exercise of powers conferred by an express term. *United Bank Ltd v Akhtar*[112] concerned the exercise of a mobility clause by employers and its effects upon the employee's right to resign and claim constructive dismissal. The terms of the mobility clause permitted the employer to require an employee to be transferred temporarily or permanently to any place of business of the bank in the UK. The employee, a junior clerk in the Leeds branch of the bank, was told on 2 June 1987 that he was to be transferred to the Birmingham branch the following Monday, 8 June. He did not receive written confirmation of this until 5 June. In the meantime, he wrote to his manager asking for a postponement of the transfer for 3 months because of personal difficulties relating to his wife's ill-health and the impending sale of his house. His request was refused. On 8 June he wrote another letter asking for 24 days' leave which was due to him in order to sort out his affairs and start work in Birmingham on 10 July. From 5 June his pay was stopped. He complained that he had been constructively dismissed. The EAT upheld the employment tribunal's decision that he had. It

---

108   [2003] EWHC 1918, [2004] ICR 697.

109   See [2004] ICR 697, at 706–709.

110   [1988] ICR 451. See also *Aparau v Iceland Frozen Foods plc* [1996] IRLR 119, where the EAT said that, although there must be some term as to the employee's place of employment in an employment contract, it is not necessary to imply a mobility term. It went on to say that, if that view was wrong, and some term as to mobility fell to be implied, there was no basis for implying a term entitling the employer to transfer the employee against his or her will.

111   [1988] ICR 451, at 462.

112   [1989] IRLR 507. Cf *White v Reflecting Roadstuds Ltd* [1991] ICR 733, in which *United Bank v Akjhtar* was distinguished: see at 741. See also *Prestwick Circuits Ltd v McAndrew* [1990] IRLR 191.

said that the tribunal was entitled to imply into the employee's contract a term that reasonable notice should be given in the exercise of the bank's powers to require mobility of its employees and that the employers' discretion under the mobility clause was one which they were bound to exercise in such a way as not to make it impossible for him to comply with his contractual obligation to move. It also upheld the tribunal's decision that the employers' conduct in relation to the employee's transfer amounted to a fundamental breach of the implied term that employers must not, without reasonable and proper cause, behave in a manner calculated or likely to destroy or seriously damage the relationship of trust and confidence between employer and employee.

4.76 A series of actions on the part of the employer may cumulatively amount to a breach of the implied contractual obligation of mutual trust and confidence, although each individual action may not. The course of conduct relied upon may include a breach of an express term of the contract committed by the employer but waived by the employee at the time. The final act, or 'last straw' as it is often called, is the one which precipitates the employee's resignation. This type of situation was considered by the Court of Appeal in *Lewis v Motorworld Garages Ltd*,[113] a case where the employers demoted the employee in breach of his contract and adversely altered his pay structure. He affirmed the contract, but over a period of 8 months the employer persistently criticised him and threatened him with dismissal if he did not improve. He eventually resigned. The employment tribunal decided that the demotion and change in pay structure became spent when the employee affirmed the contract and that the subsequent criticisms and threats did not amount to a repudiation. The Court of Appeal, however, held that the demotion and alteration could be relied upon as part of the course of conduct which cumulatively amounted to a repudiatory breach and that the employment tribunal should have considered the continuing effect of the demotion and change in pay structure.

4.77 In the later case of *Logan v Commissioners of Customs and Excise*,[114] the Court of Appeal said that in cases such as this, what is required is a view of the totality of the whole course of conduct in order to see whether the actions of the employer constitute together a breach of the implied duty of trust and confidence.

4.78 Once the employment tribunal has decided that there has been a breach or repudiation and that it was sufficiently serious to entitle the employee to end the contract immediately, it must then be satisfied that the employee's departure was caused by the breach.[115] In this context questions may arise as to whether

---

113 [1986] ICR 157. See also Glidewell LJ's remarks at 169–170.

114 [2003] EWCA Civ 1068, [2004] IRLR 63. See Ward LJ at [33]. See also *Omilaju v Waltham Forest London Borough Council* [2004] EWCA Civ 1493, [2005] ICR 481, in which the Court of Appeal considered the nature and quality of the final straw.

115 *British Leyland UK Ltd v McQuilken* [1978] IRLR 245; and *Walker v Josiah Wedgwood & Sons Ltd* [1978] ICR 744. See also *Jones v F Sirl & Son (Furnishers) Ltd* [1997] IRLR 493.

the employee need give a reason for leaving and whether that reason need be the real reason for his or her departure. In *Weathersfield Ltd v Sargent*[116] Pill LJ said:[117]

'Acceptance of a repudiation of a contract of employment will usually take the form of the employee leaving and saying why he is leaving but it is not necessary in law for the reason to be given at the time of leaving. The fact-finding tribunal is entitled to reach its own conclusion, based on the "acts and conduct of the party" as to the true reason ... [Employment] tribunals will ... be astute to discover the true reason for the employee leaving and reject those claims in which alleged conduct by the employer is no more than a pretext or cover for leaving on other grounds.'

4.79   The tribunal must be satisfied also that he or she has not waived the right to terminate by staying on too long after the conduct in question or by subsequently accepting an alternative job with the employer.[118] Otherwise he or she may be taken to have elected to affirm the contract.[119] In the event of a subsequent resignation, it will not be possible to claim constructive dismissal. In *WE Cox Toner (International) Ltd v Crook*[120] Browne-Wilkinson J said:[121]

'Mere delay by itself (unaccompanied by any express or implied affirmation of the contract) does not constitute affirmation of the contract; but if it is prolonged it may be evidence of an implied affirmation. Affirmation of the contract can be implied. Thus, if the innocent party calls on the guilty party for further performance of the contract, he will normally be taken to have affirmed the contract since his conduct is only consistent with the continued existence of contractual obligation ... However, if the innocent party further performs the contract to a limited extent but at the same time makes it clear that he is reserving his right to accept the repudiation ... such further performance does not prejudice his rights subsequently to accept the repudiation.'

4.80   The employee must also accept a repudiation unequivocally.[122] An example of a failure to accept a repudiation unequivocally is *Harrison v Norwest Holst Group Administration Ltd*.[123] The employers wrote to the employee stating that he would lose his directorship in 2 weeks' time. The employee responded with a letter headed 'Without Prejudice'. The employers

---

116   [1999] ICR 425. Cf *Holland v Glendale Ltd* [1998] ICR 493.

117   [1999] ICR 425, at 432.

118   An example of the latter situation is *Bunning v GT Bunning and Sons Ltd* [2005] EWCA Civ 983.

119   *Western Excavating (ECC) Ltd v Sharp* [1978] ICR 221, at 226, per Lord Denning MR. See also *Bashir v Brillo Manufacturing Co Ltd* [1979] IRLR 295; and *WE Cox Toner (International) Ltd v Crook* [1981] ICR 823; *Wilton v Cornwall & Isles of Scilly Health Authority* (19 May 1993, CA) (IDS Brief 499); *Abbey National plc v Robinson* (EAT 743/99) (IDS Brief 680); and *El-Hoshi v Pizza Express Restaurants Ltd* EAT 0857/03 (IDS brief 768).

120   [1981] ICR 823.

121   [1981] ICR 823, at 828–829.

122   In *Rai v Somerfield Stores Ltd* [2004] ICR 656 the EAT said that the presentation of a complaint to a tribunal is not communication to the employers of the employee's acceptance of repudiatory conduct by them.

123   [1985] ICR 668. See also *Lewis v Motorworld Garages Ltd* [1986] ICR 157; *Shook v London Borough of Ealing* [1986] ICR 314; and *Day v Pickles Farms* [1999] IRLR 217. In the last case, the EAT said that there must be 'unequivocal communication' of the acceptance of the repudiation.

later withdrew their threat to deprive him of his directorship, but the employee left anyway. The Court of Appeal treated the original threat as an anticipatory breach but said that the employee's letter was not sufficiently unequivocal to amount to an acceptance of the repudiation. Because the repudiation had not been accepted, the contract continued to run and, during the continued currency of the contract, it was open to the employers to withdraw their threat of breach.

Dismissals for reasons connected with the transfer

4.81 Dismissals on the transfer of an undertaking are now governed by reg 7 of TUPE 2006.[124] Regulation 7(1) provides that an employee dismissed either before or after a relevant transfer will be treated as automatically unfairly dismissed, if the 'sole or principal reason' for the dismissal is the transfer itself or a reason connected with it that is not an economic, technical or organisational reason entailing changes in the workforce. The regulation applies to employees both of the transferor and the transferee. Regulation 7(2) disapplies reg 7(1) where there is an 'economic, technical or organisational reason entailing changes in the workforce or either the transferor or transferee either before or after a relevant transfer' and that is the reason or principal reason for dismissing the employee. This provision and the way it operates are considered at **4.87**.

4.82 It is clear from the wording of the regulation and from the decisions of the EAT that the correct approach is to consider, first, whether reg 7(1) applies so as to make the dismissals automatically unfair; if it does not, then the tribunal should consider whether reg 7(2) applies. It should be noted, however, that liability under reg 7 will only pass to the transferee if the employee was employed in the transferred undertaking immediately before the transfer within the meaning of reg 4(3),[125] as interpreted by the House of Lords in the *Litster* case.[126] This matter, together with the relevant cases, has been fully considered in **chapter 3**: see **3.24**.

4.83 One issue which has now been resolved by the House of Lords, in the consolidated appeals in *Wilson v St Helens Borough Council* and *Meade and Baxendale v British Fuels Ltd*,[127] concerned the effect of a dismissal brought about by the transfer of an undertaking in relation to employees re-engaged under different terms and condition by the transferee. The decision has already been discussed in relation to the interpretation of Art 4 of the Directive and its effect on reg 7: see **4.9**. In the *Wilson* case, the dismissal fell within what is now reg 7(2), the dismissals involved being dismissals for an economic or technical reason; in the *Meade and Baxendale* case, reg 7(1) applied, the dismissals being

---

124 Formerly reg 8 of TUPE 1981. The wording of reg 8(1) was different, in that it contained no reference to the reason not being an economic, technical or organisation reason entailing changes in the workforce. The change of wording in the new reg 7(1) does not appear to be a change of substance.

125 Formerly reg 5(3) of TUPE 1981.

126 *Litster v Forth Dry Dock & Engineering Co Ltd (in receivership)* [1989] ICR 341.

127 [1998] ICR 1141.

for a reason connected with the transfer and thus within what is now reg 7(1). The Court of Appeal held[128] that what is now reg 7(1) fell to be construed in the light of Art 4(1) of the Acquired Rights Directive and that, so construed, it made a dismissal covered by its terms void and ineffective rather than merely automatically unfair. In the House of Lords, Lord Slynn of Hadley gave the main speech, which is considered in more detail at **4.9**. It centred round the issue whether a dismissal of an employee brought about by a transfer of an undertaking is or is not a nullity. He took the view that the provisions of reg 7(1) and (2) (as they now are) point to a dismissal being effective and not a nullity and do not create an automatic obligation on the part of the transferee to continue to employ employees who have been dismissed by the transferor. He then went on to consider whether TUPE complies with the Directive. Having considered the relevant case-law of the ECJ,[129] he concluded that the Directive does not create a Community law right to continue in employment which does not exist in national law and that TUPE gives effect to and is consistent with the Directive. The decision restores the law to the position that had been understood to obtain before the decision of the Court of Appeal in 1997. Thus, if an employee is dismissed by the transferor and re-engaged by the transferee, the latter will assume any liability for dismissals incurred by the transferor. The employee will not be able to insist on the observance by the transferee of his or her previous terms or conditions and will be bound by the terms and conditions agreed with the transferee. The dismissal will thus be unfair by virtue of reg 7(1), but not ineffective; liability for it will pass to the transferee by virtue of reg 4(2).

4.84   Regulation 7(1) apples, as has been seen, where the 'sole or principal reason' for the dismissal is '(a) the transfer itself; or (b) a reason connected with the transfer itself that is not an economic, technical or organisational reason entailing changes in the workforce'. In *Norris v Brown and Root Ealing Technical Services Ltd*,[130] the EAT upheld the tribunal's decision that a dismissal which took place more than 2 years after the transfer and was a consequence of cash-flow difficulties caused by under-funding was not for a reason connected with the transfer. The EAT made it clear that the question of what is the reason or principal reason for a dismissal is a question of fact and that the EAT cannot interfere 'unless the findings of fact by the Employment Tribunal were not a permissible option on the basis of the evidence before it'.[131] The EAT also held that the tribunal was justified in relying on the words of Lord Slynn of Hadley in *Wilson v St Helens Borough Council*:[132]

> 'However, it seems that there must, or at least may, come a time when the link with the transfer is broken or can be treated as no longer effective.'

---

128   [1998] ICR 387.
129   *Wendelboe v LJ Music ApS* [1985] ECR 457; *Foreningen af Arbejdsledere I Danmark v A/S Danmols Inventar* [1985] ECR 2639; *P Bork International A/S v Foreningen af Arbejdsledere I Danmark* [1988] ECR 3057; and *Foreningen af Arbejdsledere I Danmark v Daddy's Dance Hall A/S* [1988] ECR 739. See **4.6**.
130   EAT/386/00.
131   EAT/386/00, at para 30.
132   [1998] ICR 1141, at 1165D.

The quotation was preceded by the words: 'The variation may still be due to the transfer and for no other reason even if it comes later,' though these do not appear to have been quoted by the tribunal or the EAT. The EAT went on to refer to decisions of the Court of Appeal in *Whitehouse v Charles A Blatchford & Sons Ltd*[133] and of the EAT in *Ralton v Havering College of Further & Higher Education,*[134] to the effect that there is no infringement of an employee's rights under reg 7(1) if the transfer is 'the occasion' for the dismissal rather than the reason for it, although it did point out that those cases were on a different point (variation rather than dismissal). (Relevant cases dealing with the link between a variation and a transfer are considered at **4.100ff.**)

4.85   It should be noted that reg 7 only applies for the purposes of the provisions in ERA 1996 dealing with unfair dismissal. It has no effect on the employee's right to claim a redundancy payment. In *Gorictree Ltd v Jenkinson,*[135] for example, the employee complained of unfair dismissal and claimed a redundancy payment. The tribunal dismissed his unfair dismissal claim, taking the view that it fell within reg 7(2) but was fair; it upheld his redundancy payment claim. In upholding the tribunal's decision, the EAT said that, although a dismissal for redundancy may fall within reg 7(2), since that is specifically stated to apply for the purposes of Part X of ERA 1996, an employee's entitlement to a redundancy payment is unaffected by the provisions of TUPE.

4.86   In cases where the transferor gives notice of dismissal but the notice expires after the transfer, any liability for the dismissal will transfer to the transferee, but the reason for the notice of termination will be that of the transferor and the date for determining the reason is the date when notice was given. So, for example, in *BSG Property Services v Tuck,*[136] the facts were that the transferor (which did not consider that a TUPE transfer was involved) gave the employees notice on 12 February 1993, the notice to expire on 15 May. On 14 May, it concluded a contract with BSG for the provision of housing maintenance services; the work previously done by the transferor's employees was to be done by self-employed members of BSG's workforce. The EAT upheld the tribunal's decision that there was a transfer within TUPE. It also held that where an employee is dismissed by the transferor with notice which expires after the date of transfer, it is the transferor who dismisses and it is the transferor's reason for the dismissal notice which is relevant, even though liability in connection with the notice to terminate is transferred to the transferee. Accordingly, the notice of termination given by the transferor for the reason of the transferor is deemed to have been a notice given by the transferee for that reason. Thus the transferee was responsible for what the transferor had done. The EAT said that the tribunal had erred in finding that the reason for the dismissal fell within reg 7(2) because BSG could have had a potentially fair reason for dismissal. In the EAT's view, BSG did not actually dismiss the employees for any reason of its own. In cases such as this, therefore, it is very likely that the dismissal will be made unfair by reg 7(1). It has to be

---

133   [2000] ICR 542. See, in particular, the observations of Buxton LJ at 555D.
134   [2001] IRLR 738. See at 750, para 83(e).
135   [1985] ICR 51.
136   [1996] IRLR 134.

said that a significant factor in the outcome of the case was that the transferor (a local authority) had taken the view that TUPE did not apply, whereas in fact it was held to apply.

Dismissals for economic, technical or organisational reasons

4.87   Regulation 7(2) applies where there is an 'economic, technical or organisational reason entailing changes in the workforce or either the transferor or transferee either before or after a relevant transfer' and that is the reason or principal reason for dismissing the employee. In that case, reg 7(1) will be disapplied[137] and the reason will be treated as being either redundancy or 'some other substantial reason' within s 98(1)(b) of ERA 1996.[138] It should be noted that both reg 7(1) and (2) use the phrase 'reason connected with the transfer'. The effect of this wording is that reg 7 can only come into play if the reason for the dismissal is one connected with the transfer. If it is not, then reg 7 will not apply at all.

4.88   Two preliminary points should be noted here. First, the burden of establishing that the reason falls within reg 7(2) is on the employer.[139] This means that, if the employer wishes to argue that reg 7(1) should be disapplied by reg 7(3)(a), it must establish that the reason was a reason connected with the transfer but was an economic, technical or organisational reason entailing changes in the workforce of the transferor or transferee. If the employer fails to discharge that burden, then reg 7(1) will apply and the dismissal will be held to be automatically unfair. Secondly, once the reason has been established as being within reg 7(2), the fairness of the decision to dismiss under ERA 1996, s 98(4) must then be considered by the tribunal. A failure to do so will amount to an error of law.[140]

4.89   The next matter to be considered is the relationship between reg 7(1) and (2).[141] In the discussion of the case-law which follows, it should be borne in mind that the old reg 8(2) was differently worded from the new reg 7(2), inasmuch as reg 7(2) now contains the phrase 'a reason connected with the transfer', which was not to be found in the old reg 8(2). The difference between the old reg 8(1) and (2) was considered by the Court of Appeal in *Warner v Adnet Ltd*.[142] In that case, the argument on behalf of the employee was that the two paragraphs are mutually exclusive and that, if the tribunal concludes that the dismissal was for a reason falling within reg 8(1), it was precluded from considering the case under reg 8(2). The Court of Appeal rejected that argument. Mummery LJ, with whom the other members of the court agreed,

---

137   Regulation 7(3)(a).
138   Regulation 7(3)(b). It should be noted that this provision corrects an omission in reg 8(2) of TUPE 1981 which said that a dismissal for an organisational, technical or organisational reason was deemed to be 'some other substantial reason' within the meaning of s 98(1)(b) of ERA 1996. It said nothing about redundancy. This new provision repairs that omission.
139   See *Litster v Forth Dry Dock & Engineering Co Ltd (in receivership)* [1989] ICR 341, at 353–354, per Lord Templeman; and *Gateway Hotels Ltd v Stewart* [1988] IRLR 287.
140   *McGrath v Rank Leisure Ltd* [1985] ICR 527.
141   Regulation 8(1) and (2) of TUPE 1981.
142   [1998] ICR 1056.

said that the Regulations must be read as a whole and that the drafting of reg 8(2) was such that it expressly contemplated circumstances in which reg 8(1) would be disapplied and where a view formed by a tribunal under reg 8(1) was not final or conclusive. He said:[143]

> 'There would be no point in including the concept of an economic, technical or organisational reason in the Directive or in the 1981 Regulations, if a finding that a dismissal was by reason of a transfer was determinative of an employee's claim for unfair dismissal. If the transfer was not the reason, there is no need to inquire further. If it is the reason, regulation 8(2) *may* apply. If it does, regulation 8(1) is disapplied and the dismissal is not *automatically* unfair.'

Henry LJ said:[144]

> 'On the construction point, I would simply say this. A purposive construction, consistent with Article 4 of the Directive, clearly requires the disapplication of paragraph 8(1) in appropriate cases. It is implicit from Regulation 8(2)(a) that the principal reason for a dismissal may be both the transfer and an ETO reason. Any construction that suggests it must be one or the other would contradict the second sentence of Article 4 of the Directive, as it would make an 8(1) finding that the principal reason of the transfer was dispositive. If that were the case, there would be no point in including the concept of the economic, technical or organisational reason within the 1981 ... Regulations ...'

4.90   This approach was followed by another division of the Court of Appeal in the later case of *Whitehouse v Charles A Blatchford & Sons Ltd*.[145] In that case, the facts were that the employee was employed as a technician at a hospital disablement centre. In 1996, the company employing him lost the contract to provide services at the centre to the respondents. The employers took on all the technicians, but, since a condition of obtaining the contract was that the number of technicians working at the centre had to be reduced by one, after making detailed assessments of all the technicians they selected the applicant for dismissal. He complained of unfair dismissal. The tribunal found that the reason was an economic, technical or organisational reason within what is reg 8(2) and that, as the selection process had been comprehensively and fairly carried out, the dismissal was not unfair. The Court of Appeal upheld the tribunal's decision. It said that, although the transfer of the undertaking was the occasion for the reduction in the hospital's requirements for the services of technicians, the transfer was not the cause of or the reason for that reduction, and it was open to the tribunal to hold that the transfer was not the reason for the dismissal. Accordingly, reg 8(1) did not apply. Since also the process of selection had been properly and fairly carried out, he had not been unfairly dismissed. Buxton LJ said of Art 4 and the then reg 8:[146]

> '[A]rticle 4 says no more than two things. First of all, a transfer cannot in itself justify a dismissal; second, in a situation involving a transfer, it is still open for dismissals to take place that would otherwise be justified according to the law of the country to which it applies. The words "dismissals ... for economic, technical or organisational reasons entailing changes in the work force" are, in my judgement,

---

143 [1998] ICR 1056, at 1064.
144 [1998] ICR 1056, at 1067.
145 [2000] ICR 542.
146 [2000] ICR 542, at 552–553.

merely a very broad description of the whole range of circumstances that might, in the law of any one of the Member States, give rise to a justification for dismissal. And it goes no further than that ...

Article 4 then has to be translated into the terms and concepts of domestic law. That is done in Regulation 8. Regulation 8(1) says, as we have seen, that where the reason for dismissal is only the transfer, such a dismissal shall be unfair. That provision, making such a dismissal automatically unfair and therefore the subject of compensation, does in fact go further than the requirements of Article 4. But of course, ... that does not in any way undermine Regulation 8(1). That is because this extension, as it seems to me, of the basic protection that might be drawn from Article 4 itself, is well in line with the objectives and *vires* of the Directive. It is however, in my judgment, a separate provision of the rules of English domestic law not imposed directly by the Directive, but still binding of course on this court as a piece of domestic legislation.

Regulation 8 goes on to say by regulation 8(2) that in any other case, other than that addressed by 8(1), an employer can only assert his normal rights, of course against the background that the transfer does not interrupt the continuity of his employment.'

4.91 This decision was applied by the EAT in *Kerry Foods Ltd v Creber*.[147] The outcome was different, however, inasmuch as the EAT concluded that the reason for the dismissal was the transfer and that the dismissal was, therefore, automatically unfair.

4.92 As was mentioned at the beginning of this discussion, the cases cited above were dealing with the provisions of reg 8(1) and (2) of TUPE 1981. The difference between those two provisions and the new provisions in reg 7(1) and (2) is that reg 8(2) did not use the phrase 'a reason connected with the transfer'. That would account for the problems of interpretation discussed in those cases. The new reg 7 has clearly been drafted with these problems in mind. Regulation 7(1) now states that it is to apply where the reason for the dismissal is a reason connected with the transfer that is *not* an economic, technical or organisational reason; reg 7(2) states that it applies where the sole or principal reason for the dismissal *is* a reason connected with the transfer 'that is an economic, technical or organisational reason ...'.

4.93 The words 'economic, technical or organisational' in what is now reg 7(2) have been considered in a number of cases. In *Gorictree Ltd v Jenkinson*[148] the EAT said that an 'economic' reason includes redundancy. Subsequently, in *Wheeler v Patel*,[149] it said that the word 'economic' is to be construed ejusdem generis with the other two adjectives and is to be given a limited meaning relating to the conduct of the business. It said that it does not include broad economic reasons for a sale, such as the desire to obtain an enhanced price or a desire to achieve a sale. The facts of the case were that the

---

147 [2000] ICR 556.
148 [1985] ICR 51.
149 [1987] ICR 631. It did not follow the previous decision in *Anderson v Dalkeith Engineering Ltd* [1985] ICR 66, where the EAT said that the words are not mutually exclusive but are alternative or cumulative reasons for dismissal and the employment tribunal is not obliged to specify which of the three reasons it is relying on. See also *Trafford v Sharpe & Fisher (Building Supplies) Ltd* [1994] IRLR 325.

applicant was employed as a sales assistant by Mr Golding. Mr Golding sold his business to Mr Patel on 20 January 1986; before completion of the sale, he dismissed the applicant with effect from 17 January. She claimed unfair dismissal against Mr Patel as transferee and Mr Golding as transferor. The tribunal concluded that she was not employed by Mr Golding immediately before the transfer and that therefore Mr Patel could not be liable. It went on to conclude that, in the light of evidence to suggest that the reason for the dismissal might have been the vendor's desire to comply with the prospective purchaser's wishes, reg 8(2) of TUPE 1981 applied. There seems to have been virtually no evidence before the tribunal in *Wheeler* as to the reasons for the dismissal of the applicant beyond the wishes of Mr Patel either to take none or to take only some of Mr Golding's employees. The EAT, presided over by Scott J (as he then was), upheld the tribunal's first conclusion that there had not been a relevant transfer. As to the second conclusion, it said:[150]

> 'There is no doubt that the transfer of the business from Mr Golding to Mr Patel was the reason or was connected with the reason for the employee's dismissal. So the case prima facie falls within Reg. 8(1) ... The question for decision then is whether this case falls within Reg. 8(2). If it does not, then by reason of para. (1) the dismissal must be held to be unfair. If the case does come within paragraph (2), para. (1) does not apply, and the further question will then arise whether the circumstances surrounding the dismissal render it ... an unfair dismissal.'

4.94   The EAT went on to hold that the word 'economic' within the phrase 'economic, technical or organisational reason' should be given a restricted meaning such that it did not apply merely because a reduction of the workforce would secure a sale of or an enhanced price for the business. It said:[151]

> 'The economic reasons apt to bring a case within paragraph (2) must, in our view, be reasons which relate to the conduct of the business. If the economic reason were no more than a desire to obtain an enhanced price, or no more than a desire to achieve a sale, it would not be a reason which related to the conduct of the business. It would not in our judgment, be an "economic" reason for the purposes of para. (2). We think that an ejusdem generis approach to construction justifies giving a limited meaning to the adjective "economic" in para. (2). We think the need to leave a sensible scope for para. (1) similarly requires a limited meaning to be given to the adjective "economic" in para. (2).'

4.95   Because on the evidence the only reason for the dismissal was Mr Golding's desire to sell the business no ETO reason had been established and the case fell within reg 8(1); the appeal succeeded against Mr Golding. The EAT has followed this approach in later cases.[152]

4.96   In *Whitehouse v Charles A Blatchford & Sons Ltd*[153] (considered at **4.90**), Beldam LJ said of *Wheeler v Patel*:[154]

---

150   [1987] ICR 631, at 638.
151   [1987] ICR 631, at 640.
152   See *Gateway Hotels Ltd v Stewart* [1988] IRLR 287; *Ibex Trading Co Ltd v Walton* [1994] ICR 907, particularly at 915; *Michael Peters Ltd v Farnfield* [1995] IRLR 190.
153   [2000] ICR 542.
154   [2000] ICR 542, at 548F.

'It seems to me that the words "economic technical or organisational reason *entailing changes in the workforce*", clearly support the conclusion that the reason must be connected with the future conduct of the business as a going concern.'

Buxton LJ said:[155]

'This case was put to us as a case which turned on the interpretation of the word "economic" in Regulation 8(2) [of TUPE 1981], and there has undoubtedly been a tendency in the cases to direct what I will call English style analysis of words such as "economic" as if they were simply a word in a piece of English domestic legislation, when in truth their origin is in the much broader concept set out in the Directive.

That difficulty is to be seen in one of the early cases of which a great deal was made in this case, *Wheeler v Patel* ... As far as I can see, there was no reference at all in that case to the terms of, or even the existence of, the Directive. If such reference had been made, it would in my view have been a great deal easier for the court to reach the conclusion that it did that the reason for dismissal must be related to the conduct of the business and a dismissal that is simply related to the sale of the business does not so qualify. In reaching that analysis, the Employment Appeal Tribunal rejected the literalistic interpretation of the word "economic" which, if adopted, would very plainly have been inconsistent with the terms of Article 4 of the Directive. Mr Linden [counsel for the employers] said that he was content to adopt that formulation in *Wheeler v Patel* as the basis on which the present appeal should proceed. I am equally content to do that, though I should not necessarily be thought as accepting that the formulation of Scott J in that case (helpful though it is) is to be treated as some sort of statutory mantra that solves all problems under the Regulations.'

4.97   In the later case of *Thompson v SCS Consulting Ltd* [156] the EAT followed *Wheeler v Patel*, as modified by the approach of the Court of Appeal in the *Whitehouse* case, and said that, in deciding whether an economic, technical or organisational reason was the reason for the dismissal, it is appropriate for the tribunal to consider whether the reason is connected with the future conduct of the business as a going concern.

4.98   A further point is that the reason will not fall within reg 7(2) unless it also entails changes in the workforce. This aspect of the regulation was considered by the Court of Appeal in *Delabole Slate Ltd v Berriman*[157] in relation to reg 8(2) of TUPE 1981. The facts were that a quarryman was employed at a guaranteed weekly wage of £100. The undertaking in which he worked was taken over and his new employers wrote to inform him that they proposed to alter his pay to accord with their existing collective agreement. This would have entailed a substantial reduction in his guaranteed weekly wage. He resigned and claimed constructive dismissal. The Court of Appeal held that reg 8(2) (now reg 7(2)) did not protect the employers. It took the view that the employer's reason (to produce standardisation of pay) did not itself involve any change either in the number or the functions of the workforce, and it was not enough that the organisational reason might lead to the dismissal of those employees who did not fall into line. The change in the workforce must be

---

155   [2000] ICR 542, at 554.
156   [2001] IRLR 801.
157   [1985] ICR 546.

part of the economic, technical or organisational reason and the employer's plan must be to achieve changes in the workforce: 'It must be an objective of the plan, not just a possible consequence of it.'[158] Browne-Wilkinson LJ also said:[159]

> '[W]e do not think that the dismissal of one employee followed by the engagement of another in his place constitutes a change in the "workforce". To our minds, the word "workforce" connotes the whole body of employees as an entity: it corresponds to the "strength" or the "establishment". Changes in the identity of the individuals who make up the workforce do not constitute changes in the workforce itself so long as the overall numbers and functions of the employees looked at as a whole remain unchanged.'

The employee's constructive dismissal was thus automatically unfair because changes in the number of the workforce or the job functions of the transferred employee were not entailed.

4.99   In following the above case, the EAT has subsequently, in *Crawford v Swinton Insurance Brokers Ltd*,[160] held that the term 'workforce' is an entity separate from the individuals who make up the workforce. It is therefore possible for there to be a change in the workforce if the same people are retained but are given different jobs to do. In that case, the employee was one of two members of staff employed on typing and clerical work by the transferors before the transfer of their business to the employers. Following the transfer she lost the use of a company car, she had to work office hours and could no longer work partly at home, and she had to change from typing and clerical work to selling insurance. She resigned and claimed constructive dismissal. In arriving at its decision the tribunal decided that there could be a change in the workforce even though the identity of the personnel remained the same. The EAT upheld that decision, following the dictum of Browne-Wilkinson LJ above. It said:[161]

> 'What, in our judgment, has to be looked at, is the workforce as an entity, that is to say, as a whole, separate from the individuals who make it up and it then has to be seen whether the reason in question is one which involves a change in that workforce, strength or establishment and we are satisfied that there can well be a change in a workforce if the same people are kept on but they are given entirely different jobs to do. We would regard a workforce that was engaged in a different occupation as being, for the purposes of regulation 8(2) [now reg 7(2)] changed if that happened as a result of an organisational change on a relevant transfer.'

---

158   [1985] ICR 546, at 551.
159   [1985] ICR 546, at 551.
160   [1990] ICR 85.
161   [1990] ICR 85, at 92.

VARIATIONS OF EMPLOYEES' CONTRACTS

The provisions of Directive 2001/23/EC

4.100   Article 3(1) provides as follows:[162]

'The transferor's rights and obligations arising from a contract of employment or from an employment relationship existing on the date of a transfer shall, by reason of such transfer, be transferred to the transferee.'

4.101   It should be noted that there is no *specific* provision in the Directive dealing with variations of contract. The issue has arisen in the context of the interpretation by the ECJ of Art 3(1). The most important case is *Foreningen af Arbejdsledere I Danmark v Daddy's Dance Hall A/S*.[163] The case involved the termination of a lease on restaurants and bars owned by Palads Teatret and the grant of a new lease by them to Daddy's Dance Hall A/S. The employees were dismissed by Irma and taken on immediately by Daddy's Dance Hall, but on different terms and conditions, particularly in relation to remuneration and notice entitlement. The first question asked by the Danish Supreme Court concerned whether the circumstances gave rise to a transfer of an undertaking within Art 1(1) of the 1977 Directive;[164] the second question asked by the Danish Court was whether a person who works for a transferee of an undertaking may waive the rights conferred upon him or her by the Directive 'if this allows him to obtain such advantages that the change in conditions of employment does not place him overall in a less favourable position'. The ECJ said that it is not possible for workers to waive the rights given to them by the mandatory provisions of the Directive, even if the disadvantages for them of such a course of action are offset by advantages so that, overall, they are not in a worse position. The ECJ said:[165]

'14 ... [T]he purpose of Directive 77/187/EEC is ensure that the rights resulting from a contract of employment or employment relationship of employees affected by the transfer of an undertaking are safeguarded. Since this protection is a matter of public policy, and therefore independent of the will of the parties to the contract of employment, the rules of the directive, in particular those concerning the protection of workers against dismissal by reason of the transfer, must be considered to be mandatory, so that it is not possible to derogate from them in a manner unfavourable to employees.

15. It follows that employees are not entitled to waive the rights conferred on them by the directive and that those rights cannot be restricted even with their consent. This interpretation is not affected by the fact that, as in this case, the employee obtains new benefits in compensation for the disadvantages resulting from an

---

162   This provision is very similar to Art 3(1) of Directive 77/187/EEC, but with the omission of the words 'within the meaning of Article 1(1)' which followed the phrase 'existing on the date of a transfer'.

163   [1988] ECR 739, [1988] IRLR 315.

164   Article 1(1)(a) of the 2001 Directive. See **chapter 2**.

165   [1988] ECR 739, at 754. See also *Foreningen af Arbejdsledere I Danmark v A/S Danmols Inventar* (Case 105/84) [1985] ECR 2639, at 2650–2651, paras 15 and 16. Note also the Advocate General's comments at 2641.

amendment to his contract of employment so that, taking the matter as a whole, he is not placed in a worse position than before ...

17. Consequently, in so far as national law allows the employment relationship to be altered in a manner unfavourable to employees in situations other than the transfer of an undertaking, in particular as regards their protection against dismissal, such an alternative is not precluded merely because the undertaking has been transferred in the meantime and the agreement has therefore been made with the new employer. Since by virtue of Article 3 (1) of the directive the transferee is subrogated to the transferor's rights and obligations under the employment relationship, that relationship may be altered with regard to the transferee to the same extent as it could have been with regard to the transferor, provided that the transfer of the undertaking itself may never constitute the reason for that amendment.'

4.102   In *Wilson v St Helens Borough Council and British Fuels Ltd v Baxendale*,[166] the House of Lords considered arguments advanced in relation to variation based on the *Daddy's Dance Hall* case. Lord Slynn of Hadley, giving the only speech in the House of Lords, said:[167]

'The question as to whether and in what situations, where there has been a transfer and employees have accepted the dismissal, claimed compensation based on it and worked for a long period after the transfer, there can be a valid variation by conduct is not an easy one. I do not accept the argument that the variation is only invalid if it is agreed on or as a part of the transfer itself. The variation may still be due to the transfer and for no other reason even if it comes later. However, it seems that there must, or at least may, come a time when the link with the transfer is broken or can be treated as no longer effective ...

[A]lthough on a transfer, the employees' rights previously existing against the transferor are enforceable against the transferee and cannot be amended by the transfer itself, it does not follow there cannot be a variation of the terms of the contract for reasons which are not due to the transfer either on or after the transfer of the undertaking. It may be difficult to decide whether the variation is due to the transfer or attributable to some separate cause. If, however, the variation is not due to the transfer it can, in my opinion, on the basis of the authorities to which I have referred, validly be made.'

4.103   The later EAT decision in *Ralton v Havering College of Further & Higher Education*[168] concerned employment contracts which did not incorporate the Silver Book terms of employees who had been employed by a local authority but ceased to be so employed after a transfer from the local authority to the College. The transfer took place on 1 April 1993. After the transfer the employees entered into fixed-term contracts with the College, the contracts incorporating the Silver Book terms. After the expiry of the contracts (in 1994) the employees were offered new contracts for an indefinite term which did not incorporate the Silver Book terms. They subsequently claimed that the College was precluded from changing the Silver Book terms for a reason connected with the transfer and was bound to continue to employ them on those terms. In other words, the variations as a result of which the Silver Book ceased to be incorporated were invalid. The employment tribunal dismissed their claims; the EAT dismissed their appeals. It said that the tribunal had

---

166   [1998] ICR 1141.
167   [1998] ICR 1141, at 1165 and 1166.
168   [2001] IRLR 738.

correctly concluded that the variations to the employees' contracts were not 'because' of the transfer within the meaning of Art 4(2) of the Directive, so as to be impermissible. It also said that the tribunal had not erred in law by taking the view that the correct test was whether the variation was solely by reason of the transfer, rather than whether it was for a reason 'connected with' the transfer. The EAT said that the approach taken by the tribunal was consistent with the speech of Lord Slynn in the *Wilson* case that there is no infringement of an employee's rights under the Directive or TUPE if the transfer is simply 'the occasion' for changes. The EAT concluded that the tribunal had not erred in its decision that the termination of the rights and obligations transferred by the transfer were attributable to, or occasioned by, the expiry of their fixed-term contracts.

Interpretations of reg 5 of TUPE 1981

4.104   The domestic court and tribunals of the UK based their interpretation of reg 5 of TUPE 1981 on the *Daddy's Dance Hall* case and the House of Lords decision in *Wilson v St Helens Borough Council*. Regulation 4(4) and (5) of TUPE 2006 effectively puts this interpretation onto a statutory basis. In this section the pre-2006 case-law will be discussed. The next section will consider the effect of the introduction of reg 4(4) and (5).

4.105   The two principal cases to deal with the issue of variations of contract under TUPE 1981 both arose from the acquisition by Credit Suisse First Boston (CSFB) of the business of Barclays de Zoete Wedd in 1997 and 1998: *Credit Suisse First Boston (Europe) Ltd v Padiachy*[169] and *Credit Suisse First Boston(Europe) Ltd v Lister*.[170] Both cases concerned the enforceability of restrictive covenants entered into by employees with CSFB as part of its purchase of Barclays de Zoete Wedd's business. There had been no such covenants in the employees' contracts with BZW. In consideration of being paid £2,000 the employees entered into non-competition covenants with CSFB whose duration was expressed to be 3 months. The question of the enforceability of the covenants arose when the employees indicated their intention of taking up employment with a competitor. In the *Padiachy* case the judge took the view on the evidence that the change in the terms of the employee's employment occurred by reason of the transfer of the undertaking.[171] He went on to conclude that the employee could not waive the rights conferred on him by TUPE 1981, even if the disadvantages of doing so were offset by advantages so that he was in no worse position, and that, therefore, the newly introduced restrictive covenant could not be enforced.

4.106   The second case, *Lister*, went to the Court of Appeal, which reached the same conclusion as had Longmore J in the *Padiachy* case. Clarke LJ gave the only judgment; Aldous and Simon Brown LJJ agreed with him. Counsel for CSFB had advanced the argument that if on a fair view of the new contract as

---

169   [1999] ICR 569.
170   [1999] ICR 794.
171   [1999] ICR 569, at 574B–574D.

a whole the employee is better off than he was before, it cannot properly be said that the new contract has derogated from his rights in an unfavourable manner. Clarke LJ said:[172]

> 'There is, in my judgment, considerable force in those submissions [made on behalf of CSFB] ... It is not clear whether the European Court of Justice had these considerations in mind when it decided *Daddy's Dance Hall*. Nevertheless it is clear that the court was considering whether it was appropriate to conduct a balancing exercise as between the old contract and the new in order to decide whether the employee was placed in no worse a position under the new contract. The argument no doubt was that if the employee was in no worse a position under the new contract it could not fairly be said that the transfer had treated him in an unfavourable manner. If the argument now advanced by [counsel for CSFB] had been regarded as correct, the Court would have held that such a balancing exercise must be carried out in order to see whether the employee was in a worse position. If it was then held that he was in no worse a position ... the terms of the new contract would prevail over the old despite the terms of the directive.

> Yet the Court did not so hold. On the contrary it held that the effect of the directive was to transfer all the rights of the employee vis-a-vis the transferor to the transferee. The employee's rights under the directive could not be waived as a matter of public policy so that all his rights under his contract with the transferor were preserved. It was irrelevant that the employee was receiving new rights which compensated him for the loss of the old. In my judgment, it is impossible to reconcile the reasoning and decision of the Court of Justice with the submission advanced by [counsel for CSFB] in this case. If those submissions were correct the Court would have answered question 2 yes, whereas it did not. It did not do so because of its conclusion that the purpose and effect of the directive was to preserve *all* the rights which the employee had before the transfer. It no doubt reached that conclusion on the footing that both the policy and wording of the directive led to the conclusion that none of the employee's rights should be adversely affected by the transfer and not merely the balance of those rights.'

4.107   Clarke LJ expressed agreement with the statement by the first instance judge, Moore-Bick J:[173]

> 'The effect of the decision in the *Daddy's Dance Hall* case is that the agreement is ineffective insofar as it purports to impose on the employee an obligation to which he was not previously subject. To that extent it is disadvantageous to him and it is no answer to say that in the instant case it also gave him a compensating benefit which more than made up for it.'

4.108   The final case to consider here is *Solectron Scotland Ltd v Roper*.[174] One of the issues in the case was whether a compromise agreement entered into at the time of a transfer was affected by the statements of principle set out in the *Daddy's Dance Hall* case and were to be held to be void. The EAT said that the compromise agreement did not arise solely, or even mainly, by reason of the transfer. Giving the judgment of the EAT, Elias J said:[175]

---

172   [1999] ICR 794, at 805.
173   [1999] ICR 794, at 806.
174   [2004] IRLR 4.
175   [2004] IRLR 4, at paras 42–45.

'What these cases[176] establish is that an employer cannot, after a transfer, vary the terms of an employee's contract if that variation is solely by reason of the transfer ...

It is, however, to be noted in this case that the effect of the compromise agreement is solely to compromise a financial claim that the employee has on the termination of his employment contract. The employer is not purporting to vary the contract but merely to compromise a dispute as to its value. Moreover, there is no change in the terms and conditions for the future by reason of the obvious fact that the contract has come to an end.

Accordingly, if one looks at the policy lying behind *Daddy's Dance Hall* and related cases it is not infringed, it seems to us, by a compromise agreement made in such circumstances as arise here. We think that, properly analysed, it cannot be said that these particular compromise agreements arise solely or even mainly by reason of the transfer.'

Regulation 4(4) and (5) of TUPE 2006

4.109   Regulation 4(4) and (5) now expressly protects rights which the employee has against the transferor so that they cannot be varied on a transfer to the transferee. Regulation 4(4) provides that any purported variation of the employee's contract will be void if the sole or principal reason is the transfer itself or a reason connected with the transfer that it not an economic, technical or organisational reason entailing changes in the workforce. Regulation 4(5), however, permits the employer and employee to agree a variation if the sole or principal reason for the variation is a reason connected with the transfer that is an economic, technical or organisational reason entailing changes in the workforce or is a reason unconnected with the transfer.

4.110   To see if these provisions are applicable to a particular variation, it is suggested that the first step is to consider whether reg 4(4) applies, by asking the following questions:

(1)   Is the sole or principal reason for the variation the transfer?

(2)   If not, is the reason connected with the transfer?

(3)   If so, is the reason an economic, technical or organisational reason entailing changes in the workforce?

4.111   If the answer to the first question is in the affirmative and the transfer is the sole or principal reason, then the purported variation will be void and cannot be rescued by reg 4(5). If the variation is connected with the transfer and is not an economic, technical or organisational reason, then again the purported variation will be void and reg 4(5) will not apply. If the variation is for a reason not connected with the transfer, or is for an economic, technical or organisational reason, then reg 4(5) will apply. In proceedings involving reg 4(4), the burden of establishing that reg 4(4) applies will be on the employee.

---

176 The cases already discussed in the preceding text.

4.112 Once it has been established that the reason for the variation does not fall within reg 4(4)(a) or (b), then one can go on to reg 4(5) and ask the following questions:

(1) Is the reason connected with the transfer or not?
(2) If it is, is it an economic, technical or organisational reason entailing changes in the workforce?

If the answer to the first question is that the variation is *not* connected with the transfer, then the agreed variation is permissible. If the answer to the second question is in the affirmative, then again the agreed variation is permissible.

4.113 Although it might be thought that reg 4(4) and (5) deal with the issues of variation in a rather long-winded way, they would appear, in general, to reflect the case-law already considered. There is one area of uncertainty, however. As has been seen, reg 4(4)(b) renders void a reason connected with the transfer which is not an economic, technical or organisational reason. It is questionable whether that goes beyond the position as stated by the ECJ in the *Daddy's Dance Hall* case and discussed by Lord Slynn of Hadley in *Wilson v St Helens Borough Council*. The cases have used the phrase 'the transfer itself may never constitute the reason' for any alteration in the employment relationship.[177] Lord Slynn talks about a time coming when the link with the transfer is broken.[178] Presumably, until the time comes when the link is broken, it can be said that any variation is, on the face of it, a reason connected with the transfer. At that point, the further question must be posed as to whether it is an economic, technical or organisational reason.

4.114 One final point to make is that the phrase 'economic, technical or organisational reason entailing changes in the workforce' is identical to that used in reg 7(2), except that reg 7(2) contains the additional phrase 'of either the transferor or the transferee' after the phrase 'entailing changes in the workforce'. That apart, the cases which have considered that phrase in the context of reg 7(1) and (2) and its predecessor would appear to be relevant in this context also. Reference should be made to **4.87**.

4.115 Variations which occur where a transferor is subject to insolvency proceedings are considered in **chapter 3**: see **3.96**.

---

177 See the *Daddy's Dance Hall* case [1988] ECR 739, at para 17. See also *Rask v ISS Kantineservice A/S* (Case C-209/91) [1993] IRLR 133, at paras 28 and 31.
178 [1998] ICR 1141, at 1165D.

Chapter 5

INFORMATION TRANSFER AND EMPLOYEE CONSULTATION

5.1 In addition to the protection of individual employment rights, the Transfer of Undertakings (Protection of Employment) Regulations (TUPE) 2006[1] contain a package of measures designed to protect collective rights and to ensure that the voice of the employees is heard during the process leading up to the transfer. The package contains provisions for the transfer of collective agreements (reg 5) and for the transfer of trade union recognition (reg 6) in much the same way that individual rights transfer pursuant to reg 4.[2] The most significant elements of the package protecting collective rights, however, are the obligations which arise under reg 13 in relation to the disclosure of information to employee representatives and in relation to consultation with those representatives prior to the transfer, imposing on employers duties similar to those which apply in circumstances where large-scale redundancies are planned.[3]

5.2 We deal also in this chapter with the provisions introduced by TUPE 2006 whereby transferor employers are obliged to deliver certain information concerning the transferring workforce to the transferee employer. Hitherto, the transferee employer had inherited a workforce without necessarily receiving any official notification of the details of the employment relationships to which it would become bound. This situation has been remedied by reg 11.

5.3 The nature of the duties under reg 13 immediately gives rise to an important practical consideration for anyone contemplating the transfer of a business, for the duty to disclose the fact of the impending transfer and the prospect of consultation with employee representatives on various aspects of the proposals is to be contrasted with the situation where TUPE 2006 does not apply to a transfer of a business entity, for example, on a sale of the shares in a company.[4] Commercially, the alternative methods of transferring a business entity by a disposal of the shares in a company or by transferring the title to the assets may achieve much the same goal, yet from an employment law perspective the choice of the form of the transaction may have significant consequences. If TUPE does not apply, a disposal could be effected without the

---

1   SI 2006/246.

2   For a discussion of regs 5 and 6, see **3.78 (reg 5) and 3.99 (reg 6)**.

3   See s 188ff of the Trade Union and Labour Relations (Consolidation) Act 1992 (TULR(C)A 1992).

4   In a share transfer the undertaking remains vested in the company – it is not transferred. Only the shares are transferred and these are bare assets rather than an undertaking. There is no change of employer and no transfer of an undertaking for the purposes of TUPE.

prior knowledge of the employees. Whilst as a matter of law the employees remain employed by the same employer following a share sale, in many cases there will be a significant change in the working environment post acquisition; yet the employees may have had no prior knowledge of what is proposed, let alone the right to be consulted. Certainly, the employees might well be the subject of proposed 'measures' which will directly affect them, but about which the employees may not have been informed nor had the right (individually or through their representatives) to be consulted.

5.4 A further issue to note is the fact that where duties arise under reg 13, the proposed acquisition will inevitably become known publicly by reason of the information disclosed to employee representatives or to the employees themselves, which may alert a competing bidder. Of course, there is a multitude of reasons why this information may already be in the public domain, but if this information remains confidential at the point at which obligations under reg 13 arise, then in such circumstances the intending purchaser may feel that it faces a harsh choice between paying the penalties for non-compliance with reg 13 and suffering the commercial consequences of alerting potential rival bidders. There are no duties to treat information received pursuant to reg 13 as confidential and indeed to so legislate would be impractical. All other things being taken into consideration, in such circumstances it may be appropriate to structure a transfer so that it falls outside the scope of TUPE to avoid these consequences and it would be open to the parties to do so without being open to the accusation that they were thereby evading their obligations under TUPE.[5]

5.5 Regulation 13, which seeks to implement Art 7 of Directive 2001/23/EC, has had something of a chequered history. The European Court of Justice (ECJ) held in *EC Commission v UK*[6] that the UK had failed properly to implement the provisions of Art 7 into national law. In its guise at the time of the case, the obligation which now arises under reg 13 only arose in circumstances where a trade union was recognised for collective bargaining purposes in respect of any employees likely to be affected by the transfer, whereas Art 7 contains no such limitation. As a consequence of the ECJ's decision, an amendment to TUPE was required from the UK Government and this was effected by the Collective Redundancies and Transfer of Undertakings (Protection of Employment) Regulations 1999.[7] These Regulations expanded the scope of what is now reg 13 to cover all transfers regardless of whether a trade union is recognised in respect of any of the employees who may be affected by the transfer, whilst at the same time providing detailed procedures in relation to the identification of employee representatives in each case and the rights of those representatives. TUPE 2006 consolidates all this material.

---

5 See *Brookes v Borough Care Services* [1998] IRLR 636 in which there was a bid to take over the management of a number of local authority care homes. When it was pointed out to the prospective purchaser that TUPE would inhibit its ability as the incoming employer to change the terms and conditions of the employees, the proposal was varied to become an acquisition of shares. The employees' challenge that this amounted to an unlawful evasion of their rights under TUPE was not upheld.

6 [1994] IRLR 392.

7 SI 1999/1925.

THE NATURE OF THE INFORMATION TO BE DISCLOSED

5.6 Regulation 13(2) lists the information which employers are obliged to disclose to employee representatives in connection with the transfer of an undertaking. This information is set out in four paragraphs as follows:

(a) The fact that the transfer is to take place, the date or proposed date of the transfer and the reasons for the transfer.

(b) The legal, economic and social implications of the transfer for any affected employees. 'Legal implications' may involve briefing uninitiated recipients of the information on the main features of TUPE and its consequences. The impact of the proposed transfer on the employees' legal rights will have to be made clear. 'Economic' could be taken to mean not only the financial consequences of the proposed transfer for the employees, but also the economic status of the transferee, so that the employees can form a view as to the worth of the transferee.[8] The phrase 'social implications' is not defined and is taken straight from the Directive. It has been suggested that 'social implications' in this context means social security implications.[9] However, in practice it is ordinarily taken to be a requirement to disclose the wider implications of the transfer on the employees' working environment.

(c) The measures which the employer of the affected employees envisages it will, in connection with the transfer, take in relation to any affected employees or, if it envisages that no measures will be so taken, that fact.

(d) If the employer is the transferor, the measures in connection with the transfer which the transferor envisages the transferee will take in relation to any affected employees who will become employees of the transferee by virtue of reg 4 or, if it envisages that no measures will be so taken, that fact.

There is no express obligation to disclose the identity of the transferee, but the obligation to disclose the legal implications of the transfer under para (b) would surely require this disclosure.

5.7 A precedent letter to employee representatives showing the form in which this information is typically provided by employers to employee representatives may be found at **appendix 17**.

ON WHOM DOES THE DUTY TO INFORM REST?

5.8 The duty to inform rests with the 'employer' of 'affected employees'. The term 'employer' for these purposes follows the definition in reg 2(1), namely the person for whom any individual works, whether under a contract of service or apprenticeship or otherwise but excluding anyone who provides services under a contract for services. The definition of 'employee' in TUPE is therefore wider than the definition of that term in the Employment Rights Act 1996 (ERA

---

8 See *NALGO v British Waterways Board* COIT 2034/124.
9 See Harvey on Industrial Relations and Employment Law at [194].

1996).[10] For example, the definition of the term in TUPE would extend to civil servants. Employees will be considered to be 'affected' if they fall within the definition set out in reg 13(1), namely if they are an employee of the transferor or the transferee of the undertaking in question, regardless of whether or not they are employed in the undertaking or the part of the undertaking to be transferred and regardless of whether they themselves will be transferred. The determinant is whether they are or may be (it is not necessary to establish that they *will be* affected – a mere likelihood is enough) affected by the transfer or by measures taken in connection with it. The scope of this provision could be very wide. It is worth bearing in mind that the courts and tribunals have been prepared to take a broad view when determining whether the actions of transferee employers can be described as being connected with a TUPE transfer. In *Taylor v Connex South Eastern Ltd*,[11] for example, the actions of the employer were held to be connected to the transfer notwithstanding that 2 years had elapsed since the transfer. Hence we might expect the courts and tribunals to take a similarly broad view of whether an employee may be affected by the transfer. 'Affected' in the Directive is qualified as referring to the conditions of work and employment of the employees.

5.9   Although the principal duty to inform and, when appropriate, to consult will rest with the transferor of the undertaking and will relate to the employees who are earmarked for transfer, it is clear that the obligation goes much wider. For example, it may be that as a consequence of disposing of a part of its business, the transferor will make changes to the way in which it operates the retained business, perhaps by way of an internal reorganisation. In these circumstances the representatives of the employees within the retained workforce who might be affected by such changes would have to be informed and consulted. It will be noted that the class of such employees who themselves are not transferring but who may fall within the scope of the duty to inform and, when appropriate, to consult is defined by whether or not they will or may be affected by 'measures' taken in connection with the transfer, a nebulous term which is considered at **5.24**.

5.10   It is often overlooked that the transferee may need to inform and to consult the representatives of its own employees in connection with the acquisition of an undertaking. They will not be transferring themselves but may well be affected by measures taken in connection with the transfer. It may be, for example, that the transferring workforce will duplicate skills within the transferee's existing workforce and as a consequence there may be redundancies or redeployment within the transferee's existing workforce. Such measures would bring existing employees of the transferee within the scope of the duty.

5.11   In the event that the transfer has extensive implications for both the transferor and the transferee of the undertaking, it is conceivable that a large number of employees on each side may be affected and hence the number of employees falling within the scope of the duty could be considerable.

---

10   See ERA 1996, s 230.
11   EAT 1243/99. See also *Bernadone v Pall Mall Services Group* [2000] IRLR 487.

5.12 The term 'transferor' must be construed widely in this context. For example, it would include the proponent of an involuntary transfer. A contractor who is unsuccessful on retender and who ceases to be engaged to deliver services as a result is a transferor for these purposes, even though there is no positive action on its part to divest itself of the undertaking. However, the term does not extend to encompass employees of associated employers unless the associated employer is itself in some way a transferor or transferee, regardless of whether there would be an impact on the employees of any such associated employer.

5.13 The transferor will only be able to comply with its duty under reg 13(2)(d) in respect of measures contemplated by the transferee if such information is sent to the transferor by the transferee, as indeed the transferee is obliged to do pursuant to reg 13(4). In the event that a claim is made against the transferor in this respect, the transferor may serve notice on the transferee that it holds the transferee responsible for a failure to fulfil its responsibilities under reg 13(4). That notice acts of itself to join the transferee to the proceedings.

WHEN HAS THE INFORMATION TO BE DISCLOSED?

5.14 The timescale for delivery of the information is not easy to determine. There is no requirement to deliver the information in connection with a consultation exercise which must begin 'in good time' or in accordance with a minimum number of days, as with the duties which apply in the case of large-scale redundancies,[12] although the phrase 'in good time' is used in the Directive.[13] Rather the obligation to inform in reg 13(2) works backwards from the date of transfer – the information is to be delivered 'long enough before [the transfer] to enable the employer of any affected employees to consult the appropriate representatives of any affected employees'. Accordingly, in order to determine the time at which information must be disclosed, a decision needs to be taken about the likely extent of the consultation required including the subject matter of those consultations. The regulation does not address the fact that in some cases there will not be any duty to consult. Equally, it does not specifically address the legal obligation to consult under reg 13 and could be read as requiring adequate time to be set aside for consultation regardless of whether there is any legal duty for consultation to take place. Some assistance on this point can be found in the decision of Millett J in *Institution of Professional Civil Servants v Secretary of State for Defence* (*IPCS*).[14] He suggests that the consultation which is referred to in reg 13(2) is voluntary consultation which may be sought by employee representatives:[15]

'The second question which was canvassed before me was the extent of the obligation to consult which is placed upon the Secretary of State. That obligation is

---

12   See TULR(C)A 1992, s 188ff.
13   Article 7(1).
14   [1987] IRLR 373.
15   [1987] IRLR 373, at 376.

imposed by subsection (8),[16] and it arises only where the Secretary of State envisages that he will be taking measures in connection with the transfer. Thus the Act evidently requires the Secretary of State to inform the unions of four different matters, but to consult them on only one of them. I was for some time oppressed by the apparent illogicality of this. Why should the Secretary of State be required to consult the unions where he envisages that he will take measures, but not when he envisages that he will take none? The unions may well wish to be consulted as much in the second case as in the first. And why is the Secretary of State required to inform the unions in time to enable effective consultations to take place of matters on which he is not required to consult them? Logically, the consultations referred to in the opening words of subsection (6)[17] must include, but cannot be confined to, those referred to in subsection (8). On the other hand, Parliament can hardly have intended to compel the employer in the private sector to consult the unions on the desirability of the transfer itself or the sufficiency of the reasons for it. These are matters of business policy for the transferring employer to decide, and the unions cannot expect to participate in the decision. The reconciliation, in my view, is this. The consultations referred to in the opening words of subsection (6) are voluntary consultations, which the unions may seek on any topic once they have the requisite information, but which the transferring employer is not compelled to grant if he chooses not to do so. The only consultations which he is obliged by law to enter into are those referred to in subsection (8).'

5.15   By reason of the fact that there will not be an obligation to consult in all circumstances and if Millett J's obiter dictum analysis in *IPCS* is not followed, it could be argued that if there is no duty to consult, then no time need be set aside for consultation. Hence the delivery of the information at the last minute prior to a transfer would appear to be adequate to satisfy the obligation in reg 13(2) in these circumstances. It is worth noting in this context that, even where there is a duty to consult, the employee representatives are not given a right of consultation over the whole scope of the information to be delivered. As will be seen below, the obligation to consult arises in connection with measures to be taken and the duty to consult is expressly tied to those measures. There is no obligation, for example, to inform employee representatives about the fact of a transfer so that the representatives may participate in consultation about the decision to transfer.

5.16   The duty to inform employee representatives of those matters set out in reg 13(2)(a) and (b) could therefore strictly be seen as no more than an obligation to establish the context of the information exchange. Alternatively and perhaps more purposefully, it can be interpreted in the way Millett J did as establishing an opportunity for voluntary consultation to take place. Were an employer to refuse such a request, the very fact of being informed would at least allow the employee representatives to attempt to exert pressure within an industrial relations context to assert the opinion of the workforce in the wider

---

16   Section 1(8) of the Dockyard Services Act 1986. This section is drafted in like terms to reg 10(5) of the Transfer of Undertakings (Protection of Employment) Regulations 1981, SI 1981/1794, broadly equivalent to reg 13(6) of TUPE 2006. References to The Secretary of State are equivalent to references to a transferor under the Regulations.

17   This may be read as a reference to the wording, to be found in reg 13(2) of TUPE 2006, that the transferor shall inform employee representatives 'long enough before a relevant transfer to enable the employer of any affected employees to consult the appropriate representatives of any affected employees ...'.

decision-making process. The knowledge that a transfer is proposed is also a precondition for the exercise of the right to opt out of the transfer under reg 4(7) (see **3.33**). In Germany, by way of example, defective information can have the effect of delaying the point at which the employee can exercise the right to opt out of the transfer. Even 12 months after a transfer, an employee might assert a right to opt out and to revert to employment with the transferor, having just become aware of correct material information about the transfer. In England and Wales, by contrast, the right to opt out cannot have retrospective effect. An employee who is not aware of the proposed transfer – for whatever reason – until it has taken place will therefore be in no position to exercise the right.

5.17 Situations will arise when the transfer of an undertaking takes place with little prior warning. In such circumstances there may be little time in which to inform and to consult with employee representatives. The question therefore arises as to whether the transfer itself must be deferred so as to allow for the completion of the process of information disclosure and consultation. This point was also considered by Millett J in *IPCS*. He interpreted the phrase 'long enough before a transfer' as meaning 'as soon as measures are envisaged and if possible long enough before the transfer'. With respect to the learned judge it is not easy to read this construction into the plain wording of the regulation:[18]

'... the company[19] is not placed under any obligation to envisage any measures which it will take in connection with the transfer, and subsection (6)(d)[20] expressly contemplates that it may not. Nor is the company placed under any obligation to envisage any measures at any particular time. For his part, the Secretary of State[21] is not placed under any obligation to provide the company with information to enable it to do so. Moreover, if the company enters into discussions with the unions, it may well wish to develop or change the measures it has previously envisaged. In such a developing situation no criticism can be made of the company if, for reasons beyond its control, particular measures are not envisaged until shortly before the transfer, when there is insufficient time for effective consultations to take place. In relation to the information described in para. (d), therefore, the opening words of subsection (6)[22] cannot sensibly be read as meaning "As soon as measures are envisaged and in any event long enough before the transfer" but rather "As soon as measures are envisaged and if possible long enough before the transfer".'

5.18 There is clearly a real risk that when a transfer takes place in circumstances where full information is not delivered or if meaningful consultation does not take place, the party in default may be liable under the provision in reg 15 for failure to comply with the obligations in reg 13. It is worth comparing the provisions of domestic legislation enacted in other EU Member States pursuant to the Acquired Rights Directive. In some countries the failure to comply with information and consultation obligations can – in an

---

18 [1987] IRLR 373, at 376.
19 The transferee.
20 For which read broadly what is now reg 13(2)(d).
21 The transferor.
22 For which read the opening words of reg 13(2).

extreme case – result in the annulment of the transaction itself (for example, in Hungary) and certainly a delay until consultation has been completed.[23]

5.19 The topic of greatest interest to many in these circumstances is the information to be disclosed pursuant to reg 13(2)(d), namely the information to be disclosed about the proposals of the transferee for the transferring workforce. That information is only available to the transferor as and when the transferee chooses to pass it to the transferor. In the event that the transferor is in breach of its duties under reg 13(2)(d) by reason of the default of the transferor, this would be a matter to be taken into account when assessing the apportionment of joint and several liability pursuant to reg 15.

5.20 There is a mechanism in reg 15(5) whereby the transferee can be joined into any proceedings brought against the transferor alleging non-compliance. The transferee may be in breach of a duty imposed on it by reg 13(4) to deliver the information to the transferor and to do so early enough so as to enable the transferor to comply with its obligations under reg 13(2)(d). Notice should be served on the transferee of the transferor's intention to make this allegation and the transferee will then be joined to the defence of any proceedings brought.

5.21 It is worth noting that the obligations under reg 13 arise in contemplation of a proposed transfer. Once the transferor is at the point that a transfer is planned, the duties arise and the parties to the transfer must consider their timetable. The fact that the transfer may or may not ultimately reach legal completion is of no consequence.[24]

METHOD OF DELIVERY OF INFORMATION

5.22 Of course, in many cases one might expect that the information could be delivered to employee representatives without the need for detailed prescription as to how this must be done. Nevertheless, there is a procedure in reg 13(5) which must be followed regardless of whether the information has also been disclosed by some other, more informal means. The information must be provided to each of the appropriate representatives and the appointed method of delivery is:

- by delivering it to them, which, taken literally would mean handing the information to the representative in person;
- by posting the information to the representative at an address which they have notified to the employer. There is no suggestion that the address need have been given to the employer for this particular purpose – for example, it may be the address current on the employer's personnel records. It would appear to exclude delivering the information to their place of work or in electronic form to an e-mail box; or

---

23 Consider, for example, the position in Italy, where there is the prospect of a court granting an injunction so as to protect the right to be informed and consulted. The court may insist on completion of this process before a transfer can proceed.

24 See *Barclays Bank v BIFU* [1987] ICR 495.

- (where the appropriate representatives are trade union representatives) by sending the information by post to the union at the address of its head or main office. In the case of large numbers of union representatives, this option has the attraction of reducing the communication to a single document.

5.23 There is no basis for the information to be given on a conditional basis, for example, providing information on the basis that it may not be disclosed to third parties. Although the role of the representative is ill-defined within TUPE, an obligation of confidentiality would nevertheless restrict the ability of employee representatives to play an active role, if they were unable to inform those they represent and to seek views on the proposals. Although the delivery of information on a conditional basis may not be open to objection in itself, it would call into question whether the employer had fulfilled its duty to consult properly. In *IPCS v Secretary of State for Defence*, Millet J remarked, in the context of the information which is to be passed by the transferee to the transferor:[25]

> 'In my view it is implicit that [the transferee] will also give the requisite information to [the transferor] in a form which will enable him to perform his statutory duty, and it is not entitled to supply it under cover of commercial confidentiality so as to disable him from complying with his duty.'

'MEASURES'

5.24 The questions of whether a duty to consult arises and the scope of the duty are governed by the nebulous term 'measures', which is not defined. The term is lifted straight from Art 7 of the Directive. Regulation 13(6) provides:

> 'An employer of an affected employee who envisages that he will take measures in relation to an affected employee, in connection with the relevant transfer, shall consult the appropriate representatives of that employee with a view to seeking their agreement to the intended measures.'

5.25 We must be grateful that in *IPCS v Secretary of State for Defence* Millet J elected to give a long, obiter dictum exposition of a number of the issues surrounding the obligation to inform and to consult. He advocated a broad approach to the term 'measures', including 'any action, step or arrangement'. A similarly broad construction is given to 'envisages' – meaning 'visualises' or 'foresees', accepting that there is a degree of uncertainty here. It need not be confined to what is inevitable or non-negotiable. However, the use of the word 'will' (as opposed to 'may') excludes 'mere hopes or possibilities'.

5.26 The learned judge doubted whether it was possible to be any more precise as a matter of definition and a more precise formulation of the scope of this term has yet to be found. The breadth of the term makes it dangerous for an employer not to consult if it is considering any change in the terms and conditions of the employees or in their working environment. Support for this formulation comes from the fact that the wording of the regulation refers to

---

25 [1987] IRLR 373, at 375.

measures in relation to the employees rather than to measures in relation to the terms and conditions of employment of the employees.

5.27   In *Baxter v Marks & Spencer*[26] the EAT drew a distinction between 'measures to be taken as a result of the transfer' (which must be the subject of information and consultation) and the 'inevitable administrative consequences' of the transfer, which fall outside this obligation.

THE OBLIGATION TO CONSULT

5.28   In addition to the obligation to inform, an employer of affected employees must – if it proposes measures in respect of those employees – consult with the appropriate representatives of those employees. It is worth noting that the obligation to consult only arises in relation to an employer of affected employees – hence there is no obligation on the future employer of transferring employees to consult in respect of measures which it proposes in respect of such employees, for the transferee is not yet the employer of such employees. Although in practice the transferor will often invite consultation with the transferee on a voluntary basis, this is a big gap in the statutory framework. The transferor need only consult in relation to the transferring employees where it envisages taking measures in relation to those employees. If, for example, a transferor intended to take no measures in relation to the transferring employees, but the transferee intended to take measures, there would be no obligation to consult concerning those measures.[27] It is worth reflecting on how toothless these provisions are. Imagine, for example, a familiar takeover situation: the business of Target is to be acquired by Predator. The central issue will concern the future of the transferring Target employees and what plans Predator will have for their future. Predator will be obliged to set out what measures it proposes and this information will need to be delivered to the employee representatives via Target. However, Predator need not be available for any consultation in respect of these measures. Furthermore, there is no obligation on Target to consult about Predator's measures. Admittedly, it would be difficult for Target to do so as it may have no further information than the words on the page. If Target is taking no measures itself in relation to the transferring employees, there would be no obligation to consult. This would further reduce the scope for employees to play any role in the transaction, for otherwise one could envisage a dialogue between Target and the employee representatives about how Target might shape the deal to accommodate some of the employees' concerns.

5.29   Some commentators have suggested that the wording of reg 13(6), which is changed from its predecessor,[28] offers a solution. The new wording imposes an obligation to consult on 'an employer of an affected employee' who envisages taking measures in relation to 'an affected employee'. The regulation does not stipulate that the 'affected employee' in respect of whom measures are proposed is one and the same as the 'affected employee' first mentioned, with

---

26   UK/EAT/0162/05/RN.
27   For an example of this point, see *AEU v Permanite* COIT 2069/225.
28   See TUPE 1981, reg 10(5).

whom there is an employment relationship. Hence, the argument goes, provided that at least some of the transferee's employees are 'affected', the transferee will have an obligation to consult in respect of the transferor's affected employees concerning the measures which the transferee proposes. Regardless of whether the purpose of the new wording was to address this point (and there is no evidence that there was such an intention), the door is left ajar for a purposive interpretation of this provision so as to close this large hole in the legislation. However, whether a court would be prepared to take this step must be open to doubt. It would involve the difficulty that the obligation to consult on the part of the transferor would only arise where the transferor was itself the employer of affected employees. This precondition would have no connection with the substance of the obligation – that is to say, the effect on the transferor's employees – and would result in the obligation to consult arising in an arbitrary manner, which would make no sense whatsoever.

5.30   Regulation 13(7) provides that the employer shall, in the course of the consultations, consider any representations made by the representatives and shall reply to them. In the event that any of the representations are to be rejected, then the reasons for the rejection must be stated. The obligation is to consult appropriate representatives with a view to seeking their agreement as to the measures which are proposed. It is submitted that the burden imposed by the phrase 'seeking their agreement' is relatively light. It merely requires the employer to put in motion a procedure that could result in agreement. It does not require the employer to take a position in the consultation which is objectively likely to result in agreement. Contrast the requirement in relation to collective redundancy consultation[29] which requires consultation 'with a view to reaching agreement'. In such circumstances it could be argued that the employer is in breach of the obligation if it does not take a position which has a reasonable prospect of resulting in agreement.

5.31   There is no specific definition of consultation in TUPE 2006. However, it is clear that, given the link with the information provisions in reg 13(2), it is envisaged to be a dialogue following from the delivery of the information and concerning at least some of that information. Moreover, the requirement for consultation on those proposals 'with a view to seeking agreement' would appear to put the onus on the employer to demonstrate both an open mind and a constructive response to the views which the employee representatives put forward. Whilst TUPE does not go as far as to make it necessary for employers and employee representatives to reach agreement (and, indeed, such a provision would not be workable), the consultation process would appear to envisage a process more akin to negotiation than a mere exchange of views. An employer is unlikely to be able to show compliance without a reasoned and reasonable response to the issues raised by the employee representatives.

5.32   It is not necessary for the employer to provide all of the information at the very outset of consultation or, indeed, in one single tranche. Whilst that might be the ideal approach, it will often not be possible. Moreover, plans are quite likely to change over the course of the planning of a transaction. There is limited case-law on the point, but what there is indicates that consultation can

---

29   See TULR(C)A 1992, s 188(2).

be deemed to have commenced provided that the employer has provided sufficient information to enable meaningful consultation to take place.[30]

5.33 By analogy with the collective redundancy consultation provisions of TULR(C)A 1992, employers must expect employment tribunals to scrutinise the adequacy of the information provided when considering whether the obligation to consult has been properly discharged.[31] Some tribunal decisions have taken a 'qualitative' approach on this point, questioning whether the employer has provided sufficient information and in a sufficiently understandable form to enable meaningful consultation to take place. This risk will be particularly acute when considering whether there has been adequate disclosure of information relating to 'measures', given that it is this information which drives the consultation process. In one case,[32] the Court of Appeal indicated that in relation to collective consultation over redundancies, it was necessary that the representatives be given an adequate opportunity to understand fully the issues over which they were being consulted. This has subsequently been interpreted as requiring 'sufficient and intelligible' information to be provided to employee representatives.[33]

5.34 The leading judgment on the definition of 'consultation' in the context of redundancy-related collective consultation is that of Glidewell LJ in *R v British Coal Corporation, ex parte Price*[34] where it was stated that 'fair consultation' means giving the body consulted a fair and proper opportunity to understand fully the matters about which it is being consulted and to express its views on those subjects, with the consultor thereafter considering those views properly and genuinely:[35]

> 'It is axiomatic that the process of consultation is not one in which the consultor is obliged to adopt any or all of the views expressed by the person or body whom he is consulting. I would respectfully adopt the tests proposed by Hodgson J in *R v Gwent County Council ex parte Bryant*, reported, as far as I know, only at [1988] Crown Office Digest p.19, when he said:
>
> "Fair consultation means:
>
> (a)　consultation when the proposals are still at a formative stage;
>
> (b)　adequate information on which to respond;
>
> (c)　adequate time in which to respond;
>
> (d)　conscientious consideration by an authority of the response to consultation."
>
> Another way of putting the point more shortly is that fair consultation involves giving the body consulted a fair and proper opportunity to understand fully the matters about which it is being consulted, and to express its views on those subjects, with the consultor thereafter considering those views properly and genuinely.'

30　*MSF v GEC Ferranti (Defence Systems) Limited (No 2)* [1994] IRLR 113, a case dealing with the similar provisions in TULR(C)A 1992, s 188.

31　See *GMB and AEEU v Campbells UK Limited* (unreported) ET case no 26787/96.

32　*Ex parte Vardy* [1993] IRLR 104.

33　See *GMB and AEEU v Campbells UK Limited* (unreported) ET case no 26787/96.

34　[1994] IRLR 72.

35　[1994] IRLR 72, at 75.

5.35 By analogy, in the context of TUPE consultation the process should begin when there is something to consult about rather than at a point where the employer's mind is made up or when the transferee has closed its mind. There must be scope for consideration or reconsideration and a willingness to be persuaded to change course if appropriate.

5.36 Failure to provide quality information will undermine the prospects of compliant consultation and there is increasing evidence over recent years of employee representatives (and trade unions in particular, given their access to funds) challenging the genuine commitment of the employer to the reg 13 process. It will not be adequate for the employer to show that it has 'gone through the hoops'; it must be seen to have done so with a sense of purpose. Regulation 13(7) sets out the minimum requirement on the employer, namely an obligation to consider any representations made by the representatives, to reply to the representations and to explain why any of them are rejected.

5.37 One issue which is not dealt with in TUPE 2006 is the nature of the duties owed by employee representatives to their constituents. By implication, one would expect a representative to inform those he or she represents during the course of the information and consultation exercise and one would expect an element of dialogue in order that the representatives might ascertain the views of the group, so as to be able to provide a truly representative view in the consultation process. However, none of this is expressly required by TUPE. There is a risk that the representatives will have neither the inclination nor the organisational skills properly to represent all of the employees in respect of whom they are the representatives. In the worst case those who they represent may be in the dark as to the transfer until they are served with a notice that they have a new employer.

5.38 There is provision within TUPE 2006 for an element of support for representatives. Regulation 13(8) provides an obligation on the employer to allow the representatives access to the employees they represent. More importantly, the same section also provides an obligation on the employer to provide the employee representatives with 'such accommodation and other facilities as may be appropriate'. The full extent of this provision has yet to be explored in the courts and tribunals but it is clear that it provides the representatives with a basis for requiring the employer to provide, at its own cost, those resources which the employee representatives might reasonably need in order to communicate with the employees during the information/consultation process. Pursuant to this clause the employee representatives might reasonably request amongst other things office space and services together with communication resources such as telephones, e-mail and postal facilities. A more generous interpretation could extend to facilities such as access to independent legal advice at the employer's expense, but there is no case-law to support such an expansive reading of the legislation.

THE CONSEQUENCES OF SUPPLYING INACCURATE INFORMATION

5.39 In addition to the need to supply information of a quality such as to facilitate a meaningful consultation exercise, there is also a need to have regard to the quality of the information disclosed in the context of how that information will be used by those to whom it is provided. In *Hagen v ICI Chemicals*[36] it was accepted that ICI would not have gone ahead with the transfer of the business unless the employees were in agreement with the proposed transaction. ICI therefore set out to persuade the employees to agree to the proposed transfer and made assurances about their rights post transfer which proved critical in this respect. It was alleged that the employees had agreed to the transfer based upon inaccurate and negligent misstatements by ICI. The court held that there was a duty of care on the part of the information provider to ensure that statements made regarding the transfer were true. The duty arises out of the contract of employment by reason of an implied duty to take reasonable care in making statements in such circumstances. Likewise there is a corresponding duty on the transferor in tort to take reasonable care in the provision of information. These duties are in addition to the duties to provide information pursuant to TUPE. They are owed to employees directly as opposed to the duties under TUPE, which are owed to the employee representatives. Hence a significant liability to compensation as a consequence of inaccurate information being provided can arise at common law. The liability in tort will not transfer to the transferee under TUPE.

5.40   The practical point emerges clearly from the case, therefore, that great care must be taken to ensure that information which is disclosed is accurate and not misleading. It is common practice to disclose information in excess of the minimum requirement of reg 13. This may take the form of employee presentations or perhaps a question and answer page on an intranet. If information is to be disseminated more widely than is absolutely necessary, it is important to be aware that this will create obligations and information must be disclosed of a quality consistent with these obligations.

WHETHER TO INVOLVE THE TRANSFEREE

5.41   The person from whom the employees will invariably want to hear and to whom they will want to talk is the transferee. The employees will naturally want to know more about their future employer and to discuss its plans for the employees post transfer. Hence the transferor may come under pressure to involve the transferee in the information and consultation process, notwithstanding that there is no requirement in TUPE 2006 for such a process, other than for the mere passing on of a statement of the transferee's intended measures, if any. This brings into question the wisdom of acceding to such pressure and of exposing the employees who will be the subject of the transfer to their future employer. It may be that this will be a positive experience and will facilitate a smooth transfer. It may help to 'win the hearts and minds' of the employees, always an important aspect of any successful migration of employees. At the same time, however, it could make the transfer more difficult. It will give rise to obligations in terms of the quality of such information disclosed, as outlined above, and in certain circumstances it could give rise to an additional concern on the part of the transferor.

---

36   [2002] IRLR 31.

5.42 It may be that the employee who would otherwise transfer does not like what he hears. If the employee anticipates that the transferee will not honour the terms and conditions of his employment contract, he may exercise the right to claim constructive dismissal. The transferor's concern will be limited by reason of the expectation that such a claim will transfer to the transferee, the source of the trouble in the first place, when the transfer takes place. However, in *Oxford University v Humphries*[37] the Court of Appeal confirmed that not only did the potential transferring employee have a claim for constructive dismissal in such circumstances, but that right could also be combined with the right to opt out of the transfer under reg 4(7). In such circumstances the liability remains with the transferor and does not transfer to the transferee, the party responsible for the subject matter of the anticipatory breach on which the claim for constructive dismissal is founded. Hence in exposing the transferring employees to the transferee prior to the transfer, the transferor employer might properly be concerned about what the transferee will say to the employees. Where the transfer is the subject of a contract between transferor and transferee, some form of warranty or indemnity should be sought that the transferee will not do or say anything which could give rise to such a constructive dismissal claim, so as to protect the transferor against the consequences in *Humphries*.

APPROPRIATE REPRESENTATIVES

5.43 The obligation is to inform and consult not the employees themselves but their representatives – the 'appropriate representatives'. Regulation 13(3) sets out the principles for determining who the appropriate representatives are in each case. There are three potential categories of representatives:

- trade union representatives;
- directly elected representatives; and
- a standing body of elected or appointed representatives not specifically elected for the purpose of TUPE consultation, but who (having regard to the original purpose of their appointment) have authority to fulfil this role.

5.44 Employers must consult trade union representatives rather than any other category of representative where the affected employees fall within a category in respect of which an independent trade union is recognised.[38] The issue is not whether the affected employees are trade union members in their own right, but whether the union is recognised in respect of the employee group.

5.45 It may be that the transferring workforce contains a group of people in respect of whom a trade union is recognised, but that there are other groups within the transferring workforce in respect of whom the union is not recognised. In such circumstances the union representatives will be the authorised representatives of that group in respect of which the union is

---

37   [2000] IRLR 183.
38   Regulation 13(3)(a).

recognised only. Information/consultation obligations may therefore involve different sets of appropriate representatives in respect of different groups of employees.

5.46 The union representatives are appropriate representatives where the union is recognised – 'recognised' is defined by reg 2(1) as recognition for the purposes of collective bargaining. The union representatives, who will be the appropriate representatives in these circumstances, are defined by reg 2(3) as 'an official or other person authorised to carry on collective bargaining with that employer by that union'.

5.47 Where no union is recognised in respect of a category of employees, the employer has a choice in respect of who shall be the representatives of those employees. The employer can choose to consult representatives directly elected by the affected employees (assuming that the employees are willing to co-operate with the election) for the purposes of TUPE consultation (although not necessarily appointed for the specific purposes of the transfer in question)[39] or 'representatives appointed or elected by the affected employees otherwise than for the purposes of [reg 13 consultation] who (having regard to the purposes for and the method by which they were appointed or elected) have authority from those employees to receive information and to be consulted about the transfer on their behalf'.[40]

5.48 In practice, where no union is recognised most employers' choice will be determined by whether there is a suitable standing body already in place. However, the election of a new group of representatives is the safer route for the employer, due to the lack of clarity in the wording of reg 13(3)(b)(i). An employer would be well advised to check carefully the basis on which the standing body has been appointed before determining whether that body is likely to meet the objective test of having the authority to act on behalf of the employees in a TUPE consultation.

5.49 There is little guidance as to how an employer can demonstrate that such a body has authority to be consulted or what is meant by 'having regard to the purposes for and the method by which they were appointed or elected'. Given the risk of an award of compensation to those affected if an employer wrongly assumes that the body was appropriate, many employers choose not to take the risk, given that the burden falls on the employer to demonstrate that he has consulted with the correct representative,[41] the representative with the necessary authority to represent the employees. One might assume that a works council might be a safe body to consult, given that its purpose would be specifically to create a forum for information and consultation on issues of significance for the employer. However, regard would have to be paid to the constitution of the works council and the circumstances of the proposed transfer.

---

39   Regulation 13(3)(b)(ii). The election must have been compliant with the procedure in
      reg 14(1).
40   Regulation 13(3)(b)(i).
41   Regulation 15(3).

5.50 The Information and Consultation of Employees Regulations 2004[42] ('ICE Regulations') provide for the establishment of 'national works councils' for the purpose of informing and consulting the workforce and allow employees to request that the employer sets up the necessary information and consultation machinery. National works councils are likely to be consulted about strategic business decisions such as business transfers at a much earlier stage than the point at which consultation under TUPE 2006 would begin. The extent of the duty to consult will depend on the terms of the agreement under which the national works council has been established.

5.51 Ordinarily, an employer will be under an obligation to inform and to consult the national works council about a TUPE transfer.[43] The time required for consultation is likely to be rather longer than under TUPE 2006 by reason of, inter alia, the obligation to allow the national works council time to prepare for the consultation. However, the ICE Regulations provide that, where the TUPE information and consultation mechanism applies, the employer can notify the national works council in writing that it will comply with its TUPE obligations in lieu of the ICE obligations, provided that this notification must be given on each occasion when the duty under TUPE arises.[44] Where the standard ICE provisions are superseded by a negotiated agreement, it is important that this interface is dealt with in the agreement, so as to avoid parallel duties to inform and consult under TUPE and the ICE Regulations.

CONDUCTING ELECTIONS

5.52 Regulation 14 of TUPE 2006 provides for the election of employee representatives in some detail. Strict adherence to these rules is appropriate to avoid the employer being left open to a claim for breach of the information and consultation requirements, however technical. The rules within reg 14 reflect the fact that it is the employer on whom the burden lies of making the running with the election arrangements, not the employees themselves. The burden lies on the employer to show that the requirements of reg 14 have been complied with.[45]

5.53 The rules can be summarised as follows:

- The employer must make such arrangements as are reasonably practicable[46] to ensure that the election is fair. Little guidance is offered in terms of what standards are expected. There is a tendency to overkill in order to ensure compliance given the punitive nature of the sanction for breach of this obligation, but this will be tempered by circumstances and by the fact that the sanction for non-compliance is at the discretion of the tribunal and may be expected to reflect the extent to which the non-compliance is material. It may be that an employer decides to call in

---

42   SI 2004/3426.
43   ICE Regulations, reg 20(c)(i)–(ii).
44   ICE Regulations, reg 20(5).
45   TUPE 2006, reg 15(4).
46   See **5.71** in relation to what is 'reasonably practical'.

a specialist ballot organiser. There is no obligation to do so, but one could see how this might make a large-scale exercise more manageable and such organisations are perhaps less likely to be the subject of a successful attack to the effect that the process was not administered fairly.

- The number of representatives to be elected is to be determined by the employer, and it should ensure that there are sufficient representatives to represent the interests of all affected employees having regard to the number and classes of those employees. The criterion for setting a number of representatives is to elect enough so that all the affected employees are represented. Much will depend upon how many different classes of employee there are and how many employees there are in each class. As a bare minimum there will need to be one representative for each class of employee so that every employee can point to a representative of his or her class, but that minimum may well not be workable in the event of illness or a clash of diaries. Hence a number of representatives from each class of employees to ensure coverage of all interests at meetings, even though all representatives are not present, would make sense. Moreover, geographical reasons or simple weight of numbers might suggest a greater number of representatives in order to ensure good communication between representatives and their constituents.

- As a general rule, where there is a substantial transfer of employees a ratio of one representative to between 25 and 50 employees is a common range, depending on the number of affected employees. The greater the number, the higher the ratio. For very large-scale exercises or very small numbers, these ratios will not be particularly helpful.

- The employer must determine whether the affected employees will be represented by representatives of all the affected employees or by representatives drawn from particular classes of those employees. There is some scope for the employer to use this provision to seek to dilute the influence of troublesome groups, notwithstanding that its flexibility is designed to accommodate the circumstances of each case. It will be appropriate to divide the affected employees into separate constituencies where they naturally fall into different categories or are affected in different ways by the employer's proposals. Otherwise, if they are treated as a single group, the outcome of the election may be that some groups of the affected employees are effectively unrepresented, either because employees within that group fail to stand for election or because they are not successful in the election. The effectiveness of consultation will be severely undermined if affected groups are not properly represented.

- The employer should determine before the election the term of office of the employee representatives, so that it is of sufficient length to enable information to be given and consultation completed. This will generally be the period until consultation closes or the transfer takes place, although there may be circumstances when a longer period will be appropriate, for example, when there are likely to be subsequent transfers. Not that it can be assumed that the group would automatically fit the circumstances of a future transfer. They may be an inappropriate body, not least because the group of affected employees may be of a different composition in a subsequent transfer.

- All candidates for election of the employee representatives must be affected employees on the date of the election. This rules out external involvement.
- No affected employee should be unreasonably excluded from standing for election. The door is open to the employer to exclude a candidate where it has good reason to do so – for example, where on a previous occasion a candidate has demonstrated his or her unsuitability, perhaps by unreasonably disrupting meetings.
- All affected employees on the date of the election are entitled to vote for employee representatives.
- Employees are entitled to vote for as many candidates as there are representatives to be elected to represent them generally or for their particular class of employee.
- The election should be conducted to ensure that, so far as is reasonably practicable,[47] voting is secret and that the votes given at the election are accurately counted. The impulse to conduct the ballot by calling the employees together in the canteen and organising a show of hands should be resisted. A common way of organising a vote quickly across a dispersed group would be to use e-mail. Given that the recipient of the e-mail can readily identify the voter who has sent the e-mail, steps should be taken to have the e-mails sent to a confidential e-mail address.

5.54 No specific timeframe is set down for the election. This is determined by what follows, given that the employer must allow enough time for meaningful consultation to take place prior to the transfer. Consultation cannot start until the representatives have been elected.

5.55 When determining how to divide employees into constituencies, employers may wish to take account of the following:

- What classes of employees are affected by the proposals? Are different constituencies appropriate given the geographical location of the affected employees, the department or business unit in which they work, the roles which they perform, the proposed selection pools or the level and grade of employee affected?
- Are the employees affected in different ways? Is the employer's proposal to make radical changes in respect of employees in some groups, while others will be affected only marginally? Do the timescales for the transfer differ for the various categories of employee?
- Where affected employees are in different geographical locations, how does this impact on the practicability of consultation as a single group? If different geographical areas are treated as a single constituency, the employer will need to bring all of the representatives together in one place for consultation. It may be difficult for the representatives to communicate effectively across different locations with the employees that they represent. On the other hand, if separate geographical constituencies are used, how appropriate will it be for the employer to consult representatives of each location independently from the others?
- Separating employees into distinct constituencies allows consultation to

---

47   See **5.71** on what is 'reasonably practicable'.

take place on specific issues which affect that group. The ability to focus consultation this way can be important, for example, where different selection criteria are to be applied to different groups of affected employees or where the issues faced differ across those groups. Consultation need not be a single process – the employer has great flexibility to progress consultation in parallel with each group and possibly to expedite consultation in some business-critical areas.

5.56 In more complex and time-critical exercises, having a larger body of representatives allows the employer the flexibility to break consultation up and to progress different aspects of the obligation to consult as discrete exercises. If such an approach is to be taken, the employer must ensure that there are adequate numbers of representatives to facilitate this form of consultation.

5.57 Regulation 14(2) of TUPE 2006 contains a provision for by-elections allowing a subsequent election to be held in circumstances where a representative ceases to act as an employee representative of a class of affected employees and as a consequence a class of affected employees would otherwise be left unrepresented.

THE EMPLOYER'S DUTY IN THE EVENT OF DELAY OR APATHY

5.58 The employer's ability to comply with its duty to deliver information to employee representatives could be frustrated by a delay in electing representatives to whom the information can be distributed. This is addressed in reg 13(10) of TUPE 2006. The employer which has invited the employees to elect representatives and has issued the invitation sufficiently far in advance to enable representatives to be elected and for the information to be delivered in time, is treated as being compliant with its duty to deliver, provided that it does so as soon as reasonably practicable after the election result is known,[48] so as to keep the delay to a minimum. In other words, if there would have been time to consult fully, but that became impracticable because the election process went on longer than it should by reason of employee delay, so that there is no longer time to consult fully, there is no obligation to delay the transfer for consultation to be completed and the employer will be considered to have consulted fully, even though the consultation remains incomplete. However, bearing in mind the duty of the employer to run the election, reliance upon the provisions of reg 13(10) is always a haven of last resort.

5.59 Note that this excuse is available to the employer even if there were, ready and available, existing representatives who could have fulfilled the role.

5.60 There may be circumstances in which there are no recognised unions, no other representatives who can be rostered for duty in respect of the transfer and where no candidates put themselves forward for election as a representative. In these circumstances the employer can do nothing by way of informing and

---

48   As regards what is 'reasonably practicable' see **5.71**.

consulting. In one respect, the employer need hardly be concerned that it will be held liable for any failings on the basis that it is most unlikely that there would be anyone interested in pursuing a claim. However, reg 13(11) sets out the employer's duty in these circumstances. Should the employees have failed to elect representatives within a 'reasonable time' following the employer's invitation to do so, then the duty of the employer is limited to circulating to each affected employee a note of the information which would otherwise be deliverable to the employee representatives. There being no representatives, there is no duty to consult. Of course, they may yet elect representatives, at which point an obligation to consult may arise, notwithstanding that there may not be enough time left to consult fully. There is no obligation to substitute individual consultation for collective consultation.[49]

5.61 The delivery of a written note of the information prescribed to be delivered to all affected employees and an offer to consult the whole group is often seen as a shortcut in relatively simple transfers. It is argued that the disclosure of information to each affected employee means that each such employee and – by definition – each person eligible to be an employee representative, has been informed. It is far from clear that this approach is appropriate in relation to information disclosure. Channelling information via representatives gives the representative the opportunity to interpret the information and to explain it to his or her constituents. Simply circulating the information is not necessarily compliant; a strict construction of the obligation would conclude that the information must be given to the representative qua representative.

5.62 However, where this approach will definitely fall down is in relation to consultation. There is, it is suggested, a difference between receiving an invitation to consultation in a personal capacity and receiving it as the representative of a group, not least in terms of the inhibitions which an employee is likely to feel in relation to speaking up during consultation in an individual capacity.

5.63 A similar shortcut is often followed where there is no obligation to consult because there are no 'measures' contemplated. This is inherently dangerous, because it is difficult to be satisfied that there are no 'measures' proposed, given the nebulous nature of that term. Again, the failure to supply information to representatives is a breach of reg 13, however technical, and the punitive nature of the compensation which may be awarded pursuant to reg 15 gives rise to the prospect of a significant liability.

TRANSFEREE OBLIGATIONS TO THE TRANSFEROR IN RESPECT OF THE DISCLOSURE OF INFORMATION REGARDING 'MEASURES'

5.64 The key information of interest to employees in the majority of transfers will be the proposals of the transferee in relation to the transferring employees

---

49 *Howard v Millrise* [2005] IRLR 84.

once they have become employees of the transferee. For this reason reg 13(4) of TUPE 2006 imposes an obligation on the transferee to provide to the transferor with information regarding such measures, thereby enabling the transferor to disclose such information pursuant to reg 13(2)(d). The information must be supplied early enough to enable the transferor to comply with its duties. This provision is difficult to follow, for the transferor is not under an obligation to consult in respect of the information concerning the transferee's measures. It requires Millet J's expansive view of this provision (see **5.14**) to make sense of this provision. Alternatively, it could be argued that the entire corpus of information disclosable under reg 13(2)(d) should be delivered long enough in advance to enable consultation to take place. The argument would run that, even though only part of the information is subject to consultation, the employee representatives should see the whole picture. In the event that a claim is made against the transferor in respect of a failure to comply with reg 13(2)(d) the transferor may serve notice to join the transferee to such proceedings.[50]

5.65 The consultation mechanism may be criticised as being a rather unimaginative process, born of a literal approach to transposing the Directive into English law rather than looking to its wider purpose. In many EU countries, consultation will involve both the transferor and the transferee. This, surely, is the only basis for a sensible dialogue concerning the issues of greatest concern.

5.66 In practice, the provisions of reg 13 are often seen as a legal minimum beyond which the parties to a transfer will need to go in order to achieve a meaningful dialogue and to facilitate a smooth transfer. In an outsourcing, the transferor will in many cases need to 'sell' the transferee to the transferring workforce. If they are unable to do so, the transaction may be imperilled. Industrial action is a not infrequent consequence of a situation where the workforce feels in danger. Interrupted service delivery is a real risk. Likewise the transferee will wish to engage with the transferring workforce prior to transfer so as to plan for transition. Hence the involvement of the transferee in consultation is a regular occurrence, but this involvement is outside regulation by TUPE. Moreover, the information flow will often far exceed what is required by TUPE. It is not unusual to encounter employee briefings, bulletins and dedicated websites.

COMPLAINANTS

5.67 In the event that an employer fails in any aspect of the duty to inform and to consult a complaint may be brought in an employment tribunal. There is a 3-month time-limit within which claims must be lodged, commencing on the date on which the transfer is completed.

5.68 A claim may be brought by any of the following classes of potential complainants, dependent on the nature of the alleged failure on the part of the employer:

---

50 Regulation 15(5).

- If the allegation is that the employer has failed in relation to the election of representatives, any affected employee of that employer may bring a claim.
- Should the alleged failure relate in any other way to employee representatives, any of the representatives to whom the alleged failure related may bring a claim.
- If the alleged failure relates to representatives of a trade union, the union itself may bring a claim.
- In all other cases any affected employee may bring a claim.

5.69 Hence it is the representatives who should bring the majority of the claims that would naturally arise out of these information and consultation duties. An affected employee who feels that the consultation has been a sham and that there has not been proper consultation with the employee representatives is not in a position to make a complaint to a tribunal – he or she is reliant upon his or her representative doing so.

5.70 In practical terms, the employer will often avoid the consequences of a failure simply by reason of a lack of willingness on the part of employees and their representatives to bring a claim. This may spring from a lack of knowledge, a degree of apathy as to the significance of the whole exercise or for reasons of cost. Should a representative feel that the employer has failed in its duties in relation to the consultation – for example, by failing to disclose a significant piece of information or failing to consult with a genuine attempt to reach agreement on proposed measures – it is perhaps unlikely that the representative is going to bring proceedings in a tribunal, bearing in mind the costs of doing so, the uncertainties of the law and the limited rewards, not least for himself. A trade union is much more likely to keep an employer on its toes.

The 'special circumstances' defence

5.71 Regulation 13(9) of TUPE 2006 provides for the 'special circumstances' defence: if in any case there are 'special circumstances which render it not reasonably practicable' for the employer to comply with the reg 13 obligations to inform and to consult and the employer can show that it took 'all such steps ... as were reasonably practicable in those circumstances' then the employer may escape censure for non-compliance with those duties. Regulation 15(2) contains a similar formula.

5.72 Where the issue arises as to whether the employer can make out the reg 13(9) defence, the burden of proof is on the employer to show two things. First, that 'special circumstances' apply. It is not enough for an employer to show that there were circumstances which rendered compliance with the relevant statutory requirements not reasonably practicable. Those circumstances must be 'special'. Secondly, special circumstances do not absolve the employer from complying with the consultation requirement if compliance was reasonably practicable. Hence the employer must show a link between the special circumstances and compliance being not reasonably practicable. The employer is still under an obligation to take all steps towards compliance with the requirement as are reasonably practicable in the circumstances of the case.

5.73   The burden of proof is on the employer to show the existence of special circumstances and also to show that such steps as *were* reasonably practicable were taken to comply with the particular requirement concerned. The existence of special circumstances is judged on the facts of the case. There is no generic category of 'special circumstances'. Again, we must seek guidance from cases concerning the collective consultation duties on redundancies under s 188ff of TULR(C)A 1992. It is well established, for example, that insolvency is not of itself a special circumstance. In *Clarks of Hove v Bakers Union*,[51] a bank suddenly stopped the employer's credit facility and appointed a receiver. The court held that whilst insolvency itself is not a 'special circumstance' it may be that the attempts of the employer to keep trading up to the last minute in the genuine hope that insolvency could be avoided did constitute special circumstances where it was not reasonably practicable to consult about redundancies. However, in *GMB v Rankin & Harrison*[52] the act of an administrative receiver dismissing employees to make a business more attractive to potential purchasers was considered to be common to any form of receivership or insolvency, and therefore not capable of giving rise to 'special' circumstances. Furthermore, the receiver's inability to sell the business and the fact that no orders were available were also held to be common incidents of insolvency, rather than special circumstances.

5.74   In *Armour v ASTMS* Lord McDonald commented as follows:[53]

> 'It is settled that insolvency is not by itself a special circumstance, although it may be. It must be something out of the ordinary, something uncommon (*The Bakers' Union v Clarks of Hove Ltd* [1978] IRLR 366). In our view an application for a government loan by a company in financial difficulties which had already received substantial financial help from government sources is a circumstance sufficiently special to make it not reasonably practicable to issue the formal written details required by s.99(5)[54] until the outcome of the application was known.'

Confidentiality and 'special circumstances'

5.75   The desire for commercial confidentiality often means that employers are reluctant to enter into consultation with staff. However, the need for confidentiality alone is unlikely to amount to special circumstances, unless there are peculiar and specific facts. The courts are unlikely to adopt an expansive view of this exception. To do so would all too readily allow employers to find a commercial excuse for excluding employee rights. Moreover, the special circumstances defence does not appear in the Directive and there must be doubts as to whether the UK has implemented the Directive appropriately in this respect.

5.76   Listed companies are subject to obligations to announce price-sensitive information to the stock exchanges on which their shares are traded before it otherwise enters the public domain. Such rules do not, however, provide a

---

51   [1977] IRLR 264.
52   [1992] IRLR 514.
53   [1979] IRLR 24, at 25.
54   Now TULR(C)A 1992, s 188(4).

defence to a failure to consult collectively under TUPE 2006. There is no express exclusion. Nor is the matter in any way special – it is a common issue for all listed companies. The FSA Handbook expressly provides that information may be provided in confidence to employee representatives for the purpose of consultation. This does rather beg the question as to whether the representatives are bound to treat the information as confidential. To be required to do so would inhibit the proper exercise of their role. Many listed companies will make Stock Exchange announcements simultaneously with communications to employees and their representatives. However, care needs to be taken to ensure that the language of such announcements is consistent with the need for consultation, referring to the plans as proposals rather than as a 'done deal'. At the same time, the FSA Handbook also provides that if information is given in confidence to employee representatives, this does not of itself give rise to an obligation to make an announcement.[55] In *MSF v Refuge Assurance*[56] the then President of the EAT, Lindsay J, referred to the argument that the requirements of secrecy contained within the Takeover Code amount to a 'special circumstance'. His comments were obiter and were made in the context of a collective redundancy consultation. It is difficult to make much of them other than to infer that this is at least a reasonable argument:

> 'At the employment tribunal the companies argued that the requirements of secrecy imposed by the Takeover Code (to which the merger was subject) were a special circumstance. The employment tribunal made no finding on this issue. The Takeover Code has not been put before us … In these circumstances we express no view on either part of s.188(7)[57] save to say that in our view it cannot be simply assumed that disclosure to, say, a senior union official on the like terms of confidence as would be applicable to the companies' directors would necessarily be so restrictive that it would be completely useless to him and that it would therefore represent a step that need not be taken by the employer, or that such an official would necessarily decline to accept information on such terms. It is to be noted that *Hamish Armour v ASTMS* [1979] IRLR 24, at paragraph 11, contemplates (without proposing) disclosure to responsible union officials on a confidential basis.'

REMEDIES

5.77 The tribunal is obliged to make a declaration where it finds in favour of a complainant.[58] The primary remedy for a failure to comply with these requirements is an award of compensation by the tribunal, which is at the discretion of the tribunal both as to scope and quantum. It is for the tribunal to set the level of compensation which is just and equitable in the circumstances having regard to the seriousness of the failure and to identify the class of employees to whom the award should apply. An employee who is the subject of such an award can then personally bring a claim in circumstances where the

---

55 FSA Handbook DR 2.5.
56 [2002] IRLR 324.
57 TULR(C)A 1992.
58 Regulation 15(7).

compensation is not paid. The tribunal's discretion to make an award of compensation is capped at 13 weeks' pay per employee. There is no limit on a week's pay for these purposes.

5.78　Whether the award is compensatory or punitive is open to doubt. It has been held, in contrast with the collective redundancy consultation provisions of s 188ff of TULR(C)A 1992 that the award should be made on a compensatory rather than a punitive basis. Hence in the case of a technical breach with no detriment suffered on the part of the employees, the EAT held that there was a power and not an obligation to make an award and due to lack of detriment no award was made – see *Baxter and Others v Marks and Spencer and Others.*[59]

5.79　However, a different division of the EAT in *Sweetin v Coral Racing*[60] has held that awards are essentially punitive and that they should be made by following the principles in *GMB v Susie Radin Ltd.*[61] Giving the judgment of the EAT, Lady Smith says as follows:[62]

> 'The wording of [the provisions relating to the awards payable in respect of a failure to inform and consult in respect of redundancies under s 188 of TULR(C)A 1992 and under the Regulations] can, accordingly, be seen to reflect each other. They both underline the importance of compliance with the duty to consult. They both, significantly, instruct the tribunal, when assessing compensation, to focus on the nature and extent of the employers' default. That gives rise to the inevitable inference that Parliament intended the awards in each case to be penal in nature, rather than solely compensatory albeit that, in our view, the use of the words "just and equitable" would entitle a tribunal also to have regard to any actual loss that a claimant employee showed that he had in fact suffered as a result of the failure to consult. Lord Justice Peter Gibson, in the Susie Radin case, draws attention to such an analysis having been made by Lord McDonald, as long ago as 1978, in the case of *Association of Patternmakers & Allied Craftsmen v Kirvin Ltd* [1978] IRLR 318:
>
> > "A tribunal, however, is specifically enjoined to determine the [protected] period and so the amount of the award by paying regard to the seriousness of the employer's default. This introduces a punitive element into the jurisdiction of an industrial tribunal and in contrast with, eg, the calculation of a compensatory award which is based upon what is just and equitable having regard to the loss sustained."
>
> He followed that approach in the Susie Radin case ...'

5.80　In the *Susie Radin* case the Court of Appeal had to consider the principles for making awards following a failure to inform and to consult collectively in relation to redundancy proposals. Those principles were set out as follows:

- The purpose of the award is to provide a sanction for an employer's breach of the obligations, not to compensate employees for any loss which they have suffered as a result of the breach.

59　UK/EAT/0162/05/RN.
60　[2006] IRLR 252.
61　[2004] IRLR 400.
62　[2006] IRLR 252, at 256.

- The tribunal has a wide discretion, but it should focus on the seriousness of the employer's default.
- The seriousness of the default will vary from a technical breach to a complete failure to consult.
- The tribunal may wish to consider whether the failure was deliberate and whether the employer had any legal advice on its consultation obligations.
- Where there has been no consultation at all, it is appropriate for the tribunal to start with the maximum award and then to establish if there are any mitigating circumstances which would justify awarding less than the maximum.

Hence the starting-point for a tribunal would be to award the maximum compensation, working down from there if there are circumstances which justify a lesser award.

5.81 This is an all too typical example of the confusion which appears to be inevitable wherever TUPE is involved – the two EAT decisions are in direct conflict and we await resolution of this conflict in subsequent cases.

5.82 Payments are computed by reference to a week's gross pay. The tax treatment of payments in the hands of the employees is unclear. Payments are not taxable as earnings.[63] Given the decision in *Susie Radin*[64] that they are punitive awards, it is arguable that they are not taxable at all. However, if they are taxable it is strongly arguable that they are made in connection with the termination of employment and hence the £30,000 exemption in respect of termination payments will be applicable. National Insurance contributions are payable.[65]

5.83 For many years, awards resulting from the failure of a transferor to inform or to consult did not transfer to the transferee by reason of TUPE.[66] However, the position changed when it was held in *Kerry Foods v Creber*[67] that such awards do transfer under TUPE. The impact of this case was not only to put on the innocent party (the transferee) the burden for the failings of the transferor, but also to remove any deterrent against the transferor simply ignoring its duties to inform and to consult on the basis that there was no sanction for its failure to do so. TUPE 2006 has changed the position once more by introducing joint and several liability as between the transferor and the transferee in respect of payments of compensation.[68] Although the transferee stands in a position akin to a guarantor, it is now the case that a tribunal can look to where the blame lies and to allocate liability accordingly.

ENFORCEMENT

5.84 Claims must be made to an employment tribunal before the end of a 3-month period beginning on the date of the completion of the transfer or, in

---

63 *Mintec Ltd v Inland Revenue Commissioners* [2001] SSCD 101.
64 [2004] IRLR 400.
65 Social Security (Contributions) (Employment Protection) Regulations 1977, SI 1977/622, reg 2(b).
66 *Angus Jowett v NUTGW* [1985] ICR 646.
67 [2000] IRLR 10.
68 Regulation 15(9).

the case of a failure to pay awards of compensation, the date of the tribunal's order.[69] Where the tribunal is satisfied that it was not reasonably practicable[70] to bring the claim within the 3-month period, the tribunal may extend the 3-month period by such additional period as it considers reasonable.

5.85 The time-limit says nothing about how early a claim may be made. In fact, the claim may be made as soon as the cause of action arises and as a consequence claims may be made before the transfer has taken place.[71] This has the result that the issue of whether there is a TUPE transfer may be determined by a tribunal in advance of the transfer taking place, acting as a declaration on the point.

5.86 The remedies of a declaration and an award of compensation are the sole remedies for breach of the information and consultation provisions.[72] An injunction to restrain the breach is not available. This limits the efficacy of the law in this area, and is to be contrasted with the position in certain other Member States of the EU whereby the transaction may be halted pending compliance with information and consultation obligations.[73]

OVERLAP WITH S 188 OF TULR(C)A 1992

5.87 It will not infrequently be the case that the transfer will involve redundancies and as a consequence obligations to inform and to consult collectively will arise in respect of redundancies and under TUPE. The issue arises as to whether the consultation process can encompass compliance with obligations under s 188ff of TULR(C)A 1992 and reg 13 TUPE 2006. In practice, if redundancies are contemplated these should be disclosed as 'measures' and will inevitably form a part of the consultation process. If the redundancies are to be made post transfer, the issue arises as to whether the redundancy consultation may begin with the transferor and conclude with the incoming transferee post transfer. Given that TUPE operates on the basis of the fiction that the incoming employer had always been from the employer, dating back to the start of the employee's relationship with the transferor, the transferee should get credit for consultation undertaken by the transferor. However, on the strict language of s 188 it cannot be said that either the transferor or the transferee is 'an employer proposing to dismiss' prior to the transfer and hence there is an element of risk in seeking to run the two processes in this way.

5.88 A similar problem arises where the question of whether there is a relevant transfer under TUPE remains in dispute. Given that this issue will be determined by a tribunal well after the transfer has taken place, the transferor is faced with the dilemma prior to the transfer of how to comply with TUPE

---

69   Regulation 15(12).
70   Note that the reg 15(2) test of reasonable practicability does not apply in respect of this provision. This is a matter for the tribunal based on all the facts of the case.
71   *South Durham Health Authority v UNISON* [1995] IRLR 407.
72   Regulation 16(1).
73   See **5.18**.

consultation obligations (assuming that there is a relevant transfer for the purposes of TUPE 2006) or with s 188ff of TULR(C)A 1992 in respect of redundancies if there is no transfer under TUPE. In those circumstances the better view is that the employer should notify the employees that their employment with the transferee will come to an end on the date of the alleged transfer either because it migrates to the transferee or because of redundancy. Information should be disclosed pursuant to the requirements of TUPE and of s 188 and consultation should cover both eventualities.

TRANSFER OF EMPLOYEE LIABILITY INFORMATION

5.89   During the period of consultation which culminated in TUPE 2006, the Government was lobbied to provide for the disclosure of employee information to the transferee employer. Two objectives lay behind the request. First, those preparing a tender for the provision of services will wish to understand the implications of their bid in terms of who they will inherit and on what terms, so that they can price accurately for the staffing costs of the delivery of the service. Secondly, the transferee will wish to be informed as to the details of the contract of employment which it inherits. The request fell upon deaf (or at least unwilling) ears in respect of the first objective, but the second objective is satisfied in reg 11. This deals with the concern that, hitherto, transferee employers had inherited employment relationships which were deemed to have always been a relationship between them (as opposed to the transferor employer) and the transferring employee and yet they may have had no knowledge of that relationship. In an extreme case they may have had no knowledge of the basic terms and conditions of employment pertaining to the relationship. The employer would be in no position to comply with its obligations to the transferring employees if it had no knowledge of what those obligations were.

5.90   The provisions of reg 11(1) set out an obligation on a transferor employer to notify the transferee (including indirectly, through a third party)[74] of certain 'employee liability information' relating to any person employed by the transferor who is assigned to the organised grouping of resources or employees which is the subject of the transfer. Hence the *Botzen*[75] test is applied as if the transfer were to take place at the time when the information is due, and it is those employees who are the subject of the disclosure obligation, notwithstanding that some such employees may not transfer, perhaps because they fall out of scope at the last minute or because they exercise their right to opt out of the transfer.

5.91   The information must be disclosed in written form or made available 'in a readily accessible form'. This would accommodate the common practice of downloading the necessary information onto a disk or CD-ROM, but could

---

74   Regulation 11(7)(b).

75   See **2.131**. Given that employees who have been dismissed may appeal successfully and be deemed to have been in employment immediately before the transfer (see *G4S Justice Services v Anstey* EAT 0698/05) it would be prudent to include information in relation to such employees in the disclosures.

also include sources such as access to a virtual data room or extranet. In an extreme case it could be that the delivery of information over the telephone could suffice.

5.92 The information which is to be disclosed is set out in reg 11(2) as follows:

(a) the identity and age of the employee;
(b) those particulars of employment that an employer is obliged to give to an employee pursuant to s 1 of ERA 1996. This provision will provide welcome certainty to the employment relationship post transfer and will also avoid the common problem of the past whereby transferee employers found themselves falling into a breach of the obligation to provide a statement of particulars pursuant to s 1. However, it is worth noting that a s 1 statement is not necessarily a complete statement of the terms and conditions of employment of a transferring employee. Hence, in situations where the transfer is the subject of a negotiated contract, transferee employers are still well advised to seek a warranty that there has been a complete disclosure of all terms and conditions of employment of the transferring employees. Key terms of the employment contract could therefore be omitted from the information disclosure. For example, the existence of an enhanced redundancy entitlement may be of great significance in the context of the transfer and yet it would not be disclosable. Moreover, there is no obligation to provide such information to employers within the first 2 months of employment. Hence these employees would appear to be outside the scope of the obligation to provide this information to the transferee.
(c) Information of any disciplinary procedure taken against an employee or grievance procedure taken by an employee within the previous 2 years, in circumstances where the Employment Act 2002 (Dispute Resolution) Regulations 2004[76] apply. This is, in fact, quite narrow and would not include oral and written warnings, for example.
(d) Information of any court or tribunal case, claim or action brought by a transferring employee against the transferor within the previous 2 years or any such claim which the transferor has reasonable grounds to believe that an employee may bring against the transferee, arising out of the employee's employment with the transferor.
(e) Information of any collective agreement which will have effect after the transfer.

5.93 This information is to be disclosed as at a specified date not more than 14 days before the date on which the information is notified to the transferee. The notification itself must be given not less than 14 days before the relevant transfer. There is a 'special circumstances' defence – where compliance is not reasonably practicable, the information must be delivered as soon as reasonably practicable thereafter. The DTI Guidance to TUPE 2006[77] quotes the example of where a service transfers at very short notice, as the type of instance where delivery of information 14 days in advance may not be possible.

---

76 SI 2004/752.
77 See http://www.dti.gov.uk/er/individual/tupeguide2006regs.pdf.

5.94 Of course, information delivered as late as 14 days prior to the transfer leaves the transferee employer with little time to react. It does, however, mean that the employees can enter into an informed relationship with their new employer from day one. It is also conceivable that a potential transferee may see this information for the first time and may wish to avoid the consequence of inheriting such a workforce with its attendant liabilities. This does, in theory at least, raise the prospect of a transferee employer pulling out of a transfer at this late stage to avoid its consequences. If a transfer is to be the subject of a simultaneous contract and completion, it may be possible for a potential transferee to manoeuvre a transferor to disclose this information before there is a contractual commitment on the part of the transferee to the transfer itself.

5.95 Once the information has been disclosed, there is a duty on the transferor employer to keep it updated pending the transfer. The provisions in this respect are a little difficult to interpret. Under reg 11(5), once the information has been notified to the transferee employer the transferor is under a duty to notify the transferee employer of any change in the information. No time-limit is attached to this duty; it would appear that the transferor employer can notify these changes at its leisure, subject to the general time-limit attached to all notifications which is not less than 14 days before the transfer.

5.96 Regulation 11(4) captures information relating to employees in respect of whom liabilities will transfer pursuant to the principle in the *Litster*[78] case.

5.97 The information will often, in practice, be supplied to the transferee's solicitor. Although the legislation does not specifically provide for this, it is likely that such delivery will amount to compliance.[79]

REMEDIES FOR NON-COMPLIANCE

5.98 When the provisions of what is now reg 11 of TUPE 2006 were first circulated for consultation, enforcement was by a claim to the High Court with an attendant fine. This proposal has been replaced in the final version of the 2006 Regulations by a right on the part of the aggrieved transferee employer to seek compensation from an employment tribunal. A transferee employer may lodge a claim at any point from the time of transfer, alleging that the transferor employer is in breach of its duties to transfer employee liability information. If upheld, the tribunal shall make a declaration to this effect and may, at its discretion, award compensation to the transferee employer.

5.99 The award of compensation shall be such as the tribunal considers just and equitable. The tribunal shall have particular regard to any loss suffered by the transferee employer as a consequence of the breach by the transferor of its obligations to transfer employee liability information. The tribunal shall also have particular regard to the terms of any contract between transferor and transferee under which the transferor is liable to pay any sum to the transferee in respect of a failure to deliver employee liability information. In practice,

---

78   [1990] 1 AC 546.
79   See *Infiniteland Ltd v Artisan Contracting Ltd* [2005] EWCA Civ 758.

where the transfer is the subject of a contract between the parties, it is usual for a transferee employer to seek an indemnity in respect of any shortcoming in terms of the delivery or accuracy of employee information.

5.100 The transferee employer is under a duty to mitigate its loss. Compensation is without limit and shall not be less than £500 per employee who is the subject of the duty and in respect of whom there has been a failure to comply, save to the extent that the tribunal feels it to be just and equitable to award a lower sum.

5.101 Complaints must be made within 3 months of the transfer save where not reasonably practicable to do so. The same test applies as governs claims made pursuant to reg 15. It is not possible to contract out of the obligation to provide this information. The extent to which that principle will impact on the enforceability of any indemnities is unclear.

5.102 Frequently, a transferee service provider will fix its price for delivery of the service on the date of the transfer by reference to the final picture as regards who will transfer and on what terms. Reliance may be placed in this respect on the information delivered pursuant to reg 11. A substantial loss could arise where information is inaccurate and is relied on in this way.

APPENDICES

LEGISLATION

Appendix 1

THE TRANSFER OF UNDERTAKINGS (PROTECTION OF EMPLOYMENT) REGULATIONS 2006, SI 2006/246

STATUTORY INSTRUMENTS

2006 NO. 246

TERMS AND CONDITIONS OF EMPLOYMENT

THE TRANSFER OF UNDERTAKINGS (PROTECTION OF EMPLOYMENT) REGULATIONS 2006

Made _ _ _	*6th February 2006*
Laid Before Parliament	*7th February 2006*
Coming into force _ _	*6th April 2006*

The Secretary of State makes the following Regulations in exercise of the powers conferred upon him by section 2(2) of the European Communities Act 1972[1] (being a Minister designated for the purposes of that section in relation to rights and obligations relating to employers and employees on the transfer or merger of undertakings, businesses or parts of businesses[2]]) and section 38 of the Employment Relations Act 1999[3].

Citation, commencement and extent

1.—(1) These Regulations may be cited as the Transfer of Undertakings (Protection of Employment) Regulations 2006.

(2) These Regulations shall come into force on 6 April 2006.

(3) These Regulations shall extend to Northern Ireland, except where otherwise provided.

Interpretation

2.—(1) In these Regulations—

"assigned" means assigned other than on a temporary basis;

"collective agreement", "collective bargaining" and "trade union" have the same meanings respectively as in the 1992 Act;

"contract of employment" means any agreement between an employee and his employer determining the terms and conditions of his employment;

references to "contractor" in regulation 3 shall include a sub-contractor;

"employee" means any individual who works for another person whether under a contract of service or apprenticeship or otherwise but does not include anyone who provides services under a contract for services and references to a person's employer shall be construed accordingly;

"insolvency practitioner" has the meaning given to the expression by Part XIII of the Insolvency Act 1986[4];

references to "organised grouping of employees" shall include a single employee;

"recognised" has the meaning given to the expression by section 178(3) of the 1992 Act;

"relevant transfer" means a transfer or a service provision change to which these Regulations apply in accordance with regulation 3 and "transferor" and "transferee" shall be construed accordingly and in the case of a service provision change falling within regulation 3(1)(b), "the transferor" means the person who carried out the activities prior to the service provision change and "the transferee" means the person who carries out the activities as a result of the service provision change;

"the 1992 Act" means the Trade Union and Labour Relations (Consolidation) Act 1992[5];

"the 1996 Act" means the Employment Rights Act 1996[6];

"the 1996 Tribunals Act" means the Employment Tribunals Act 1996[7];

"the 1981 Regulations" means the Transfer of Undertakings (Protection of Employment) Regulations 1981[8].

(2) For the purposes of these Regulations the representative of a trade union recognised by an employer is an official or other person authorised to carry on collective bargaining with that employer by that trade union.

(3) In the application of these Regulations to Northern Ireland the Regulations shall have effect as set out in Schedule 1.

A relevant transfer

3.—(1) These Regulations apply to—
    (a)   a transfer of an undertaking, business or part of an undertaking or business situated immediately before the transfer in the United Kingdom to another person where there is a transfer of an economic entity which retains its identity;
    (b)   a service provision change, that is a situation in which—
        (i)   activities cease to be carried out by a person ("a client") on his own behalf and are carried out instead by another person on the client's behalf ("a contractor");

> (ii)   activities cease to be carried out by a contractor on a client's behalf (whether or not those activities had previously been carried out by the client on his own behalf) and are carried out instead by another person ("a subsequent contractor") on the client's behalf; or
>
> (iii)   activities cease to be carried out by a contractor or a subsequent contractor on a client's behalf (whether or not those activities had previously been carried out by the client on his own behalf) and are carried out instead by the client on his own behalf,

and in which the conditions set out in paragraph (3) are satisfied.

(2) In this regulation "economic entity" means an organised grouping of resources which has the objective of pursuing an economic activity, whether or not that activity is central or ancillary.

(3) The conditions referred to in paragraph (1)(b) are that—

> (a)   immediately before the service provision change—
>
> > (i)   there is an organised grouping of employees situated in Great Britain which has as its principal purpose the carrying out of the activities concerned on behalf of the client;
> >
> > (ii)   the client intends that the activities will, following the service provision change, be carried out by the transferee other than in connection with a single specific event or task of short-term duration; and
>
> (b)   the activities concerned do not consist wholly or mainly of the supply of goods for the client's use.

(4) Subject to paragraph (1), these Regulations apply to—

> (a)   public and private undertakings engaged in economic activities whether or not they are operating for gain;
>
> (b)   a transfer or service provision change howsoever effected notwithstanding—
>
> > (i)   that the transfer of an undertaking, business or part of an undertaking or business is governed or effected by the law of a country or territory outside the United Kingdom or that the service provision change is governed or effected by the law of a country or territory outside Great Britain;
> >
> > (ii)   that the employment of persons employed in the undertaking, business or part transferred or, in the case of a service provision change, persons employed in the organised grouping of employees, is governed by any such law;
>
> (c)   a transfer of an undertaking, business or part of an undertaking or business (which may also be a service provision change) where persons employed in the undertaking, business or part transferred ordinarily work outside the United Kingdom.

(5) An administrative reorganisation of public administrative authorities or the transfer of administrative functions between public administrative authorities is not a relevant transfer.

(6) A relevant transfer—

> (a)   may be effected by a series of two or more transactions; and

(b)   may take place whether or not any property is transferred to the transferee by the transferor.

(7) Where, in consequence (whether directly or indirectly) of the transfer of an undertaking, business or part of an undertaking or business which was situated immediately before the transfer in the United Kingdom, a ship within the meaning of the Merchant Shipping Act 1995[9] registered in the United Kingdom ceases to be so registered, these Regulations shall not affect the right conferred by section 29 of that Act (right of seamen to be discharged when ship ceases to be registered in the United Kingdom) on a seaman employed in the ship.

Effect of relevant transfer on contracts of employment

4.—(1) Except where objection is made under paragraph (7), a relevant transfer shall not operate so as to terminate the contract of employment of any person employed by the transferor and assigned to the organised grouping of resources or employees that is subject to the relevant transfer, which would otherwise be terminated by the transfer, but any such contract shall have effect after the transfer as if originally made between the person so employed and the transferee.

(2) Without prejudice to paragraph (1), but subject to paragraph (6), and regulations 8 and 15(9), on the completion of a relevant transfer—

(a)   all the transferor's rights, powers, duties and liabilities under or in connection with any such contract shall be transferred by virtue of this regulation to the transferee; and

(b)   any act or omission before the transfer is completed, of or in relation to the transferor in respect of that contract or a person assigned to that organised grouping of resources or employees, shall be deemed to have been an act or omission of or in relation to the transferee.

(3) Any reference in paragraph (1) to a person employed by the transferor and assigned to the organised grouping of resources or employees that is subject to a relevant transfer, is a reference to a person so employed immediately before the transfer, or who would have been so employed if he had not been dismissed in the circumstances described in regulation 7(1), including, where the transfer is effected by a series of two or more transactions, a person so employed and assigned or who would have been so employed and assigned immediately before any of those transactions.

(4) Subject to regulation 9, in respect of a contract of employment that is, or will be, transferred by paragraph (1), any purported variation of the contract shall be void if the sole or principal reason for the variation is—

(a)   the transfer itself; or

(b)   a reason connected with the transfer that is not an economic, technical or organisational reason entailing changes in the workforce.

(5) Paragraph (4) shall not prevent the employer and his employee, whose contract of employment is, or will be, transferred by paragraph (1), from agreeing a variation of that contract if the sole or principal reason for the variation is—

(a) a reason connected with the transfer that is an economic, technical or organisational reason entailing changes in the workforce; or

(b) a reason unconnected with the transfer.

(6) Paragraph (2) shall not transfer or otherwise affect the liability of any person to be prosecuted for, convicted of and sentenced for any offence.

(7) Paragraphs (1) and (2) shall not operate to transfer the contract of employment and the rights, powers, duties and liabilities under or in connection with it of an employee who informs the transferor or the transferee that he objects to becoming employed by the transferee.

(8) Subject to paragraphs (9) and (11), where an employee so objects, the relevant transfer shall operate so as to terminate his contract of employment with the transferor but he shall not be treated, for any purpose, as having been dismissed by the transferor.

(9) Subject to regulation 9, where a relevant transfer involves or would involve a substantial change in working conditions to the material detriment of a person whose contract of employment is or would be transferred under paragraph (1), such an employee may treat the contract of employment as having been terminated, and the employee shall be treated for any purpose as having been dismissed by the employer.

(10) No damages shall be payable by an employer as a result of a dismissal falling within paragraph (9) in respect of any failure by the employer to pay wages to an employee in respect of a notice period which the employee has failed to work.

(11) Paragraphs (1), (7), (8) and (9) are without prejudice to any right of an employee arising apart from these Regulations to terminate his contract of employment without notice in acceptance of a repudiatory breach of contract by his employer.

Effect of relevant transfer on collective agreements

5.—Where at the time of a relevant transfer there exists a collective agreement made by or on behalf of the transferor with a trade union recognised by the transferor in respect of any employee whose contract of employment is preserved by regulation 4(1) above, then—

(a) without prejudice to sections 179 and 180 of the 1992 Act (collective agreements presumed to be unenforceable in specified circumstances) that agreement, in its application in relation to the employee, shall, after the transfer, have effect as if made by or on behalf of the transferee with that trade union, and accordingly anything done under or in connection with it, in its application in relation to the employee, by or in relation to the transferor before the transfer, shall, after the transfer, be deemed to have been done by or in relation to the transferee; and

(b) any order made in respect of that agreement, in its application in relation to the employee, shall, after the transfer, have effect as if the transferee were a party to the agreement.

Effect of relevant transfer on trade union recognition

6.—(1) This regulation applies where after a relevant transfer the transferred organised grouping of resources or employees maintains an identity distinct from the remainder of the transferee's undertaking.

(2) Where before such a transfer an independent trade union is recognised to any extent by the transferor in respect of employees of any description who in consequence of the transfer become employees of the transferee, then, after the transfer—

    (a)   the trade union shall be deemed to have been recognised by the transferee to the same extent in respect of employees of that description so employed; and

    (b)   any agreement for recognition may be varied or rescinded accordingly.

Dismissal of employee because of relevant transfer

7.—(1) Where either before or after a relevant transfer, any employee of the transferor or transferee is dismissed, that employee shall be treated for the purposes of Part X of the 1996 Act (unfair dismissal) as unfairly dismissed if the sole or principal reason for his dismissal is—

    (a)   the transfer itself; or

    (b)   a reason connected with the transfer that is not an economic, technical or organisational reason entailing changes in the workforce.

(2) This paragraph applies where the sole or principal reason for the dismissal is a reason connected with the transfer that is an economic, technical or organisational reason entailing changes in the workforce of either the transferor or the transferee before or after a relevant transfer.

(3) Where paragraph (2) applies—

    (a)   paragraph (1) shall not apply;

    (b)   without prejudice to the application of section 98(4) of the 1996 Act (test of fair dismissal), the dismissal shall, for the purposes of sections 98(1) and 135 of that Act (reason for dismissal), be regarded as having been for redundancy where section 98(2)(c) of that Act applies, or otherwise for a substantial reason of a kind such as to justify the dismissal of an employee holding the position which that employee held.

(4) The provisions of this regulation apply irrespective of whether the employee in question is assigned to the organised grouping of resources or employees that is, or will be, transferred.

(5) Paragraph (1) shall not apply in relation to the dismissal of any employee which was required by reason of the application of section 5 of the Aliens Restriction (Amendment) Act 1919[10] to his employment.

(6) Paragraph (1) shall not apply in relation to a dismissal of an employee if the application of section 94 of the 1996 Act to the dismissal of the employee is excluded by or under any provision of the 1996 Act, the 1996 Tribunals Act or the 1992 Act.

Insolvency

8.—(1) If at the time of a relevant transfer the transferor is subject to relevant insolvency proceedings paragraphs (2) to (6) apply.

(2) In this regulation "relevant employee" means an employee of the transferor—

    (a)   whose contract of employment transfers to the transferee by virtue of the operation of these Regulations; or

    (b)   whose employment with the transferor is terminated before the time of the relevant transfer in the circumstances described in regulation 7(1).

(3) The relevant statutory scheme specified in paragraph (4)(b) (including that sub-paragraph as applied by paragraph 5 of Schedule 1) shall apply in the case of a relevant employee irrespective of the fact that the qualifying requirement that the employee's employment has been terminated is not met and for those purposes the date of the transfer shall be treated as the date of the termination and the transferor shall be treated as the employer.

(4) In this regulation the "relevant statutory schemes" are—

    (a)   Chapter VI of Part XI of the 1996 Act;

    (b)   Part XII of the 1996 Act.

(5)   Regulation 4 shall not operate to transfer liability for the sums payable to the relevant employee under the relevant statutory schemes.

(6) In this regulation "relevant insolvency proceedings" means insolvency proceedings which have been opened in relation to the transferor not with a view to the liquidation of the assets of the transferor and which are under the supervision of an insolvency practitioner.

(7) Regulations 4 and 7 do not apply to any relevant transfer where the transferor is the subject of bankruptcy proceedings or any analogous insolvency proceedings which have been instituted with a view to the liquidation of the assets of the transferor and are under the supervision of an insolvency practitioner.

Variations of contract where transferors are subject to relevant insolvency proceedings

9.—(1) If at the time of a relevant transfer the transferor is subject to relevant insolvency proceedings these Regulations shall not prevent the transferor or transferee (or an insolvency practitioner) and appropriate representatives of assigned employees agreeing to permitted variations.

(2) For the purposes of this regulation "appropriate representatives" are—

    (a)   if the employees are of a description in respect of which an independent trade union is recognised by their employer, representatives of the trade union; or

    (b)   in any other case, whichever of the following employee representatives the employer chooses—

        (i)   employee representatives appointed or elected by the assigned employees (whether they make the appointment or election alone or with others) otherwise than for the purposes of this regulation, who (having regard to the purposes for, and the method by which they were appointed or elected) have authority from those employees to agree permitted variations to contracts of employment on their behalf;

(ii)   employee representatives elected by assigned employees (whether they make the appointment or election alone or with others) for these particular purposes, in an election satisfying requirements identical to those contained in regulation 14 except those in regulation 14(1)(d).

(3) An individual may be an appropriate representative for the purposes of both this regulation and regulation 13 provided that where the representative is not a trade union representative he is either elected by or has authority from assigned employees (within the meaning of this regulation) and affected employees (as described in regulation 13(1)).

(4) In section 168 of the 1992 Act (time off for carrying out trade union duties) in subsection (1), after paragraph (c) there is inserted—

", or

(d)   negotiations with a view to entering into an agreement under regulation 9 of the Transfer of Undertakings (Protection of Employment) Regulations 2006 that applies to employees of the employer, or

(e)   the performance on behalf of employees of the employer of functions related to or connected with the making of an agreement under that regulation.".

(5) Where assigned employees are represented by non-trade union representatives—

(a)   the agreement recording a permitted variation must be in writing and signed by each of the representatives who have made it or, where that is not reasonably practicable, by a duly authorised agent of that representative; and

(b)   the employer must, before the agreement is made available for signature, provide all employees to whom it is intended to apply on the date on which it is to come into effect with copies of the text of the agreement and such guidance as those employees might reasonably require in order to understand it fully.

(6) A permitted variation shall take effect as a term or condition of the assigned employee's contract of employment in place, where relevant, of any term or condition which it varies.

(7) In this regulation—

"assigned employees" means those employees assigned to the organised grouping of resources or employees that is the subject of a relevant transfer;

"permitted variation" is a variation to the contract of employment of an assigned employee where—

(a)   the sole or principal reason for it is the transfer itself or a reason connected with the transfer that is not an economic, technical or organisational reason entailing changes in the workforce; and

    (b)   it is designed to safeguard employment opportunities by ensuring the survival of the undertaking, business or part of the undertaking or business that is the subject of the relevant transfer;

"relevant insolvency proceedings" has the meaning given to the expression by regulation 8(6).

Pensions

10.—(1) Regulations 4 and 5 shall not apply—

    (a)   to so much of a contract of employment or collective agreement as relates to an occupational pension scheme within the meaning of the Pension Schemes Act 1993[11]; or

    (b)   to any rights, powers, duties or liabilities under or in connection with any such contract or subsisting by virtue of any such agreement and relating to such a scheme or otherwise arising in connection with that person's employment and relating to such a scheme.

(2) For the purposes of paragraphs (1) and (3), any provisions of an occupational pension scheme which do not relate to benefits for old age, invalidity or survivors shall not be treated as being part of the scheme.

(3) An employee whose contract of employment is transferred in the circumstances described in regulation 4(1) shall not be entitled to bring a claim against the transferor for—

    (a)   breach of contract; or

    (b)   constructive unfair dismissal under section 95(1)(c) of the 1996 Act,

arising out of a loss or reduction in his rights under an occupational pension scheme in consequence of the transfer, save insofar as the alleged breach of contract or dismissal (as the case may be) occurred prior to the date on which these Regulations took effect.

Notification of Employee Liability Information

11.—(1) The transferor shall notify to the transferee the employee liability information of any person employed by him who is assigned to the organised grouping of resources or employees that is the subject of a relevant transfer—

    (a)   in writing; or

    (b)   by making it available to him in a readily accessible form.

(2) In this regulation and in regulation 12 "employee liability information" means—

    (a)   the identity and age of the employee;

    (b)   those particulars of employment that an employer is obliged to give to an employee pursuant to section 1 of the 1996 Act;

    (c)   information of any—

        (i)   disciplinary procedure taken against an employee;

        (ii)   grievance procedure taken by an employee,

        within the previous two years, in circumstances where the Employment Act 2002 (Dispute Resolution) Regulations 2004[12] apply;

    (d)   information of any court or tribunal case, claim or action—

       (i)   brought by an employee against the transferor, within the previous two years;

       (ii)   that the transferor has reasonable grounds to believe that an employee may bring against the transferee, arising out of the employee's employment with the transferor; and

  (e)   information of any collective agreement which will have effect after the transfer, in its application in relation to the employee, pursuant to regulation 5(a).

(3) Employee liability information shall contain information as at a specified date not more than fourteen days before the date on which the information is notified to the transferee.

(4) The duty to provide employee liability information in paragraph (1) shall include a duty to provide employee liability information of any person who would have been employed by the transferor and assigned to the organised grouping of resources or employees that is the subject of a relevant transfer immediately before the transfer if he had not been dismissed in the circumstances described in regulation 7(1), including, where the transfer is effected by a series of two or more transactions, a person so employed and assigned or who would have been so employed and assigned immediately before any of those transactions.

(5) Following notification of the employee liability information in accordance with this regulation, the transferor shall notify the transferee in writing of any change in the employee liability information.

(6) A notification under this regulation shall be given not less than fourteen days before the relevant transfer or, if special circumstances make this not reasonably practicable, as soon as reasonably practicable thereafter.

(7) A notification under this regulation may be given—

  (a)   in more than one instalment;

  (b)   indirectly, through a third party.

Remedy for failure to notify employee liability information

12.—(1) On or after a relevant transfer, the transferee may present a complaint to an employment tribunal that the transferor has failed to comply with any provision of regulation 11.

(2) An employment tribunal shall not consider a complaint under this regulation unless it is presented—

  (a)   before the end of the period of three months beginning with the date of the relevant transfer;

  (b)   within such further period as the tribunal considers reasonable in a case where it is satisfied that it was not reasonably practicable for the complaint to be presented before the end of that period of three months.

(3) Where an employment tribunal finds a complaint under paragraph (1) well-founded, the tribunal—

  (a)   shall make a declaration to that effect; and

  (b)   may make an award of compensation to be paid by the transferor to the transferee.

(4) The amount of the compensation shall be such as the tribunal considers just and equitable in all the circumstances, subject to paragraph (5), having particular regard to—

    (a)   any loss sustained by the transferee which is attributable to the matters complained of; and

    (b)   the terms of any contract between the transferor and the transferee relating to the transfer under which the transferor may be liable to pay any sum to the transferee in respect of a failure to notify the transferee of employee liability information.

(5) Subject to paragraph (6), the amount of compensation awarded under paragraph (3) shall be not less than £500 per employee in respect of whom the transferor has failed to comply with a provision of regulation 11, unless the tribunal considers it just and equitable, in all the circumstances, to award a lesser sum.

(6) In ascertaining the loss referred to in paragraph (4)(a) the tribunal shall apply the same rule concerning the duty of a person to mitigate his loss as applies to any damages recoverable under the common law of England and Wales, Northern Ireland or Scotland, as applicable.

(7) Section 18 of the 1996 Tribunals Act (conciliation) shall apply to the right conferred by this regulation and to proceedings under this regulation as it applies to the rights conferred by that Act and the employment tribunal proceedings mentioned in that Act.

Duty to inform and consult representatives

13.—(1) In this regulation and regulations 14 and 15 references to affected employees, in relation to a relevant transfer, are to any employees of the transferor or the transferee (whether or not assigned to the organised grouping of resources or employees that is the subject of a relevant transfer) who may be affected by the transfer or may be affected by measures taken in connection with it; and references to the employer shall be construed accordingly.

(2) Long enough before a relevant transfer to enable the employer of any affected employees to consult the appropriate representatives of any affected employees, the employer shall inform those representatives of—

    (a)   the fact that the transfer is to take place, the date or proposed date of the transfer and the reasons for it;

    (b)   the legal, economic and social implications of the transfer for any affected employees;

    (c)   the measures which he envisages he will, in connection with the transfer, take in relation to any affected employees or, if he envisages that no measures will be so taken, that fact; and

    (d)   if the employer is the transferor, the measures, in connection with the transfer, which he envisages the transferee will take in relation to any affected employees who will become employees of the transferee after the transfer by virtue of regulation 4 or, if he envisages that no measures will be so taken, that fact.

(3) For the purposes of this regulation the appropriate representatives of any affected employees are—

    (a)   if the employees are of a description in respect of which an independent trade union is recognised by their employer, representatives of the trade union; or

    (b)   in any other case, whichever of the following employee representatives the employer chooses—

        (i)   employee representatives appointed or elected by the affected employees otherwise than for the purposes of this regulation, who (having regard to the purposes for, and the method by which they were appointed or elected) have authority from those employees to receive information and to be consulted about the transfer on their behalf;

        (ii)   employee representatives elected by any affected employees, for the purposes of this regulation, in an election satisfying the requirements of regulation 14(1).

(4) The transferee shall give the transferor such information at such a time as will enable the transferor to perform the duty imposed on him by virtue of paragraph (2)(d).

(5) The information which is to be given to the appropriate representatives shall be given to each of them by being delivered to them, or sent by post to an address notified by them to the employer, or (in the case of representatives of a trade union) sent by post to the trade union at the address of its head or main office.

(6) An employer of an affected employee who envisages that he will take measures in relation to an affected employee, in connection with the relevant transfer, shall consult the appropriate representatives of that employee with a view to seeking their agreement to the intended measures.

(7) In the course of those consultations the employer shall—

    (a)   consider any representations made by the appropriate representatives; and

    (b)   reply to those representations and, if he rejects any of those representations, state his reasons.

(8) The employer shall allow the appropriate representatives access to any affected employees and shall afford to those representatives such accommodation and other facilities as may be appropriate.

(9) If in any case there are special circumstances which render it not reasonably practicable for an employer to perform a duty imposed on him by any of paragraphs (2) to (7), he shall take all such steps towards performing that duty as are reasonably practicable in the circumstances.

(10) Where—

    (a)   the employer has invited any of the affected employee to elect employee representatives; and

    (b)   the invitation was issued long enough before the time when the employer is required to give information under paragraph (2) to allow them to elect representatives by that time,

the employer shall be treated as complying with the requirements of this regulation in relation to those employees if he complies with those requirements as soon as is reasonably practicable after the election of the representatives.

(11) If, after the employer has invited any affected employees to elect representatives, they fail to do so within a reasonable time, he shall give to any affected employees the information set out in paragraph (2).

(12) The duties imposed on an employer by this regulation shall apply irrespective of whether the decision resulting in the relevant transfer is taken by the employer or a person controlling the employer.

Election of employee representatives

14.—(1) The requirements for the election of employee representatives under regulation 13(3) are that—

    (a)   the employer shall make such arrangements as are reasonably practicable to ensure that the election is fair;

    (b)   the employer shall determine the number of representatives to be elected so that there are sufficient representatives to represent the interests of all affected employees having regard to the number and classes of those employees;

    (c)   the employer shall determine whether the affected employees should be represented either by representatives of all the affected employees or by representatives of particular classes of those employees;

    (d)   before the election the employer shall determine the term of office as employee representatives so that it is of sufficient length to enable information to be given and consultations under regulation 13 to be completed;

    (e)   the candidates for election as employee representatives are affected employees on the date of the election;

    (f)   no affected employee is unreasonably excluded from standing for election;

    (g)   all affected employees on the date of the election are entitled to vote for employee representatives;

    (h)   the employees entitled to vote may vote for as many candidates as there are representatives to be elected to represent them or, if there are to be representatives for particular classes of employees, may vote for as many candidates as there are representatives to be elected to represent their particular class of employee;

    (i)   the election is conducted so as to secure that—

        (i)   so far as is reasonably practicable, those voting do so in secret; and

        (ii)   the votes given at the election are accurately counted.

(2) Where, after an election of employee representatives satisfying the requirements of paragraph (1) has been held, one of those elected ceases to act as an employee representative and as a result any affected employees are no longer represented, those employees shall elect another representative by an election satisfying the requirements of paragraph (1)(a), (e), (f) and (i).

Failure to inform or consult

15.—(1) Where an employer has failed to comply with a requirement of regulation 13 or regulation 14, a complaint may be presented to an employment tribunal on that ground—

(a)   in the case of a failure relating to the election of employee representatives, by any of his employees who are affected employees;

(b)   in the case of any other failure relating to employee representatives, by any of the employee representatives to whom the failure related;

(c)   in the case of failure relating to representatives of a trade union, by the trade union; and

(d)   in any other case, by any of his employees who are affected employees.

(2) If on a complaint under paragraph (1) a question arises whether or not it was reasonably practicable for an employer to perform a particular duty or as to what steps he took towards performing it, it shall be for him to show—

(a)   that there were special circumstances which rendered it not reasonably practicable for him to perform the duty; and

(b)   that he took all such steps towards its performance as were reasonably practicable in those circumstances.

(3) If on a complaint under paragraph (1) a question arises as to whether or not an employee representative was an appropriate representative for the purposes of regulation 13, it shall be for the employer to show that the employee representative had the necessary authority to represent the affected employees.

(4) On a complaint under paragraph (1)(a) it shall be for the employer to show that the requirements in regulation 14 have been satisfied.

(5) On a complaint against a transferor that he had failed to perform the duty imposed upon him by virtue of regulation 13(2)(d) or, so far as relating thereto, regulation 13(9), he may not show that it was not reasonably practicable for him to perform the duty in question for the reason that the transferee had failed to give him the requisite information at the requisite time in accordance with regulation 13(4) unless he gives the transferee notice of his intention to show that fact; and the giving of the notice shall make the transferee a party to the proceedings.

(6) In relation to any complaint under paragraph (1), a failure on the part of a person controlling (directly or indirectly) the employer to provide information to the employer shall not constitute special circumstances rendering it not reasonably practicable for the employer to comply with such a requirement.

(7) Where the tribunal finds a complaint against a transferee under paragraph (1) well-founded it shall make a declaration to that effect and may order the transferee to pay appropriate compensation to such descriptions of affected employees as may be specified in the award.

(8) Where the tribunal finds a complaint against a transferor under paragraph (1) well-founded it shall make a declaration to that effect and may—

(a)   order the transferor, subject to paragraph (9), to pay appropriate compensation to such descriptions of affected employees as may be specified in the award; or

(b)   if the complaint is that the transferor did not perform the duty mentioned in paragraph (5) and the transferor (after giving due notice) shows the facts so mentioned, order the transferee to pay appropriate compensation to such descriptions of affected employees as may be specified in the award.

(9) The transferee shall be jointly and severally liable with the transferor in respect of compensation payable under sub-paragraph (8)(a) or paragraph (11).

(10) An employee may present a complaint to an employment tribunal on the ground that he is an employee of a description to which an order under paragraph (7) or (8) relates and that—

    (a)   in respect of an order under paragraph (7), the transferee has failed, wholly or in part, to pay him compensation in pursuance of the order;

    (b)   in respect of an order under paragraph (8), the transferor or transferee, as applicable, has failed, wholly or in part, to pay him compensation in pursuance of the order.

(11) Where the tribunal finds a complaint under paragraph (10) well-founded it shall order the transferor or transferee as applicable to pay the complainant the amount of compensation which it finds is due to him.

(12) An employment tribunal shall not consider a complaint under paragraph (1) or (10) unless it is presented to the tribunal before the end of the period of three months beginning with—

    (a)   in respect of a complaint under paragraph (1), the date on which the relevant transfer is completed; or

    (b)   in respect of a complaint under paragraph (10), the date of the tribunal's order under paragraph (7) or (8),

or within such further period as the tribunal considers reasonable in a case where it is satisfied that it was not reasonably practicable for the complaint to be presented before the end of the period of three months.

Failure to inform or consult: supplemental

16.—(1) Section 205(1) of the 1996 Act (complaint to be sole remedy for breach of relevant rights) and section 18 of the 1996 Tribunals Act (conciliation) shall apply to the rights conferred by regulation 15 and to proceedings under this regulation as they apply to the rights conferred by those Acts and the employment tribunal proceedings mentioned in those Acts.

(2) An appeal shall lie and shall lie only to the Employment Appeal Tribunal on a question of law arising from any decision of, or arising in any proceedings before, an employment tribunal under or by virtue of these Regulations; and section 11(1) of the Tribunals and Inquiries Act 1992[13] (appeals from certain tribunals to the High Court) shall not apply in relation to any such proceedings.

(3) "Appropriate compensation" in regulation 15 means such sum not exceeding thirteen weeks' pay for the employee in question as the tribunal considers just and equitable having regard to the seriousness of the failure of the employer to comply with his duty.

(4) Sections 220 to 228 of the 1996 Act shall apply for calculating the amount of a week's pay for any employee for the purposes of paragraph (3) and, for the purposes of that calculation, the calculation date shall be—

    (a)   in the case of an employee who is dismissed by reason of redundancy (within the meaning of sections 139 and 155 of the

1996 Act) the date which is the calculation date for the purposes of any entitlement of his to a redundancy payment (within the meaning of those sections) or which would be that calculation date if he were so entitled;

(b)   in the case of an employee who is dismissed for any other reason, the effective date of termination (within the meaning of sections 95(1) and (2) and 97 of the 1996 Act) of his contract of employment;

(c)   in any other case, the date of the relevant transfer.

Employers' Liability Compulsory Insurance

17.—(1) Paragraph (2) applies where—

(a)   by virtue of section 3(1)(a) or (b) of the Employers' Liability (Compulsory Insurance) Act 1969[14] ("the 1969 Act"), the transferor is not required by that Act to effect any insurance; or

(b)   by virtue of section 3(1)(c) of the 1969 Act, the transferor is exempted from the requirement of that Act to effect insurance.

(2) Where this paragraph applies, on completion of a relevant transfer the transferor and the transferee shall be jointly and severally liable in respect of any liability referred to in section 1(1) of the 1969 Act, in so far as such liability relates to the employee's employment with the transferor.

Restriction on contracting out

18.—Section 203 of the 1996 Act (restrictions on contracting out) shall apply in relation to these Regulations as if they were contained in that Act, save for that section shall not apply in so far as these Regulations provide for an agreement (whether a contract of employment or not) to exclude or limit the operation of these Regulations.

Amendment to the 1996 Act

19.—In section 104 of the 1996 Act (assertion of statutory right) in subsection (4)—

(a)   the word "and" at the end of paragraph (c) is omitted; and

(b)   after paragraph (d), there is inserted—

", and

(e)   the rights conferred by the Transfer of Undertakings (Protection of Employment) Regulations 2006.".

Repeals, revocations and amendments

20.—(1) Subject to regulation 21, the 1981 Regulations are revoked.

(2) Section 33 of, and paragraph 4 of Schedule 9 to, the Trade Union Reform and Employment Rights Act 1993[15] are repealed.

(3) Schedule 2 (consequential amendments) shall have effect.

Transitional provisions and savings

21.—(1) These Regulations shall apply in relation to—

(a)   a relevant transfer that takes place on or after 6 April 2006;

(b)   a transfer or service provision change, not falling within sub-paragraph (a), that takes place on or after 6 April 2006 and is regarded by virtue of any enactment as a relevant transfer.

(2) The 1981 Regulations shall continue to apply in relation to—
    (a)   a relevant transfer (within the meaning of the 1981 Regulations) that took place before 6 April 2006;
    (b)   a transfer, not falling within sub-paragraph (a), that took place before 6 April 2006 and is regarded by virtue of any enactment as a relevant transfer (within the meaning of the 1981 Regulations).

(3) In respect of a relevant transfer that takes place on or after 6 April 2006, any action taken by a transferor or transferee to discharge a duty that applied to them under regulation 10 or 10A of the 1981 Regulations shall be deemed to satisfy the corresponding obligation imposed by regulations 13 and 14 of these Regulations, insofar as that action would have discharged those obligations had the action taken place on or after 6 April 2006.

(4) The duty on a transferor to provide a transferee with employee liability information shall not apply in the case of a relevant transfer that takes place on or before 19 April 2006.

(5) Regulations 13, 14, 15 and 16 shall not apply in the case of a service provision change that is not also a transfer of an undertaking, business or part of an undertaking or business that takes place on or before 4 May 2006.

(6) The repeal of paragraph 4 of Schedule 9 to the Trade Union Reform and Employment Rights Act 1993 does not affect the continued operation of that paragraph so far as it remains capable of having effect.

6th February 2006
Gerry Sutcliffe
Parliamentary Under Secretary of State for
Employment Relations and Consumer Affairs
Department of Trade and Industry

SCHEDULE 1

Regulation 2

APPLICATION OF THE REGULATIONS TO NORTHERN IRELAND

1. These Regulations shall apply to Northern Ireland, subject to the modifications in this Schedule.

2. Sub-paragraph (1)(b) of regulation 3 and any other provision of these Regulations insofar as it relates to that sub-paragraph shall not apply to Northern Ireland.

3. Any reference in these Regulations—
    (a)   to an employment tribunal shall be construed as a reference to an Industrial Tribunal; and
    (b)   to the Employment Appeal Tribunal shall be construed as a reference to the Court of Appeal.

4. For the words from "Paragraph (1)" to "the 1992 Act" in regulation 7(6) there is substituted—

"Paragraph (1) shall not apply in relation to a dismissal of an employee if the application of Article 126 of the Employment Rights (Northern Ireland) Order 1996[16] to the dismissal of the employee is excluded by or under any provision of that Order, the Industrial Tribunals (Northern Ireland) Order 1996[17] or the 1992 Act insofar as it extends to Northern Ireland, the Industrial Relations (Northern Ireland) Order 1992[18] or the Trade Union and Labour Relations (Northern Ireland) Order 1995[19]".

5. For the words from "In this Regulation" to "Part XII of the 1996 Act" in regulation 8(4) there is substituted—

"In this Regulation the "relevant statutory schemes" are—
> (a) Chapter VI of Part XII of the Employment Rights (Northern Ireland) Order 1996 ("the 1996 Order");
> (b) Part XIV of the 1996 Order".

6. For paragraph (4) of regulation 9 there is substituted—

"In article 92 of the 1996 Order (time off for carrying out trade union duties) in paragraph (1), for the full stop at the end of sub-subparagraph (c) there is inserted—
> "(d) negotiations with a view to entering into an agreement under regulation 9 of the Transfer of Undertakings (Protection of Employment) Regulations 2006 that applies to employees of the employer, or
> (e) the performance on behalf of employees of the employer of functions related to or connected with the making of an agreement under that regulation.".".

7. For the words from "Paragraph (2)" to "the employee's employment with the transferor" in regulation 17 there is substituted—

"Paragraph (2) applies where—
> (a) by virtue of article 7(a), 7(aa) or 7(b) of the Employers' Liability (Defective Equipment and Compulsory Insurance) (Northern Ireland) Order 1972[20] ("the 1972 Order"), the transferor is not required by that Order to effect any insurance; or
> (b) by virtue of article 7(c) of the 1972 Order, the transferor is exempted from the requirement of that Order to effect insurance.

(2) Where this paragraph applies, on completion of a relevant transfer the transferor and the transferee shall be jointly and severally liable in respect of any liability referred to in article 5(1) of the 1972 Order, in so far as such liability relates to the employee's employment with the transferor".

8. In regulation 2 for "the 1992 Act" there is substituted "the Industrial Relations (Northern Ireland) Order 1992" and for "Part XIII of the Insolvency Act 1986" there is substituted "Part XII of the Insolvency (NI) Order 1989[21]".

9. In regulation 5 for "sections 179 and 180 of the 1992 Act" there is substituted "Article 26 of the Industrial Relations (NI) Order 1992 No.807 (N.I. 5)".

10.—(1) In regulation 10 for "the Pensions Schemes Act 1993" there is substituted "the Social Security Pensions (Northern Ireland) Order 1975[22]".

(2) In regulation 11 for "the Employment Act 2002 (Dispute Resolution) Regulations 2004" there is substituted "the Employment (Northern Ireland) Order 2003 (Dispute Resolution) Regulations (NI) 2004[23]".

(3) In regulation 12 for " "Section 18 of the 1996 Tribunals Act" there is substituted "Article 20 of the Industrial Tribunals (NI) Order 1996 No.1921 (NI 18)".

(4) In regulation 16—
   (a)   for "Section 18 of the 1996 Tribunals Act" there is substituted "Article 20 of the Industrial Tribunals (NI) Order 1996 No.1921 (NI 18)"; and
   (b)   for any reference to "those Acts" there is substituted a reference to "those Orders".

11. For a reference to a provision of the 1996 Act in column one of Table 1 there is substituted the corresponding reference to the Employment Rights (Northern Ireland) Order 1996 in column two of Table 1—

Table 1

Column 1	Column 2
Provision of the Employment Rights Act 1996	**Equivalent Provision in the Employment Rights (Northern Ireland) Order 1996**
Part X	Part XI
Section 98(4)	Article 130(4)
Section 98(1)	Article 130(1)
Section 135	Article 170(I)
Section 98(2)(c)	Article 130(2)(c)
Section 95(1)(c)	Article 127(1)(c)
Section 1	Article 33
Section 205(1)	Article 247(I)
Sections 220–228	Articles 16–24
Section 139	Article 174
Section 155	Article 190
Section 95(1)	Article 127(1)
Section 95(2)	Article 127(2)
Section 97	Article 129
Section 203	Article 245
Section 104	Article 135

12. Any expression used in this Schedule which is defined in the Interpretation Act (Northern Ireland) 1954[24] shall have the meaning assigned by that Act.

SCHEDULE 2

Regulation 20

CONSEQUENTIAL AMENDMENTS

References to the 1981 Regulations

1. In the following provisions, for "Transfer of Undertakings (Protection of Employment) Regulations 1981" or "Transfer of Undertakings (Protection of Employment) Regulations 1981 (S.I. 1981/1794)" there is substituted "Transfer of Undertakings (Protection of Employment) Regulations 2006"—

(a)   section 2(2) of the Property Services Agency and Crown Suppliers Act 1990[25];

(b)   paragraph 8 of Schedule 1 to the New Roads and Street Works Act 1991[26];

(c)   paragraph 5 of Schedule 1 to the Ports Act 1991[27];

(d)   section 9(1) of the Export and Investment Guarantees Act 1991[28];

(e)   section 168(1)(c) of the Trade Union and Labour Relations (Consolidation) Act 1992[29];

(f)   paragraph 8 of Schedule 2 to the Roads (Northern Ireland) Order 1993[30];

(g)   paragraph 6 of Schedule 1 to the Ports (Northern Ireland) Order 1994[31];

(h)   section 129(1)(b) of the Education Act 2002[32];

(i)   section 102(8) of the Local Government Act 2003[33];

(j)   sections 3(6)(a) and 32(6)(b) of, and paragraph 12(1) of Schedule 3 to, the Horserace Betting and Olympic Lottery Act 2004[34];

(k)   section 90(4) of the Clean Neighbourhoods and Environment Act 2005[35];

(l)   section 39(5) of the Equality Act 2006.

Industrial Training Act 1982

2.—(1) Section 3B of the Industrial Training Act 1982[36] (transfer of staff employed by industrial training boards) is amended as follows.

(2) In subsection (2), for "Transfer of Undertakings (Protection of Employment) Regulations 1981" there is substituted "Transfer of Undertakings (Protection of Employment) Regulations 2006".

(3) In subsection (3)(a), for "within the meaning of those Regulations" there is substituted "to which those Regulations apply".

Ordnance Factories and Military Services Act 1984

3.—(1) Paragraph 2 of Schedule 2 to the Ordnance Factories and Military Services Act 1984[37] (application of 1981 Regulations to ordnance factories transfer schemes) is amended as follows.

(2) In sub-paragraph (1), for the words from "for" to the end there is substituted "for a transfer that is a relevant transfer for the purposes of the 2006 regulations".

(3) In sub-paragraphs (2) and (6), for "1981 regulations", in both places where it occurs, there is substituted "2006 regulations".

(4) In sub-paragraph (3) for the words from "the 1981 regulations" to the end there is substituted "the 2006 regulations as if, immediately before the appointed day, they were employed in the entity subject to the transfer".

(5) In sub-paragraph (4)(b)—

   (a)   for "with the undertaking or part" there is substituted "with the entity subject to the transfer", and

   (b)   for the words from "the 1981 regulations" to "or part" there is substituted "the 2006 regulations as if he were employed in the entity subject to the transfer".

(6) In sub-paragraph (7), for the definition of "the 1981 regulations" there is substituted—

""the 2006 regulations" means the Transfer of Undertakings (Protection of Employment) Regulations 2006."

Dockyard Services Act 1986

4.—(1) Section 1 of the Dockyard Services Act 1986[38] (transfer of persons engaged in dockyard services) is amended as follows.

(2) In subsection (4)—

   (a)   for the words from the beginning to "Regulations 1981" there is substituted "The Transfer of Undertakings (Protection of Employment) Regulations 2006",

   (b)   for the words from "an undertaking" to "those Regulations" there is substituted "an undertaking to whose transfer those Regulations apply", and

   (c)   for the words from "a part" to "a business" there is substituted "a part of that undertaking to whose transfer those Regulations apply".

(3) In subsection (5)—

   (a)   for the words from the beginning to "Regulations 1981" there is substituted "The Transfer of Undertakings (Protection of Employment) Regulations 2006",

   (b)   for "regulation 10", in both places where it occurs, there is substituted "regulation 13", and

   (c)   for "regulation 11" there is substituted "regulations 15 and 16".

Dartford-Thurrock Crossing Act 1988

5.—(1) Schedule 5 to the Dartford-Thurrock Crossing Act 1988[39] (transfers of staff) is amended as follows.

(2) In paragraphs 3(1) and 4, for "the Employment Transfer Regulations", in both places where it occurs, there is substituted "the Transfer of Undertakings (Protection of Employment) Regulations 2006".

(3) In paragraph 4, for "Regulation 7" there is substituted "Regulation 10".

(4) In paragraph 6—

(a)   in sub-paragraph (2), for "this Schedule", in both places where it occurs, there is substituted "Part 1 of this Schedule", and

(b)   after that sub-paragraph there is inserted—

"(3) Expressions used in Part 2 of this Schedule to which a meaning is given by the Transfer of Undertakings (Protection of Employment) Regulations 2006 have the same meaning in Part 2 of this Schedule."

Atomic Weapons Establishment Act 1991

6.—(1) Section 2 of the Atomic Weapons Establishment Act 1991[40] (provisions applying to the transfer of certain employees) is amended as follows.

(2) In subsection (1)—

(a)   for the words from the beginning to "Regulations 1981" there is substituted "The Transfer of Undertakings (Protection of Employment) Regulations 2006", and

(b)   for the words from "an undertaking" to "those Regulations" there is substituted "an undertaking to whose transfer those Regulations apply".

(3) In subsection (2), for the words from "a part" to "a business" there is substituted "a part of that undertaking to whose transfer those Regulations apply".

Railways Act 1993

7. In section 151 of the Railways Act 1993[41] (general interpretation), in subsection (6), for the words from "the Transfer" to the end there is substituted "the Transfer of Undertakings (Protection of Employment) Regulations 2006, in their application in relation to a relevant transfer within the meaning of those regulations".

Employment Tribunals Act 1996

8. In section 4 of the Employment Tribunals Act 1996[42] (composition of a tribunal), in subsection (3)(ca), for the words from "regulation 11(5)" to "Regulations 1981" there is substituted "regulation 15(10) of the Transfer of Undertakings (Protection of Employment) Regulations 2006".

Industrial Tribunals (Northern Ireland) Order 1996

9. In Article 6 of the Industrial Tribunals (Northern Ireland) Order 1996[43] (composition of a tribunal), in paragraph (3)(ab), for the words from "regulation 11(5)" to "Regulations 1981" there is substituted "regulation 15(10) of the Transfer of Undertakings (Protection of Employment) Regulations 2006".

Employment Rights Act 1996

10. In each of the following provisions of the Employment Rights Act 1996[44], for the words from "Regulations 10" to "Regulations 1981" there is substituted "regulations 9, 13 and 15 of the Transfer of Undertakings (Protection of Employment) Regulations 2006"—

(a)   section 47(1)(a) and (1A);

(b)   section 61(1)(a);

(c)   section 103(1)(a) and (2).

Employment Rights (Northern Ireland) Order 1996

11. In each of the following provisions of the Employment Rights (Northern Ireland) Order 1996[45] for the words from "Regulations 10" to "Regulations 1981" there is substituted "regulations 9, 13 and 15 of the Transfer of Undertakings (Protection of Employment) Regulations 2006"—

(a)   Article 70(1)(a) and (1A);

(b)   Article 89(1)(a);

(c)   Article 134(1)(a) and (2).

Income Tax (Earnings and Pensions) Act 2003

12.—(1) The Income Tax (Earnings and Pensions) Act 2003[46] is amended as follows.

(2) In section 498 (no charge on shares ceasing to be subject to share incentive plan in certain circumstances), in subsection (2)(c), for the words from "a transfer" to the end there is substituted "a relevant transfer within the meaning of the Transfer of Undertakings (Protection of Employment) Regulations 2006".

(3) In Schedule 2 (approved share incentive plans), in paragraph 32(2)(c), for the words from "a transfer" to the end there is substituted "a relevant transfer within the meaning of the Transfer of Undertakings (Protection of Employment) Regulations 2006".

Pensions Act 2004

13.—(1) Section 257 of the Pensions Act 2004[47] (conditions for pension protection) is amended as follows.

(2) In subsection (1), for paragraph (a) there is substituted—

     "(a)   there is a relevant transfer within the meaning of the TUPE regulations,".

(3) Subsection (6) is omitted.

(4) In subsection (8), in the definition of the "TUPE Regulations", for the words from "Transfer" to the end there is substituted "Transfer of Undertakings (Protection of Employment) Regulations 2006".

Energy Act 2004

14.—(1) Paragraph 10 of Schedule 5 to the Energy Act 2004[48] (supplementary provisions about nuclear transfer schemes) is amended as follows.

(2) In sub-paragraphs (1), (2) and (3), in each place where it occurs, for "1981 regulations" there is substituted "2006 regulations".

(3) In sub-paragraph (1)—

     (a)   after "an undertaking", in both places where it occurs, there is inserted "or business", and

(b)   for "that undertaking or part" there is substituted "that undertaking or business or that part of an undertaking or business".

(4) After sub-paragraph (1), there is inserted—

> "(1A) The 2006 regulations apply to a service provision change—
>> (a) in accordance with a nuclear transfer scheme, or
>> (b) in accordance with a modification agreement,
>
> as if (in so far as that would not otherwise be the case) the references in those regulations to the transferor were references to the person by whom the activities affected by the service provision change were carried out immediately before the coming into force of the service provision change."

(5) In sub-paragraph (2), after "a transfer" there is inserted "(or service provision change)".

(6) In sub-paragraph (3), after "transfer", in both places where it occurs, there is inserted "(or service provision change)".

(7) In sub-paragraph (4), for the definition of "undertaking" there is substituted—

> "references to a service provision change are references to a service provision change falling within regulation 3(1)(b) of the 2006 regulations."

EXPLANATORY NOTE

(This note is not part of the Regulations)

These Regulations implement Council Directive 2001/23/EC ("the Directive") on the approximation of the law relating to business transfers. They revoke the Transfer of Undertakings (Protection of Employment) Regulations 1981 ("the 1981 Regulations"). The provisions introduced by these regulations are similar to those included in the 1981 Regulations. They also include provisions taking advantage of certain policy options conferred by the Directive.

To the extent that the Regulations implement the Directive, they are made under section 2(2) of the European Communities Act 1972. To the extent that they relate to the treatment of employees, and related matters, in relation to a service provision change (in circumstances other than those to which the Directive applies), they are made under section 38 of the Employment Relations Act 1999 ("the 1999 Act").

These Regulations apply to the UK. However to the extent that they are made under section 38 of the 1999 Act they do not apply to Northern Ireland (paragraph 2 of Schedule 1).

The Regulations make provision for the treatment of employees, and related matters, on the transfer of an undertaking or business or a service provision change.

The principal provisions of the Regulations provide as follows—

(1) Regulation 3 defines a transfer to which these Regulations apply (described as a relevant transfer). The two categories of relevant transfer (which are not mutually exclusive) are the transfer of an undertaking or business to another person and a service provision change.

(2) Regulation 4 provides that a relevant transfer shall not operate to terminate the contract of employment of a person employed by the transferor and assigned to the organised grouping of resources or employees subject to a relevant transfer but that any such contract shall have effect after the transfer as if originally made between the person so employed and the transferee. The transferor's powers, duties, rights and liabilities under or in connection with that employment contract shall transfer to the transferee. A variation to that employment contract by reason of the transfer is prohibited but that shall not prevent the employer and his employee from agreeing a variation to the contract for a reason unconnected with the transfer or a reason connected with the transfer that is an economic, technical or organisational reason entailing changes in the workforce.

(3) Regulation 5 provides that a collective agreement made by a transferor with a recognised trade union shall, after the transfer, have effect as if made by the transferee with that trade union. Regulation 6 provides for the transfer of recognition of an independent trade union.

(4) Regulation 7 provides that the dismissal of an employee by reason of the transfer is unlawful but that a dismissal for a reason connected with the transfer that is an economic technical or organisational reason entailing changes in the workforce is potentially lawful.

(5) Regulation 8 applies where, at the time of the transfer, the transferor is subject to relevant insolvency proceedings, as defined in regulation 8(6). It provides that certain of an employer's pre-existing debts to employees do not pass to the transferee but are instead met by the National Insurance Fund.

(6) Regulation 9 provides greater scope for the transferee to vary, subject to certain requirements, the terms and conditions of employment of transferring employees in circumstances where the transferor is subject to relevant insolvency proceedings.

(7) Regulation 10 provides that regulations 4 and 5 shall not apply to so much of a contract of employment or collective agreement as relates to any provision of an occupational pension scheme relating to old age, survivors or invalidity benefits.

(8) Regulation 11 provides that the transferor shall provide employee liability information in respect of employees assigned to the organised grouping of resources or employees that is subject to a relevant transfer to the transferee in advance of a relevant transfer.

(9) Regulation 12 provides a remedy to a transferee for the failure of a transferor to comply with regulation 11.

(10) Regulation 13 imposes a duty on an employer to provide information to appropriate representatives of affected employees about a relevant transfer and measures he envisages taking in respect of it, long enough before a relevant transfer to enable the employer to consult those representatives with a view to

seeking their agreement to the intended measures. Regulation 14 makes provision for the election of employee representatives where there is no recognised independent trade union. Regulations 15 and 16 provide a remedy for a failure of an employer to comply with regulations 13 or 14.

(11) Regulation 21 provides that these Regulations shall apply to a relevant transfer that takes place on or after 6 April 2006 whilst the 1981 Regulations will apply to a transfer to which the 1981 Regulations applied that took place before 6 April 2006.

(12) Schedule 1 provides modifications in the application of the Regulations to Northern Ireland.

(13) Schedule 2 provides amendments consequential on these Regulations.

(14) A Regulatory Impact Assessment of the effect these Regulations will have on business costs, and Transposition Notes showing how Council Directive 2001/23/EC has been implemented in the United Kingdom are available to the public, free of charge, from the Employment Relations Directorate, TUPE Unit, 3rd Floor, Department of Trade and Industry, 1 Victoria Street, London SW1H 0ET, and from the DTI website on the links shown below. Copies of each have also been placed in both Houses of Parliament.

http://www.dti.gov.uk/er/individual/tupe_transposition_note_2006.pdf and

http://www.dti.gov.uk/er/individual/tupe_ria_2006.pdf

Notes:

[1]   1972 c.68.
[2]   See the European Communities (Designation) (No.2) Order 1977 (S.I. 1977/1718).
[3]   1999 c.26.
[4]   1986 c.45; section 388, which explains the meaning of acting as insolvency practitioner, was amended by the Insolvency Act 2000 (c.39) sections 4(1), 4(2)(a), 4(2)(b), 4(2)(c), the Bankruptcy (Scotland) Act 1993 section 11(1), S.I. 1994/2421, S.I. 2002/1240 and S.I. 2002/2708.
[5]   1992 c.52.
[6]   1996 c.18.
[7]   1996 c.17; section 18, which defines conciliation, was amended by the Employment Rights (Dispute Resolution) Act 1998 (c.8) sections 1(2)(a), 11(1), 15 and Schedule 1, the National Minimum Wage Act 1998 (c.39) sections 24 and 30(1), the Employment Act 2002 (c.22) sections 24(2), 53 and Schedule 7, the Employment Relations Act 2004 (c.24) section 57(1) and Schedule 1, S.I. 1998/1833, S.I. 1999/3323, S.I. 2000/1299, S.I. 2000/1551, S.I. 2001/1107, S.I. 2002/2034, S.I. 2003/1660, S.I. 2003/1661, S.I. 2003/1673, S.I. 2003/3049, S.I. 2004/2326, S.I. 2004/1713 and S.I. 2004/3426.
[8]   S.I. 1981/1794, amended by the Dock Work Act 1989 (c.13) section 7(2), the Trade Union Reform and Employment Rights Act 1993 (c.19) sections 33, 51 and Schedule 10, the Employment Rights (Dispute Resolution) Act 1998 (c.8) section 1(2)(a), S.I. 1987/442. S.I. 1995/2587, S.I. 1998/1658, S.I. 1999/1925 and S.I. 1999/2402.

[9]   1995 c.21.
[10] 1919 c.92; section 5 was amended by the Former Enemy Aliens (Disabilities Removal) Act 1925 section 1 and Schedule 2, the Merchant Shipping Act 1970 section 100(3) and Schedule 5 and the Merchant Shipping Act 1995 section 314 and Schedule 12.
[11] 1993 c.48; section 1, which defines occupational pension scheme, was amended by the Welfare Reform & Pensions Act 1999 (c.30) section 18 and Schedule 2, the Pensions Act 2004 (c.35) section 239 and S.I. 1999/1820.
[12] S.I. 2004/752.
[13] 1992 c.53; section 11(1) was amended by the Sea Fish (Conservation) Act 1992 (c.60) section 9, the Special Educational Needs and Disability Act 2001 (c.10) section 42(1) and Schedule 8 and S.I. 2001/3649.
[14] 1969 c.57.
[15] 1993 c.19.
[16] S.I. 1996/1919 (N.I. 16).
[17] S.I. 1996/1921 (N.I. 18).
[18] S.I. 1992/807 (N.I. 5).
[19] S.I. 1995/1980 (N.I. 12).
[20] S.I. 1992/963 (N.I. 6).
[21] S.I. 1989/2405 (N.I. 19).
[22] S.I. 1995/1503 (N.I. 15).
[23] S.R. 2004 No. 521.
[24] 1954 c.33 (N.I).
[25] 1990 c.12.
[26] 1991 c.22.
[27] 1991 c.52.
[28] 1991 c.67.
[29] 1992 c.52.
[30] S.I. 1993/3160 (N.I. 15).
[31] S.I. 1994/2809 (N.I. 16).
[32] 2002 c.32.
[33] 2003 c.26.
[34] 2004 c.25.
[35] 2005 c.16.
[36] 1982 c.10.
[37] 1984 c.59.
[38] 1986 c.52.
[39] 1988 c.20.
[40] 1991 c.46.
[41] 1993 c.43.
[42] 1996 c.17.
[43] S.I. 1996/1921 (N.I. 18).
[44] 1996 c.18.
[45] S.I. 1999/1919 (N.I. 16).
[46] 2003 c.1.
[47] 2004 c.35.
[48] 2004 c.20.

Appendix 2

THE TRANSFER OF EMPLOYMENT (PENSION PROTECTION) REGULATIONS 2005, SI 2005/649

STATUTORY INSTRUMENTS

2005 NO. 649

PENSIONS

THE TRANSFER OF EMPLOYMENT (PENSION PROTECTION) REGULATIONS 2005

Made _ _ _	*10th March 2005*
Laid Before Parliament	*16th March 2005*
Coming into force _ _	*6th April 2005*

The Secretary of State for Work and Pensions, in exercise of the powers conferred upon him by sections 258(2)(c)(ii) and (7), 315(2) and 318(1) of the Pensions Act 2004[1] and all other powers enabling him in that behalf, by this instrument, which contains regulations made before the end of the period of six months beginning with the coming into force of the provisions by virtue of which they are made[2], hereby makes the following Regulations:

Citation, commencement, application and interpretation

1.—(1) These Regulations may be cited as the Transfer of Employment (Pension Protection) Regulations 2005 and shall come into force on 6th April 2005.

(2) These Regulations apply in the case of a person ("the employee") in relation to whom section 257 of the Act (conditions for pension protection) applies, that is to say a person who, in the circumstances described in subsection (1) of that section, ceases to be employed by the transferor of an undertaking or part of an undertaking and becomes employed by the transferee.

(3) In these Regulations "the Act" means the Pensions Act 2004.

Requirements concerning a transferee's pension scheme

2.—(1) In a case where these Regulations apply, and the transferee is the employer in relation to a pension scheme which is not a money purchase scheme, that scheme complies with section 258(2)(c)(ii) of the Act (alternative standard for a scheme which is not a money purchase scheme) if it provides either—

> (a) for members to be entitled to benefits the value of which equals or exceeds 6 per cent. of pensionable pay for each year of employment together with the total amount of any contributions made by them, and, where members are required to make contributions to the scheme, for them to contribute at a rate which does not exceed 6 per cent. of their pensionable pay; or

> (b) for the transferee to make relevant contributions to the scheme on behalf of each employee of his who is an active member of it.

(2) In this regulation—

> "pensionable pay" means that part of the remuneration payable to a member of a scheme by reference to which the amount of contributions and benefits are determined under the rules of the scheme.

Requirements concerning a transferee's pension contributions

3.—(1) In a case where these Regulations apply, the transferee's pension contributions are relevant contributions for the purposes of section 258(2)(b) of the Act in the case of a money purchase scheme, section 258(3) to (5) of the Act in the case of a stakeholder pension scheme, and regulation 2(1)(b) above in the case of a scheme which is not a money purchase scheme, if—

> (a) the contributions are made in respect of each period for which the employee is paid remuneration, provided that the employee also contributes to the scheme in respect of that period, and

> (b) the amount contributed in respect of each such period is—

>> (i) in a case where the employee's contribution in respect of that period is less than 6 per cent. of the remuneration paid to him, an amount at least equal to the amount of the employee's contribution;

>> (ii) in a case where the employee's contribution in respect of that period equals or exceeds 6 per cent. of the remuneration paid to him, an amount at least equal to 6 per cent. of that remuneration.

(2) In calculating the amount of an employee's remuneration for the purposes of paragraph (1)—

> (a) only payments made in respect of basic pay shall be taken into account, and bonus, commission, overtime and similar payments shall be disregarded, and

> (b) no account shall be taken of any deductions which are made in respect of tax, national insurance or pension contributions.

(3) In calculating the amount of a transferee's pension contributions for the purposes of paragraph (1) in the case of a scheme which is contracted-out by

virtue of section 9 of the Pension Schemes Act 1993[3], minimum payments within the meaning of that Act shall be disregarded.

Signed by authority of the Secretary of State for Work and Pensions.

Malcolm Wicks
Minister of State, Department for Work and Pensions

10th March 2005

EXPLANATORY NOTE

(This note is not part of the Regulations)

These Regulations concern the obligations of an employer under section 258 of the Pensions Act 2004 (c. 35) towards a person in relation to whom section 257 of that Act applies.

Section 257 applies to a person ("the employee") who becomes the employee of a new employer ("the transferee") by virtue of a transfer to which the Transfer of Undertakings (Protection of Employment) Regulations 1981 (S.I. 1981/1794) apply, and who had actual or contingent rights in relation to an occupational pension scheme immediately before the transfer.

Under section 258, the transferee is required to secure that the employee is, or is eligible to become, an active member of an occupational pension scheme (as defined in section 1 of the Pension Schemes Act 1993 (c. 48) as substituted by section 239 of the 2004 Act) in relation to which the transferee is the employer and, if it is a money purchase scheme, to make "relevant contributions" to it. Alternatively, the transferee must make such contributions to a stakeholder pension scheme of which the employee is a member (or offer to contribute to a stakeholder scheme of which he is eligible to be a member).

Section 258(2)(c) provides that a scheme in relation to which the transferee is the employer, if it is not a money purchase scheme, must satisfy a standard provided for in the Pension Schemes Act 1993, or, if regulations so provide, comply with prescribed requirements. For the purposes of this provision, regulation 2 requires that either the value of the benefits provided for by the transferee's scheme must be at least 6% of pensionable pay for each year of employment in addition to any contributions made by him or that the scheme must provide for the employer to make relevant contributions on behalf of his employees.

Section 258(7) provides for "relevant contributions" to be defined in regulations. Regulation 3 provides that such contributions must be made in respect of each period for which the employee contributes to the pension scheme, and that the amount contributed must equal the employee's contribution subject to an upper limit of 6% of basic pay.

As these Regulations are made before the expiry of the period of six months beginning with the coming into force of the provisions of the Pensions Act 2004 by virtue of which they are made, the requirement for the Secretary of State to consult such persons as he considers appropriate does not apply.

An assessment of the impact on business, charities and the voluntary sector of the provisions in these Regulations is included in the Regulatory Impact Assessment that accompanied the Pensions Act 2004. A copy of that assessment has been placed in the libraries of both Houses of Parliament. Copies may be obtained from the Department for Work and Pensions, Regulatory Impact Unit, Adelphi, 1–11 John Adam Street, London WC2N 6HT.

Notes:

[1] 2004 c.35; section 318(1) is cited for the definitions of "prescribed" and "regulations".

[2] See section 317(2)(c) of the Pensions Act 2004 which provides that the Secretary of State must consult such persons as he considers appropriate before making regulations by virtue of the provisions of that Act (other than Part 8). This duty does not apply where regulations are made before the end of six months beginning with the coming into force of the provisions of that Act by virtue of which the regulations are made.

[3] 1993 c.48; section 9 was amended by the Pensions Act 1995 (c.26), section 136(3), and the Pensions Act 2004, section 283.

Appendix 3

PENSIONS ACT 2004 (C 35), SS 257–258

257 Conditions for pension protection

(1) This section applies in relation to a person ("the employee") where—

    [(a)   there is a relevant transfer within the meaning of the TUPE regulations,]

    (b)   by virtue of the transfer the employee ceases to be employed by the transferor and becomes employed by the transferee, and

    (c)   at the time immediately before the employee becomes employed by the transferee—

        (i)   there is an occupational pension scheme ("the scheme") in relation to which the transferor is the employer, and

        (ii)   one of subsections (2), (3) and (4) applies.

(2) This subsection applies where—

    (a)   the employee is an active member of the scheme, and

    (b)   if any of the benefits that may be provided under the scheme are money purchase benefits—

        (i)   the transferor is required to make contributions to the scheme in respect of the employee, or

        (ii)   the transferor is not so required but has made one or more such contributions.

(3) This subsection applies where—

    (a)   the employee is not an active member of the scheme but is eligible to be such a member, and

    (b)   if any of the benefits that may be provided under the scheme are money purchase benefits, the transferor would have been required to make contributions to the scheme in respect of the employee if the employee had been an active member of it.

(4) This subsection applies where—

    (a)   the employee is not an active member of the scheme, nor eligible to be such a member, but would have been an active member of the scheme or eligible to be such a member if, after the date on which he became employed by the transferor, he had been employed by the transferor for a longer period, and

    (b)   if any of the benefits that may be provided under the scheme are money purchase benefits, the transferor would have been required to make contributions to the scheme in respect of the employee if the employee had been an active member of it.

(5)   For the purposes of this section, the condition in subsection (1)(c) is to be regarded as satisfied in any case where it would have been satisfied but for any action taken by the transferor by reason of the transfer.

(6)   ...

(7)   In the case of a scheme which is contracted-out by virtue of section 9 of the Pension Schemes Act 1993 (c 48), the references in subsections (2)(b), (3)(b) and (4)(b) to contributions mean contributions other than minimum payments (within the meaning of that Act).

(8)   In this section—

> the "TUPE Regulations" means the [Transfer of Undertakings (Protection of Employment) Regulations 2006];
>
> references to the transferor include any associate of the transferor, and section 435 of the Insolvency Act 1986 (c 45) applies for the purposes of this section as it applies for the purposes of that Act.

Amendments. Subsection substituted by SI 2006/246, reg 20(3), Sch 2, para 13(1), (2). Subsection repealed by SI 2006/246, reg 20(3), Sch 2, para 13(1), (3). Words inserted by SI 2006/246, reg 20(3), Sch 2, para 13(1), (4).

258 Form of protection

(1)   In a case where section 257 applies, it is a condition of the employee's contract of employment with the transferee that the requirements in subsection (2) or the requirement in subsection (3) are complied with.

(2)   The requirements in this subsection are that—
   (a)   the transferee secures that, as from the relevant time, the employee is, or is eligible to be, an active member of an occupational pension scheme in relation to which the transferee is the employer, and
   (b)   in a case where the scheme is a money purchase scheme, as from the relevant time—
      (i)   the transferee makes relevant contributions to the scheme in respect of the employee, or
      (ii)   if the employee is not an active member of the scheme but is eligible to be such a member, the transferee would be required to make such contributions if the employee were an active member, and
   (c)   in a case where the scheme is not a money purchase scheme, as from the relevant time the scheme—
      (i)   satisfies the statutory standard referred to in section 12A of the Pension Schemes Act 1993 (c 48), or
      (ii)   if regulations so provide, complies with such other requirements as may be prescribed.

(3)   The requirement in this subsection is that, as from the relevant time, the transferee makes relevant contributions to a stakeholder pension scheme of which the employee is a member.

(4)   The requirement in subsection (3) is for the purposes of this section to be regarded as complied with by the transferee during any period in relation to which the condition in subsection (5) is satisfied.

(5) The condition in this subsection is that the transferee has offered to make relevant contributions to a stakeholder pension scheme of which the employee is eligible to be a member (and the transferee has not withdrawn the offer).

(6) Subsection (1) does not apply in relation to a contract if or to the extent that the employee and the transferee so agree at any time after the time when the employee becomes employed by the transferee.

(7) In this section—

"the relevant time" means—
  (a)   in a case where section 257 applies by virtue of the application of subsection (2) or (3) of that section, the time when the employee becomes employed by the transferee;
  (b)   in a case where that section applies by virtue of the application of subsection (4) of that section, the time at which the employee would have been a member of the scheme referred to in subsection (1)(c)(i) of that section or (if earlier) would have been eligible to be such a member;

"relevant contributions" means such contributions in respect of such period or periods as may be prescribed;

"stakeholder pension scheme" means a pension scheme which is registered under section 2 of the Welfare Reform and Pensions Act 1999 (c 30).

Appendix 4

COUNCIL DIRECTIVE 2001/23/EC

COUNCIL DIRECTIVE 2001/23/EC

of 12 March 2001

**on the approximation of the laws of the Member States relating to the safeguarding of employees'
rights in the event of transfers of undertakings, businesses or parts of undertakings or businesses**

THE COUNCIL OF THE EUROPEAN UNION,

Having regard to the Treaty establishing the European Community, and in particular Article 94 thereof,

Having regard to the proposal from the Commission,

Having regard to the opinion of the European Parliament (1),

Having regard to the opinion of the Economic and Social Committee (2),

Whereas:

(1)   Council Directive 77/187/EEC of 14 February 1977 on the approximation of the laws of the Member States relating to the safeguarding of employees' rights in the event of transfers of undertakings, businesses or parts of undertakings or businesses (3) has been substantially amended (4). In the interests of clarity and rationality, it should therefore be codified.

(2)   Economic trends are bringing in their wake, at both national and Community level, changes in the structure of undertakings, through transfers of undertakings, businesses or parts of undertakings or businesses to other employers as a result of legal transfers or mergers.

(3)   It is necessary to provide for the protection of employees in the event of a change of employer, in particular, to ensure that their rights are safeguarded.

(4)   Differences still remain in the Member States as regards the extent of the protection of employees in this respect and these differences should be reduced.

---

1   Opinion delivered on 25 October 2000 (not yet published in the Official Journal).
2   OJ C 367, 20.12.2000, p. 21.
3   OJ L 61, 5.3.1977, p. 26.
4   See Annex I, Part A.

(5) The Community Charter of the Fundamental Social Rights of Workers adopted on 9 December 1989 ('Social Charter') states, in points 7, 17 and 18 in particular that: 'The completion of the internal market must lead to an improvement in the living and working conditions of workers in the European Community. The improvement must cover, where necessary, the development of certain aspects of employment regulations such as procedures for collective redundancies and those regarding bankruptcies. Information, consultation and participation for workers must be developed along appropriate lines, taking account of the practice in force in the various Member States. Such information, consultation and participation must be implemented in due time, particularly in connection with restructuring operations in undertakings or in cases of mergers having an impact on the employment of workers'.

(6) In 1977 the Council adopted Directive 77/187/EEC to promote the harmonisation of the relevant national laws ensuring the safeguarding of the rights of employees and requiring transferors and transferees to inform and consult employees' representatives in good time.

(7) That Directive was subsequently amended in the light of the impact of the internal market, the legislative tendencies of the Member States with regard to the rescue of undertakings in economic difficulties, the case-law of the Court of Justice of the European Communities, Council Directive 75/129/EEC of 17 February 1975 on the approximation of the laws of the Member States relating to collective redundancies ([5]) and the legislation already in force in most Member States.

(8) Considerations of legal security and transparency required that the legal concept of transfer be clarified in the light of the case-law of the Court of Justice. Such clarification has not altered the scope of Directive 77/187/EEC as interpreted by the Court of Justice.

(9) The Social Charter recognises the importance of the fight against all forms of discrimination, especially based on sex, colour, race, opinion and creed.

(10) This Directive should be without prejudice to the time limits set out in Annex I Part B within which the Member States are to comply with Directive 77/ 187/EEC, and the act amending it,

HAS ADOPTED THIS DIRECTIVE:

CHAPTER I

Scope and definitions

Article 1

1. (a) This Directive shall apply to any transfer of an undertaking, business, or part of an undertaking or business to another employer as a result of a legal transfer or merger.

(b) Subject to subparagraph (a) and the following provisions of this Article,

---

5   OJ L 48, 22.2.1975, p. 29. Directive replaced by Directive 98/ 59/EC (OJ L 225, 12.8.1998, p. 16).

there is a transfer within the meaning of this Directive where there is a transfer of an economic entity which retains its identity, meaning an organised grouping of resources which has the objective of pursuing an economic activity, whether or not that activity is central or ancillary.

(c)   This Directive shall apply to public and private undertakings engaged in economic activities whether or not they are operating for gain. An administrative reorganisation of public administrative authorities, or the transfer of administrative functions between public administrative authorities, is not a transfer within the meaning of this Directive.

2.   This Directive shall apply where and in so far as the undertaking, business or part of the undertaking or business to be transferred is situated within the territorial scope of the Treaty.

3.   This Directive shall not apply to seagoing vessels.

Article 2

1.   For the purposes of this Directive:

(a)   'transferor' shall mean any natural or legal person who, by reason of a transfer within the meaning of Article 1(1), ceases to be the employer in respect of the undertaking, business or part of the undertaking or business;

(b)   'transferee' shall mean any natural or legal person who, by reason of a transfer within the meaning of Article 1(1), becomes the employer in respect of the undertaking, business or part of the undertaking or business;

(c)   'representatives of employees' and related expressions shall mean the representatives of the employees provided for by the laws or practices of the Member States;

(d)   'employee' shall mean any person who, in the Member State concerned, is protected as an employee under national employment law.

2.   This Directive shall be without prejudice to national law as regards the definition of contract of employment or employment relationship.

However, Member States shall not exclude from the scope of this Directive contracts of employment or employment relationships solely because:

(a)   of the number of working hours performed or to be performed,

(b)   they are employment relationships governed by a fixed-duration contract of employment within the meaning of Article 1(1) of Council Directive 91/383/EEC of 25 June 1991 supplementing the measures to encourage improvements in the safety and health at work of workers with a fixed-duration employment relationship or a tempory employment relationship ([6]), or

(c)   they are temporary employment relationships within the meaning of Article 1(2) of Directive 91/383/EEC, and the undertaking, business or part of the undertaking or business transferred is, or is part of, the temporary employment business which is the employer.

---

6   OJ L 206, 29.7.1991, p. 19.

CHAPTER II

Safeguarding of employees' rights

Article 3

1.   The transferor's rights and obligations arising from a contract of employment or from an employment relationship existing on the date of a transfer shall, by reason of such transfer, be transferred to the transferee.

Member States may provide that, after the date of transfer, the transferor and the transferee shall be jointly and severally liable in respect of obligations which arose before the date of transfer from a contract of employment or an employment relationship existing on the date of the transfer.

2.   Member States may adopt appropriate measures to ensure that the transferor notifies the transferee of all the rights and obligations which will be transferred to the transferee under this Article, so far as those rights and obligations are or ought to have been known to the transferor at the time of the transfer. A failure by the transferor to notify the transferee of any such right or obligation shall not affect the transfer of that right or obligation and the rights of any employees against the transferee and/or transferor in respect of that right or obligation.

3.   Following the transfer, the transferee shall continue to observe the terms and conditions agreed in any collective agreement on the same terms applicable to the transferor under that agreement, until the date of termination or expiry of the collective agreement or the entry into force or application of another collective agreement.

Member States may limit the period for observing such terms and conditions with the proviso that it shall not be less than one year.

4. (a) Unless Member States provide otherwise, paragraphs 1 and 3 shall not apply in relation to employees' rights to old-age, invalidity or survivors' benefits under supplementary company or intercompany pension schemes outside the statutory social security schemes in Member States.

(b)   Even where they do not provide in accordance with subparagraph (a) that paragraphs 1 and 3 apply in relation to such rights, Member States shall adopt the measures necessary to protect the interests of employees and of persons no longer employed in the transferor's business at the time of the transfer in respect of rights conferring on them immediate or prospective entitlement to old age benefits, including survivors' benefits, under supplementary schemes referred to in subparagraph (a).

Article 4

1.   The transfer of the undertaking, business or part of the undertaking or business shall not in itself constitute grounds for dismissal by the transferor or the transferee. This provision shall not stand in the way of dismissals that may take place for economic, technical or organisational reasons entailing changes in the workforce.

Member States may provide that the first subparagraph shall not apply to certain specific categories of employees who are not covered by the laws or practice of the Member States in respect of protection against dismissal.

2.   If the contract of employment or the employment relationship is terminated because the transfer involves a substantial change in working conditions to the detriment of the employee, the employer shall be regarded as having been responsible for termination of the contract of employment or of the employment relationship.

Article 5

1.   Unless Member States provide otherwise, Articles 3 and 4 shall not apply to any transfer of an undertaking, business or part of an undertaking or business where the transferor is the subject of bankruptcy proceedings or any analogous insolvency proceedings which have been instituted with a view to the liquidation of the assets of the transferor and are under the supervision of a competent public authority (which may be an insolvency practitioner authorised by a competent public authority).

2.   Where Articles 3 and 4 apply to a transfer during insolvency proceedings which have been opened in relation to a transferor (whether or not those proceedings have been instituted with a view to the liquidation of the assets of the transferor) and provided that such proceedings are under the supervision of a competent public authority (which may be an insolvency practioner determined by national law) a Member State may provide that:

(a)   notwithstanding Article 3(1), the transferor's debts arising from any contracts of employment or employment relationships and payable before the transfer or before the opening of the insolvency proceedings shall not be transferred to the transferee, provided that such proceedings give rise, under the law of that Member State, to protection at least equivalent to that provided for in situations covered by Council Directive 80/987/EEC of 20 October 1980 on the approximation of the laws of the Member States relating to the protection of employees in the event of the insolvency of their employer (7), and, or alternatively, that,

(b)   the transferee, transferor or person or persons exercising the transferor's functions, on the one hand, and the representatives of the employees on the other hand may agree alterations, in so far as current law or practice permits, to the employees' terms and conditions of employment designed to safeguard employment opportunities by ensuring the survival of the undertaking, business or part of the undertaking or business.

3.   A Member State may apply paragraph 20(b) to any transfers where the transferor is in a situation of serious economic crisis, as defined by national law, provided that the situation is declared by a competent public authority and open to judicial supervision, on condition that such provisions already existed in national law on 17 July 1998.

---

7   OJ L 283, 20.10.1980, p. 23. Directive as last amended by the 1994 Act of Accession.

The Commission shall present a report on the effects of this provision before 17 July 2003 and shall submit any appropriate proposals to the Council.

4.   Member States shall take appropriate measures with a view to preventing misuse of insolvency proceedings in such a way as to deprive employees of the rights provided for in this Directive.

Article 6

1.   If the undertaking, business or part of an undertaking or business preserves its autonomy, the status and function of the representatives or of the representation of the employees affected by the transfer shall be preserved on the same terms and subject to the same conditions as existed before the date of the transfer by virtue of law, regulation, administrative provision or agreement, provided that the conditions necessary for the constitution of the employee's representation are fulfilled.

The first subparagraph shall not supply if, under the laws, regulations, administrative provisions or practice in the Member States, or by agreement with the representatives of the employees, the conditions necessary for the reappointment of the representatives of the employees or for the reconstitution of the representation of the employees are fulfilled.

Where the transferor is the subject of bankruptcy proceedings or any analoguous insolvency proceedings which have been instituted with a view to the liquidation of the assets of the transferor and are under the supervision of a competent public authority (which may be an insolvency practitioner authorised by a competent public authority), Member States may take the necessary measures to ensure that the transferred employees are properly represented until the new election or designation of representatives of the employees.

If the undertaking, business or part of an undertaking or business does not preserve its autonomy, the Member States shall take the necessary measures to ensure that the employees transferred who were represented before the transfer continue to be properly represented during the period necessary for the reconstitution or reappointment of the representation of employees in accordance with national law or practice.

2.   If the term of office of the representatives of the employees affected by the transfer expires as a result of the transfer, the representatives shall continue to enjoy the protection provided by the laws, regulations, administrative provisions or practice of the Member States.

CHAPTER III

Information and consultation

Article 7

1.   The transferor and transferee shall be required to inform the representatives of their respective employees affected by the transfer of the following:

— the date or proposed date of the transfer,
— the reasons for the transfer,
— the legal, economic and social implications of the transfer for the employees,
— any measures envisaged in relation to the employees.

The transferor must give such information to the representatives of his employees in good time, before the transfer is carried out.

The transferee must give such information to the representatives of his employees in good time, and in any event before his employees are directly affected by the transfer as regards their conditions of work and employment.

2. Where the transferor or the transferee envisages measures in relation to his employees, he shall consult the representatives of this employees in good time on such measures with a view to reaching an agreement.

3. Member States whose laws, regulations or administrative provisions provide that representatives of the employees may have recourse to an arbitration board to obtain a decision on the measures to be taken in relation to employees may limit the obligations laid down in paragraphs 1 and 2 to cases where the transfer carried out gives rise to a change in the business likely to entail serious disadvantages for a considerable number of the employees.

The information and consultations shall cover at least the measures envisaged in relation to the employees.

The information must be provided and consultations take place in good time before the change in the business as referred to in the first subparagraph is effected.

4. The obligations laid down in this Article shall apply irrespective of whether the decision resulting in the transfer is taken by the employer or an undertaking controlling the employer.

In considering alleged breaches of the information and consultation requirements laid down by this Directive, the argument that such a breach occurred because the information was not provided by an undertaking controlling the employer shall not be accepted as an excuse.

5. Member States may limit the obligations laid down in paragraphs 1, 2 and 3 to undertakings or businesses which, in terms of the number of employees, meet the conditions for the election or nomination of a collegiate body representing the employees.

6. Member States shall provide that, where there are no representatives of the employees in an undertaking or business through no fault of their own, the employees concerned must be informed in advance of:

— the date or proposed date of the transfer,
— the reason for the transfer,
— the legal, economic and social implications of the transfer for the employees,
— any measures envisaged in relation to the employees.

CHAPTER IV

Final provisions

Article 8

This Directive shall not affect the right of Member States to apply or introduce laws, regulations or administrative provisions which are more favourable to employees or to promote or permit collective agreements or agreements between social partners more favourable to employees.

Article 9

Member States shall introduce into their national legal systems such measures as are necessary to enable all employees and representatives of employees who consider themselves wronged by failure to comply with the obligations arising from this Directive to pursue their claims by judicial process after possible recourse to other competent authorities.

Article 10

The Commission shall submit to the Council an analysis of the effect of the provisions of this Directive before 17 July 2006. It shall propose any amendment which may seem necessary.

Article 11

Member States shall communicate to the Commission the texts of the laws, regulations and administrative provisions which they adopt in the field covered by this Directive.

Article 12

Directive 77/187/EEC, as amended by the Directive referred to in Annex I, Part A, is repealed, without prejudice to the obligations of the Member States concerning the time limits for implementation set out in Annex I, Part B.

References to the repealed Directive shall be construed as references to this Directive and shall be read in accordance with the correlation table in Annex II.

Article 13

This Directive shall enter into force on the 20th day following its publication in the Official Journal of the European Communities.

Article 14

This Directive is addressed to the Member States.

Done at Brussels, 12 March 2001.

For the Council
The President
B. RINGHOLM

———————

ANNEX I

PART A

Repealed Directive and its amending Directive

(referred to in Article 12)

Council Directive 77/187/EEC (OJ L 61, 5.3.1977, p. 26)

Council Directive 98/50/EC (OJ L 201, 17.7.1998, p. 88)

PART B

Deadlines for transposition into national law

(referred to in Article 12)

Directive	Deadline for transposition
77/187/EEC	16 February 1979
98/50/EC	17 July 2001

———————

ANNEX II

CORRELATION TABLE

Directive 77/187/EEC	This Directive
Article 1	Article 1
Article 2	Article 2
Article 3	Article 3
Article 4	Article 4
Article 4a	Article 5
Article 5	Article 6
Article 6	Article 7
Article 7	Article 8
Article 7a	Article 9

Article 7b	Article 10
Article 8	Article 11
—	Article 12
—	Article 13
—	Article 14
—	Annex I
—	Annex II

GUIDANCE NOTES, ETC

Appendix 5

EXPLANATORY MEMORANDUM TO
TUPE 2006

EXPLANATORY MEMORANDUM TO THE
TRANSFER OF UNDERTAKINGS (PROTECTION OF EMPLOYMENT)
REGULATIONS 2006

2006 No. 246

1. This explanatory memorandum has been prepared by the Department of Trade and Industry and is laid before Parliament by Command of Her Majesty.

2. **Description**

    2.1 The Transfer of Undertakings (Protection of Employment) Regulations 2006 revoke the Transfer of Undertakings (Protection of Employment) Regulations 1981[1] – commonly known as the TUPE Regulations – and implement Council Directive 2001/23/EC on the approximation of the laws of the Member States relating to the safeguarding of employees' rights in the event of transfers of undertakings or businesses. They provide that the transferor's rights and obligations arising from a contract of employment or from an employment relationship shall by reason of a transfer be transferred to the transferee. They provide protection for employees from dismissal by the transferor or the transferee by sole or principal reason of the transfer itself. They allow a dismissal for a reason connected with the transfer where that reason is an economic, technical or organisational one entailing changes in the workforce.

3. **Matters of special interest to the Joint Committee on Statutory Instruments**

    3.1 These Regulations are laid under the power contained in section 2(2) of the European Communities Act 1972 to the extent that they implement obligations under, and options conferred by, Council Directive 2001/23 EC (please see attached Transposition Note for detail). To the extent that they do more than implement an obligation under, or an option conferred by, that Directive, they are laid under the power in section 38 of the Employment Relations Act 1999. That section empowers the Secretary of State to make provision by statutory instrument for employees to be given the same or similar treatment in circumstances falling outside the scope of the Acquired Rights Directive as employees are given under the UK's

---

1   SI 1981/1794.

implementing legislation in circumstances falling within the scope of the Directive. In other words, the power in section 38 is exercisable in circumstances other than those to which the Community obligation under the Directive applies.

3.2   Section 38 is used restrictively. It is used principally to make Regulation 3(1)(b), which applies TUPE to what are described as "service provision changes" (which includes situations where a client business outsources or contracts out a service to a contractor). Many service provision changes will also constitute the transfer of an undertaking or business within the meaning of Regulation 3(1)(a). Provision made in respect of a transfer that is a relevant transfer falling within Regulation 3(1)(b) but outside Regulation 3(1)(a) is identical to that made in respect of a relevant transfer within Regulation 3(1)(a). Insofar as the Regulations make provision for that narrow category of service provision change that is not also a relevant transfer within Regulation 3(1)(a), they are made under section 38.

3.3   Section 38 does not extend to Northern Ireland and Schedule 1 provides that Regulation 3(1)(b) and consequential provisions do not extend to Northern Ireland.

4.   Legislative Background

4.1   Council Directive 77/187/EEC was amended in 1998, by Council Directive 1998/50/EC and subsequently consolidated under 2001/23/EC. The 2006 TUPE Regulations revoke the Transfer of Undertakings (Protection of Employment) Regulations of 1981 and implement the revised Directive. (See Transposition Note attached)

5.   Extent

5.1   This instrument applies to all of the United Kingdom save for the provisions relating to service provision changes which do not apply to Northern Ireland, as described in paragraph 3.3 above Modifications in the application of the Regulations to Northern Ireland are listed at Schedule 1.

6.   European Convention on Human Rights

6.1   Mr Gerry Sutcliffe, Parliamentary Under Secretary of State for Employment Relations and Consumer Affairs, has made the following statement regarding Human Rights:

In my view the provisions of the Transfer of Undertakings (Protection of Employment) Regulations 2006 are compatible with the Convention rights.

7.   Policy background

7.1   The aim of the revised Regulations is to implement options contained in the revised Directive and to update UK legislation in the light of case law. Preparations and preliminary steps toward the reform of the Regulations have been in train for a number of years. Throughout that time, the Department of Trade and Industry has engaged in a process of thorough consultation (both formal and informal) with key stakeholders, such as the CBI, TUC, Business Services Association (BSA) and the Engineering Employers' Federation (EEF), as well as other government departments and the TUPE Forum (a group of organisations representing business and employees convened to provide views on the Regulations to Government). Specific policy proposals were put forward in a formal public consultation document, and a supporting background paper, in September 2001. The responses to that consultation were evaluated and a set of draft Regulations were prepared. Further consultation took place on the draft revised Regulations between March and June, 2005.

7.2 The main changes that will be effected by the revised Regulations are:-

(a) bringing a wider range of "service provision changes" (i.e. contracting-out and similar exercises involving business services) within the scope of the Regulations;

(b) clarification of the effect of the Regulations in relation to the key issues of transfer-related dismissals and changes to terms and conditions;

(c) the introduction of a requirement on the old employer (the transferor) to provide information about the transferring employees to the new employer (the transferee) in advance of the transfer. That information is termed "employee liability information);

(d) greater flexibility in the application of the Regulations in cases where the transferor is insolvent.

(a) Service provision changes

7.3 The scope of the legislation is the most extensively debated and litigated aspect of the existing Regulations, both nationally and at a European level. The Government considers that, ideally, everyone should know where they stand when a business sale or reorganisation, or a contracting-out or similar exercise, takes place, so that employers can plan effectively in a climate of fair competition and affected employees are protected as a matter of course.

7.4 The term "service provision change" describes situations where a contract to provide a client (public or private sector) with a business service, e.g. office cleaning is: a) awarded to a contractor ("contracted out" or "outsourced"); b) re-let to a new contractor on subsequent re-tendering ("reassigned"); or c) ended with the bringing "in house" of the service activities in question ("contracted in" or "insourced").

7.5 In most cases, service provision changes fall within the scope of the Directive and the existing Regulations; however, not all do. In some cases, uncertainty arises, leading to unnecessary disputes and litigation. The rationale for the new measure is that it would reduce such uncertainty in practice by establishing a position in which service provision changes would be comprehensively covered by the legislation, subject to certain specified exceptions. A major reason for introducing Section 38 of the Employment Relations Act 1999 was to ensure that adequate order-making powers were in place to enable the Government to achieve this extension of the existing scope through secondary legislation.

7.6 Businesses and employees will thus be clearer where they stand when such changes occur, and will be insulated to a significant extent from the effects of any further developments in ECJ jurisprudence on the application of the Directive itself in relation to such cases. The Government's intention is to ensure a "level playing field" for contractors bidding for service contracts, so that tendering decisions are taken on commercial merit rather than on differing views as to the employment rights of employees, and so that transaction risks and costs are reduced. Therefore, under the revised Regulations if:

- a service provision change (as described above) takes place; and
- prior to the change, there are employees assigned to an organised grouping the principal purpose of which is to carry out the service activities in question on behalf of the client concerned;

then:

- the employees assigned to the organised grouping shall be treated in the same way as in cases where the TUPE Regulations have historically applied; and
- the party responsible for the carrying out of the service activities before the change shall be treated as the transferor and the party responsible for the carrying out of the service activities after the change shall be treated as the transferee.

(b) Dismissals and changes to terms and conditions of employment

7.7   In the light of conflicting case law and confusion surrounding the meaning of the existing provisions the Government decided to update and clarify the effect of the Regulations in relation to dismissals and changes to terms and conditions of employment. The aim is to set out clearly how dismissals or variations of contract are to be treated in three different sets of circumstance:

- first, dismissals or variations for which the sole or principal reason is the transfer itself or a reason connected with the transfer that is not an economic, technical or organisational reason entailing changes in the workforce (an "ETO" reason) will be unlawful;
- secondly, dismissals or variations for which the sole or principal reason is not the transfer itself, but is a reason connected with the transfer that is an ETO reason will be potentially lawful;
- thirdly, dismissals or variations for which the sole or principal reason is unconnected with the transfer will be potentially lawful.

(c) Notification of employee liability information

7.8   Member States were given a new option in the revised Directive to introduce provisions requiring the transferor to notify the transferee of the rights and obligations in relation to employees that will be transferred, so far as those rights and obligations are or ought to be known to the transferor at the time of the transfer.

7.9   The introduction of these new provisions will entitle transferees to full, accurate information about the employees, and the associated rights and obligations, that they are taking on in a relevant transfer, and so are well placed to honour those rights, obligations etc. The Government considers that this will be of benefit not only to the employees who transfer but also to the transferees themselves as it would help transferees prepare more fully at an earlier stage for the incoming staff.

7.10   The employee liability information must be in writing or in another form which is accessible to the transferee. After the information in question has been notified, any changes in that information must also be notified. The information can be notified in instalments, and can be passed between contractors via the client in a service provision change case.

7.11   Where the transferor breaches the requirement, the transferee will be able to present a complaint to the employment tribunal. If the tribunal finds in the transferee's favour, it will be required to make a declaration to that effect and to award compensation for any loss which cannot be mitigated. However, a minimum amount of compensation must be awarded (£500 per employee involved), unless the tribunal considers that it would be just or equitable to award a smaller sum.

(d) Insolvency

7.12   The revised Directive gives Member States two options in cases where its requirements are applied in relation to "insolvency proceedings … under the supervision of a competent public authority (which may be an insolvency practitioner determined by national law)". The two new options are to provide that:

- in cases giving rise to protection for employees at least equivalent to that provided for in situations covered by the EC Insolvency Payments Directive (80/987/EEC), the transferor's pre-existing debts toward the employees do not pass to the transferee; and/or
- employers and employee representatives may agree changes to terms and conditions of employment by reason of the transfer itself, provided that this is in accordance with current law and practice and with a view to ensuring the survival of the business and thereby preserving jobs.

7.13   The underlying aim of these options is to allow Member States to promote the sale of insolvent businesses as going concerns and to promote the "rescue culture".

7.14   The statutory insolvency payments provisions in Part XII of the Employment Rights Act 1996 and equivalent Northern Ireland provisions (as amended from time to time) will in future apply to relevant employees who transferred to the transferee notwithstanding the fact that they were not dismissed by the transferor, as would normally be a prerequisite for entitlement under those provisions.

7.15   Where the transferor is in one of the types of insolvency proceedings described in Article 5.2, all relevant employees – those who transferred to the transferee and those who were unfairly dismissed by the transferor by reason of the transfer itself or a non-ETO reason connected with the transfer – will in future be entitled to receive payments from the

Secretary of State in respect of relevant debts incurred by the transferor. In cases where the relevant employee has transferred, the date of transfer will be treated as the date of dismissal for the purposes of calculating insolvency payments in respect of which the "appropriate date" is the date of dismissal (section 185 of the Employment Rights Act 1996).

7.16   The liability for any other debts owed by the insolvent transferor to relevant employees – i.e. debts that either fall outside the categories payable under the relevant statutory schemes or exceed the statutory upper limits on payments under those provisions – will still pass to the transferee in the relevant transfer, as they would do under the existing Regulations.

7.17   Where the transferor is in one of the types of insolvency proceedings described in Article 5.2 of the Directive, the Regulations will in future not stand in the way of the transferor or transferee (or insolvency practitioner) agreeing "permitted variations" to terms and conditions with appropriate representatives of the employees. "Permitted variation" means a variation that would normally be rendered unlawful under the Regulations (because, say, the sole or principal reason for it is either the transfer itself or a reason connected with the transfer that is not an ETO reason) and is designed to safeguard employment opportunities by ensuring the survival of the organised grouping involved in the relevant transfer.

8.   Impact

8.1   A Regulatory Impact Assessment is attached to this memorandum.

8.2   There is no real impact on the public sector, as far as the extension of scope is concerned, as the practical impact of this change is essentially confined to purely private sector transfers. This is because TUPE-type requirements are already applied comprehensively when public sector contracts change hands between private sector contractors by virtue of the public policy set out in the Cabinet Office Statement of Practice "Staff Transfers in the Public Sector". In addition, extending the scope of the legislation in "service provision change" cases will reduce significantly the proportion of cases in which disputes, involving legal proceedings, arise. This would mean savings to employers of up to £1.6 million per year. Taking together all the quantifiable costs and savings identified gives total additional quantifiable cost to business of a maximum of £9.5 million to £24.3 million each year. However, it is expected that the figure is likely to be at the lower end of the range. Also, there will be other unquantifiable but significant benefits and savings resulting from the change and these will offset the expected cost.

8.3   As far as the insolvency provision are concerned, then there is likely to be a saving to business of £6.5 million to £14.5 million each year in redundancy payments.

9.   Contact

Mr Bernard Carter at the Department for Trade and Industry Tel: 020 7215 2760 or e-mail: Bernard.Carter@dti.gsi.gov.uk can answer any queries regarding the instrument.

Appendix 6

FINAL REGULATORY IMPACT ASSESSMENT

REVISION OF THE TRANSFER OF UNDERTAKINGS (PROTECTION OF EMPLOYMENT) REGULATIONS 1981

January 2006
http://www.dti.gov.uk/er

1. The Transfer of Undertakings (Protection of Employment) Regulations 1981, commonly known as the TUPE Regulations, implement the EU Acquired Rights Directive and safeguard employees' rights when the business in which they work changes hands between employers.

Purpose and intended effect

Objective

2. The aims of the legislation are to:
    -   assist the smooth management of necessary business restructuring and public sector modernisation by securing the interests and commitment of the employees affected;
    -   promote a co-operative, partnership approach toward change; and
    -   help create a level playing field, and reduce transaction risks and costs, in business acquisitions and in contracting operations in the business services sector.
3. There are at present, however, a number of problems with the way the Regulations operate, and transfers can be the subject of confusion and dispute. The Government has therefore decided to amend the Regulations with the objective: a) to improve and simplify their operation, remedying some widely recognised shortcomings and reducing the potential for disputes and litigation; and b) to take advantage of some additional flexibilities afforded by a number of new Member State options introduced in a revised version of the Directive adopted in June 1998, following successful negotiations under the UK Presidency.

Background

4. The 1981 TUPE Regulations provide that when an undertaking or business, or part of one, is transferred from one employer to another:
    -   The employment contracts of the employees, along with all the rights, powers, duties and liabilities of the old employer (transferor) pass automatically to the transferee

- Employees of the transferor or of the new employers (transferee) may not be lawfully dismissed by reason of, or for a reason connected with the transfer. However, the Regulations provide that that prohibition shall not prevent lawful dismissals for an economic, technical or organisational reason entailing a change in the workforce; the employer will remain under a duty to act reasonably in the circumstances.

- Both the old and the new employer must inform employee representatives and consult them about the legal, economic and social implications of the transfer and any measures envisaged in relation to any of the employees affected by the transfer.

5. At the end of 2001, the Government carried out formal public consultation on a package of proposals for reform of the Regulations. This was both preceded by and followed by extensive informal consultation with key stakeholders and TUPE specialists. In February 2003, the Secretary of State for Trade and Industry announced the Government's decisions as to how the reform would be taken forward.

6. In March 2005, the DTI issued another consultation document containing new draft TUPE Regulations[1], seeking views as to whether or not the draft Regulations correctly and effectively implement the policy decisions taken in February 2003.

7. The 2005 public consultation document included a Partial RIA. The present RIA has been developed from that, in the light of comments received on the proposed measures.

Rationale for government intervention

8. The Regulations are widely regarded, by all groups whose interests are affected by them, as less than satisfactory in their present state. For instance:

    - The scope of the legislation is the most extensively debated and litigated aspect of the current Regulations. Ideally, everyone should know where they stand, so that employers can plan effectively in a climate of fair competition and affected employees are protected as a matter of course. In the past, however, this has not always been the case. There are two particular areas which have been a frequent source of dispute – avoidance devices and service provision changes.

    - It is often difficult for the transferee to understand the rights and obligations of employees conferred by the transferor. This increases the degree of uncertainty of the transfer market, thus leading to unnecessary barriers.

    - There are a number of disputes that arise because of a lack of clarity of whether dismissal by reason of a transfer of an undertaking is always unlawful.

    - It is unclear in which circumstances the regulations allow transfer related changes to terms and conditions that arise for an economic, technical or organisational reason entailing changes in the workforce. This results in uncertainty and unnecessary disputes.

---

1   TUPE Draft Revised Regulations: Public Consultation Document, Employment Relations Directorate, DTI, March 2005, URN 05/926

- Around 69 per cent of insolvencies result in the break-up of the assets of the company, thus resulting in job losses and a loss of productive potential.[2] There are a number of barriers that could potentially prevent a rescue of an insolvent business that could be reduced by changes to the TUPE regulations.

9. Failure to introduce the revised Regulations would mean that their shortcomings remained unaddressed, contrary to the Government's commitment to review and where necessary reform outdated and deficient regulation that imposes undue burdens on business. It would also mean that the valuable new flexibilities in the revised Directive, successfully negotiated by the UK in 1998, were not taken advantage of. It would impact negatively on policy priorities not only of the Department of Trade and Industry (DTI) but also of a number of other government departments.

Consultation

(i) Within government

10. These proposals have been developed in consultation with interested government departments including HM Treasury, The Department for Work and Pensions and Cabinet Office.

(ii) Public consultation

11. In 1997, the Government made it a social affairs priority for the then forthcoming UK Presidency of the EU to secure a revision of the Acquired Rights Directive, so as to: a) clarify the meaning of certain provisions by incorporating elements of the jurisprudence of the European Court of Justice (ECJ); and b) give the UK – and other Member States – increased flexibility in tailoring national implementing legislation to domestic circumstances. The DTI carried out a formal public consultation exercise to canvass views on the UK's stance in the negotiations leading up to the revision.

12. In September 2001, the DTI published another formal public consultation document, accompanied by a detailed background paper, setting out specific policy proposals for the reform of the Regulations.

13. In the light of those consultations, the Government announced in February 2003 that it would proceed with its policy proposals. Since that date, the Government has been working on a new set of TUPE Regulations to replace the existing ones, and, as part of that exercise, it has undertaken extensive prior consultations with interested parties.

14. On 15 March 2005, the DTI issued another consultation document containing new draft TUPE Regulations. It sought views as to whether or not the draft Regulations correctly and effectively implement the policy decisions taken in February 2003. The consultation document made it clear that the Government was not seeking views on the policy proposals, except in relation to a few outstanding issues such as the exemption of "professional services" from the scope of the Regulations. The document

---

2   Source: R3 (2004) 12th Corporate Insolvency Survey. Available at www.r3.org.uk/publications.

was therefore aimed principally at TUPE specialist groups such as legal advisers, trade unions, employer's organisations and experts with knowledge of the operation of the Regulations.

15.   The consultation closed on 7 June 2005. There were 72 responses to the consultation overall. However no concerns were raised with respect to the estimated costs and benefits presented in the Partial Regulatory Impact Assessment.

Options

16.   A range of options was considered in the 2001 consultation These were mainly concerned with the provision of pensions (which have been addressed in the Pensions Act 2004) but also included the costing of policy recommendations to deal with the problems described above. The results of the formal and informal consultation, have enabled the drafting of legislation on the following measures to, briefly:

   - give more comprehensive coverage to service contracting operations, with the aim of improving the operation of the market, promoting business flexibility and reducing insecurity for employees affected by such operations;

   - introduce a requirement on the transferor to notify the transferee of the employees and associated employment liabilities that it will be transferring, thus increasing the transparency of the transfer process and combating 'sharp practice';

   - clarify the circumstances in which employers can lawfully make transfer-related dismissals and negotiate transfer-related changes to terms and conditions of employment for 'economic, technical or organisational' (ETO) reasons; and

   - introduce new flexibility into the Regulations' application in relation to the transfer of insolvent businesses, giving a worthwhile boost to the promotion of the 'rescue culture'.

Costs and benefits

Assumptions

17.   The RIA considers the different aspects of the revision of the Regulations individually. Some of the assumptions are common. We use evidence from the Workplace Employee Relations survey 1998 (WERS 98) and from the Small Business Survey business database to establish the proportion and numbers of employees and undertakings likely to be affected.

18.   WERS 98 questioned managers of workplaces with over 25 employees about whether or not there had been a change of ownership in their workplace over the past 5 years. 312 responded 'yes', and of those, 94 implied that a private sector to private sector TUPE transfer was involved.[3] The latter equates to 4.3 per cent of those surveyed, or about 1 per cent per annum. Anecdotal evidence shows – as would be expected –

---

3   The takeovers included in the analysis include 'sold by parent organisation' and 'management

that small firms are less likely to be involved in transfers. We assume therefore that those affected comprise: between 0.1 per cent and 0.5 per cent of businesses with 1–9 employees; between 0.5 per cent and 0.9 per cent of businesses with 10–19 employees; and 1 per cent of businesses with 20 or more employees.

19. This indicates that between at least 2,500 and 7,100 businesses with between about 200,000 and 220,000 employees will benefit each year from the changes to the legislation. The true figure will be somewhat higher, however, as while the WERS data gives a good indication of the incidence of businesses changing hands through ordinary sales and buy-outs, it probably does not capture transfers occurring through contracting-out and analogous operations. The proportion of such operations to which the Regulations will apply in future will be increased by the changes. The numbers likely to be affected in these cases are considered further below.

20. We assume that there would be no additional implementation costs to companies. Companies who are involved in a TUPE transfer, would in any case be referring to lawyers on what they can and cannot do, so would incur the costs with or without the changes in the Regulations.

Extension of scope

21. The aim of this aspect of the revision of the Regulations is to reduce the high degree of uncertainty felt by the parties involved in service provision changes, as to whether or not the Regulations apply in relation to their particular case.[4] The measure will involve the scope of the Regulations being extended to give more comprehensive coverage to service provision changes.

22. The practical impact of this change will be essentially confined to purely private sector transfers, i.e. transfers not involving a public sector or former public sector service. This is because TUPE-type requirements are already applied comprehensively when public sector service contracts change hands between private sector contractors, by virtue of the public policy set out in the Cabinet Office Statement of Practice "Staff Transfers in the Public Sector". The Government remains committed to this policy. The Local Government Act 2003 confers powers on the Secretary of State, the National Assembly of Wales and Scottish Ministers to require best value authorities in England, Wales and Scotland to deal with staff matters in accordance with Directions. The purpose of these powers was to enable the provisions of the Statement of Practice to be made a statutory requirement for those authorities. No Directions have yet been issued under these powers.

23. The change will entail new provisions being made to the effect that if:
   ● a service provision change is to take place; and
   ● prior to the change, there are employees assigned to an organized

---

buyout'. See Annex A for details. It should be pointed out that WERS 98 was not a survey conducted to answer TUPE questions.

4 'Service provision changes' is a term coined to describe a) contracting-out ("outsourcing"); b) reassignment of a contract ("re-tendering") and c) contracting-in ("insourcing") of labour-intensive services.

grouping the principal purpose of which is to perform the service activities in question specifically on behalf of the client concerned;

then, subject to certain specified exceptions:

- the employees assigned to the organized grouping shall be treated in the same way as in cases where the TUPE Regulations normally apply; and
- the party with responsibility for the carrying out of the service activities before the change shall be treated as the transferor, and the party with responsibility for this after the change shall be treated as the transferee.

24. The measure is expected to impact principally on private sector clients for, and contractors providing, 'blue collar' services such as office cleaning, workplace catering, security guarding, maintenance, and some computer services; and on the employees of such clients and contractors.

25. To estimate the numbers of businesses and employees involved in this type of service provision we use statistics from a selection of industry sectors.[5] We then make assumptions about the number of times that service providers are changed, including being contracted-in. Annex B provides details.

26. We estimate that between about 2,500 and 4,500 businesses employing between about 60,000 and 100,000 employees are involved each year in a service provision change not involving a public sector service.

27. We further assume that 65 per cent of these service provision changes are, at the point when they actually take place, clearly TUPE transfers under the current Regulations, and are generally recognized and treated as such by all parties concerned. We also assume that 10 per cent of cases are clearly not TUPE transfers under the current legislation. This implies that in 25 per cent of cases it is, at present, legally uncertain and unclear to the parties involved whether or not the change involves a TUPE transfer. Some of the cases in this category will in fact involve TUPE transfers (and may eventually be established to do so by way of legal action); others not. It is impossible to say exactly where the dividing line currently falls, owing to the legal uncertainty. 25 per cent is, in effect, the margin of uncertainty.

28. It should be noted that this considerably understates the true degree of uncertainty surrounding service provision changes as, although the majority – as indicated in the preceding paragraph, we assume 65 per cent – are clearly TUPE transfers at the point when they actually take place, they may well have been subject to uncertainty at an earlier stage. This is because the uncertainty arises mainly where the new service provider declines, or seeks to decline, to take over a major part (in terms of numbers or skills) of the old service provider's workforce, and it may not be known at the outset – for instance, at the stage when a client invites contractors to bid for a contract – whether or not any given case will ultimately fall into this category. The parties themselves can however take steps to reduce the chances of their case ultimately falling into the 25 per cent margin of uncertainty. The client, for instance, can make clear in initiating a tendering exercise that it will exclude bids that contemplate

---

5   See Annex B.

the existing workforce not being taken over; and, even where the client makes no such stipulation, the contractor can choose to bid on a basis that will almost certainly involve a TUPE transfer (provided of course that the bid is successful, and that the contractor is not undercut by a competitor bidding on a purported 'non TUPE' basis).

29. The extension of scope is expected to bring clearly within the coverage of the Regulations the majority of cases that are currently within the assumed 25 per cent margin of uncertainty. It will also bring within the coverage of the Regulations a proportion of the assumed 10 per cent of cases that are, at the moment, clearly not TUPE cases. We assume that, under the new Regulations, 85 per cent to 90 per cent of cases will be clearly TUPE cases, and 5 per cent clearly not TUPE cases. This will leave 5 per cent to 10 per cent of cases in which there will still be uncertainty over whether or not the Regulations apply. The change will thus bring certainty to an additional 15 per cent to 20 per cent of cases, involving the transfer of 390 to 880 businesses with between 9,000 to 21,000 employees per annum[6] – a considerable reduction in the margin of uncertainty.

30. We assume that, of this subset of cases, 10 per cent will already apply the full TUPE Regulations even if they do not have to. This may, on first consideration, seem a low percentage. However, as explained above, where the new service provider in a service provision change does in fact take over a major part (in terms of numbers and skills) of the old service provider's existing workforce, this generally, in practice, has the effect of causing the Regulations clearly to apply – i.e. of avoiding those cases falling within the margin of uncertainty in the first place. There are, where a labour-intensive service is concerned, only a relatively narrow range of circumstances in which the new service provider might take over a major part of the existing workforce and treat them as if TUPE applies, when in fact TUPE does not apply. An example might be a case where the business is completely reorganized following the change, so that the undertaking does not 'retain its identity' in the hands of the new service provider – part of the test for the transfer of an undertaking under the Directive and the existing Regulations.

31. This leaves the net numbers likely to be affected at between 350 and 790 businesses with (prior to the service provision changes) between 8,000 and 19,000 employees in total. Again, however, these estimates understate the benefits of the change in terms of avoiding disputes, because: a) disputes would at present arise in a proportion of the 10 per cent of cases where, notwithstanding the uncertainty, TUPE was ultimately applied; and b) because – for reasons explained in the following paragraph – the 5 per cent to 10 per cent of cases in which legal uncertainty will remain following the change will be the types of cases in which disputes are, in practice, relatively unlikely to arise.

32. It is unavoidable that some uncertainty will remain following the extension of scope, because the precise facts will be different in every case and it is impossible to draft provisions that draw an absolutely clear line

---

6   These results are obtained by applying the percentages to the numbers of service provision changes that we estimate will be affected each year, as set out – after rounding – in paragraph 19.

between those that fall within the Regulations' coverage and those that do not. There could potentially be uncertainty about such matters as whether or not there was, prior to the change, an organised grouping of employees dedicated to meeting the needs of one particular client.

33.   The main benefits of making this change are that it will:
   - help to ensure that all parties involved in service provision changes know where they stand from the outset, and thereby:
     o reduce transaction risks and costs for clients and contractors, and allow for services to be provided more cheaply, in part because of a reduction in the cost of commercial indemnity insurance;
     o help 'take the fear out of transfer' and reduce insecurity for affected employees;
     o reduce the number of TUPE-related employment tribunal and court cases;
   - help to create a 'level playing field' for contract bids and promote fair competition, encouraging *bona fide* potential bidders (including small firms) to become involved in service contracting while deterring 'cowboys' who would seek to compete by cutting employees' terms and conditions;
   - minimise the risk to employees of facing redundancy, and to contractors of facing large associated redundancy payment liabilities, when contracts reach the end of their term;
   - help to insulate contractors, clients and employees from possible future upheavals in the case law on this aspect of the scope of the Directive, such as occurred when the European Court of Justice gave its unexpected judgment in the *Suzen* case in 1997;

34.   Set against this, there will be some marginal costs arising from the additional protections that employees will gain in the 350 to 790 cases per annum in which the change will have a direct impact (i.e. in which the legal position will change, leaving aside the indirect impact of providing greater certainty and helping to avoid disputes in cases where the legal position will remain the same). Even leaving aside the – unquantifiable – benefits described in the preceding paragraph, these will be largely offset by savings. A more detailed analysis of quantifiable costs and savings follows.

35.   Redundancy payments: In cases where the change results in TUPE being applied, and where otherwise it would not have been, there is likely to be a significant reduction in the number of redundancies made. This is because:

> a. the workforce will pass from the old service provider to the new along with the contract whereas, but for the application of the Regulations, all those who could not be redeployed by the old service provider on other work would have had to be made redundant by the old service provider; and

> b. this is likely to result in more employment stability in these sectors as new contractors will have less freedom, and less incentive, to undercut using cheaper labour on worse terms and conditions.

36.   We assume below that, if TUPE did not apply, only 5 per cent of the workforce on average would be able to be redeployed by the old service

provider. (Some of the others might subsequently be taken on, on new contracts, by the new service provider; but this would not avoid the necessity for the old service provider to make them redundant and pay them – subject to the normal qualifying conditions – a statutory, or possibly an enhanced contractual, redundancy payment.)

37. The new service provider might still wish to make some redundancies following the transfer, however, if this is warranted by increased efficiency, meaning that fewer employees are required. We assume that, on average, there would be a reduction of 25 per cent in the number of employees engaged in carrying out the service activities, and that these employees would all be shed through redundancy (although it would be wrong to suppose that they would necessarily all be employees who had transferred from the old service provider, as there would need to be a fair redundancy selection exercise). This compares with 95 per cent of employees being made redundant by the old service provider if TUPE did not apply – i.e. a 70 per cent reduction in the total number of redundancies. This will result in a saving to business of £6.5million to £14.5 million each year in redundancy payments.[7] The cost of redundancy payments for the 25 per cent of employees who were made redundant would shift from the old service provider to the new. This would be a shift of £2 million to £5 million each year.

38. <u>Number of tribunal applications:</u> Currently there are 1,428 applications each year to the Employment Tribunals Service that include a claim of unfair dismissal under TUPE and 1,321 that include a claim regarding failure to inform and consult under TUPE.[8] A certain proportion of breach of employment contract claims (which are generally heard in the civil courts rather than the Employment Tribunals), claims for unauthorized deductions from wages and redundancy payment claims will also be claims arising from a dispute over the application of the TUPE Regulations, but these are not separately identified in the statistics that are collected and cannot be quantified – hence the analysis below understates the benefits of the change in terms of reducing costs associated with legal proceedings. We assume therefore that the number of cases that include either types of claim to be between 1,400 and 2,700 each year.

39. A certain proportion of these TUPE-related claims arise from the current uncertainty over the Regulations' scope in relation to service provision changes. As discussed above, extending the scope of the Regulations is expected to reduce significantly the proportion of cases in which disputes, and consequent legal proceedings, arise. This will mean savings to employers and the Exchequer. On average, a tribunal application costs the employer involved £3,000[9] and the Exchequer £990.

40. On the other hand, broadening the scope of the legislation will mean

---

7   We assume an average duration of employment of 4 years. The calculation is therefore: 8,000 x £280 x 4 x 0.70 = £6.546 million, 19,000 x £280 x 4 x 0.70 = £14.546 million. This is based on the assumption that employers only pay the statutory minimum of £280 per year of service. They may choose to pay more.

8   Source: Employment Tribunal Service Annual Report 2003/04.

9   This is an estimate of the median cost of an employment tribunal to an employer. This includes the cost of legal services as well as the cost of staff time. The estimates are based on

more cases in which there is potential to make a claim; particularly a claim regarding an alleged transfer-related change to terms and conditions. We assume however, that this effect will be overshadowed by the impact of making the Regulations clearer.

41.   If we assume that the changes result in a reduction of between 10 per cent and 20 per cent in applications, this is equivalent to between 140 and 540 applications per year. This will result in a saving to employers of up to £1.6 million and to the exchequer of up to £0.5million each year.

42.   Changes in terms and conditions: If there is no TUPE transfer, the new employer can essentially determine the terms and conditions of new employees, subject to market conditions. We assume that the average total employment package is worth 110 per cent of gross wages. On average this would be about £382 per week.[10] If, but for the application of TUPE, the service provision change would lead to the employees in the new workforce having a remuneration package worth 15 per cent less than the employees in the old workforce (who would be mostly different individuals), this would mean a 'loss' of about £3,000 per employee per year. It was assumed above that, if TUPE applied, the new service provider would reduce the total workforce by 25 per cent. We now further assume that if TUPE did not apply, the new service provider would reduce the workforce by 30 per cent – in other words, that the application of TUPE would, mainly as a result of the transfer of redundancy payments liabilities, act as a marginal disincentive on the new service provider to reduce the size of the workforce. The additional costs falling to the transferee as a result of the extension of scope would thus be: a) the full cost of the remuneration package, i.e. £382 per week, for 5 per cent of the old workforce; and b) the difference between the old remuneration package and the new, i.e. 15 per cent x £382 =£57 per week, for 70 per cent of the old workforce. This totals between £17 million and £39 million[11] each year. This is a direct transfer from the new employer to the employees. All or part of it may have an influence on the price of the contract, and so effectively be 'passed back' to the transferee.

43.   Information and consultation: In the case of a TUPE transfer the old employer has to inform and consult employee representatives. For those extra 350 to 790 businesses that will now fall under TUPE Regulations this would have cost implications. We assume that the consultation process takes three days of management and worker representative's time. This includes a consultation meeting as well as discussions before and after. We estimate the daily cost of a manager's time to be about £152 and that of an employee representative about £85.[12] The total cost per

---

information from the Survey of Employment Tribunal Applications 2003 and the Annual Survey of Hours and Earnings 2004 (available at www.statistics.gov.uk).

10   Source: Annual Survey of Hours and Earnings 2004. Average (median) gross weekly earnings for full and part time workers (including overtime) in United Kingdom is £346.90. 110% of this is £382.

11   £57 per week x 52 weeks x 8,000 to 19,000 employees affected x 70% = £17.4 million to £38.7 million.

12   Median weekly rate for managers is £583.20, source Annual Survey of Hours and Earnings 2004. Therefore daily cost of managers time is £583.20 x 1.3 /5 = £151.63.

business will therefore be about £710.[13] This will bring the costs to all businesses to £0.3 million to £0.6 million each year.

44. Summary of costs and benefits: Taking together all the quantifiable costs and savings identified above gives total additional quantifiable costs to business of a maximum of £9.5 million to £24.3 million each year. Table 1 gives a breakdown of how this figure is derived.

1. Summary of costs and benefits of extending the scope of the legislation

	Annual benefits (£m)	Annual Costs (£m)
Firms		
Redundancy payments	6.4–14.5	
Tribunal applications	1.6	
Terms and conditions		17–39
Information and consultation		0.3–0.6
Total net impact		9.5–24.3
Individuals		
Redundancy payments		6.4–14.5
Terms and conditions	17–39	
Total net impact	10.8–24.1	
Exchequer		
Tribunal applications	0.5	

45. It should be noted however that the assumptions used in this analysis have – as explained in the appropriate paragraphs – consistently understated the savings and overstated the costs that will flow from the change. It is therefore likely that the true additional quantifiable costs associated with the change will be at the lower end of this range, i.e. a maximum of around £10 million per annum. This must also be viewed in the light of the fact that there will be other, unquantifiable but nonetheless significant, benefits and savings resulting from the change, as discussed in paragraphs above. It is likely that these will more than offset the estimated maximum £10 million per annum quantifiable costs, so that, overall, the effects of the measure will be positive for business and for the operation of the market as well as for the affected employees. This is certainly the strong view of consultation respondents closely involved in the service-contracting sector – including for example the Business Services Association, which represents many private sector contractors for services. The contracting industry in general strongly supports the measure to extend the scope of the Regulations.

46. Employees would benefit by about £11 million to £24 million each year (see Table 1 for details).

Weekly cost of employee representatives time is £327.60. Therefore daily costs of employee reps time is £327.60/5 x 1.3 = £85.18.

13 (£152 + £85) x 3 = £710.

47. The following sections address specific Regulations where there are potential cost and benefit issues arising.

Notification of employee liability information

48. The consultation document dealt with the flow of information from the transferor to the transferee regarding the transfer of employment liabilities.

49. At present, there is no legal obligation on the transferor to pass any information to the transferee. Under the revised Regulations, however, the transferor will be obliged to give the transferee information about the employees who are to transfer, and all the associated rights and obligations towards them. The information will need to be provided at least fourteen days before the transfer, or, if special circumstances mean that that is not reasonably practicable, as soon as reasonably practicable thereafter. If the details change between the time they have first been notified to the transferee and the actual completion of the transfer, the transferor has to inform the transferee.

50. In light of responses the 2005 consultation, the Regulations have been amended to identify the main categories of information which should be supplied. These include the age and the employment particulars of each transferred individual. As much of this information is already collected by employers under other information obligations, this should reduce the administrative burden on the transferor. Simplifications have also been made to the means of transferring data: the Regulations now allow for the non-written notification of the information, as long as such other forms of communication can be accessed by the transferee.

51. The intended effect of the measure is to increase transparency for the transferee as well as for the employees, and to reduce the number of cases in which the transferee feels obliged to seek commercial indemnities from the transferor to afford cover against exposure to unforeseen liabilities. In cases where no commercial indemnities are or would be agreed, the measure will protect the transferee, and indirectly its employees, against acquiring such unforeseen liabilities and suffering adverse consequences –including potentially, in extreme cases, insolvency – as a result. The measure also aims at increasing competition as it introduces a strong disincentive to hide any relevant information about a business to be transferred. This might have an effect on the price of a business. If there were significant unusual liabilities toward employees this would reduce the price. This benefit to the transferee would be a cost to the transferor. We cannot quantify this effect, but assume that it would mainly support the functioning of the market.

52. We assume that even at present, in the absence of a legal requirement, equivalent information is already in most cases (90–95 per cent) made accessible in writing to the transferee. The benefit of the measure in those cases will thus be to increase security for the parties against the risk that the information provided may be incomplete or inaccurate, and to reduce the need for commercial indemnities (which can be time consuming and costly for the parties to negotiate and agree). In the other 5–10 per cent of

cases – i.e. 240 to 1,100 transfers per annum[14] – the new measure will have the additional effect of causing the transferor to incur costs through time spent identifying the information and writing it down.

53.   In the Partial RIA that accompanied the public consultation document we assumed that this would not take more than one day of management time. In light of the simplifications discussed above we now assume that the time needed is reduced by one-quarter. At a daily cost of £152 for senior management this would cost up to £0.125 million each year in total for all transfers.[15]

Dismissal by reason of a transfer of an undertaking

54.   The consultation document raised the issue of the circumstances in which transfer-related dismissals may be lawfully made for economic, technical or organisational reasons entailing a change in the workforce (ETO reasons), and indicated that the Government intended to change the wording of the Regulations in order to clarify the legal position. There has been no change to that position.

55.   This aspect of the current Regulations has been subject to uncertainty. We would expect the clarification to reduce the number of disputes over this issue and so save businesses and employees the costs arising from such disputes, including in some instances the costs of contesting court and tribunal cases (and the associated costs to the Exchequer).

56.   There were 1,428 transfer-related unfair dismissal cases brought by employees to employment tribunals in 2003/04,[16] either as a main or other jurisdiction. This is 0.5 per cent of all employees affected by a transfer. This is about the same as the general proportion of all employees making a tribunal application. Therefore even though we expect a reduction, this is likely to be modest. We assume about 5 per cent, or about 70 cases.

57.   An employment tribunal case costs business on average £3,000. A reduction of 70 cases would therefore reduce costs to employers by about £0.2 million each year. There would be additional benefits: a reduction in uncertainty over when transfer-related dismissals can be lawfully made would also give employers the ability to make people redundant etc, where necessary, with more confidence, and therefore reduce risks and transaction costs around transfers. These are important benefits but it is not possible to quantify them.

Changes to the terms and conditions of employment affected employees

58.   The consultation document also raised the issue of transfer-related changes to the terms and conditions of affected employees and, again, indicated that the Government aimed to clarify the legal position. The Government has now reaffirmed its view that there should be greater

---

14   These are 5 to 10% of the 4,800 to 11,000 transfers (including TUPE transfers under new regulations) taking place every year.

15   Calculation: 240 x 0.75 x £152 = £27,360 to 1,100 x 0.75 x £152 = £125,400.

16   The official figure for TUPE related unfair dismissal cases may underestimate the actual figure as some of these cases may be filed under other unfair dismissal cases. We do not know the size of this effect. Source of official data: ETS annual report 2003/04.

scope in the new Regulations for the transferee to be able to vary contracts after the transfer for an economic, technical or organisational reason connected with the transfer.

59. The effects of this increased clarity and flexibility in the Regulations will be to:

- reduce the number of disputes over this issue and so save businesses and employees the costs arising from such disputes, including in some cases the costs (and the costs to the Exchequer) of contesting court and tribunal cases;

- give employers the confidence to negotiate changes to terms and conditions, and potentially gain improvements in business efficiency (for example, more logical payment systems with lower administration costs), in some cases where they would otherwise have refrained from doing so because of the perceived legal risk;

- reduce a perverse incentive for employers to make transfer-related dismissals, and attempt to rely on the ETO defence in any resulting unfair dismissal claims, simply in order to be able to offer the employees re-engagement on new terms and conditions (and thereby achieve changes by the 'back door'); and

- reduce employers' risks and transaction costs associated with transfers.

60. These benefits would be significant, but are unquantifiable.

Application of the legislation in relation to insolvency proceedings

61. The consultation document discussed the situation of an insolvent business. It indicated that the Government had decided to take advantage of two new derogations in this regard in the revised Acquired Rights Directive.

62. The Regulations have been revised to provide that, in transfers of businesses in certain types of formal insolvency proceedings:

- the debts that, but for the transfer, would have been met by the Secretary of State for Trade and Industry from the National Insurance Fund under the insolvency payments provisions of the Employment Rights Act 1996, will in future remain with the insolvent transferor and still be met by the state in this way even though a transfer has occurred (although debts outside the categories or in excess of the amounts covered under the insolvency payments provisions will transfer as at present); and/or

- employers and employees may (subject to certain specified safeguards) agree transfer-related changes to the terms and conditions even where there are no ETO reasons that would render them potentially lawful in any event.

63. The intended effect of taking up these derogations is to support the 'rescue culture' by reducing burdens on the transferee. This will create an additional incentive to rescue a business, or parts of it, reducing the proportion of insolvent businesses that are simply wound-up and saving at least some of the jobs of their employees. It will also increase the chances of a rescued business remaining viable after the transfer.

(i) Pre-existing debts not passed to transferee

64. The benefits to business and to employees flowing from the first of the two changes described above will be achieved at the cost of some deadweight expenditure falling to the National Insurance Fund.

65. Under the insolvency payments provisions, employees of formerly insolvent businesses may claim from the state, up to eight weeks' arrears of wages and up to six weeks' arrears of holiday pay, subject to a statutory upper limit on the amount of a week's pay that may be taken into account for these purposes, plus certain other amounts that are largely irrelevant in the present context.[17] If, however, the business is rescued and transfers to a solvent transferee, then – under the current TUPE Regulations – the transferee has to pay any wages or holiday pay owed to the transferred employees and the state is relieved of this liability. Under the new Regulations, where businesses in certain specified types of insolvency proceedings are concerned (these types of insolvency proceedings being dictated by the scope of the derogation in the Directive), the state will continue to pay the debts that it would have paid in the absence of a transfer, even though a transfer has occurred. We estimate that this will result in an increase in payments for the state in this category of about 12 per cent. This is equivalent to about £6.6 million per annum.[18] See Annex C for details of calculations. These will be benefits for the transferee.

66. It is anticipated that insolvent businesses will be easier to sell with one level of debts less. We assume that the measure will increase the preservation rate of businesses in the specified types of insolvency proceedings by between 2 and 3 percentage points. This compares with the current average preservation rate for all insolvencies of about 30 per cent.[19] This implies an increase in the number of insolvent businesses rescued through TUPE transfers of between 240 and 360 per annum.[20]

67. The 240–360 additionally rescued businesses would have between 4,900 and 7,300 employees.[21] Not all of these would keep their jobs. We assume that about 50 per cent (2,400 to 3,700) of them would do so.

68. The rescue of 240 to 360 additional businesses per annum would benefit the taxpayer. Benefits would include savings in redundancy payments (only between 2,400 to 3,700 employees would claim such payments from the National Insurance Fund), reduced levels of unemployment payments to those who would otherwise not have been able to find another job, and future tax payments. The latter are the consequence of a successful

---

17 For detailed information please see www.dti.gov.uk/access/job_1/pl718/insolv2.htm.

18 The Insolvency Service paid about £56 million in compensation for arrears in pay and holiday pay. 12 per cent of this is about £6.6 million.

19 Source: R3 (2004) 12th Corporate Insolvency Survey. Available at www.r3.org.uk/publications

20 Relating this to the number of insolvent business (in the relevant categories) being sold or partly sold as an ongoing concern of around 3,000 the increased rescue of between 240 and 360 enterprises seems reasonable.

21 There are 1.22 million businesses with employees in the UK with 24.8m employees. If the employee distribution of the rescued businesses is the same as for the population of businesses as a whole then this would mean between (240 x 24.8m / 1.22m) = 4,879 and (360 x 24.8m / 1.22m) =7,318 employees in additional rescued businesses.

business. In every individual case these benefits would be significant for the jobholder. Overall we cannot quantify these benefits.

(ii) Transfer-related changes to terms and conditions

69.   Under the second of the two changes impacting on the transfer of insolvent businesses, transfer-related changes to the terms and conditions of employment of affected employees would be lawful, even in the absence of ETO reasons, if:

●   they were agreed between the transferor or the transferee and appropriate employee representatives;

●   they were designed to safeguard employment opportunities by ensuring the survival of the undertaking; and

●   they were not otherwise contrary to UK law (e.g. the National Minimum Wage Act).

70.   This measure would have the effect of increasing flexibility for the transferee and would thereby support the 'rescue culture' that the Government is keen to foster.

71.   The main benefit for employers would be that there would be the potential to secure agreement to less favourable terms and conditions and enable businesses to be rescued in cases where unaffordable terms and conditions were responsible, or partly responsible, for their becoming insolvent in the first place. The terms and conditions of employees include a large area of benefits apart from pay, such as holiday entitlement, additional maternity and parental leave, company cars etc. If the annual net value for the benefits were to be reduced by £100 for all the employees involved in this type of transfer, benefits to the transferee would be up to £3 million per annum.[22] These would be costs to the employees.

72.   The benefit for employees would be that in some cases they would keep their jobs where otherwise they would have lost them. The same principle applies as under the first of the two measures in this area. The benefits to employees would be reduced by any worsening in their terms and conditions. The benefits for the taxpayer would be similar to those under the first measure.

Equity and fairness

73.   The Regulations will affect employees in a number of ways. They will increase protection for employees when subject to a transfer of services provision, they will increase certainty when subject to any TUPE transfer and they will increase the chance of keeping a job when the firm that they work for becomes insolvent. Any distributional impacts will depend of the proportions of certain groups (low income, ethnic minorities, women) that are affected.

74.   The extension of TUPE to certain types of service provision changes is likely to have an impact on employees in catering, cleaning, security and certain types of computer related services. On the whole these are made

---

22   This is £100 times the estimated number of employees that are currently transferred to another company as a result of insolvency.

up of workers that earn below average wages, both on an hourly and a weekly basis.[23] Giving these workers some protection will have a positive equity impact, firstly through the protection of their incomes and secondly through the increase in their labour market attachment.

Small firms impact test

75. The Regulations will affect small firms, like all firms, in several ways. The extension of scope to certain service provision changes that are not considered as TUPE transfers will allow them to bid for contracts in a more certain environment. The requirement for notification of employee liability for all TUPE transfers will increase transparency at a modest cost to some transferors. The clarification of when ETO reasons for redundancy and when changes to terms and conditions of employment can apply, will reduce the number of tribunals and reduce uncertainty. And lastly the changes in relation to insolvency proceedings will increase the chances of rescue.

76. The question that we need to answer for the Small firms impact test is whether small firms are likely to be affected disproportionately by these changes to the regulations. To answer this question the Small firms impact test draws on the following:

- our assessment of the relative numbers of small firms that are involved in TUPE transfers which involve a straight purchase;
- how many small firms are likely to be involved in transfers of services;
- the rescue rate of small firms after an insolvency;
- evidence on implementation costs for small firms;
- responses from small firms to our previous formal consultation;
- informal discussions with small firms and organizations that represent small firms amongst others.

77. We do not have any figures on the number of small firms that are currently involved in a TUPE transfer which involves a sale or management buy-out. However, anecdotal evidence suggests that small firms are less likely to be involved in transfers and in particular are less likely to be the transferee.

78. In terms of transfers of service provision (private sector to private sector), we have looked at the proportion of small firms in the affected sectors (cleaning, catering, security and some computer related activities) and compared this with the population of small firms in all sectors. The result shows that small firms are not overly represented in these sectors.[24]

79. However, surveys have shown that preservation rates in the case of an insolvency are lower the smaller the company.[25] This is probably not

23 In the UK the average (median) gross hourly rate (excluding overtime) in 2004 for kitchen and catering assistants was £5.13, for cleaners and domestics £5.33, for security guards/related occupations £6.75, for database assistants and clerks was is £7.22. Source Office of National Statistics, Annual Survey of Hours and Earnings 2004. Available at www.statistics.gov.uk.

24 Of the affected sectors 96% are small firms employing between 1 and 49 employees, compared with 97% for all sectors. Source: Small Business Service.

25 Source: R3 (1992) A decade of change (10th annual company survey). Available at www.r3.org.uk/publications.

surprising as small firms are more likely to be subject to compulsory liquidations, where preservation rates are low. There is also some concern about the prevalence of insolvency amongst small firms. These statistics would tend to support a view that small firms stand to gain most from changes in the regulations whereby the National Insurance Fund takes on the debts to employees (up to the normal limits) where there is a buy-out.

80. Consultation has revealed no particular concerns from small firms.

Competition assessment

81. We have applied the Competition Filter and this did not reveal any concerns overall. However that is not to say that these measures will have a neutral effect on the markets for transfers generally, changes in service provisions, rescues and on the labour market. We have outlined these impacts in the text. This section summarizes the impacts.

82. The overall effect on the market for transfers would be positive as it would
    - increase transparency by improving information on the extent of employee liabilities;
    - clarify the circumstances under which it is lawful to make transfer related dismissals for ETO reasons;

83. There would also be improvements to the workings of the market for service provisions such as cleaning and catering by increasing the certainty of when a transfer is a TUPE transfer and when it is not. This would encourage more and possibly smaller bidders for service provision tenders by giving them a greater understanding of their potential liabilities.

84. Extra protection for employees in the service provision markets would maintain the overall value of their terms and conditions. This could be seen as anti-competitive in that it acts a barrier to new entrants, who are prepared to work for less. One could argue that this will give some existing employees some extra market power, resulting in wages that are uncompetitively high. On the other hand redundancy can serve to weaken the labour market attachment of workers resulting in a shrinking of the labour supply.

85. The market wages for the types of workers that the extension of the legislation is designed to protect are at present above the minimum wage, but not by much. Maintaining minimum standards at work is important in maintaining incentives for those that are out of employment.

86. Our conclusion is that although there may be some short-term costs in terms of reduced labour market flexibility, in the longer term these measures will act to prevent a reduction in the labour supply and are hence on balance positive.

Enforcement, sanctions and monitoring

87. Enforcement continues to be through the Employment Tribunals and the courts.

Implementation and delivery plan

88. The revised draft Regulations will be laid before Parliament in late 2005, to come into effect on 6 April 2006. To assist understanding and implementation, the Department will also publish guidance on the revised Regulations.

Post implementation review

89. Monitoring the effectiveness of the legislation will take place through the talking to stakeholders, monitoring tribunal statistics, data from baseline surveys and case law developments. Officials will also monitor insolvency statistics and any reports into look into the rescue of insolvent companies.

Summary

90. The Government has consulted widely on a number of changes to the Transfer of Undertakings (Protection of Employment) Regulations 1981. The proposed changes are likely to have an impact on employees, firms and the Exchequer. The quantifiable costs and benefits are outlined in Table 2.

2. Summary of costs and benefits of changes to TUPE Regulations

	Annual benefits (£m)	Annual Costs (£m)
Firms		
Extension of scope		9.5–24.3
Employee liability information	0.13	
Dismissal by reason of a transfer	0.2	
Insolvency	3	
Individuals		
Extension of scope	11–24	
Insolvency		3
Exchequer		
Insolvency		6.6

91. There will also be unquantifiable benefits to firms and individuals deriving from the increased certainty that the changes to the Regulations will bring, and the increased chances of a successful rescue after insolvency.

Gerry Sutcliffe
Parliamentary Under Secretary of State for
Employment Relations and Consumer Affairs

Signature:

Date:

Contact point:

Bernard Carter
Employment Relations Directorate
Bay 3124
Department of Trade and Industry
1 Victoria Street,
London SW1H 0ET
Tel: 0207 215 2760
Bernard.Carter@dti.gsi.gov.uk

Annex A

Of 2,191 workplaces surveyed in WERS 98, there had been 312 changes in ownership. These were disaggregated into 8 categories which were not mutually exclusive.

A1. Takeovers over the last 5 years

	Number of workplaces	% of changes
Agreed takeover	110	35.2
Takeover/merger formally opposed	2	0.6
Sold by parent organisation	63	20.2
Ex public sector, now privatised/denationalised	9	2.9
Management buy out	31	9.9
Buy out by employees	0	0
Change in partners/major shareholders	86	27.6
Other	36	11.5

Source: Workplace Employee Relations Survey 1998, Department of Trade and Industry

For TUPE-related transfers we include 'sold by parent organization' and 'management buy out'. This means that up to 94 of the 312 changes of ownership could be relevant. This equates to 4.3 per cent of those surveyed, or about 1 per cent per annum. These questions were only asked of workplaces with 25 or more employees. Anecdotal evidence shows – as would be expected – that small firms are less likely to be involved in transfers. We assume therefore that those affected comprise: between 0.1 per cent and 0.5 per cent of businesses with 1–9 employees; between 0.5 per cent and 0.9 per cent of businesses with 1019 employees; and 1 per cent of businesses with 20 or more employees.

A2. Total number of businesses in UK, by number of employees

	Number of businesses by number	Number of employees (000s)
1 – 4	802,860	1,733
5 – 9	215,260	1,403
10 19	112,780	1,515
20 – 49	59,015	1,790
50 – 99	17,740	1,234
100 – 199	9,155	1,270
200 – 249	1,855	413
250 – 499	3,770	1,315
500 +	4,485	13,326
1 or more	1,207,995	23,618

Source: Small Business Service: Small and Medium sized Enterprises in the UK 2003 (http://www.statistics.gov.uk/)

Table A3 takes the numbers of businesses and employees in each firm size band and multiplies this by the expected proportion of transfers to get an estimate of the number of businesses and employees affected by a TUPE transfer each year.

A3. Number of businesses and employees affected by a TUPE transfer each year

	Number of businesses	Number of employees
1- 9	1,020 – 5,090	3,140 – 15,680
10 – 19	560 – 1,020	7,580 – 13,640
20 and over	960	193,480
total	2,540 – 7,070	204,200 – 222,800

Source: DTI estimates. Figures may not add up due to rounding

Annex B

Details of calculations due to changes in service provision in the private sector.

The following outlines details of the estimates of the number of firms and employees in service sectors which are likely to be affected by the extension of TUPE.

B1. Number of firms and employment in sectors affected

Industry Sector	Number of businesses	Numbers in employment	Number of employees*
Canteens and catering	4,695	214,000	211,000
Investigation and security services	3,760	155,000	153,000

Industrial Cleaning	10,355	372,000	365,000
Software consultancy and supply	23,710	299,000	286,000
Maintenance and repair of office, accounting and computer machinery	1,230	16,000	16,000
Total	43,750	1,056,000	1,031,000

Source: Office of National Statistics (www.statistics.gov.uk) * DTI estimate taking into account the likely number of non-employees

We assume that the firms in these sectors are providing services for other companies, mainly in the private sector. These services are provided under contracts which will be periodically reviewed and as a result service providers may change, or may even be brought in-house. By making assumptions of the average duration of contracts and the chances of a change in provider after expiry of a contract, we come to an estimate of the number of firms and employees that are affected each year.

B2. Estimate of number of firms and employees affected by extension to TUPE

	Low scenario	High scenario
Duration of an average contract for services	5	4
Chances of contract expiring in year (%)	20	25
Chance of change in service provider after expiry of contract (%)	30	40
Chance of change of contract per year (%)	6	10
Number of firms affected each year	2,625	4,375
Number of employees affected each year	62,000	103,000
Source: DTI estimates		

Annex C

Details of calculations from changes in relation to insolvencies

The table below shows changes to the case load of the Insolvency Service as a result of pre-existing debt not passed to the transferee. Although company liquidations are not within the scope of the legislation, they are already covered by other legislation. For voluntary arrangements and administrations we assume that only in the case of a partial recovery would the Insolvency Service need to pay pre-existing debt. The partial recovery rate for these types of cases is 40 per cent of all recoveries. Receiverships are not covered.

C1. Impact of changes to Regulations on the Insolvency Service

Type of insolvency	Covered under the legislation?	Numbers (average over three years)	Recovery rate	Numbers of cases picked up by insolvency service now	Numbers picked up by insolvency service after new Regs
Company liquidations	N	5,824	10%	5,824	5,824
Creditor voluntary liquidations	Y	9,083	10%	8,175	9,083
Voluntary arrangements	Y	663	76%	159	361
Administrations	Y	2,241	76%	538	1,219
Receiverships	N	1,326	76%	318	318
Total				15,011	16,800

Source: DTI (data on insolvencies) 2002 to 2004, and R3 12th Corporate Insolvency Survey (data on recovery rates)

The estimates show that the insolvency service would have a 12 percent increase in its caseload.[26]

Annex D – Detailed note on the rationale for, and impact of, the extension of scope in relation to service provision changes

Rationale for the extension of scope

1. At present, in some cases where a service provision change takes place – i.e. a contract to provide a client with a service is: a) awarded to a contractor; b) re-let to a new contractor on subsequent re-tendering; or c) ended with the bringing 'in house' of the service activities in question – uncertainty arises as to whether or not the TUPE Regulations apply. This is due to conflicting and unsettled case-law on the scope of the Regulations and of the EU Acquired Rights Directive. The uncertainty centres mainly on service provision changes involving labour-intensive, blue collar services – e.g. office cleaning, workplace catering, refuse collection – where the new contractor declines to take over a major part of the existing workforce from the old contractor. There are essentially two competing views in the case law on the existing legislation. On one view, failure to take over a major part of the existing workforce in a case such as this conclusively avoids the application of the legislation – so that its application is essentially 'voluntary'. On the other view, such a failure may point toward the conclusion that the legislation does not apply, but is only one factor to be weighed up in the overall assessment, along with other factors such as, in particular, what the new contractor's motive was for failing to take over the workforce (which can be difficult to assess). In the absence of further ECJ

---

26   16,800/15,011 = 1.12 or 112 per cent.

jurisprudence to resolve this case law conflict, it is a moot point to what extent the Directive and the Regulations already apply to the category of 'problem cases' described above.

2.   This uncertainty has a number of negative consequences. If the new contractor fails to take over a major part of the existing workforce from the old contractor and maintains that TUPE does not apply, but the old contractor and/or the employees or their representatives disagree, all parties concerned – the two clients, the contractor and the employees – are left 'in limbo' until the dispute is resolved, which can often be achieved only months later through legal action. If the new contractor ultimately succeeds in the argument that TUPE did not apply, the old contractor is landed with a large unanticipated redundancy liability toward his or her former employees, many of whom may be left without jobs. If, on the other hand, the tribunal or court finds that TUPE did apply, the old contractor's workforce will be entitled to return to their jobs or – more realistically, given that the new contractor will usually, by this point, have taken on a new workforce in order to carry out the contract – to claim unfair dismissal, landing the new contractor with a large unanticipated compensation bill.

3.   In addition, the possibility of avoiding the application of the legislation by failing to take over a major part of the existing workforce creates a perverse incentive for contractors to bid for contracts on this 'non-TUPE' basis, so that they can undercut competitors by taking on a new workforce on inferior terms and conditions. This tends to place the focus of the competition on the question of which contractor can keep labour costs to the lowest level, rather than which contractor can deliver the best management and the greatest efficiency savings.

4.   The rationale for the extension of scope is that it will establish in the Regulations themselves that (other than in certain exceptional circumstances) they do apply in the 'problem cases' described above, reducing significantly the number of instances in which uncertainty arises in practice. This will help all parties to know where they stand from the outset and avoid unnecessary disputes and employment tribunal and court proceedings.

Anticipated impact of the extension of scope

5.   The extension of scope will ensure that service provision changes are (except in certain exceptional circumstances) clearly covered by TUPE. The new contractor will thus be obliged to take over the existing workforce from the old. In general, therefore, contractors will no longer be able to bid for contracts on the basis that they could carry them out with a new workforce on poorer terms and conditions. The estimated cost of the proposed measure (see Annex B) mainly represents the difference between the TUPE-protected terms and conditions of the existing workforce and the inferior terms and conditions that the newly-recruited workforce would otherwise have had in this minority of 'problem cases'. These costs would be offset by savings.

6.   The application of the Regulations in such cases will not prevent the making of genuine redundancies for 'economic, technical or organisational reasons entailing a change in the workforce' (ETO reasons), e.g. where the new

contractor considers that the contract could be carried out with fewer employees. Where there is a surplus of staff, the responsibility for carrying out the redundancy selection exercise (which will naturally have to be done on a fair basis), making the dismissals and paying any redundancy payments due will generally fall to the new contractor – who can, however, be expected to have been aware of the surplus when bidding for the contract, and to have factored these associated costs into the bid. If the new contractor is simply concerned about the competence or efficiency of employees transferring from the old contractor, these issues can be addressed through training and development and, if necessary, inefficiency action. Transfers should not, in the Government's view, be used as a device for removing underperforming employees 'by the back door'.

7.   As far as service employees are concerned, the comprehensive application of TUPE in such cases will reduce insecurity and help to 'take the fear out of transfer'. This can be expected to smooth the transfer process, improving workplace relations and partnership and promoting business flexibility.

Competitiveness considerations

8.   The extension of scope will not, in the Government's view, adversely affect competitiveness in the service contracting market. On the contrary, it will go a long way towards removing a perverse market distortion and creating a 'level playing field' for contract bids, increasing fairness and transparency. Responsible contractors who bid for contracts on the basis that they can deliver improved management and efficiency will no longer be at risk of being undercut by 'cowboys' who bid on the basis that they can slash labour costs. The Government wishes to discourage such 'low cost, low quality' competition.

9.   Although there is perhaps an argument that contractors should take steps to protect themselves, through commercial indemnities or other means, against incurring redundancy liabilities on the loss of a contract, or of becoming involved in a legal dispute not of their own making, this does not always happen in practice. It is also something with which small firms, with little in-house expertise and limited bargaining power, are particularly ill-equipped to cope. Maintaining the status quo would thus perpetuate a disincentive for small firms to become involved in bidding for service contracts, at odds with the Government's 'think small first' philosophy. Even where well-advised contractors do negotiate commercial indemnities, this adds to the transaction costs. The comprehensive application of TUPE in service provision change cases will reduce these costs.

10.   A contractor bidding for a service contract will not normally have a large surplus workforce that it can readily assign to that contract if successful. The choice it faces, as things stand under the existing Regulations, is normally between taking over a major part of the existing workforce or recruiting a new workforce from scratch. The extension of scope will in most cases close off the latter option for the minority of contractors who would prefer to take it. This will not disadvantage the sitting contractor in the bidding for the contract, as all bidders will have to work on the basis that the existing workforce will

continue to carry out the contract on their established terms and conditions, with no wholesale redundancies being necessary.

11.   Contractors and their representative bodies, along with many clients for services, strongly supported the extension of scope in their replies to the 2001 public consultation document, and in other informal representations. There is, in addition, no evidence to suggest that the similar approach already being taken as a matter of policy in the public sector – by virtue of the Cabinet Office Statement of Practice *Staff Transfers in the Public Sector* and, in local government, the extended legal protections introduced under powers in the Local Government Act 2003 – has had any adverse effect on competitiveness within public service contracting.

Appendix 7

TRANSPOSITION OF COUNCIL DIRECTIVE 2001/23/EC

TRANSPOSITION OF COUNCIL DIRECTIVE 23 OF 2001 (EC)

The Transfer of Undertakings (Protection of Employment) Regulations 2006 implement the EC Acquired Rights Directive, now revised and consolidated in EC Directive 23 of 2001. They safeguard employees' rights when the business in which they work changes hands between employers.

These regulations do what is necessary to implement the Directive, including making consequential changes to domestic legislation to ensure its coherence in the area to which they apply.

Transposition of 2001. 23 EC by the Transfer of Undertakings (Protection of Employment) Regulations 2006 ("TUPE")

Article	Regulations
1.1(a) – This Directive shall apply to any transfer of an undertaking or business, or part of an undertaking or business to another employer as a result of a legal transfer or merger.	3(1)(a) and 3(2) Regulation 3(1)(a) provides that these regulations apply to the transfer of an undertaking, business or part of an undertaking or business situated immediately before the transfer in the United Kingdom to another employer where there is a transfer of an economic entity which retains its identity.
1.1(b) – The Directive applies where there is a transfer of an economic entity which retains its identity, meaning an organised grouping of resources which has the objective of pursuing an economic activity.	3(1)(a) and 3(2).

1.1(c) – The Directive applies to public and private undertakings engaged in economic activities.	3(4)(a)
1.2 This Directive shall apply where and in so far as the undertaking, business or part of the undertaking or business to be transferred is situated within the territorial scope of the Treaty.	3(1)(a) and 3(4)(b) 3(1)(a) – the provision is set out above. Regulation 3(4)(b) provides that the Regulations apply – to a transfer or service provision howsoever effected notwithstanding that the transfer is governed or effected by the law of a country or territory outside the United Kingdom; that persons employed in the undertaking or part transferred ordinarily work outside the United Kingdom or that the employment of any of those persons is governed by any such law.
1.3 This Directive shall not apply to seagoing vessels.	3(7) Regulation 3(7) provides that where, in consequence (whether directly or indirectly) of the transfer of an undertaking or part of one which was situated immediately before the transfer in the United Kingdom, a ship within the meaning of the Merchant Shipping Act 1995 registered in the United Kingdom ceases to be so registered, these Regulations shall not affect the right conferred by section 5 of that Act (right of seamen to be discharged when ship ceases to be registered in the United Kingdom) on a seaman employed in the ship.
2.1(a) "transferor" shall mean any natural or legal person who, by reason of a transfer within the meaning of Article 1(1), ceases to be the employer in respect of the undertaking, business or part of the undertaking or business.	2(1) and 3(1) Regulation 2(1) provides that a "relevant transfer" means a transfer to which these Regulations apply in accordance with regulation 3 and "transferor" and "transferee" shall be construed accordingly. Regulation 3(1) as set out above provides for the scope of the Regulations.
2.1(b) "transferee" shall mean any natural or legal person who, by reason of a transfer within the meaning of Article 1(1) becomes the employer in respect of the undertaking, business or part of the undertaking or business.	2(1) The definition of "relevant transfer" as set out above includes a definition of "transferor" and "transferee".

2.1 (c) "representatives of employees" and related expressions shall mean the representatives of the employees provided for by the laws of practices of the member States	9, 13 and 14 If the employees are of a description in respect of which an independent trade union is recognised by their employer, employee representatives are representatives of that trade union. In other circumstances, provisions for the appointment and election of employee representatives are set out in regulations 9(2), 13(1) and 14.
2.1 (d) "employee" shall mean any person who, in the Member State concerned, is protected as an employee under national law.	2(1) "employee" means any individual who works for another person whether under a contract of service or apprenticeship or otherwise but does not include anyone who provides services under a contract for services and references to a person's employer shall be construed accordingly.
2.2 This Directive shall be without prejudice to national law as regards the definition of contract of employment relationship. However Member States shall not exclude from the scope of this Directive contracts of employment or employment relationships solely because: (a) of the number of working hours performed or to be performed. (b) they are employment relationships governed by a fixed-duration contract of employment within the meaning of Article 1(1) of Council Directive 91/383/EEC of 25 June 1991 supplementing the	2(1) Regulation 2(1) provides that a "contract of employment" means any agreement between an employee and his employer determining the terms and conditions of his employment. Such contracts/employment relationships are not soexcluded from the scope of the TUPE Regulations.

measures to encourage improvements in the safety and health at work of workers with a fixed-duration employment relationship or a temporary relationship, or they are temporary employment relationships within the meaning of Article 1(2) of Directive 91/383/EEC, and the undertaking, business or part of the undertaking or business transferred is, or is part of, the temporary employment business which is the employer.	
3.1 The transferor's rights and obligations arising from a contract of employment relationship existing on the date of a transfer shall, by reason of such transfer, be transferred to the transferee. Member States may provide that, after the date of transfer, the transferor and the transferee shall be jointly and severally liable in respect of obligations, which arose before the date of transfer from a contract of employment or an employment relationship existing on the date of the transfer.	4(1), 4(2), 4(4) and 4(5). Regulation 4(1) provides that a relevant transfer shall not operate so as to terminate the contract of employment of any person employed by the transferor or in the undertaking or part transferred but any such contract which would otherwise have been terminated by the transfer shall have effect after the transfer as if originally made between the person so employed and the transferee. Regulation 4(2) provides that on the completion of a relevant transfer – (a) all the transferor's rights, powers, duties and liabilities under or in connection with any such contract shall be transferred by virtue of this Regulation to the transferee; and (b) Anything done before the transfer is completed by or in relation to the transferor in respect t of that contract or a person employed in that undertaking or part shall be deemed to have been done by or in relation to the transferee. Regulation 4(4) provides that in respect of a contract of employment that is, or will be, transferred by paragraph (1) described further up any purported variation of the contract shall be void if the sole or principal reason for the variation is:

	(a) the transfer itself, or
	(b) a reason connected with the transfer that is not an economic, technical or organisational reason entailing changes in the workforce.
	Regulation 4(5) provides that paragraph (4) shall not prevent the employer and his employee, whose contract of employment is, or will be, transferred by paragraph (1) (set out above), from agreeing a variation of that contract if the sole or principal reason for the variation is -
	(a) A reason connected with the transfer that is an economic, technical or organisational reason entailing changes in the workforce, or
	(b) a reason unconnected with the transfer.
3.2 Member States may adopt appropriate measures to ensure that the transferor notifies the transferee of all rights and obligations which will be transferred to the transferee under this Article, so far as those rights and obligations are or ought to have been known to the transferor at the time of the transfer. A failure by the transferor to notify the transferee of any such right or obligation shall not affect The transfer of that right or obligation and the rights of any employees against the transferee and/or transferor in respect of that right or obligation.	11 and 12 This is an option that has been exercised at Regulations 11 and 12. Regulation 11 introduces a new duty on the transferor to notify the transferee of the rights and obligations in relation to the employees to be transferred. Regulation 12 provides a remedy of a complaint to an employment tribunal where a transferor has failed to comply with Regulation 11.

3.3 Following the transfer, the transferee shall continue to observe the terms and conditions agreed in any collective agreement on the same terms applicable to the transferor under that agreement, until the date of termination or expiry of the collective agreement or the entry into force or application of another collective agreement.	**5** Regulation 5 provides that where at the time of a relevant transfer there exists a collective agreement made by or on behalf of the transferor with a trade union recognised by the transferor in respect of any employee whose contract of employment is preserved by regulation 4(1) above, then tat agreement shall have effect in its application in relation to the employee after the transfer as if it were made with the transferee. Regulation 5(b) provides that any order made in respect of that agreement, in its application in relation to the employee, shall, after the transfer, have effect as if the transferee were a party to the agreement.
3.4 (a) Unless Member States provide otherwise, paragraphs 1 and 3 shall not apply in relation to employees' rights to old-age, invalidity or survivors' benefits under supplementary company or intercompany pension schemes outside the statutory social security schemes in Member States. (b) Even where they do not provide in accordance with subparagraph (a) that paragraphs 1and 3 apply in relation to such rights, Member States shall adopt the measures necessary to protect the interests of employees and of persons no longer employed in the transferor's business	**10** Article 3.4(a) gives Member States an option to include the right to an occupational pension scheme as a right which transfers, but otherwise it is excluded. The UK Government considers there is no need for it in the light of the ECJ's judgements in Beckmann and Martin cases. Those judgements merely interpreted the requirements of the Directive. Regulation 10 provides that Regulations 4 and 5 above shall not apply to so much of a contract of employment or collective agreement as relates to an occupational pension scheme within the meaning of the Pension Schemes Act 1993 or the Social Security Pensions (Northern Ireland) Order 1975; or to any rights, powers, duties or liabilities under or in connection with any such contract or subsisting by virtue of any such agreement and relating to such scheme or otherwise arising in connection with that person's employment and relating to such a scheme. Regulation 10(2) provides that for the purposes of paragraph (1) above any provisions of an occupational pension scheme which do not relate to benefits for old age, invalidity or survivors shall be treated as not being part ofthe scheme.

at the time of the transfer in respect of rights conferring on them immediate or prospective entitlement to old age benefits, including survivors' benefits, under supplementary schemes referred to in subparagraph (a).	
4.1 The transfer of the undertaking, business or part of the undertaking or business shall not in itself constitute grounds for dismissal by the transferor or the transferee. This provision shall not stand in the way of dismissals that may take place for economic, technical or organisational reasons entailing changes ion the workforce. Member States may provide that the first subparagraph shall not apply to certain specific categories of employees who are not covered by the laws or practice of the Member States in respect of protection against dismissal.	7(1) The UK Government has implemented this article through Regulation 7 by providing a right to automatic unfair dismissal if the sole or principal reason is the transfer itself or a reason connected with the transfer that is not an economic, technical or organisational reason entailing changes in the workforce. This fits in with the UK's existing remedies for breach of employment rights. In accordance with the second paragraph of the Article, those who are excluded from protection are those who are not protected by the unfair dismissal legislation in the UK. This shall not prevent a dismissal being potentially lawful where it is for a reason connected to the transfer that is an economic, technical or organisational reason entailing changes in the workforce. 7(5) provides that paragraph (1) above shall not apply in relation to the dismissal of any employee which was required by reason of the application of s 5 of the Aliens Restriction (Amendment) Act 1919 (10) to his employment. 7(6) provides that paragraph (1) above shall not apply in relation to a dismissal of an employee if the application of section 94 of the 1996 Act to the dismissal of the employee is excluded by or under any provision of the 1996 Act, the 1996 Tribunals Act or the 1992 Act.

4.2 If the contract of employment or the employment relationship is terminated because the transfer involves as substantial change in working conditions to the detriment of the employee, the employer shall be regarded as having been responsible for termination of the contract of employment or of the employment relationship.	4(9) Regulation 4(9) provides that where a relevant transfer involved or would involve a substantial change in working conditions to the detriment of a person whose contract of employment was or would be transferred under Regulation 4(1), such an employee may treat the contract of employment as having been terminated, and the employee shall be treated for any purpose as having been dismissed with notice by the employer.
5.1 Unless Member States provide otherwise, Article 3 and 4 shall not apply to any transfer of an undertaking, business or part of an undertaking or business where the transferor is the subject of bankruptcy proceedings or any analogous insolvency proceedings which have been instituted with a view to the liquidation of the assets of the transferor and are under the supervision of a competent public authority (which may be an insolvency practitioner authorised by a competent public authority.	8(7) This is implemented through Regulation 8(7) which provides that Regulations 4 and 7 above do not apply to any relevant transfer where the transferor is the subject of bankruptcy proceedings or any analogous proceedings which have been instituted with a view to the liquidation of the assets of the transferor and are under the supervision of an insolvency practitioner.

5.2 This provides options to Member States to provide additional assistance and flexibility to transferees of insolvent undertakings by providing that certain debts will not transfer and that certain changes to terms and conditions can be agreed with the workforce.	8 and 9 The UK Government has decided to exercise these options in the new regulations. Regulations 8 and 9 contain special rescue provisions in insolvency situations – by ensuring that pre-existing debts do not transfer to the transferee and providing greater scope to vary terms and conditions of contract.
5.3 This provides an option to Member States whose national law provides for a "situation of serious economic crisis".	UK national law does not provide for "a situation of serious economic crisis", so Article 5.3 is not relevant to the UK.
5.4 Member States shall take appropriate measures with a view to preventing misuse of insolvency proceedings in such a way as to deprive employees of the rights provided for in this Directive.	The UK Government has reviewed its existing insolvency legislation and considers that sufficient safeguards are already in place. The relevant legislation is the Insolvency Act 1986 (as amended).

6.1	6
If the undertaking, business or part of an undertaking or business preserves its autonomy, the status and function of the representatives or of the representation of the employees affected by the transfer shall be preserved on the same terms and subject to the same conditions as existed before the date of the transfer by virtue of law, regulation, administrative provision or agreement, provided that the conditions necessary for the constitution of the employee's representation are fulfilled. The first subparagraph shall not apply if, under the laws, regulations, administrative provisions or practice in the Member States, or by agreement with the representatives of the employees, the conditions necessary for the reappointment of the representatives of the employees or for the reconstitution of the employees are fulfilled. Where the transfer is the subject of bankruptcy proceedings or any analogous insolvency proceedings which have been instituted with a view to the	This regulation relates only to voluntary agreement. Regulations are to be made in due course, under section 169B of the Trade Union and labour relations (Consolidation) Act 1992, inserted by section 18 of the Employment Relations Act 2004, to ensure that declarations made by CAC as to recognition, under statutory trade union recognition procedure are preserved in the event of a change of employer, including by reason of a transfer. Regulation 6 applies where after a relevant transfer the transferred organised grouping of resources or employees maintains an identity distinct from the remainder of the transferee's undertaking. It provides that in such a circumstance, where before such a transfer an independent trade union is recognised to any extent by the transferor in respect of employees of any description who in consequence of the transfer become employees of the transferee, then, after the transfer- (a) the union shall be deemed to have been recognised by the transferee to the same extent in respect of employees of that description so employed; and (b) any agreement for recognition may be varied or rescinded accordingly. The third paragraph introduces a new option which the UK Government has not taken up. Other than representation for health and safety purposes and under the Information and Consultation Regulations 2004, UK legislation only provides for employees to be represented temporarily and for specific purposes such as on transfer of an undertaking or when redundancies are being considered. Insofar as any need arises for such representatives, transferred employees are in the same position after the transfer as they are before, in that appropriate representatives for them would be elected as and when they are needed, rather than on a permanent basis. The UK Government does not consider it necessary or appropriate to provide for transferred employees to be given permanent representation for these purposes when they did not have such representation before the transfer and indeed no other employees have such representation. However, the Commission may wish to note that the concept of general representation for all employees is currently under review in the UK. UK law gives all employees the right to be represented at all times for health and safety matters. All employers are a duty to consult safety representatives concerning arrangements for employees' health and safety. In respect of unionised employees, safety representatives are appointed by the union in accordance with the Safety Representatives and Safety Committees Regulations 1977. In respect of non-unionised employees, employers are obliged to consult elected representatives, or if there are

liquidation of the assets of the transferor and are under the supervision of a competent public authority (which may be) an insolvency practitioner authorised by a competent public authority), Member States may take the necessary measures to en- sure that the transferred employees are properly represented until the new election or designation of representatives of the employees. If the undertaking, business or part of an undertaking or business does not preserve its autonomy, the member States shall take the necessary measures to ensure that the employees transferred who were represented before the transfer continue to be properly represented during the period necessary for the reconstitution or reappointment of the representation of employees in accordance with national law or practice.	no elected representatives, the employees themselves, concerning health and safety matters by virtue of the Health and Safety (Consultation with Employees) Regulations 1996. Union appointed safety representatives are entitled to paid time off for training and to carry out their duties and are protected against unfair dismissal and victimisation. Following a transfer employees are covered by the transferee's arrangements for health and safety representation from the moment they transfer. There is no time during which they are not properly represented. The UK Government therefore considers that it is not necessary to take further measures. In the case of Information and Consultation issues, transferred employees may make use of the provision in the Information and Consultation Regulations to seek a negotiated information and consultation agreement with the new employer or make use of the standard procedures provided for in those Regulations. The employer may also have existing arrangements which will apply to the transferred employees.

6.2 If the term of office of the representatives of employees affected by the transfer expires as a result of the transfer, the representatives shall continue to enjoy the protection provided by the laws, regulations, administrative provisions or practice of the Member States.	The protections afforded to the employee representatives are set out in Employment Rights Act 1996 as follows: Section 47(1)(a): An employee has the right not to be subjected to any detriment by any act, or any deliberate failure to act, by his employer done on the ground that being an employee representative for the purposes of Regulations 9,13 and 15 of the Transfer of Undertakings (Protection of Employment Regulations) 2006 he performed (or proposed to perform) any functions or activities as such an employee representative or candidate. Section 47(1A): An employee has the right not to be subjected to any detriment by any act, or by any deliberate failure to act, by his employer done on the ground of his participation in an election of employee representatives for the purposes of Regulations 9,13 and 15 of the Transfer of Undertakings (Protection of Employment Regulations) 2006. Section 103(1)(a): An employee who is dismissed shall be regarded for the purposes of this Part as unfairly dismissed if the reason (or, if more than one, the principal reason) for the dismissal is that the employee, being ... an employee representative for the purposes of Regulations 9,13 and 15 of the Transfer of Undertakings (Protection of Employment Regulations) 2006 performed (or proposed to perform) any functions or activities as such an employee representative or candidate. Section 103(2): An employee who is dismissed shall be regarded for the purposes of this Part as unfairly dismissed if the reason (or, if more than one, the principal reason) for the dismissal is that the employee took part in an election of employee representatives for the purposes of Regulations 9,13 and 15 of the Transfer of Undertakings (Protection of Employment Regulations) 2006. The UK Government considers that these protections apply equally to a former employee representative who is subjected to detriment or dismissed because of his activities in that capacity as to a current one. There is therefore no need to make further provision to implement Article 6.2 There are also provisions entitling employee representatives to paid time off to carry out duties under TUPE in Trade Union and Labour Relations (Consolidation) Act 1992 ss 168 and 169 (union representatives) and considers that these would enable a former employee representative to recover pay for time spent in activities under TUPE if it had not been paid by the time he/she ceased to be a representative.

7.1	13(2)
The transferor and transferee shall be required to inform the representatives of their respective employees affected by the transfer of the following: the date or proposed date of the transfer; the reasons for the transfer; the legal, economic and social implications of the transfer for the employees; any measures envisaged in relation to the employees. The transferor must give such information to the representatives of his employees in good time, before the transfer is carried out. The transferee must give such information to the representatives of his employees in good time, and in any event before his employees are directly affected by the transfer as regards their conditions of work and employment.	Regulation 13(2) provides: Long enough before a relevant transfer to enable the employer of any affected employees to consult all the persons who are appropriate representatives of any of those affected employees, the employer shall inform those representatives of- (a) The fact that the relevant transfer is to take place, the date or proposed date of the transfer and the reason for it; (b) the legal, economic and social implications of the transfer for the affected employees; (c) the measures which he envisages he will, in connection with the transfer, take in relation to those employees or, if he envisages that no measures will be so taken, that fact; and

7.2 Where the transferor or the transferee envisages measures in relation to his employees, he shall consult the representatives of his employees in good time on such measures with a view to reaching an agreement.	13(2)(d), 13(4) and 13(6) Regulation 13(2)(d) provides that if the employer is the transferor, the measures which the transferee envisages he will, in connection with the transfer, take in relation to such of those employees as, by virtue of regulation 4 above, become employees of the transferee after the transfer or, if he envisages that no measures will be so taken, that fact. 13(4) the Transferee shall give to the transferor such information at such a time as will enable the transferor to perform the duty imposed on him by virtue o paragraph 2(d) above. Regulation 13(6) provides that where an employer of any affected employees envisages that he will, in connection with the transfer, be taking measures in relation to any such employees he shall consult all the persons who are appropriate representatives of any of the affected employees in relation to whom he envisages taking measures with a view to seeking their agreement to measures to be taken.
7.4 The obligations laid down in this Article shall apply irrespective of whether the decision resulting in the transfer is taken by the employer or an undertaking controlling the employer. In considering alleged breaches of the information and consultation requirements laid down by this Directive, the argument that such a breach occurred because the information was not provided by an undertaking controlling the employer shall not be accepted as an excuse.	13(12) The duties imposed ion an employer by this regulation shall apply irrespective of whether the decision resulting in the relevant transfer is taken by the employer or a person controlling the employer.

7.6 Member States shall provide that, where there are no representatives of the employees in an undertaking or business through no fault of their own, the employees concerned must be informed in advance of: the date or proposed date of the transfer the reason for the transfer the legal, economic and social implications of the transfer for the employees any measures envisaged in relation to the employees.	13(11) Regulation 13(11) provides that if, after the employer has invited affected employees to elect representatives, they fail to do so within a reasonable time, he shall give to each affected employee the information set out in paragraph (2).
8 – 14 These are Final Provisions not requiring to be implemented, other than article 9 (which concerns remedies).	

9 Member States shall introduce into their national systems such measures as are necessary to enable all employees and representatives of employees who consider themselves wronged by failure to comply with the obligations arising from this Directive to pursue their claims by judicial process after possible recourse to other competent authorities.	The main remedy in the UK is a claim for unfair dismissal which can be brought in the Employment Tribunals. TUPE provides employees who are dismissed by reason of the transfer or for a reason connected with the transfer where there is no economic, technical or organisational reason with a right to claim that they have been automatically unfairly dismissed (see Article 4.1 above). The remedy for unfair dismissal is reinstatement, re-engagement or compensation. The unfair dismissal legislation is contained in Part X of the Employment Rights Act 1996. In addition there are the following remedies for specific breaches of TUPE. Regulation 12 provides a remedy for failure on the part of the transferee to notify employee liability information. Regulation 15 provides a remedy for failure to inform or consult employee representatives (as required by Article 7 of the Directive). There are also the following rights and remedies in connection with employee representatives and their election (also referred to at Article 6.2 above) which are included in the UK legislation other than TUPE- Section 47 of the Employment Rights Act 1996 ("ERA 1996"): This gives employees the right not to suffer detriment by their employer because of their activities as an employee representative, or the fact that they have participated in an election of employee representatives. Sections 61–63 ERA 1996: This gives non-union representatives the right to paid time off to carry out their duties in that capacity, and the right to complain to an Employment Tribunal if the employer is in breach of this. Section 103 ERA 1996: This provides that where an employee is dismissed because he/she has performed activities as an employee representative the dismissal shall be regarded as unfair. Section 168 of Trade Union and Labour relations (Consolidation) Act 1992: This gives union representatives the right to paid time off to carry out their duties as appropriate representatives under TUPE and the right to complain to an Employment Tribunal if their employer is in breach of this.

Appendix 8

DTI GUIDE TO THE 2006 TUPE REGULATIONS FOR EMPLOYEES, EMPLOYERS AND REPRESENTATIVES

EMPLOYMENT RIGHTS ON THE TRANSFER OF AN UNDERTAKING

A GUIDE TO THE 2006 TUPE REGULATIONS FOR EMPLOYEES, EMPLOYERS AND REPRESENTATIVES

This guide tells you about the provisions of the Transfer of Undertakings (Protection of Employment) Regulations 2006 (commonly known as the TUPE Regulations). It is not a legal document and for further advice see contacts on pages 35 and 36.

CONTENTS

PART 5 – INFORMATION AND CONSULTATION RIGHTS

(a) Disclosure of "employee liability information" to the transferee employer

(b) Consultations with the affected workforce

Who should be consulted about the transfer?

Arrangements for elections

Rights of employee representatives

PART 6 – THE POSITION OF INSOLVENT BUSINESSES

PART 7 – REMEDIES

(a) Employee and Consultation Rights

Complaining to an employment tribunal

Awards made by an employment tribunal

(b) The right of the transferee employer to "employee liability information"

SOURCES OF FURTHER INFORMATION

INTRODUCTION – THE REVISED 2006 TUPE REGULATIONS

On 6 April 2006, the revised Transfer of Undertakings (Protection of Employment) Regulations (called 'the TUPE Regulations' in this guidance) come into force.[1] The box at the end of this Section summarises the main changes to the previous 1981 TUPE Regulations which the revised 2006 Regulations introduce.

These Regulations provide employment rights to employees when their employer changes as a result of a transfer of an undertaking. They implement the European Community Acquired Rights Directive (77/187/EEC, as amended by Directive 98/50 EC and consolidated in 2001/23/EC).

This document provides guidance to employees, employers and their representatives in order to help them understand the Regulations and to help parties comply with their legal requirements. It gives general guidance only and should not be regarded as a complete or authoritative statement of the law.

The guidance in this publication applies equally to men and women but, for simplicity, the masculine pronoun is used throughout.

Other rights already conferred by existing employment legislation are not affected by the Regulations and are explained in other documents in guidance material produced by the DTI. This material can be found on the DTI's web site at www.dti.gov.uk/er/regs.htm and some of the most relevant pieces of guidance are listed at the end of this document.

---

1   The Regulations are entitled the Transfer of Undertakings (Protection of Employment) Regulations 2006 (SI 246). They update the Transfer of Undertakings (Protection of Employment) Regulations 1981 (SI 1794), as amended.

If, when you have read this document, you have any questions about the Regulations, you should contact the Advisory, Conciliation and Arbitration Service (Acas) on 08457 474747 or at www.acas.org.uk.

Main Changes in the 2006 TUPE Regulations

The 2006 Regulations introduce:

– a widening of the scope of the Regulations to cover cases where services are outsourced, insourced or assigned by a client to a new contractor (described as "service provision changes");

– a new duty on the old transferor employer to supply information about the transferring employees to the new transferee employer (by providing what is described as "employee liability information");

– special provisions making it easier for insolvent businesses to be transferred to new employers;

–provisions which clarify the ability of employers and employees to agree to vary contracts of employment in circumstances where a relevant transfer occurs;

– provisions which clarify the circumstances under which it is unfair for employers to dismiss employees for reasons connected with a relevant transfer.

The rights and obligations in the 1981 Regulations remain in place, though the 2006.

Regulations contain revised wording at some points to make their meaning clearer, as well as reflecting developments in case law since 1981.

PART 1 – OVERVIEW OF THE TUPE REGULATIONS

Subject to certain qualifying conditions, the Regulations apply:

(a) when a business or undertaking, or part of one, is transferred to a new employer; or

(b) when a "service provision change" takes place (for example, where a contractor takes on a contract to provide a service for a client from another contractor).

These two circumstances are jointly categorised as "relevant transfers".

Broadly speaking, the effect of the Regulations is to preserve the continuity of employment and terms and conditions of those employees who are transferred to a new employer when a relevant transfer takes place. This means that employees employed by the previous employer (the "transferor") when the transfer takes effect <u>automatically</u> become employees of the new employer (the "transferee") on the same terms and conditions (except for certain occupational pensions rights). It is as if their contracts of employment had originally been made with the transferee employer. However, the Regulations provide some limited opportunity for the transferee or transferor to vary, with the agreement of the employees concerned, the terms and conditions of employment contracts for a range of stipulated reasons connected with the transfer.

The Regulations contain specific provisions to protect employees from dismissal before or after a relevant transfer.

Representatives of affected employees have a right to be informed about a prospective transfer. They must also be consulted about any measures which the transferor or transferee employer envisages taking concerning the affected employees.

The Regulations also place a duty on the transferor employer to provide information about the transferring workforce to the transferee employer before the transfer occurs.

The Regulations make specific provision for cases where the transferor employer is insolvent by increasing, for example, the ability of the parties in such difficult situations to vary contracts of employment, thereby ensuring that jobs can be preserved because a relevant transfer can go ahead.

The Regulations can apply regardless of the size of the transferred business: so the Regulations equally apply to the transfer of a large business with thousands of employees or of a very small one (such as a shop, pub or garage). The Regulations also apply equally to public or private sector undertakings and whether or not the business operates for gain, such as a charity.

PART 2 – RELEVANT TRANSFERS: THE SCOPE OF THE REGULATIONS

The Regulations apply to "relevant transfers".

A "relevant transfer" can occur when –

- a business, undertaking or part of one is transferred from one employer to another as a going concern (a circumstance defined for the purposes of this guidance as a "business transfer"). This can include cases where two companies cease to exist and combine to form a third;

- when a client engages a contactor to do work on its behalf, or reassigns such a contract – including bringing the work "in-house" (a circumstance defined as a "service provision change").

These two categories are not mutually exclusive. It is possible – indeed, likely – that some transfers will qualify both as a "business transfer" and a "service provision change". For example, outsourcing of a service will often meet both definitions.

Business transfers

To qualify as a business transfer, the identity of the employer must change. The Regulations do not therefore apply to transfers by share take-over because, when a company's shares are sold to new shareholders, there is no transfer of a business or undertaking: the same company continues to be the employer. Also, the Regulations do not ordinarily apply where only the transfer of assets, but not employees, is involved. So, the sale of equipment alone would not be covered. However, the fact that employees are not taken on does not prevent TUPE applying in certain circumstances.[2]

To be covered by the Regulations and for affected employees to enjoy the rights under them, a business transfer must involve the transfer of an "economic entity which retains its identity". In turn, an "economic entity" means "an

---

2   See, for example, the decision of the Court of Appeal in RCO Support Services v Unison [2002] EWCA Civ 464 and ECM v Cox [1999] IRLR 559.

organised grouping of resources which has the objective of pursuing an economic activity, whether or not that activity is central or ancillary".

Q. What business transfers are therefore covered by the Regulation?

A. The precise application of the Regulations will be a matter for the tribunals or courts to decide, depending on the facts of each case. However, the economic entity test would generally mean that the Regulations apply where there is a identifiable set of resources (which includes employees) assigned to the business or to a part of the business which is transferred, and that set of resources retains its identity after the transfer. Where just a part of a business is transferred, the resources do not need to be used exclusively in the transferring part of the business and by no other part. However, where resources are applied in a variable pattern over several parts of a business, then there is less likelihood that a transfer of any individual part of a business would qualify as a business transfer under the Regulations.

Service provision changes

"Service provision changes" concern relationships between contractors and the clients who hire their services. Examples include contracts to provide such labour-intensive services as office cleaning, workplace catering, security guarding, refuse collection and machinery maintenance.

The changes to these contracts can take three principal forms:

- where a service previously undertaken by the client is awarded to a contractor (a process known as "contracting out" or "outsourcing");
- where a contract is assigned to a new contractor on subsequent re-tendering; or
- where a contract ends with the service being performed "in house" by the former client ("contracting in" or "insourcing").

The Regulations apply only to those changes in service provision which involve "an organised grouping of employees ... which has as its principal purpose the carrying out of the activities concerned on behalf of the client". This is intended to confine the Regulations' coverage to cases where the old service provider (i.e. the transferor) has in place a team of employees to carry out the service activities, and that team is essentially dedicated to carrying out the activities that are to transfer (though they do not need to work exclusively on those activities). It would therefore exclude cases where there was no identifiable grouping of employees. This is because it would be unclear which employees should transfer in the event of a change of contractor, if there was no such grouping. So, if a contractor was engaged by a client to provide, say, a courier service, but the collections and deliveries were carried out each day by various different couriers on an ad hoc basis, rather than by a n identifiable team of employees, there would be no "service provision change" and the Regulations would not apply.

A service provision change will often capture situations where an existing service contract is re-tendered by the client and awarded to a new contractor. It would also potentially cover situations where just some of those activities in the original service contract are re-tendered and awarded to a new contractor, or where the original service contract is split up into two or more components, each of which is assigned to a different contractor. In each of these cases, the key test is whether an organised grouping has as its principal purpose the carrying out of the activities that are transferred.

It should be noted that a "grouping of employees" can constitute just one person, as may happen, say, when the cleaning of a small business premises is undertaken by a single person employed by a contractor.

Q. Are there any other exceptions?

A. Yes, the Regulations do not apply in the following circumstances.

- *where a client buys in services from a contractor on a "one off" basis, rather than the two parties entering into an ongoing relationship for the provision of the service.*

So, the Regulations should not be expected to apply where a client engaged a contractor to organise a single conference on its behalf, even though the contractor had established an organised grouping of staff – e.g. a "project team" – to carry out the activities involved in fulfilling that task. Thus, were the client subsequently to hold a second conference using a different contractor, the members of the first project team would not be required to transfer to the second contractor.

To qualify under this exemption, the one-off service must also be "of short-term duration". To illustrate this point, take the example of two hypothetic contracts concerning the security of an Olympic Games or some other major sporting event. The first contract concerns the provision of security advice to the event organisers and covers a period of several years running up to the event; the other concerns the hiring of security staff to protect athletes during the period of the event itself. Both contracts have a one-off character in the sense that they both concern the holding of a specific event. However, the first contract runs for a significantly longer period than the second; therefore, the first would be covered by the TUPE Regulations (if the other qualifying conditions are satisfied) but the second would not.

- *where the arrangement between client and contractor is wholly or mainly for the supply of goods for the client's use.*

So, the Regulations are not expected to apply where a client engaged a contractor to supply, for example, sandwiches and drinks to its canteen every day, for the client to sell on to its own staff. If, on the other hand, the contract was for the contractor to run the client's staff canteen, then this exclusion would not come into play and the Regulations might therefore apply.

Transfers within public administrations

Both the Acquired Right Directive and the TUPE Regulations make it clear that a reorganisation of a public administration, or the transfer of administrative functions between public administrations, is not a relevant transfer within the meaning of the legislation. Thus, most transfers within, say, central or local government are not covered by the Regulations. However, such intra-governmental transfers are covered by the Cabinet Office's Statement of Practice *"Staff Transfers in the Public Sector"*,[3] which in effect guarantees TUPE-equivalent treatment for the employees so transferred.

---

3   This document may be found online at http://www.civilservice.gov.uk/publications/staff_
     transfers/publications_and_forms/pdf/stafftransfers.pdf.

Q. Are there any other statutory protections which may apply to employees transferring between public administrations?

A. Yes. Section 38 of the Employment Relations Act 1999[4] provides a regulation-making power to the Secretary of State to provide TUPE-equivalent protections to cases or classes of cases falling outside the scope of the Acquired Rights Directive. As at January 2006, the Secretary of State has made two sets of regulations under this power.[5] In addition, protections may be provided in case-specific legislation where that legislation effects a particular transfer within public administrations.

Q. What is the treatment of transfers from the public sector to the private sector?

A. These are covered by the Regulations in just the same way as transfers between private sector employers. In addition, there are other protections which apply to transfers from the public sector to the private sector. For example, the Cabinet Office's Statement of Practice 'Staff Transfers in the Public Sector" affords TUPE-style protections comprehensively to employees whose jobs transfer to the private sector, or whose job subsequently transfers between private sector employers. In this regard, the Local Government Act 2003 confers powers on the Secretary of State, the National Assembly of Wales and Scottish Ministers to require best value authorities in England, Wales and Scotland to deal with staff matters in accordance with Directions. The purpose of securing these powers was to enable the provisions of the Statement of Practice to be made a statutory requirement for those authorities. No Directions have ye been issued. The Local Government Act 2003 can be viewed on the ODPM website at www.odpm.gov.uk.

The effect of the Regulations where employees work outside the UK

The Regulations apply to the transfer of an undertaking situated in the UK immediately before the transfer, and, in the case of a service provision change, where there is an organised grouping of employees situated in the UK immediately before the service provision change.

However, the Regulations may still apply notwithstanding that persons employed in the undertaking ordinarily work outside the United Kingdom. For example, if there is a transfer of a UK exporting business, the fact that the sales force spends the majority of its working week outside the UK will not prevent the Regulations applying to the transfer, so long as the undertaking itself (comprising, amongst other things, premises, assets, fixtures & fittings, goodwill as well as employees) is situated in the UK.

In the case of a service provision change, the test is whether there is an organised grouping of employees situated in the UK (immediately before the service provision change). For example, where a contract to provide website

---

4   Section 38 of the Employment Relations Act 1999 empowers the Secretary of State to make provision by statutory instrument, subject to the negative resolution procedure, for employees to be given the same or similar treatment in specified circumstances falling outside the scope of the Acquired Rights Directive as they are given under the UK's legislation implementing that Directive.

5   The Transfer of Undertakings (Protection of Employment) (Rent Officer Service) Regulations 1999, SI 1999/2511 and the Transfer of Undertakings (Protection of Employment) (Transfer of OFCOM) Regulations 2003, SI 2003/2715.

maintenance comes to an end and the client wants someone else to take over the contract, if in the organised grouping of employees that has performed the contract, one of the IT technicians works from home, which is outside the UK, that should not prevent the Regulations applying to the transfer of the business. However if the whole team of IT technicians worked from home which was outside the UK, then a transfer of the business for which they work would not fall within the Regulations as there would be no organised grouping of employees situated in the United Kingdom.

PART 3 – CONTRACTS OF EMPLOYMENT

The employer's position

When a relevant transfer takes place, the position of the previous employer and the new employer in respect of the contracts of the transferred employees is as follows:

– The new employer (i.e. the transferee) takes over the contracts of employment of all employees who were employed in the "organised grouping of resources or employees" immediately before the transfer, or who would have been so employed if they had not been unfairly dismissed by reason of the transfer.[6] The transferee employer cannot pick and choose which employees to take on. It follows that the transferee cannot terminate contracts and dismiss employees just because the transfer has occurred (see Part 4 below for more detail). However, the new employer does not take over the contracts of any employees who are only temporarily assigned to the "organised grouping". Whether an assignment is "temporary" will depend on a number of factors, such as the length of time the employee has been there and whether a date has been set by the transferor for his return or re-assignment to another part of the business or undertaking.

– The transferee employer takes over all rights and obligations arising from those contracts of employment, except for criminal liabilities and some benefits under an occupational pension scheme [see below]. This means that the transferee employer will inherit any outstanding liabilities incurred by the transferor employer by his failure to observe the terms of those contracts or for failure to observe employment rights. So, an employee may make a claim to a court or an employment tribunal against the transferee employer for, say, breach of contract, personal injury or sex discrimination, even though the breach of contract, injury or discrimination occurred before the transfer took place.

– The transferee employer takes over any collective agreements made by or on behalf of the transferor employer in respect of any transferring employees and in force immediately before the transfer.

---

6   The words "or who would have been so employed had they not been unfairly dismissed for a
     reason connected with the transfer" appear in the Regulations to prevent employers from
     dismissing the employees immediately before the relevant transfer takes place to make the
     business a more attractive proposition to a purchaser.

– Where the transferor employer voluntarily recognised an independent trade union (or unions) in respect of some or all of the transferred employees, then the transferee employer will also be required to recognise that union (or unions) to the same extent after the transfer takes place. However, this requirement only applies if the organised grouping of transferred employees maintains an identity distinct from the remainder of the transferee's business. If the undertaking does not keep its separate identity, the previous trade union recognition lapses, and it will then be up to the union and the employer to renegotiate a new recognition arrangement. It should be noted that where at the time of the transfer a union is recognised by the transferor employer via the statutory recognition procedure, then different arrangements apply.[7]

Q. Can the transferor employer select the employees who transfer across?

A. No. He cannot retain individuals who were assigned to the organised grouping immediately before the transfer. However, this does not prevent the transferor from retaining those individuals whom he had permanently re-assigned to other work outside the "organised grouping" in advance of a transfer.

Q. Does this mean that the transferee must actually employ a person who was unfairly dismissed before the transfer where they had previously worked in the entity or grouping which then transferred?

A .No. There is no obligation on the transferee to provide a job to such former employees of the transferor. However, the transferee is responsible for all outstanding liabilities relating to such persons which result from their former employment. So, the transferee would be the respondent should a former employee complain to an employment tribunal that he was unfairly dismissed. The employment tribunal may order reinstatement or re-engagement.

Q. How can the transferee employer ensure he does not suffer a loss for a failure of the transferor employer prior to the transfer?

A. It is a common practice for the transferee employer to require the transferor employer to indemnify him against any losses from such pre-transfer breaches of contracts or employment law. Also, the Regulations require the transferor to inform the transferee in advance of the transfer about such liabilities towards the employees. (See Part 5 below).

The employee's position

When a relevant transfer takes place, the position of the employees of the transferor and transferee employer is as follows:

– Employees employed in the "organised grouping" immediately before the transfer automatically become employees of the transferee. However, an employee has the right to object to the automatic transfer of their contract of

---

7   The statutory recognition procedure is positioned in Schedule A1 of the Trade Union and Labour Relations (Consolidation) Act 1992, and under the procedure, the Central Arbitration Committee (CAC) is empowered to award recognition to independent trade unions. Regulations are to be made, in due course, under paragraph 169B of Schedule A1, inserted by section 18 of the Employment Relations Act 2004, to ensure that declarations made by the CAC, and applications made to the CAC, are appropriately preserved in the event of a change in the identity of the employer.

employment if he so wishes, as long as they inform either the transferor or the transferee that he objects to the transfer of his contract to the transferee. In that case, the objection terminates the contract of employment and the employee is not treated for any purpose as having been dismissed by either the transferor or the transferee. Moreover, the employee is considered to have resigned and would therefore not be entitled to a redundancy payment. The transferor may re-engage the employee on whatever terms they agree, though the continuity of employment will be broken.

–An employee's period of continuous employment is not broken by a transfer and, for the purposes of calculating entitlement to statutory employment rights, the date on which the period of continuous employment started would usually be the date on which the employee started work with the old employer.[8] This should be stated in the employee's written statement of terms and conditions; if it is not, or if there is a dispute over the date on which the period of continuous employment started, the matter can be referred to an employment tribunal. (For further details, see the DTI booklet *Written statement of employment particulars* (PL700)).

– Transferred employees retain all the rights and obligations existing under their contracts of employment with the previous employer and these are transferred to the new employer. This means that their previous terms and conditions of employment carry over to the transferee employer. The main exception to this rule concerns the treatment of occupational pensions.

Q. How are occupational pensions treated when a relevant transfer occurs?

A. Occupational pension rights earned up to the time of the transfer are protected by social security legislation and pension trust arrangements. The transferee employer is not required to continue identical occupational pension arrangements for the transferred employees. However, where transferred employees were entitled to participate in an occupational pension scheme prior to the transfer, the transferee employer must establish a minimum level of pension provision for the transferred employees. This minimum 'safety net' requires the transferee to match employee contributions, up to 6 per cent of salary, into a stakeholder pension, or offer an equivalent alternative.[9] In the public sector, the Government will continue to follow the policy set out in the HM Treasury note "A Fair Deal for Staff Pensions". As explained in Part 2, the Local Government Act 2003 contains provisions for Directions to be issued to best value authorities concerning contracting-out exercises. The Act also provides that those Directions should make certain provisions concerning pension benefits for the local authority staff affected by those exercises. The Directions have not yet been issued.

Changes to terms and conditions

The Regulations ensure that employees are not penalised when they are transferred by being placed on inferior terms and conditions. So, not only are

---

8   It may be earlier, for example, where the employee had been subject to a previous TUPE transfer.

9   These arrangements were introduced by the Pensions Act 2004, Further information on these aspects of the Act can be found on the Department for Work and Pensions (DWP) website (www.dwp.gov.uk)

their pre-existing terms and conditions transferred across on the first day of their employment with the transferee, but the Regulations also impose limitations on the ability of the transferee and employee to agree a variation to terms and conditions thereafter. In particular, the transferee must never vary contracts where the sole or principal reason is:

– the transfer itself; or

– a reason connected with a transfer which is not "an economic, technical or organisational reason entailing changes in the workforce".

If contracts are varied for these reasons, then those variations are rendered void by the Regulations.

The same restrictions apply to the transferor where he contemplates changing terms and conditions of those employees who will transfer to the new employer in anticipation of the transfer occurring.

Q. What is the difference between an action that is by reason of the transfer itself and that which is for a reason which "is connected with" the transfer?

A. Where an employer changes terms and conditions simply because of the transfer and there are no extenuating circumstances linked to the reason for that decision, then such a change is prompted by reason of the transfer itself. However, where the reason for the change is prompted by a knock-on effect of the transfer – say, the need to re-qualify staff to use the different machinery used by the transferee – then the reason is "connected to the transfer".

Q. What is an "economic, technical or organisational" reason?

A. There is no statutory definition of this term, but it is likely to include

(a) a reason relating to the profitability or market performance of the transferee's business (i.e. an economic reason);

(b) a reason relating to the nature of the equipment or production processes which the transferee operates (i.e. a technical reason); or

(c) a reason relating to the management or organisational structure of the transferee's business (i.e. an organisational reason).

Q. What is meant by the phrase "entailing changes in the workforce"?

A. There is no statutory definition of this term, but interpretation by the courts has restricted it to changes in the numbers employed or to changes in the functions performed by employees. A functional change could involve a new requirement on an employee who held a managerial position to enter into a non-managerial role, or to move from a secretarial to a sales position.

The Regulations also provide some freedom for a transferee or transferor to agree with an employee to vary an employment contract before or after a transfer. The employer and employee can agree to vary an employment contract where the sole or principal reason is:

– a reason unconnected with the transfer; or

– a reason connected with the transfer which is "an economic, technical or organisational reason entailing changes in the workforce".

A reason unconnected with a transfer could include the sudden loss of an expected order by a manufacturing company or a general upturn in demand for a particular service or a change in a key exchange rate.

It must be remembered that other elements of employment law continue to apply to contracts in the context of a TUPE transfer. Therefore an employer cannot validly impose new terms and conditions without the agreement of employees. Any changes would have to be agreed by the employee or by his union representatives on his behalf.

Q. Does this freedom to vary contracts permit the transferee employer to harmonise the terms and conditions of the transferred workers to those of the equivalent grades and types of employees he already employs?

A. No. According to the way the courts have interpreted the Acquired Rights Directive, the desire to achieve "harmonisation" is by reason of the transfer itself. It cannot therefore constitute "an ETO reason connected with a transfer entailing changes in the workforce".

Q. Is there a time period after the transfer where it is "safe" for the transferee to vary contracts because the reason for the change cannot have been by reason of the transfer because of the passage of time?

A. There is likely to come a time when the link with the transfer can be treated as no longer effective. However, this must be assessed in the light of all the circumstances of the individual case, and will vary from case to case. There is no "rule of thumb" used by the courts or specified in the Regulations to define a period of time after which it is safe to assume that the transfer did not impact directly or indirectly on the employer's actions.

Q. How do the Regulations affect annual pay negotiations or annual pay reviews?

A. These should be little affected, and should continue under the transferee employer in much the same way as they operated with the transferor employer.

PART 4 – DISMISSALS AND REDUNDANCIES

The general law on unfair dismissal and redundancies applies in situations where a relevant transfer occurs or is in prospect. For example, the employer must follow the appropriate procedures when handling the dismissals, and act in accordance with the Dispute Resolution Regulations which came into force on 1 October 2004 (see the DTI publication *"Resolving disputes at work: new procedures for discipline and grievance"*, which is available on the DTI's web site). The TUPE Regulations also provide some additional protections which limit the ability of employers to dismiss employees when transfers arise.

The additional TUPE protections

Neither the new employer (the transferee) nor the previous one (the transferor) may fairly dismiss an employee

– because of the transfer itself; or

– for a reason connected with the transfer, unless that reason is an "economic, technical or organisational (ETO) reason entailing changes in the workforce."

If there is no such reason, the dismissal will be automatically unfair.

If there is such a reason, and it is the cause or main cause of the dismissal, the dismissal will be fair as long as an employment tribunal decides that:

– the employer acted reasonably in the circumstances in treating that reason as sufficient to justify dismissal; and

– the employer met the other requirements of the general law on unfair dismissal.

Also, if the dismissal occurred for reason of redundancy, then the usual redundancy arrangements will apply, and the dismissed employee could be entitled to a redundancy payment.

The onus lies on the dismissing employer to show that the dismissal falls within the ETO exemption to the automatic unfairness rule. Neither the Regulations nor the Acquired Rights Directive define what an ETO reason may be. The courts and tribunals have not generally sought to distinguish between each of the three ETO categories, but rather have treated them as a single concept.

To qualify as an ETO defence, an economic, technical or organisational reason must be one "entailing changes in the workforce." The courts have held that this means a change in the <u>numbers</u> of people employed or a change in employees' particular <u>functions</u>.

Dismissal by a substantial change to working conditions

As described in Part 3, employees can object to a transfer and, by doing so, the employees terminate their contracts. In many cases, those employees will not be able to claim unfair dismissal because they have in effect resigned and therefore have not been "dismissed". However, those transferred employees who find that there has been or will be a "substantial change" for the worse in their working conditions as a result of the transfer have the right to terminate their contract and claim unfair dismissal before an employment tribunal on the grounds that the actions or proposed actions of the employer had constituted or would constitute a de facto termination of their employment contract. An employee who resigns in reliance on this right cannot make a claim for pay in lieu of a notice period to which they were entitled under their contract.

This statutory right exists independently of an employee's common law right to claim constructive dismissal for an employer's repudiatory breach of contract.

Q. What might constitute a 'substantial change in working conditions"?

A. This will be a matter for the courts and the tribunals to determine in the light of the circumstances of each case. What might be a trivial change in one setting might constitute a substantial change in another. However, a major relocation of the workplace which makes it difficult or much more expensive for an employee to transfer, or the withdrawal of a right to a tenured post, is likely to fall within this definition.

Q. Does this mean it is unlawful for the transferee to make such "substantial changes in working conditions" and it is automatically unfair when an employee resigns because such a change has taken place?

A. No. The Regulations merely classify such resignations as "dismissals". This can assist the employee if he subsequently complains on unfair dismissal because

he does not need to prove he was "dismissed". However, to determine whether the dismissal was unfair, the tribunal will still need to satisfy itself that the employer had acted unreasonably, and there is no presumption that it is unreasonable for the employer to make changes. Also, because the statutory dismissal procedures do not apply in these circumstances, any failure by the employer to follow those procedures does not make the "dismissal" automatically unfair.

TUPE and redundancy

Dismissals on the grounds of redundancy are permitted by TUPE, as they will normally be for an ETO reason, although the transferee will need to make sure that the redundancy is fair within other employment legislation: e.g. selection for redundancy is fair, and not based simply on the fact that the person is a transferred employee.

Dismissed employees may also be entitled to a redundancy payment if they have been employed for two years or more. Employers must also ensure that the required period for consultation with employees' representatives is allowed. More details are in the DTI documents *Redundancy consultation and notification (PL833)* and *Redundancy Entitlement: Statutory Rights (PL808)*. Entitlement to redundancy payments will not be affected by the failure of any claim which an employee may make for unfair dismissal compensation.

Where there are redundancies and it is unclear whether the Regulations apply, it will also be unclear whether the previous or the new employer is responsible for making redundancy payments. In such cases employees should consider whether to make any claims against both employers at an employment tribunal.

PART 5 – INFORMATION AND CONSULTATION RIGHTS

This section discusses:

(a) the requirements in the Regulations for the transferor employer to provide information to the transferee employer about the transferred employees before the relevant transfer takes place; and

(b) the requirements in the Regulations on both the transferee and transferor employers to consult representatives of the affected workforce before the relevant transfer takes place.

These requirements are discussed in turn.

(a) Disclosure of "employee liability information" to the transferee employer

The transferor employer must provide the transferee with a specified set of information which will assist him to understand the rights, duties and obligations in relation to those employees who will be transferred. This should help the transferee employer to prepare for the arrival of the transferred employees, and the employees also gain because their new employer is made aware of his inherited obligations towards them. The information in question is:

– the identity of the employees who will transfer;

– the age of those employees;

– information contained in the "statements of employment particulars" for those employees;

– information relating to any collective agreements which apply to those employees;

– instances of any disciplinary action within the preceding two years taken by the transferor in respect of those employees in circumstances where the statutory dispute resolution procedures apply,[10]

– instances of any grievances raised by those employees within the preceding two years in circumstances where the statutory dispute resolution procedures apply;[11] and

– instances of any legal actions taken by those employees against the transferor in the previous two years, and instances of potential legal actions which may be brought by those employees where the transferor has reasonable grounds to believe such actions might occur.

If any of the specified information changes between the time when it is initially provided to the transferee and the completion of the transfer, then the transferor is required to give the transferee written notification of those changes.

The information must be provided in writing or in other forms which are accessible to the transferee. So, it may be possible for the transferor to send the information as computer data files as long as the transferee can access that information, or provide access to the transferor's data storage. Likewise, in cases where a very small number of employees are transferring and small amounts of information may be involved, it might be acceptable to provide the information by telephone. However, it would be a good practice for the transferor to consult the transferee first to discuss the methods which he can use.

The specified information may be given in several instalments, but all the information must be given. The information may also be provided via a third party. For example, where a client is re-assigning a contract from an existing contractor to a new contractor, that client organisation may act as the third party in passing the information to the new contractor.

This information should be given at least two weeks before the completion of the transfer. However, if special circumstances make this not reasonably practicable, the information must be supplied as soon as is reasonably practicable.

Q. What is the "statement of employment particulars"?

A. All employers are under a legal obligation to provide each employee in writing with basic information about their employment. That information is called the

---

10   These circumstances are set out in the Employment Act 2002 (Dispute Resolution) Regulations 2004.

11   Ditto.

"written statement of employment particulars" (see DTI publication "Written Statement of Employment Particulars (PL700)"). Among other things, the written statement must set out the remuneration package, the hours of work and holiday entitlements.

Q. What are grievances to which the statutory dispute resolution procedures apply?

A. Broadly speaking, these are grievances which could give rise to any subsequent complaint to an employment tribunal about a breach of a statutory entitlement. Guidance on the statutory dispute procedures is provided in the DTI publication "Resolving disputes at work: new procedures for discipline and grievance".

Q. What is the "disciplinary action" which must be notified to the transferee?

A. This is action taken under formal disciplinary procedures which the employer is required to follow under the Employment Act 2002 (Dispute Resolution) Regulations 2004. They do not include oral or written warnings or suspensions on full pay. For guidance on those Regulations, see the DTI publication "Resolving disputes at work: new procedures for discipline and grievance".

Q. How will the transferee decide whether it is reasonable to believe that a legal action could occur?

A. This is a matter of judgment and depends on the characteristics of each case. So, where an incident seems trifling – say, where an employee slipped at work but did not take any time off as a result – then there is little reason to suppose that a claim for personal injury damages would result. In contrast, if a fall at work led to hospitalisation over a long period or where a union representative raised the incident as a health and safety concern, then the transferor should inform the transferee accordingly.

Q. Can the transferor supply some information in the form of staff handbooks, sample contracts or the texts of collective agreements?

A. It is open to the transferor to provide such documentation if it would assist. Providing information in that form might also be easier for both parties to handle. Again, it would make sense for parties to discuss in advance how information should be provided.

Q. What are the circumstances where it may not be reasonably practicable to provide the information two weeks in advance of the transfer occurring?

A. These would be various depending on circumstances. But, clearly, it would not be reasonably practicable to provide the information in time, if the transferor did not know the identity of the transferee until very late in the process, as might occur when service contracts are re-assigned from one contractor to another by a client, or, more generally, when the transfer takes place at very short notice.

Q. Can the transferor and the transferee agree between themselves that this information should not be provided by contracting out of the requirement?

A. No. There is no entitlement to contract out of the duty to supply employee liability information because that would disadvantage the employees involved.

(b) Consultations with the affected workforce

The Regulations place a duty on both the transferor and transferee employers to inform and consult representatives of their employees who may be affected by the transfer or measures taken in connection with the transfer. Those affected employees might include:

(a) those individuals who are to be transferred;

(b) their colleagues in the transferor employer who will not transfer but whose jobs might be affected by the transfer; or

(c) their new colleagues in employment with the transferee whose jobs might be affected by the transfer.

Long enough before a relevant transfer to enable the employer to consult with the employees' representatives, the employer must inform the representatives:

- that the transfer is going to take place, approximately when, and why;
- the legal, economic and social implications of the transfer for the affected employees;
- whether the employer envisages taking any action (reorganisation for example) in connection with the transfer which will affect the employees, and if so, what action is envisaged;
- where the previous employer is required to give the information, he or she must disclose whether the prospective new employer envisages carrying out any action which will affect the employees, and if so, what. The new employer must give the previous employer the necessary information so that the previous employer is able to meet this requirement.

If action is envisaged which will affect the employees, the employer must consult the representatives of the employees affected about that action. The consultation must be undertaken with a view to seeking agreement of the employee representatives to the intended measures.

During these consultations the employer must consider and respond to any representations made by the representatives. If the employer rejects these representations he must state the reasons.

If there are special circumstances which make it not reasonably practicable for an employer to fulfil any of the information or consultation requirements, he must take such steps to meet the requirements as are reasonably practicable.

Who should be consulted about the transfer?

Where employees who may be affected by the transfer are represented by an independent trade union recognised for collective bargaining purposes, the employer must inform and consult an authorised official of that union. This may be a shop steward or a district union official or, if appropriate, a national or regional official. The employer is not required to inform and consult any other employee representatives in such circumstances, but may do so if the trade union is recognised for one group of employees, but not for another.

Where employees who may be affected by the transfer are not represented by a trade union as described above, the employer must inform and consult other appropriate representatives of those employees. These may be either existing representatives or new ones specially elected for the purpose. It is the employer's responsibility to ensure that consultation is offered to appropriate representatives. If they are to be existing representatives, their remit and method of election or appointment must give them suitable authority from the employees concerned. It would not, for example, be appropriate to inform and consult a committee specially established to consider the operation of a staff canteen about a transfer affecting, say, sales staff; but it may well be appropriate to inform and consult a fairly elected or appointed committee of employees, such as a works council, that is regularly informed or consulted more generally about the business's financial position and personnel matters.

Arrangements for elections

If the representatives are to be specially elected ones, certain election conditions must be met:

- The employer shall make such arrangements as are reasonably practical to ensure the election is fair;
- The employer shall determine the number of representatives to be elected so that there are sufficient representatives to represent the interests of all the affected employees, having regard to the number and classes of those employees;
- The employer shall determine whether the affected employees should be represented either by representatives of all the affected employees or by representatives of particular classes of those employees;
- Before the election the employer shall determine the term of office as employee representatives so that it is of sufficient length to enable relevant information to be given and consultations to be completed;
- The candidates for election as employee representatives are affected employees on the date of the election;
- No affected employee is unreasonably excluded from standing for election; and
- All affected employees on the date of the election are entitled to vote for employee representatives.

The employees entitled to vote may vote as many candidates as there are representatives to be elected to represent them; or, if there are to be representatives for particular classes of employees, for as many candidates as there are representatives to be elected to represent their particular class of employee.

The election is conducted so as to secure that:

- so far as reasonably practicable, those voting do so in secret; and
- the votes given at the election are accurately counted.

Where an employee representative is elected in accordance with these rules but subsequently ceases to act as such and, in consequence, certain employees are no longer represented, another election should be held satisfying the rules set out as above.

The legislation does not specify how many representatives must be elected or the process by which they are to be chosen. An employment tribunal may wish to consider, in determining a claim that the employer has not informed or consulted in accordance with the requirements, whether the arrangements were such that the purpose of the legislation could not be met. An employer will therefore need to consider such matters as whether:

- the arrangements adequately cover all the categories of employees who may be affected by the transfer and provide a reasonable balance between the interests of the different groups;
- the employees have sufficient time to nominate and consider candidates;
- the employees (including any who are absent from work for any reason) can freely choose who to vote for;
- there is any normal company custom and practice for similar elections and, if so, whether there are good reasons for departing from it.

<u>Rights of employee representatives</u>

Representatives and candidates for election have certain rights and protections to enable them to carry out their function properly. The rights and protections of trade union members, including officials, are in some cases contained in separate provisions to those of elected representatives but are essentially the same as those of elected representatives described below. (For further details of the rights of trade union members see the DTI publication *Union membership: rights of members and non-members (PL871)*).

The employer must allow access to the affected workforce and to such accommodation and facilities, e.g. use of a telephone, as is appropriate. What is "appropriate" will vary according to circumstances.

The dismissal of an elected representative will be automatically unfair if the reason, or the main reason, related to the employee's status or activities as a representative. An elected representative also has the right not to suffer any detriment short of dismissal on the grounds of their status or activities. Candidates for election enjoy the same protection. Where an employment tribunal finds that a dismissal was unfair, it may order the employer to reinstate or re-engage the employee or make an appropriate award of compensation (see also *Unfairly dismissed? (PL712)*). Where an employment tribunal finds that a representative or a candidate for election has suffered detriment short of dismissal it may order that compensation be paid.

An elected representative also has a right to reasonable time off with pay during normal working hours to carry out representative duties. Representatives should be paid the appropriate hourly rate for the period of absence from work. This is arrived at by dividing the amount of a week's pay by the number of normal working hours in the week. The method of calculation is similar to that used for computing redundancy payments (see *Redundancy Entitlement: Statutory Rights (PL808)*).

PART 6 – THE POSITION OF INSOLVENT BUSINESSES

To assist the rescue of failing businesses, the Regulations make special provision where the transferor employer is subject to insolvency proceedings.

First, the Regulations ensure that some of the transferor's pre-existing debts to the employees do not pass to the transferee. Those debts concern any obligations to pay the employees statutory redundancy pay or sums representing various debts to them, such as arrears of pay, payment in lieu of notice, holiday pay or a basic award of compensation for unfair dismissal.[12] In effect, payment of statutory redundancy pay and the other debts will be met by the Secretary of State through the National Insurance Fund. However, any debts over and above those that can be met in this way will pass across to the transferee.

Second, the Regulations provide greater scope in insolvency situations for the transferee to vary terms and conditions after the transfer takes place. As was discussed in Part 3, the Regulations place significant restrictions on transferees when varying contracts because of the transfer or a reason connected with the transfer. These restrictions are in effect waived, allowing the transferor, the transferee or the insolvency practitioner in the exceptional situation of insolvency to reduce pay and establish other inferior terms and conditions after the transfer. However, in their place, the Regulations impose other conditions on the transferee when varying contracts:

- the transferor, transferee or insolvency practitioner must agree the "permitted variation" with representatives of the employees. Those representatives are determined in much the same way as the representatives who should be consulted in advance of relevant transfers (see Part 5 for more details);

- the representatives must be union representatives where an independent trade union is recognised for collective bargaining purposes by the employer in respect of any of the affected employees. Those union representatives and the transferor, transferee or insolvency practitioner are then free to agree variations to contracts, though the speed of their negotiations may be faster than usual in view of pressing circumstances associated with insolvency;

- in other cases, non-union representatives are empowered to agree permitted variations with the transferor, transferee or insolvency practitioner. However, where agreements are reached by non-union representatives, two other requirements must be met. **First**, the agreement which records the permitted variation must be in writing and signed by each of the non-union representatives (or by an authorised person on a representative's behalf where it is not reasonably practicable for that representative to sign). **Second**, before the agreement is signed, the employer must provide all the affected employees with a copy of the agreement and any guidance which the employees would reasonably need in order to understand it;

- the new terms and conditions agreed in a "permitted variation"

---

12   The Regulations also provide for the payment of these sums on the date of the transfer even though they may not have actually been dismissed by the transferor on or before that date, as would normally be a requirement for such payments.

must not breach other statutory entitlements. For example, any agreed pay rates must not be set below the national minimum wage; and

- a "permitted variation" must be made with the intention of safeguarding employment opportunities by ensuring the survival of the undertaking or business or part of the undertaking or business.[13]

Q. What types of insolvency proceedings are covered by these aspects of the Regulations?

A. These provisions are found in Regulations 8 and 9. Those two Regulations apply where the transferor is subject to "relevant insolvency proceedings" which are insolvency proceedings commenced in relation to him but not with a view to the liquidation of his assets. The Regulations do not attempt to list all these different types of procedures individually. It is the Department's view that "relevant insolvency proceedings" mean any collective insolvency proceedings in which the whole or part of the business or undertaking is transferred to another entity as a going concern. That is to say, it covers an insolvency proceeding in which all creditors of the debtor may participate, and in relation to which the insolvency office-holder owes a duty to all creditors. The Department considers that "relevant insolvency proceedings" does not cover winding-up by either creditors or members where there is no such transfer.

PART 7 – REMEDIES

This document has set out a number of rights and duties for employees, their representatives and a right for the transferee employer to receive information from the transferor employer. This section describes how these rights can be enforced and remedies obtained.

(a) Rights for employees and their representatives

If any employee considers that their contractual rights have been infringed, they may be able to seek redress through the civil courts or the employment tribunals. However, before doing so employees are advised to discuss these issues with the Advisory, Conciliation & Arbitration Service (Acas) on 08457 474747 or at www.acas.org.uk. or to seek their own independent legal advice, through their trade union, from a local office of the Citizens' Advice Bureau or from a local law centre.

Complaining to an employment tribunal

An employee can make a claim to an employment tribunal by completing a claim form, available from jobcentres, law centres and Citizens' Advice Bureaux, or online at www.employmenttribunals.gov.uk. This will generally need to be done within a specified time limit.

---

13 In addition, the sole or principal reason for the permitted variation must be the transfer itself or a reason connected with the transfer which is not an economic, technical or organisational reason.

You can complain to an employment tribunal if you are:

- an employee who has been dismissed or who has resigned in circumstances in which they consider they were entitled to resign because of the consequences or anticipated consequences of the transfer (see Part 4). An employee must complain within three months of the date when their employment ended. (The method of calculating this date is explained in *Unfairly dismissed? (PL712)*). It may be unclear whether claims should be made against the previous or the new employer. In such cases, employees should consider whether to claim against both employers;

- an elected or trade union representative, if the employer does not comply with the information or consultation requirements (see Part 5). A representative must complain within three months of the date of the transfer;

- a representative or candidate for election who has been dismissed, or suffered detriment short of dismissal. A complaint must be made within three months of the effective date of termination (or, in the case of a detriment short of dismissal, within three months of the action complained of);

- a representative who has been unreasonably refused time off by an employer, or whose employer has refused to make the appropriate payment for time off. A complaint must be made within three months of the date on which it is alleged time off should have been allowed or was taken;

- an affected employee where the employer has not complied with the information or consultation requirements other than in relation to a recognised trade union or an elected representative. A complaint must be made within three months of the date of the transfer.

In any one of the above cases the tribunal can extend the time limit if it considers that it was not reasonably practicable for the complaint to be made within three months. Also, the time limits can be varied to allow for part or all of the statutory dispute resolution procedures to be used (for further detail, see the DTI publication *"Resolving disputes at work: new procedures for discipline and grievance"*).

- an employee who wishes to claim a redundancy payment. The application should normally be made within six months of the dismissal (see *Redundancy Entitlement – Statutory Rights (PL808)*).

If a representative complains to an employment tribunal that an employer has not given information about action proposed by a prospective new employer, and if the employer wishes to show that it was "not reasonably practicable" to give that information because the new employer failed to hand over the necessary information at the right time, the employer must tell the new employer that he or she intends to give that reason for non-compliance. The effect of this will be to make the new employer a party to the tribunal proceedings.

An employee must have at least 12 months' continuous service before they can make a complaint of unfair dismissal for a TUPE-related reason.[14]

Awards made by an employment tribunal

If complaints are upheld, awards may be made against the previous or new employer, depending on the circumstances of the transfer as follows:

a) Unfair dismissal awards

Employment tribunals may order reinstatement or re-engagement of the dismissed employee if the complaint is upheld, and/or make an award of compensation. Further details are in *Unfairly dismissed? (PL712)*.

b) Detriment awards

The employer may be ordered to pay compensation to the person(s) concerned. The compensation will be whatever amount the tribunal considers just and equitable in all the circumstances having regard for any loss incurred by the employee.

c) Information and consultation awards

The defendants in consultation cases may be either the transferor or transferee employer, or both of them – the choice is for the complainant to make. Where either the transferor or the transferee employer is the sole defendant, he may seek to join the other employer to the case. Where joining occurs, both the transferor and the transferee employer are liable to pay compensation to each affected employee for a failure to consult. In such cases, it will be a matter for the tribunal fairly to apportion the compensation between the two parties.[15] The compensation cannot exceed 13 weeks' pay (the value of a week's pay is capped by the Employment Rights Act 1996).[16] If employees are not paid the compensation, they may present individual complaints to the tribunal, which may order payment of the amount due to them. These complaints must be presented within three months from the date of the original award (although the tribunal may extend the time-limit if it considers that it was not reasonably practicable for the complaint to be presented within three months).

Q. Are there any procedures which a complainant may need to follow before making an application to the employment tribunal?

A. Yes, for some of the jurisdictions mentioned above. The Dispute Resolution Regulations came into force on 1 October 2004 giving new rights and responsibilities to both employer and employee. See "Resolving disputes at work: new procedures for discipline and grievance". If an employee does not follow the procedures laid out in the Regulations then a tribunal may not be able to hear the claim or the amount of any money awarded may be reduced.

---

14 Exceptionally, this qualifying period does not apply where an employee claims that he was unfairly dismissed for asserting his TUPE rights.

15 Alternatively, where judgment is given against a sole defendant, that employer may be able to recover a contribution from the other employer by suing him in the civil courts.

16 As at February 2006, the value of a week's pay was £290.

(b) The right of the transferee employer to be provided with employee liability information

This entitlement is described in Part 5. If the transferor does not comply, then the transferee can present a complaint to an employment tribunal. If the tribunal finds in favour of the transferee it will make a declaration to that effect. Also, the tribunal may award compensation for any loss which the transferee has incurred because the employee liability information was not provided.

The level of compensation must be no less than £500 for each employee for whom the information was not provided, or the information provided was defective. So, if information was not provided for 10 of the transferring employees, then the minimum compensation would be £5,000. However, the tribunal may award a lesser sum if it considers that it would be unjust or inequitable to award this default minimum payment.

Q. When would the tribunal not award the minimum award of compensation because it was unjust or inequitable?

A. That would of course be a matter for the tribunal. But it might be fair to assume that trivial or unwitting breaches of the duty may lead to a tribunal waiving what would otherwise be a minimum award of compensation.

SOURCES OF FURTHER INFORMATION

Acas
Helpline: 08457 47 47 47 or at www.acas.org.uk
Helpline for text phone users: 08456 06 16 00

Office of the Deputy Prime Minister (ODPM)
Enquiry Helpdesk: 020 7944 4400 or www.odpm.gov.uk

Department of Trade and Industry (DTI)
Enquiry Line: 020 7215 5000 or www.dti.gov.uk

Department of Work and Pensions (DWP)
www.dwp.gov.uk

Employment Tribunal Service (ETS)
Enquiry Helpline: 0845 795 9775 or www.employmenttribunals.gov.uk

Relevant DTI Publications

Written statement of employment particulars (PL700)
www.dti.gov.uk/er/individual/statement-pl700.htm

Unfairly Dismissed? (PL712)
www.dti.gov.uk/er/individual/unfair-pl712.htm

Redundancy consultation and notification (PL833)
www.dti.gov.uk/er/redundancy/consult-pl833.htm

Redundancy entitlement – statutory rights (PL808)
www.dti.gov.uk/er/redundancy/payments-pl808.htm

Resolving disputes at work: new procedures for discipline and grievance
www.dti.gov. uk/er/employee_guide.pdf

Union membership: rights of members and non-members (PL871)
www.dti.gov.uk/er/union/membership-pl871.htm

Other Publications

Cabinet Office's Statement of Practice *"Staff transfers in the public sector"*
www.civilservice.gov.uk/publications/staff_transfers/publications_and_forms/pdf/
stafftransfers.pdf

Appendix 9

TUPE 2006 – REDUNDANCY AND INSOLVENCY PAYMENTS (DTI NOTE URN 06/1368)

THE TRANSFER OF UNDERTAKINGS (PROTECTION OF EMPLOYMENT) REGULATIONS 2006

REDUNDANCY AND INSOLVENCY PAYMENTS

Purpose of Guidance

1.   The purpose of this guidance is to set out the Secretary of State's view of the application and effects of the Transfer of Undertakings (Protection of Employment) Regulations 2006 ("the 2006 TUPE Regulations") in the context of payments made by the Secretary of State to employees under the provisions of:

●   Part XI of the Employment Rights Act 1996 (redundancy payments) and
●   Part XII of the 1996 Act (payments on insolvency of employer).

2.   This guidance is not an authoritative interpretation of the provisions of the 2006 TUPE Regulations. Only the tribunals and courts can give this. It however sets out the approach that the Secretary of State will apply in determining whether he is liable to make payments under the Employment Rights Act 1996 in the context of the 2006 TUPE Regulations. The 2006 TUPE Regulations apply to business and similar transfers on or after 6th April 2006 and replace the earlier 1981 Regulations. This guidance replaces earlier guidance in relation to the 2006 TUPE Regulations and insolvency.

2006 TUPE Regulations – Overview in the context of payments under the Employment Rights Act 1996

3.   The 2006 Regulations apply to transfers of the whole or part of a business or undertaking or a change in a service provider (referred to in this note as "a relevant transfer") subject to certain exceptions. Regulation 4 provides that a relevant transfer does not operate to terminate the contract of employment of employees who were working in the business at the time of the transfer but transfers their contracts to the transferee. Those who would have been so employed by the transferor had they had not been dismissed in a manner described by Regulation 7(1) (see below) also have their contract of employment transferred to the transferee. This means that the transferor's powers, rights and liabilities under or in connection with the contract of employment are transferred to the new employer (subject to certain exceptions

– see further below). Where an employee's contract of employment is transferred pursuant to regulation 4 and his employment continues with the transferee, no redundancy payment will be payable as the employee has not been dismissed.

4.   Regulation 7 provides that a dismissal because of the transfer or a reason connected with the transfer that is not an economic, technical or organisational one is automatically an unfair dismissal. Regulation 8 makes a number of alterations in relation to insolvency. In summary these are as follows:

- Regulations 4 and 7 do not apply where the transferor is subject to "bankruptcy proceedings or any analogous insolvency proceedings which have been instituted with a view to the liquidation of the assets of the transferor".

- Where there is a relevant transfer and the transferor is subject to "relevant insolvency proceedings" (defined as insolvency proceedings which have been opened in relation to the transferor not with a view to the liquidation of the assets) regulations 4 and 7 do apply. However regulation 8 provides for sums of the kinds described in Part XII of the Employment Rights Act 1996 which are owed at the date of the transfer to employees who transfer to the transferee to be payable by the Secretary of State rather than the transferee.

In addition regulation 9 provides a procedure whereby appropriate representatives of employees who transfer under the Regulations and the transferor or transferee may agree variation of contracts of employment where the transferor is subject to relevant insolvency proceedings.

Application of the 2006 TUPE Regulations to specific types of insolvency proceedings

5.   The position regarding specific types of insolvency proceedings is as follows:

Bankruptcy

Where a trustee in bankruptcy sells a business that was run by the bankrupt there is no question of the employees' contracts of employment passing to the purchaser. In such a case there will be a redundancy of the employees and redundancy and insolvency payments owed to employees will be payable by the Secretary of State in accordance with the provisions of Parts XI and XII of the Employment Rights Act 1996. The reason for this is that regulation 8(7) provides that neither regulation 4 nor regulation 7 is to apply to bankruptcy proceedings.

Compulsory liquidation

Where a company is wound up by an order of the court on grounds that it is unable to pay its debts, regulations 4 and 7 of the 2006 TUPE Regulations do not apply as such proceedings are liquidation proceedings under the supervision of an insolvency practioner that are analogous to bankruptcy proceedings. The position under case law was that on the making of a winding-up order this operates to terminate the contracts of employment of any employees as at the date of the making of the order.

Employees will be entitled to insolvency and redundancy payments out of the National Insurance Fund in accordance with the provisions of the Employment Rights Act 1996.

Creditors' voluntary liquidation

Where a liquidator sells a business run by a company that is in creditors' voluntary liquidation regulation 4 and regulation 7 will not apply. These provisions are disapplied by regulation 8(7) by virtue of the fact that creditors' voluntary liquidations are liquidation proceedings under the supervision of an insolvency practioner that are analogous to bankruptcy proceedings. Accordingly a transfer of a business by the liquidator in a creditors' voluntary liquidation would cause the dismissal of those employees who immediately prior to the transfer were employed by the company unless prior to the transfer there is an agreement between the parties (including the employees) that the transferee is to be substituted as their employer. In the absence of any agreement substituting the transferee as their employer, employees whose contracts of employment with the transferee are terminated will be entitled to be paid redundancy payments and arrears of wages etc. from the National Insurance Fund in accordance with the provisions of the 1996 Act.

Members' voluntary liquidation

Members' voluntary liquidation is not an insolvency proceeding. It is by definition a solvent winding up. Therefore regulations 4 and 7 apply if there is a relevant transfer and regulation 8 is not applicable at all.

Administration

The Secretary of State takes the view that regulations 4 and 7 will always apply in relation to a relevant transfer that is made in the context of an administration. He takes the view that such proceedings do not fall within regulation 8(7). For this exception to apply the proceedings must be analogous to bankruptcy proceedings and involve the liquidation of the assets under the supervision of an insolvency practitioner. Administration is not in the view of the Secretary of State analogous to bankruptcy proceedings. The correct approach is to look at the main or sole purpose of the procedure rather than its outcome in a specific instance. The main purpose of bankruptcy proceedings is to realise the free assets of an insolvent debtor and share the proceeds after deduction of costs and expenses amongst all the debtor's creditors. This is not the main purpose of administration. It follows that Regulation 8(7) will not apply to administration. It is also the view of the Secretary of State that regulations 8(2) to (6) will apply to administration so that liabilities owed to transferring employees at the transfer date of the kinds described in Part XII of the Employment Rights Act 1996 would fall to be paid out of the National Insurance Fund by the Secretary of State and not by the transferee.

Voluntary Arrangements

A transfer in the context of a voluntary arrangement is subject to regulations 4 and 7 for the same reasons referred to in relation to administration. In a voluntary arrangement the debtor is left in control of the assets and the function of the insolvency practitioner is merely to supervise the arrangement. Regulations 8(2) to (6) will apply in relation to a relevant transfer where the transferor is subject to a voluntary arrangement. Liabilities owed to transferring employees at the transfer date of the kinds described in Part XII of the Employment Rights Act 1996 do not transfer to the transferee and would fall to be paid by the Secretary of State out of the National Insurance Fund.

Administrative Receivership

Regulations 4 and 7 will apply to administrative receiverships. They are not analogous to bankruptcy proceedings since they are not collective proceedings and the exception in regulation 8(7) will accordingly not apply. Where there is a relevant transfer regulations 8(2) to (6) will apply so that liabilities owed at the transfer date to transferring employees of the kinds described in Part XII of the Employment Rights Act 1996 do not transfer to the transferee and would fall to be paid by the Secretary of State out of the National Insurance Fund.

Other types of receivership

Other types of receivership are not insolvency proceedings and so the provisions of regulation 8 do not apply to them. A relevant transfer by a receiver will therefore be subject to regulations 4 and 7.

Proceedings in other jurisdictions where a relevant transfer occurs in Great Britain

In this case it is necessary to consider whether the foreign proceedings are analogous to bankruptcy proceedings. If they are then the exception in regulation 8(7) will apply.

Appendix 10

REDUNDANCY PAYMENTS OFFICE GUIDANCE LETTER

APRIL 2006

Dear Insolvency Practitioner

EMPLOYMENT RIGHTS ACT 1996

I hope the following will be helpful to your administration and staff who deal with redundancy and insolvency claims.

Revised Transfer of Undertakings (Protection of Employment) Regulations 2006[1]

As you are aware the new regulations come into force on 6 April 2006. It may be helpful if I set out the RPOs understanding of the changes to the regulations in respect of insolvent transferors.

The aim of the transfer regulations is to protect employees who are in an undertaking when it transfers to a new owner. There is no change to the way a relevant transfer is identified. The new regulations are expanded to expressly include a change of service provider. What the regulations do is give continuity of employment to the employees who transfer to the new owner, who will assume liability for contracts transferred to him. There is no redundancy situation, as the employees have not been dismissed. They also protect those who have been unfairly dismissed because of the transfer. They also clarify that employees dismissed for economic, technical or organisational (ETO) reasons may be classed as being dismissed for redundancy reasons rather than 'some other substantial reason' under the unfair dismissal provisions of the Employment Rights Act 1996. What this means is that rather be classed as automatically unfairly dismissed, they can now be treated as redundant and claim redundancy pay.

The regulations have changed in respect of *insolvent* transferors. Neither the wording in regs 8(6) and 8(7), nor the DTI guidance lists the types of insolvency procedures within their scope. This means that the uncertainty of the tests in the ECJ case law, where the purposes of the insolvency proceedings is not easily discernible, still remains. It is the RPOs understanding that the Regulations will not apply to an insolvency where the undertaking is, as a matter of fact, wound up and the proceeds are distributed to creditors. The Regulations will apply to insolvencies where the undertaking, or part of one, is transferred to a new owner. It is our view that the only type of insolvency

---

1   SI 2006/246.

definitely outside the scope of the TUPE Regulations is a compulsory winding up by the courts. In all other types of insolvency it is possible for the undertaking (or part of it) to be transferred to a new owner and therefore [be] capable of fitting the 'purposive' definition in reg 8(6). It is inevitable that an employment tribunal will eventually determine this point. In the meantime the RPO is adopting the pragmatic approach and the test of whether assistance from the National Insurance Fund is given will depend on *whether or not a transfer has occurred in actual fact*.

What the employees will be entitled to claim will depend on the following circumstances:

(1) *Whether they transfer to the new owner*;

If the employer is insolvent on the transfer date, to assist the rescue at all, or part, of an insolvent business, the Secretary of State will pay wages and holidays taken prior to the insolvency date but unpaid up to the statutory limits to employees who transfer to the new owner. No redundancy pay, accrued holiday, entitlement or notice pay will be paid as there is no dismissal – the contract continues with the new employer. The transferee will pay the residual contract debt. The Secretary of State's debt will stay with the insolvent company – it cannot be recovered from the transferee.

(2) *Whether they are unfairly dismissed because of the transfer*;

Employees who are unfairly dismissed because of the transfer will also be paid wages and holiday pay (as for those who transfer). RP and notice will not be paid, as they were not dismissed by reason of redundancy. Employees may make a claim to ET for an unfair dismissal award and breach of contract (notice). It will be for the ET to determine on the joint and several liabilities between the transferor and transferee.

(3) *Whether the dismissal is for ETO reason*;

There is no change to the payment procedure where the employee's dismissal is transfer related but is for ETO reasons entailing changes in the workforce. They are considered to be redundant and the RPO will pay redundancy, wages, holiday pay (including accrued holiday entitlement) and notice pay as usual.

(4) *Whether the employees have refused to transfer*;

There is no change to the procedure for those who refuse to transfer. Wages and holidays will be paid. RP and CNP will be rejected as there is not redundancy and they are treated as having left employment of their own accord.

In *cases where the transfer date is prior to the insolvency date*, no payments for wages and holiday pay will be made by the RPO to employees who transfer, or those who are unfairly dismissed. It will be treated as a transfer under the solvent TUPE provisions. Employees dismissed for ETO reasons will be considered in the usual way and if the liability rests with the insolvent transferor, payment may be made to employees.

There are no special RP1 forms – the current form/booklet can be used. We will be updating in due course, along with our other publications and forms. It would be helpful if you would explain to those employees who transfer that they should only complete the forms in respect of wages and holiday taken but not paid when you issue the booklets.

One of the new requirements under the TUPE regs is the notification of employee liability information from the transferor to the transferee. We would also be grateful for a copy of the information about employees given to the transferee with the RP14 form as it will assist in sorting out who has transferred and who is unfairly dismissed, etc.

Revised RP14a

For those of you who use Turnkey, an electronic version of the RP14a has been produced and will be accepted by the RPO. The ordinary RP14a forms will be updated shortly to reflect the changes.

Appendix 11

CABINET OFFICE STATEMENT OF PRACTICE – STAFF TRANSFERS IN THE PUBLIC SECTOR

JANUARY 2000

STAFF TRANSFERS IN THE PUBLIC SECTOR STATEMENT OF PRACTICE

Guiding Principles

- The Government is committed to ensuring that the public sector is a good employer and a model contractor and client. The people employed in the public sector, directly and indirectly, are its biggest asset and critical in developing modern, high quality, efficient, responsive, customer focused and environmentally friendly public services.

- The Government's approach to modernising public services is a pragmatic one, based on finding the best supplier who can deliver quality services and value for money for the taxpayer. This involves some services or functions being provided by, or in partnership with, the private or voluntary sector, or restructured and organised in a new way within the public sector. The involvement, commitment and motivation of staff are vital for achieving smooth and seamless transition during such organisational change.

- Public Private Partnerships and the process of modernisation through organisational change in the public sector will be best achieved by clarity and certainty about the treatment of staff involved. The Government is committed to ensuring that staff involved in all such transfers are treated fairly and consistently and their rights respected. This will encourage a co-operative, partnership approach to the modernisation of the public sector with consequential benefits for all citizens.

Introduction

1. In order to meet these guiding principles the Government believes that there must be a clear and consistent policy for the treatment of staff, founded upon the provisions of the Transfer of Undertaking (Protection of Employment) Regulations 1981 (as amended) (TUPE). This Statement of

Practice[1] sets out the framework that the Government expects all public sectororganisations to work within to achieve this aim (see paragraph 6 for the coverage of this Statement).

2.   TUPE implements the 1977 European Council Acquired Rights Directive. In broad terms, TUPE protects employees' terms and conditions (except occupational pension arrangements) when the business in which they work is transferred from one employer to another. Employment with the new employer is treated as continuous from the date of the employee's start with the first employer. Terms and conditions cannot be changed where the operative reason for the change is the transfer although changes for other reasons may be negotiated.

3.   The Government takes a positive attitude towards TUPE, regarding it as an important aspect of employment rights legislation with the potential to promote a co-operative, partnership approach towards business restructuring and change in the public sector. It has, however, acknowledged that TUPE is less than satisfactory in its current form and, following amendments to the Acquired Rights Directive agreed in June 1998, will be shortly consulting on proposals for revising it.

4.   The Government's strategy in revising this legislation is based on the principle that it must be made to work effectively for all those whose interests depend upon it. This mirrors the approach that the Government is adopting in deciding policy on employment relations issues generally.

5.   In the area of Public Private Partnerships and change in the public sector, the consultations that the Government has undertaken and the representations which have been made, have showed a strong consensus between private sector employers, the voluntary sector, employee representatives and public sector organisations for the application of TUPE to all general situations where a service or function is contracted out, then retendered, brought back into the public sector, transferred within the public sector, or restructured and organised in a new way in a different part of the public sector. It is accepted that there will be some genuinely exceptional circumstances where TUPE will not apply but attempts to orchestrate a non-TUPE situation in other circumstances should not be tolerated. The policy in this Statement of Practice is therefore based on the following principles:

●   contracting-out exercises with the private sector and voluntary organisations and transfers between different parts of the public sector, will be conducted on the basis that staff will transfer and TUPE should apply, unless there are genuinely exceptional reasons not to do so;

●   this includes second and subsequent round contracts that result in a new contractor and where a function is brought back into a public sector organisation where, in both cases, when the contract was first awarded staff transferred from the public sector;

●   in circumstances where TUPE does not apply in strict legal terms to certain types of transfer between different parts of the public sector, the principles of TUPE should be followed (where possible using legislation

---

1   Further copies of this Statement can be obtained from tel. 0207 270 5774, by e-mail to S McDonald, or on the Cabinet Office web-site at www.cabinet-office.gov.uk/civilservice/ 2000/tupe/stafftransfers.pdf.

to effect the transfer) and the staff involved should be treated no less favourably than had the Regulations applied; and

- there should be appropriate arrangements to protect occupational pensions, redundancy and severance terms of staff in all these types of transfer. Attached at Annex A is HM Treasury's Statement of Practice on Staff Transfers from Central Government "A fair deal for Staff Pensions" which sets out the policy on staff pensions announced by the Chief Secretary on 14 June 1999 that must be followed by Central Government Departments and Agencies, and which Ministers expect to be adopted by other public sector employers.[2]

Coverage

6.   This Statement of Practice sets out a framework to be followed by public sector organisations to implement the Government's policy on the treatment of staff transfers where the public sector is the employer when contracting out or the client in a subsequent retendering situation. It applies directly to central government departments and agencies and to the NHS. The Government expects other public sector organisations to follow this Statement of Practice. Local government is subject to some different considerations particularly the current restrictions in legislation contained in Parts I and II of the Local Government Act 1988. However abolition of CCT from January 2000 and proposals to modify Section 17 of the 1988 Act, as part of the introduction of Best Value, will remove in part obstacles to local authorities following this Statement of Practice. However, in doing so, they must have regard to the need to comply with their best value duties. The Personnel and Human Resources panel of the Local Government Association support the principles set out in this Statement of Practice and have encouraged their adoption by individual local authorities.

7.   The Statement of Practice covers the following types of situation that may involve transfers of staff:

- Public Private Partnerships (e.g. following Better Quality Service reviews). This includes contracting-out; market testing; PFI; privatisation and other outsourcing and contracting exercises, (paragraph 10–16);
- Second and subsequent generation contracting where, when the contract was first awarded, staff transferred from the public sector, (paragraph 12);
- Reorganisations and transfers from one part of the public sector to another, (paragraph 1720); and
- Reorganisations and transfers within the civil service (where TUPE cannot apply because there is no change in employer but TUPE principles should be followed), (paragraphs 21 and 22).

8.   This Statement deals only with the policy framework for the treatment of staff involved in such transfers. It does not offer policy advice or guidance on:

- assessing the options for a particular service or function;
- project appraisal or procurement (except on the application of TUPE);
- managing a contracting exercise;

---

2   Separate consideration is being given to the protection of pensions in staff transfers from local government.

- how to discharge the obligations when TUPE applies or not; or
- how to secure appropriate pension provision, redundancy or severance terms.

Nor does it remove the need to seek legal advice in each individual case.

9.   Detailed guidance on these aspects is provided separately, often tailored for different parts of the public sector to reflect their different needs, and for different types of Public Private Partnership. A list of relevant guidance for these aspects is at Annex B.

Transfers as a Result of Public Private Partnerships

10.   This section of the Statement deals with the policy that should be adopted for the transfer of staff from the public sector to a private sector employer or a voluntary sector body. This will be as a result of a Public Private Partnership where a service or function currently performed by the public sector will in future be carried out by a private sector organisation. This may, for example, be a result of a PFI initiative, strategic contracting out or market testing exercises. All will involve some sort of contracting exercise where the public sector organisation (not necessarily the one in which the staff are employed) is the contracting authority.

11.   In such transfers the application of TUPE will always be a matter of law based on the individual circumstances of the particular transfer. However, the policy adopted in defining the terms of the contracting exercise can help ensure that staff should be protected by TUPE and that all parties have a clear understanding that TUPE should apply and will be followed. In such transfers, therefore, the public sector contracting authority should, except in genuinely exceptional circumstances (see paragraph 14), ensure that:

- at the earliest appropriate stage in the contracting exercise, it states that staff are to transfer and this should normally have the effect of causing TUPE to apply, although legal advice should always be taken to confirm the applicability of TUPE in individual cases;
- at the earliest appropriate stage staff and recognised unions (or, if none, other independent staff representatives) are informed in writing of the intention that staff will transfer (and where possible when the transfer will take place) and that TUPE should apply;
- potential bidders are then invited to tender, drawing their attention in the Invitation to Tender letter to the intention that staff will transfer and TUPE should apply. Potential bidders should be also advised that they can, if they wish, submit bids where staff do not transfer and TUPE not apply, but that these will only be accepted if they fall within the genuinely exceptional circumstances i.e. unless the bid falls within one of the exceptions at paragraph 14 it must comply with the condition that staff transfer and TUPE should apply;
- the contracting exercise is then operated on the basis that the intention is that staff will transfer and TUPE should apply. Public sector contracting authorities should however consider all bids received. If a tenderer considers that staff should not transfer, they should be asked to give their reasons for this. Tenderers should be reminded if they do not consider

that staff should transfer and the contract does not fall within the exceptions in paragraph 14, the contracting authority reserves the right not to accept the tender;

- in a very few cases bids made on the basis staff will not transfer and TUPE not apply will fall within the genuinely exceptional circumstances set out in paragraph 14 and cause the authority to accept the bid. The costs of redeploying staff and redundancies costs to the public sector employer must be taken into account when assessing such a bid. In all other cases the bid should not be accepted as it will not conform to the contracting authority's view that staff should transfer and TUPE apply; and

- where there is then a contractual requirement that staff should transfer, the requirements of TUPE should be scrupulously followed by the public sector contracting authority who should also ensure that it is satisfied that bidders' proposals fully meet the requirements of TUPE.

Second and subsequent transfers

12.   This part of the Statement also extends to the retendering of contracts where, when the contract was first awarded staff transferred from the public sector (irrespective of whether TUPE applied at the time). Where a public contracting authority retenders such a contract then, except in exceptional circumstances (and where the incumbent contractor is successful), staff working on the contract should transfer and TUPE should apply. Views should be sought from the current contractor as to whether, from their point of view, there are any exceptional circumstances why staff should not transfer (by reference to paragraph 14). The retendering exercise should then be conducted as described above in paragraph 11.

Transfer of services or functions back into the public sector

13.   There may also be circumstances that require a function contracted-out to a private sector contractor or voluntary sector body to be brought back into the public sector on the termination of the contract. If, when the contract was first awarded staff transferred from the public sector (irrespective of whether TUPE applied at the time), then the public sector organisation should ensure that staff working on the contract transfer (and TUPE should therefore apply) into its organisation unless there are genuinely exceptional reasons not to do so. Views should be sought from the current contractor as to whether, from their point of view, there are any exceptional circumstances why staff should not transfer (by reference to paragraph 14). For transfers into the Civil Service, where TUPE applies, then the recruitment provisions of the Civil Service Order in Council and Civil Service Commissioners Recruitment Code as well as Civil Service Nationality rules are not relevant[3].

Exceptions

14.   There may be a small number of cases where the policy set out in para 11–13 may not be followed and TUPE may not apply. There must be genuinely exceptional reasons why this should be the case. Circumstances that may qualify for such exceptions are, broadly:

---

3   Civil Service Management Code.

- where a contract is for the provision of both goods and services, but the provision of services is ancillary in purpose to the provision of the goods; or
- where the activity for which the public sector organisation is contracting is essentially new or a one off project; or
- where services or goods are essentially a commodity bought "off the shelf" and no grouping of staff are specifically and permanently assigned to a common task; or
- where the features of the service or function subject to the contracting exercise are significantly different from the features of the function previously performed within the public sector, or by an existing contractor e.g. a function to be delivered electronically and in such a way that it requires radically different skills, experience and equipment.

15.   Where a public sector organisation believes such genuinely exceptional circumstances exist then it should be prepared to justify this, and the departure from the Government's policy (para 11–13), publicly, if challenged. In central government, the agreement of the relevant departmental Ministers may need to be obtained before such an exception is made.

16.   In such exceptional cases where staff do not transfer and TUPE does not apply, the public sector organisation should, in the case of first generation contracts, seek to identify as soon as possible with the contractor any staff that will be taken on voluntarily by the contractor;[4] and then, where possible, to redeploy those members of staff remaining within the public sector organisation (the costs of such redeployments and possible resulting redundancy payments must be taken into account when evaluating the bid).

Transfers and Reorganisations within the public sector

17.   TUPE can apply to the transfers of a function from one part of the public sector to another where there is a change of employer. This, for example, can include[5]:

- Transfers between local government and Civil Service Departments and Agencies
- Transfers between local government and NDPBs
- Transfers between local government and the NHS
- Transfers between the NHS and Civil Service Departments and Agencies
- Transfers between the NHS and NDPBs
- Transfers between NDPBs and Civil Service Departments and Agencies

18.   The application of TUPE will, again, always be a matter of law based on the individual circumstances of the particular transfer. The amended Acquired Rights Directive directly legislates the *Henke* judgement of the European Court of Justice that: an administrative reorganisation of public administrative authorities or the transfer of administrative function is not a transfer and, therefore, as a matter of law, does not fall within the Directive. Recent case law suggests that it excludes from the legislation's application only a relatively

---

4   Public Sector organisations should be aware that the transfer of a major part of the workforce, in terms of numbers or skills, may cause TUPE to apply.

5   This list is not exhaustive.

limited range of situations involving the transfer of entities pursuing non-economic objectives within the public sector. Nevertheless the issue has still to be tested fully in the tribunals and courts. The *Henke* exception has been thought to apply where: the reason for a transfer is only because there is a change of geographical boundaries and the type of public sector body carrying out the function does not change (e.g. the transfer of administrative staff as a result of changes to police authority boundaries); or where the main function is a judicial, quasi-judicial or quasi-judicial regulatory function (e.g. the creation of the Financial Services Authority) and incapable of being performed other than by a public sector authority. Officeholders who are not workers are also excluded from the scope of the Directive.

19.   However, transfers at the instigation and under the control of central government will usually be effected through legislation, in particular those involving Officeholders. Provision can then be made for staff to transfer on TUPE terms, irrespective of whether the transfer is excluded from the scope of the Directive implemented by TUPE. Departments must therefore ensure that legislation effecting transfers of functions between public sector bodies makes provision for staff to transfer and on a basis that follows the principles of TUPE along with appropriate arrangements to protect occupational pension, redundancy and severance terms.

20.   Section 38 of the Employment Relations Act also includes a power that can be used to apply the requirements of TUPE specifically to some such transfers e.g. Transfer of Undertakings (Protection of Employment) (Rent Officer Service) Regulations 1999 (SI 2511/1999). Where, for whatever reason, this power or other legislation is not used there will be no legal requirement or obligation in such cases for staff to transfer to another part of the public sector where the function is to be performed (as to attempt to compel them would, in effect, constitute a unilateral change in their employment contract by imposing a change of employer). In such cases, as a matter of policy, public sector bodies should ensure that the principles of TUPE are followed and staff are offered the opportunity to transfer on terms that are, overall, no less favourable than had TUPE applied. They should also ensure appropriate pension provision and redundancy and severance terms. Staff who choose not to transfer should, where possible, be redeployed within the transferring public sector organisation.

Transfers and Reorganisations within the Civil Service

21.   Reorganisation and transfers between central government departments and agencies (i.e. within the Civil Service) do not involve a change in employer and TUPE therefore cannot apply. However, terms and conditions of employment do vary between different departments and many of the considerations addressed in the Statement for other types of transfer may also apply.

22.   As a matter of policy, therefore, such reorganisations and transfers between central government departments will be conducted on the basis that:

- as a general rule, when functions are transferred from one department to another staff will be transferred with the work;
- departments should, however, make every effort to provide an opportunity for those who wish to stay with or return to their original

department to do so, having regard to ensuring consistent treatment of staff affected and the needs of the work;

- departments should ensure that wherever possible the principles of TUPE are followed. The existing terms and conditions of staff cannot be changed unilaterally;
- staff and their recognised unions are informed at the earliest appropriate stage of the reorganisation and transfer; and
- over time, the receiving department may aim to move, through negotiation with staff, towards fuller alignment of the terms of transferred staff to those of the main body of staff.

Cabinet Office
January 2000

ANNEX A

H M Treasury   *June 1999*

STAFF TRANSFERS FROM CENTRAL GOVERNMENT:

A FAIR DEAL FOR STAFF PENSIONS

Guidance to Departments and Agencies

Introduction

This paper sets out in general terms how pensions issues are to be handled in future when staff from central government Departments and Agencies are transferred to a new employer as part of a business transfer. The new approach set out here builds upon earlier guidance, and extends and strengthens its application in order to ensure that staff are treated fairly. It is mainly concerned with transfers between the Government and the private sector when contracts are awarded under public-private partnership (PPP) deals.

2. *Better Quality Services* gives guidance on the treatment of staff pensions in PFI and PPP deals, and there are also policy statements and guidance issued by the Treasury Task Force covering, for instance, the Government's continuing commitment to dialogue with staff and other interested parties about the way in which PPP projects are managed.

3. This new guidance should be reflected in procurement practice as soon as is practicable without disruption to projects which are already at an advanced stage. Detailed guidance will be issued to contracting authorities later this year.

Background

4. Pensions are often an important element in the overall remuneration of staff, particularly within the public services where there are occupational pension schemes offering a high quality of benefits. Sometimes public service schemes require very low employee contributions to earn pension benefits, such as in the

Principal Civil Service Pension Scheme (PCSPS) where employee contributions are set at only 1½% of pay, and in these cases employee pay is somewhat lower than it would otherwise be, to reflect the value of the pension scheme.

5. If appropriate arrangements were not made for staff pensions as part of business transfers, the result could be disadvantageous to public service staff who were transferring to the new employer. Not only are pension arrangements an important subject, but they are complex and likely to cause confusion and apprehension if not handled openly and consistently by the contracting authority. It is not in the interests of the contracting authority, or the new employer, or the taxpayer, for staff to be alarmed about the prospects for their pensions in a business transfer which depends upon staff motivation for delivery of good quality public services.

6. Occupational pensions are not covered by the Transfer of Undertaking (Protection of Employment) Regulations 1981 (the TUPE regulations). The new EU Acquired Rights Directive gives Member States the option of including occupational pensions within the terms which are protected by national legislation when an undertaking transfers between employers, and the Government is reviewing whether and if so, how, to include pensions within new TUPE regulations.

7. Independently of the TUPE review, and without prejudice to its conclusions, this paper sets out the standard practices which the Government will follow when its own staff are transferred to other employers. Contracting authorities in other parts of the public sector will continue to make their own arrangements consistent with the law and good employment practice. It would be welcome if they adopted approaches comparable to those set out here. Separate consideration is being given to staff transfers from local government.

8. The principles which Government will apply as a contracting authority in relation to the pensions of transferring staff are:

– to treat staff fairly;
– to do so openly and transparently;
– to involve staff and their representatives fully in consultation about the process and its results; and
– to have clear accountability within Government for the results.

9. There are two separate but related aspects to treatment of pensions in a business transfer:

– first, staff should continue to have access after the transfer to a good quality occupational pension scheme under which they can continue to earn pension benefits through their **future service**;
– second, staff should be given options for the handling of the **accrued benefits** which they have already earned.

Each of these aspects is discussed, in turn, in the following sections.

FUTURE SERVICE

10. The focus of this guidance is upon those cases, likely to be in the majority, where a business transfer means that staff have to be 'early leavers' of the occupational pension scheme associated with their former employment. The Government has no plans to seek amendment to the Superannuation Act 1972

to broaden the categories of employees eligible for membership of the PCSPS. Where Civil Servants transfer to private sector employment they will therefore cease to be eligible for PCSPS membership, and their ability to earn further occupational pension benefits through future service will depend upon the occupational pension arrangements offered by the new employer.

11. Not all private sector employers offer occupational pension schemes which are as valuable to employees as the public service schemes, and where good quality pension schemes are offered they typically differ in major respects: for instance, the age of normal retirement, the rate of accrual of pension entitlements, provision of a lump sum on retirement, the degree of indexation of pensions increases, and so on. If care were not taken over staff pensions, the unintended upshot of a business transfer might be a detriment to staff pension benefits.

12. The terms of the business transfer should specifically protect staff pensions. The arrangements made to achieve this need to be considered within the overall context of the business transfer negotiations between the contracting authority and prospective private sector partners and should not be so cumbersome or expensive to administer as to militate against finding a justifiable business solution.

13. To require that the new employer should offer transferring staff access to a pension scheme which is in all respects identical to the public service scheme which they are leaving would be unduly restrictive. It would add to administrative costs and it could hamper harmonisation of terms and conditions. In the case of the PCSPS it would be an unrealistic requirement, because a non-statutory scheme which was identical to the PCSPS would not qualify for tax exemption. A requirement for an identical scheme would also prevent employers from offering different benefit packages, more in line with private sector standards, which might overall be of greater value to many transferring employees.

14. The guiding principle should be that the new employer offers transferring staff membership of a pension scheme which though not identical is '**broadly comparable**' to the public service pension scheme which they are leaving. To satisfy the criteria for broad comparability there must be a rigorous scrutiny of the alternative pension arrangements by a professionally qualified actuary which compares the alternative scheme with the public service scheme in detail. A broadly comparable scheme will be one which, in the professional opinion of the actuary, satisfies the condition that there are no identifiable employees who will suffer material detriment overall in terms of their future accrual of pension benefits under the alternative scheme. The PCSPS takes actuarial advice from the Government Actuary's Department, as do a number of other public service pension schemes.

15. There may be cases where although there are no identifiable classes of employee who would be materially worse off overall, transfer to the new scheme might be materially detrimental to a few individuals. In such cases it will be a matter of judgement whether the new scheme should be adjusted, or whether it would be better simply to make appropriate compensation arrangements to protect the disadvantaged individual(s).

16. Each case should be considered on its merits. There may be exceptional circumstances where there are special reasons for not providing a broadly comparable pension scheme. The strength of those reasons should be tested rigorously and it would then be necessary for the terms of the business transfer to ensure appropriate compensation for all the staff. Actuarial advice should be taken by the contracting authority on the calculation of any compensation in these exceptional circumstances if a broadly comparable scheme is not to be provided, or if there are identified individuals who would be materially worse off overall in the new scheme. In all cases the preference should be for the new employer to offer transferring staff membership of a broadly comparable scheme, and this should be a contract condition in the procurement. Only in exceptional circumstances should the combination of pension arrangements which are less than broadly comparable plus appropriate compensation for employees be accepted.

17. This principle is already being followed by the Government. Its practical application will now be strengthened, extended and made more open:

(i) for transfers of staff from Government Departments and Agencies it will continue to be a requirement for the Government Actuary's Department (GAD) to certify the broad comparability of specified alternative pension arrangements before any contractual commitment is made;

(ii) if for exceptional reasons the requirement for broad comparability is to be waived, GAD advice on appropriate compensation to staff must be followed;

(iii) GAD will follow a published Statement of Practice in certifying broad comparability (attached). This sets out clearly the principles which are already being followed. Publishing these principles in the form of this Statement for the first time will increase transparency and accountability;

(iv) GAD will provide to the contracting authority an analysis of the key differences between the alternative pension scheme and the public service scheme, and the ways in which the differences balance out overall to satisfy the condition of no material detriment overall, by reference to the different groups of employees identified in the staff to be transferred;

(v) the full GAD analysis will be made available to trades unions and staff representatives, and GAD will respond to any queries or observations which staff representatives have. A reasonable period will be allowed by the contracting authority for discussion, if requested, of any points arising from the GAD analysis;

(vi) at the conclusion of this period, if any points of concern about the suitability of the proposed alternative pension arrangements remain which cannot be settled by discussion between staff representatives and the contracting authority, staff representatives may raise their concerns directly with a nominated Minister responsible for the affairs of the Department or Agency;

(vii) no contractual commitments will be made whilst this process of review and consultation is underway, but a reasonable time limit may be set by the contracting authority;

(viii) the contract for the business transfer must specifically require the implementation of the alternative pension arrangements which have been accepted.

18. In practice this will mean that in order to avoid delay or having to retrace steps, contracting authorities will need to be satisfied about the broad comparability of alternative pension arrangements well in advance of moving a procurement to selection of short-listed bidders or a preferred bidder. Bidders will need to provide GAD with detailed specifications of their proposed pension arrangements in good time to allow the analysis required and, if necessary, subsequent discussion of it with staff representatives. Contracting authorities will have to reflect this in their procurement logistics. There can be no proper evaluation of options for public-private partnership without a full analysis of the future staff pension arrangements.

19. Ministers will not authorise a procurement contract, and contractual commitments should not be made under delegated powers, if the conditions set out in paragraph 17 (above) have not been satisfied. This provides a guarantee to staff that the process of identifying acceptable alternative pension arrangements will be fair and open and carried out in full consultation with their representatives.

Subsequent transfers of staff

20. Current practice restricts the contracting authority's concern about broad comparability to transfers from Government to another employer. Once staff have transferred to a new employer, they may be involved in subsequent business transfers. As a contracting authority, the Government will usually not be involved directly as a party to those arrangements. A contracting authority cannot take responsibility for the treatment of its former staff throughout the remainder of their working lives. But a contracting authority does take an interest in the conduct of business transfers which occur as the direct consequence of actions which it takes as a contracting authority.

21. Therefore:

(i) where a contract for services is terminated and the work is given to another contractor, the contracting authority will require that pension arrangements are made for staff transferring from the first contractor to the second contractor which would at least be broadly comparable with the public service pension scheme which those staff were in originally. The requirement will be limited to staff originally transferred from the contracting authority, although employers may find it convenient to harmonise terms and conditions in the workforce; and

(ii) where a primary contractor under a Government contract transfers staff whose work is integral to performance of the contract to a sub-contractor in consequence of the terms of the primary contractor's obligations to the Government, it should be a condition of that subcontracting that broadly comparable pension arrangements are made for the transferring staff who were originally in the employ of the contracting authority.

ACCRUED BENEFITS

22. The treatment in procurement practice of the accrued pension benefits of transferring staff is more complex, but raises issues of equal importance. Regulations applicable to pension schemes require 'early leavers' to be given the option of 'preserving' their accrued benefits in the pension scheme which they are leaving, or transferring them to another pension arrangement. In the

former case (preservation), the early leavers become 'deferred pensioners' of the scheme which they are leaving. The value of their benefits in that scheme will be uprated by price inflation until they come into payment at normal retirement age. This option may often be preferred by staff, especially those who are closer to retirement and do not expect significant future real earnings growth. In the latter case, where accrued benefits are transferred, the transferor scheme makes a transfer payment to the transferee scheme which extinguishes its liability to the early leaver; in return the new employer's scheme awards a past service credit to the individual. (If the transfer were made to a personal pension plan instead, it would be invested in the normal way.)

23. Regulations stipulate a basis for calculating a minimum transfer value where accrued credits are transferred. Typically this will not result in individuals securing full credits in the new employer's scheme in relation to the credits they are surrendering in the transferor scheme, unless there is a specific agreement between the two pension schemes that they should do so. Typically there is then a different basis for calculation of the transfer value involving the transferor scheme in making higher transfer payments. Such agreements between pension schemes are called **'bulk transfer agreements'** (although they may in fact cover only a few members of staff, or just one). A bulk transfer agreement specifies the basis for calculating the transfer payment and the size of the transfer credits it will secure.

24. It is desirable where staff are obliged by a transfer of undertaking to be early leavers of a public service pension scheme for there to be bulk transfer agreements covering the award of past service credits by the new employer's pension scheme. Current practice, as set out in Better Quality Services is to treat the absence of a bulk transfer agreement as a significant disadvantage of a bid. In practice this means that bids should be unlikely to succeed unless there is a very good prospect of a bulk transfer agreement being concluded to cover transferring staff. But it is still possible for the business transfer to become dissociated from negotiation of the bulk transfer agreement between the two pension schemes, leaving staff uncertain about the arrangements which will eventually be made.

25. The existing approach will therefore now be strengthened by making it a condition for the business transfer that there will be a bulk transfer agreement under which the pension scheme of the new employer will provide day for day past service credits (or an equivalent recommended by the Government Actuary's Department as a suitable reflection of differences in benefit structures between the schemes) to staff choosing to transfer their accrued credits.

26. It will therefore be essential in future that negotiations between the public service pension scheme and the new employer's pension scheme are settled at a sufficiently early stage in the procurement. The contracting authority should then be able to explain to staff and their representatives what the terms for award of past service credits will be. Staff representatives will be able to discuss this with the contracting authority and GAD, and they will have a reasonable period in which to make any observations and, if necessary, to make representations directly to the Minister nominated as responsible for the project.

27. Only in exceptional circumstances should staff transfers be contemplated where the contract terms will not ensure appropriate bulk transfer terms. If there are exceptional circumstances justifying a waiver of this contract requirement, these should be explained and discussed with staff representatives at an early stage.

28. As in current practice, staff should normally be given a three month period following the issue to them of pension option forms in which to elect whether to preserve their accrued benefits or transfer them. Pension option forms should be issued as soon as practicable following the staff transfer.

29. Further guidance will be issued to contracting authorities concerning the mechanics of bulk transfer negotiations.

Subsequent transfers

30. Where a public service pension scheme associated with the public contracting authority is not a party to a bulk transfer agreement involving a further transfer of former public servants, the position is substantially more complicated. But appropriate bulk transfer terms should be sought for staff in transfers arising from second-round and subsequent contracting, and sub-contracting. Further guidance will be issued to contracting authorities concerning appropriate contractual safeguards covering availability of bulk transfer terms in subsequent TUPE transfers involving staff who in initial transfers from the Government were the subject of bulk transfer payments by a public service pension scheme.

* * * * *

31. Making these reforms to procurement arrangements will ensure fair treatment of staff pensions in public-private partnerships. It will continue to be important to look at each case on its merits, and to allow contractual mechanisms to continue to evolve towards better practice. The new approaches described above will guide current practice and new developments to ensure that staff are treated consistently on terms which are fair and predictable, and that there is in every case an opportunity for staff to understand fully the implications for their pensions and to make any representations they wish to the responsible Minister *well before* a Government contracting authority makes final arrangements for a business transfer involving the transfer of staff.

32. The Government will be ready to consider any further reforms which may be needed to cope with developments. In addition, for the longer term, it will review with representatives of employers and employees the scope for simplifying the administration of public – private partnerships, for instance by developing 'model schemes' or industry-wide multi-employer schemes which are broadly comparable with public service schemes and can facilitate transfers of staff between employers more easily as public – private partnership arrangements become more important to the delivery of public services.

ASSESSMENT OF BROAD COMPARABILITY OF PENSION RIGHTS

STATEMENT OF PRACTICE BY THE GOVERNMENT ACTUARY

The Government has issued a Code of Practice entitled *"Transfers of Government Staff: A Fair Deal for Pensions*, describing the key steps which the Government is taking when staff are transferred within the public service, or from the public service to the private sector, with their work. Central to the process is the requirement for an assessment of whether pension arrangements being offered to employees by their new employer are "broadly comparable" to those provided by their existing employers. This requirement relates only to the period of employment after the change of employer. Exceptionally, if comparability is not available, there is a requirement for the valuation of any detriment on pensions to be offset by elements of the remuneration package outside the pension scheme.

This Statement of Practice sets out the principles on which the Government Actuary's Department (GAD) undertakes its assessments of broad comparability.

Assessments may be commissioned by a public service employer, or by a contracting authority, on a one-off basis in relation to a specific group of staff. They may also be commissioned by a private sector employer with a view to obtaining a "passport" that his pension scheme is broadly comparable to a specific public service scheme for any group of employees who may transfer from that scheme to his employment over a given period. In either case, the principles are the same. For a passport, where a specific group of employees cannot be identified, the tests are conducted using a very large range of employee profiles containing different characteristics affecting the value of pension rights, for example age, gender, salary level and service length.

Benefits Against Which Assessment Is Made

The assessment will be made against those benefits provided as a right from the current employer's pension scheme, for which the employees are eligible, and the contributions which employees pay towards that scheme. The assessment will not take account of any benefits which are payable solely as a result of a member being declared redundant, either compulsorily or voluntarily, where those exceed the normal benefits available to an individual who resigns from employment at that time.

The assessment excludes the injury benefits payable by public service employers which provide a minimum income guarantee as a result of injury or death while in the service of the employer.

It is recognised that there is uncertainty over the legal protection for benefits available on redundancy and injury within the Transfer of Undertakings (Protection of Employment) Regulations 1981. If so requested by a public service employer or contracting authority, an additional assessment of comparability of the arrangements being offered by the new employer against a base of those on offer with the existing public service employer will be undertaken.

General Principles

The general principles on which the assessment of broad comparability is made on transfers from the public service to the private sector are set out below. Corresponding principles apply on other transfers. It must be recognised that there is a very wide range of possible remuneration packages, including pensions, and that some flexibility may need to be applied in the practical implementation of these principles.

Value

- The overall value of the new scheme should be equal to or greater than that of the current scheme.
- In addition to the test of overall value, assessments of value will be made separately for different types of individual, e.g. for different pay levels, for different ages, and for any other characteristics which could reasonably be expected to have a material impact on the value of pension benefits.
- Value is assessed by calculating, on consistent assumptions and methods, the underlying employer costs, in excess of the employee's share of the cost, of providing the benefits under the scheme which will accrue over the remaining working life.
- Value is considered as that in the hands of the employee gross of any liability to tax.

Contributions

- Schemes with higher employee contributions, will not be deemed broadly comparable because of the implied reduction in net pay (unless a compensating pay rise is proposed).

Benefits

- The range of benefits provided under the new schemes must at least match that provided by the current scheme.
- Benefits must be available from the new scheme in respect of the same events and at the same time as would have arisen in the existing scheme.
- In some cases, the amount of benefit may be lower on a particular contingency than under the current scheme, but this will need to be balanced by better benefits on other contingencies.
- Normal retirement age – at which full unreduced retirement benefits are available without employer consent and at which deferred benefits are payable – will be no greater than in current scheme.
- The initial rate of pension at normal retirement age should normally be no lower than that in the former scheme.
- Shortfalls in the level of pensions increases offered must be offset by better benefits elsewhere.
- In defined benefit schemes, benefits and contributions must be calculated on a definition of pensionable pay of at least the value of that applying in the current scheme.
- Under the arrangements for contracting-out of the State

Earnings-Related Pension Scheme currently in place, schemes which are either contracted-out or not contracted-out will be considered for broad comparability.

- Time spent with the current employer which would have counted towards qualification for benefits in the existing scheme will count in the new employer's scheme as qualifying service, regardless of whether or not accrued rights are transferred to the new scheme.

Membership

- All those eligible to participate in the current scheme will automatically be admitted to the new scheme from the date of transfer of employment without medical examination. This would not interfere with an employee exercising his/her right to choose to opt out of scheme membership.

Security

- It is recognised that the security of a private sector scheme cannot be provided in the same form as that applying in the public service, but specific safeguards will be sought in the following areas:
  - member representation on trustee bodies
  - protection of accrued rights, on an on-going basis, on any rule change
  - changes inspired by the employer, including loss of the contract, involving joining another pension scheme will trigger the offer of a bulk transfer payment or enhancement of benefits within the scheme, to a level commensurate with existing benefits.

Type of Scheme

- Only defined benefit schemes will be certified as broadly comparable to defined benefit schemes; only defined contribution schemes will be certified as broadly comparable to defined contribution schemes.
- A test of adequacy of contribution (for a defined contribution scheme) or of benefit design where broad comparability cannot apply (for a defined benefit scheme) will be carried out with the aim, but not the certainty, of ensuring benefits of similar value are expected to emerge.
- When the transfer is between defined benefit and defined contribution schemes, (or vice versa), specific provision should be made for death benefits.

Certification

Pension proposals which satisfy my view of broad comparability will be certified as such. The onus, as set out in the certificate, will be on the current employer to ensure that the pension promises made by the prospective new employer are delivered for the staff concerned.

The certificate will detail the key design features of the proposed pension arrangement and any associated undertakings provided by the new employer. It will be written in plain English. It will be in a form which can be distributed to the employees and their representatives.

Where a passport application is being considered an interim certificate will be issued if the formal documentation and approvals from regulatory bodies are not in place.

C D Daykin   **26 May 1999**
Government Actuary
London

ANNEX B

OVERVIEW

12 Guiding Principles in Using Market Testing and Contracting Out, Hansard, 4 November 1997, Col 94

Better Quality Services – a Handbook on creating Public/Private Partnerships through Market Testing and Contracting Out, The Stationery Office July 1998, ISBN 0-11-630964-4

Better Quality Services: Guidance for Senior Managers, The Stationery Office, July 1998 ISBN 0-11130152-2 A summary of the above handbook Efficiency Plans – Guidance for Development and Use, Cabinet Office, November 1995, ISBN 07115 0305 2 and amendments, November 1996 – describes the various efficiency techniques

Appraisal and Evaluation in Central Government, the "Green Book", HM Treasury, 1997

Keeping an Eye on the Government's Own Costs, useful ideas on assessing and comparing performances, HM Treasury, 1997

Deregulation and Contracting Out Act 1994 – An Explanatory Guide, Cabinet Office (originally issued by the Department of Trade and Industry), 1994

Procurement Policy Guidance and Procurement Practice Guidance (CUP Guidance, as was), HM Treasury (various dates)

Guidance on Agency Reviews, Cabinet Office, 1995

Towards Best Practice: An evaluation of the Public Sector Benchmarking Project 1996–98, Cabinet Office, 1998

Partnership for Prosperity: The Private Finance Initiative, HM Treasury, 1997

Selling Government Services into Wider Markets – policy and guidance notes, HM Treasury, 1998

CUP Guidance Note: No 40

CUP Guidance Note: No 44

The Duties of an Accounting Officer, HM Treasury, 1994

A Guide to Quality Schemes for the Public Sector, Cabinet Office, 1999

Public Sector Benchmarking Project Brochure of Services Available, version 3, Cabinet Office, 1999

Assessing Excellence, Cabinet Office, 1999

HOW TO SUCCEED

Competing for Quality Policy Review, HMSO 1996, ISBN 0-11-430142-5

Service First – The New Charter Programme, Cabinet Office, 1998

CUP Guidance Note: No 40

CUP Guidance Note: No 46 Quality Assurance

CUP Guidance Note: No 53 Procurement Training

CUP Guidance Note: No 55

CUP Guidance Note: No 56

CUP Guidance Note: No 59

CUP Guidance Note: No 61

Code of Practice on Access to Government Information, 2nd Edition, 1997

Guidance on Interpretation of Code of Practice on Access to Government Information, 2nd Edition, 1997

"Dear Procurement Officer" Letter DPO (98) 2, of 13 January 1998

Consultants: How to Use Them, in the Pay and Grading Guidance Notes, Cabinet Office, 1996

Use of External Management Consultants, Efficiency Unit Scrutiny, Cabinet Office, 1995

Setting New Standards, Cm 2840

MANAGING STAFF

The Transfer of Undertakings (Protection of Employment) Regulations 1981, as amended

Code of Practice for TUPE Transfers in MOD Contracts, Ministry of Defence 1998

For Your Future Security – Your Pension Scheme Benefits Explained, 1996, published by the Civil Service Pensions Division, Cabinet Office, Office of Public Service

OPS Pay Delegation Guidance Note 32: Trade Union Recognition and Bargaining Arrangements, September 1994, amendment, November 1995

Guidance on Privatisations and Redundancy Guarantees: letter from HM Treasury to Principal Establishment and Finance Officers, 2 March 1994

Health and Safety Executive's Infoline: tel 0541 545500

PREPARING THE GROUND – SCOPING AND ASSESSING FEASIBILITY

Setting New Standards – A Strategy for Government Procurement Cm 2840 HMSO May 1995, ISBN 0-10128402-0

Maximising Value from Public Sector Assets: Selling Services into Wider Markets, HM Treasury

Competing for Quality Policy Review, HMSO July 1996, ISBN 0-11-430142-5

CUP Guidance Note: No 40

CUP Guidance Note: No 51

CUP Guidance Note: No 57 Strategic Partnering in Government, HM Treasury, Procurement Group

Towards Best Practice: An evaluation of the first two years of the Public Sector Benchmarking project 199698, Cabinet Office, 1996

Partnerships for Prosperity: The Private Finance Initiative, HM Treasury Taskforce, 1997

INVITING BIDS

CUP Guidance Note 27 Approved Suppliers (Vendors and Contractors) Lists

CUP Guidance Note 30, Specification Writing

CUP Guidance Note 40, the Competitive Tendering Process

CUP Guidance Note 44, Service Legal Agreements

Trade Sales including Management Buy Outs, HM Treasury (1996 – new edition expected)

Maximising Value from Public Sector Assets: Selling Services into Wider Markets, HM Treasury

Government Opportunities, Business Information Publications Ltd, Glasgow

CUP Guidance Note 51, Introduction to the EC Procurement Rules

CUP Guidance Note 59: Supplier Appraisal Questionnaire; Invitation to Appraisal Interview; Invitation to Tender

CUP Guidance Notes: Nos 59A – 59D CUP Guidance Note 60, Supplier Appraisal

RESPONDING TO INVITATIONS TO TENDER

Trade Sales including Management Buy Outs (MBOs), HM Treasury

Selling Government Services into Wider Markets – policy and guidance notes, HM Treasury, 1998

Market Testing Costing Guidance, HM Treasury, 1994

Fees and Charges Guide, HM Treasury

CUP Guidance Note: No 35, Life Cycle Costing

CUP Guidance Note: No 59C, Documentation: Model Invitation to Tender

Appraisal and Evaluation in Central Government, "The Green Book" HM Treasury, 1997

EVALUATING BIDS

CUP Guidance Note: No 40 The Competitive Tendering Process

CUP Guidance Note: No 48

CUP Guidance Note: No 55 Debriefing

CUP Guidance Note: No 56

CUP Guidance Note: No 60 Supplier Appraisal

Appraisal and Evaluation in Central Government: "The Green Book", HM Treasury, 1997

Market Testing Costing Guidance, HM Treasury, 1994

CONTRACTS

Competing for Quality Policy Review, HMSO, 1996, ISBN 0-11-430142-5

CUP Guidance Note: No 1

CUP Guidance Note: No 19

CUP Guidance Note 30: Specification Writing

CUP Guidance Note 61: Contract Management

CUP Guidance Note 51: Disputes Resolution

CUP Guidance Note 58: Incentivisation

CUP Guidance Note 59D: Documentation: Model Conditions of Contract

CUP Guidance Note 61: Contract Management

RETENDERING

CUP Guidance Note 43: Project Evaluation

Civil Service Commissioners' Recruitment Code

Civil Service Management Code

LOCAL GOVERNMENT

DETR Circular 16/97 Local Government Act 1992: Competition in the Provision of Local Authority Services – Guidance on the Conduct of Compulsory Competitive Tendering (para 29 to 33)

Department of Environment Issues Paper: Handling TUPE matters in relation to CCT (21 January 1994)

Handling of Pension Matters in Relation to TUPE (15 March 1995)

Handling of Pensions Matters in Relation to CCT (28 June 1995)

TREASURY TASKFORCE GUIDANCE

Partnerships for Prosperity (November 97)

A Step by step guide to the PFI procurement process (April 98)

Policy Statement No1: PFI and Public Expenditure Allocations (October 97)

Policy Statement No2: Public Sector Comparators and Value for Money (March 98)

Policy Statement No3: PFI and Public Expenditure Allocations for Non-departmental Public Bodies (August 98)

Policy Statement No 4: Disclosure of Information and Consultation with Staff and other Interested Parties (August 98)

Technical Note No 1: How to account for PFI Transactions (September 97) – update expected shortly

Technical Note No 2: How to follow EC Procurement Procedure and advertise in the OJEC (June 98)

Technical Note No 3: How to appoint and manage Advisers (August 98)

Case study material

Private Finance and IS/IT: case study – "TAFMIS ... and after" (Cabinet Office March 98)

Colfox School Dorset – A Case Study on the first DBFO School Project (HM Treasury Taskforce March 98)

Appendix 12

CODE OF PRACTICE ON WORKFORCE MATTERS IN PUBLIC SECTOR SERVICE CONTRACTS

1. This document sets out an approach to workforce matters in public sector service contracts which involve a transfer of staff from the public sector organisation to the service provider, or in which staff originally transferred out from the public sector organisation as a result of an outsourcing are TUPE transferred to a new provider under a retender of a contract. This Code will form part of the service specification and conditions for all such contracts, except those where the Best Value Code of Practice on Workforce Matters in Local Authority Service Contracts applies, or where other exemptions have been announced.[1]

2. The Code recognises that there is no conflict between good employment practice, value for money and quality of service. On the contrary, quality and good value will not be provided by organisations who do not manage workforce issues well. The intention of the public sector organisation is therefore to select only those providers who offer staff a package of terms and conditions which will secure high quality service delivery throughout the life of the contract. These must be sufficient to recruit and motivate high quality staff to work on the contract and designed to prevent the emergence of a 'two-tier workforce', dividing transferees and new joiners working beside each other on the same contracts.

3. Service providers who intend to cut costs by driving down the terms and conditions for staff, whether for transferees or for new joiners taken on to work beside them, will not be selected to provide services for the public sector organisation. However, nothing in this Code should discourage public sector organisations or service providers from addressing productivity issues by working with their workforces in a positive manner to achieve continuous improvement in the services they deliver.

Treatment of transferees

4. In its contracting-out of services, the public sector organisation will apply the principles set out in the Cabinet Office Statement of Practice on Staff Transfers in the Public Sector and the annex to it, A Fair Deal for Staff

---

1   Exemptions include: public corporations and trading funds, Independent Sector Treatment Centres, transfers where the Retention of Employment Model for NHS PFI contracts applies, higher and further education institutions and Academies.

Pensions. The service provider will be required to demonstrate its support for these principles and its willingness to work with the public sector organisation fully to implement them.

5. The intention of the Statement is that staff will transfer and that TUPE should apply, and that in circumstances where TUPE does not apply in strict legal terms, the principles of TUPE should be followed and the staff involved should be treated no less favourably than had the Regulations applied.

6. The annex to the Statement requires the terms of a business transfer specifically to protect the pensions of transferees. **Transferring staff should be offered membership of a pension scheme which is broadly comparable to the public service pension scheme which they are leaving.**

Treatment of new joiners to an outsourced workforce

7. Where the service provider recruits new staff to work on a public service contract alongside staff transferred from the public sector organisation, it will offer employment on fair and reasonable terms and conditions which are, overall, no less favourable than those of transferred employees. The service provider will also offer reasonable pension arrangements (as described at paragraph 10 below).

8. The principle underpinning the provisions of paragraph 7 is to consider employees' terms and conditions (other than pensions arrangements which are dealt with in paragraph 10) in the round – as a 'package'. This Code does not prevent service providers from offering new recruits a package of non-pension terms and conditions which differs from that of transferred staff, so long as the overall impact of the changes to this package meets the conditions in paragraph 7. The aim is to provide a flexible framework under which the provider can design a package best suited to the delivery of the service, but which will exclude changes which would undermine the integrated nature of the team or the quality of the workforce.

9. The service provider will consult representatives of a trade union where one is recognised, or other elected representatives of the employees where there is no recognised trade union, on the terms and conditions to be offered to such new recruits.

(References to 'trade unions' throughout this code should be read to refer to other elected representatives of the employees where there is no recognised trade union.) The arrangements for consultation will involve a genuine dialogue. The precise nature of the arrangements for consultation is for agreement between the service provider and the recognised trade unions. The intention is that contractors and recognised trade unions should be able to agree on a particular package of terms and conditions, in keeping with the terms of this Code, to be offered to new joiners.

Pension arrangements for new joiners to an outsourced workforce

10. The service provider will be required to offer new recruits taken on to work on the contract beside transferees one of the following pension provision arrangements:

- membership of a good quality employer pension scheme, either being a contracted out, final-salary based defined benefit scheme, or a defined contribution scheme. For defined contribution schemes the employer must match employee contributions up to 6%, although either could pay more if they wished;

- a stakeholder pension scheme, under which the employer will match employee contributions up to 6%, although either could pay more if they wished.

On a retender of a contract to which this Code applies the new service provider will be required to offer one of these pensions options to any staff who transfer to it and who had prior to the transfer a right under the Code to one of these pension options.

Monitoring arrangements

11. Throughout the length of the contract, the service provider will provide the public sector organisation with information as requested which is necessary to allow the public sector organisation to monitor compliance with the conditions set out in this Code. This information will include the terms and conditions for transferred staff and the terms and conditions for employees recruited to work on the contract after the transfer.

12. Such requests for information will be restricted to that required for the purpose of monitoring compliance, will be designed to place the minimum burden on the service provider commensurate with this, and will respect commercial confidentiality. The service provider and the public sector organisation will also support a review of the impact of the Code, drawn up in consultation with representatives of the public sector organisations, contractors, trade unions and will provide information as requested for this purpose. Such requests will follow the same principles of proportionality and confidentiality.

Enforcement

13. The public sector organisation will enforce the obligations on the service provider created under this Code. Employees and recognised trade unions should, in the first instance, seek to resolve any complaints they have about how the obligations under this Code are being met, directly with the service provider. Where it appears to the public sector organisation that the service provider is not meeting its obligations, or where an employee of the service provider or a recognised trade union writes to the authority to say that it has been unable to resolve a complaint directly with the service provider, the public sector organisation will first seek an explanation from the service provider. If the service provider's response satisfies the public sector organisation that the Code is being followed, the public sector organisation will inform any complainant of this. If the response does not satisfy the public sector organisation it will ask the service provider to take immediate action to remedy this. If, following such a request, the service provider still appears to the public sector organisation not to be complying with the Code, the public sector organisation will seek to enforce the terms of the contract, which will incorporate this Code. In addition, where a service provider has not complied with this Code, the public sector organisation will not be bound to consider that provider for future work.

14. The contract shall include a provision for resolving disputes about the application of this Code in a fast, efficient and cost-effective way as an

alternative to litigation, and which is designed to achieve a resolution to which all the parties are committed. The service provider, public sector organisation and recognised trade unions or other staff representatives, shall all have access to this 'alternative dispute resolution' (ADR) process (Annex A to this Code sets out the ADR mechanism).

15. Alongside this Code, the appropriate Government Department will publish contact details for employees or trade unions to seek advice in cases where they consider that the public sector organisation has failed to meet its responsibilities under paragraph 13.

Sub-contractors

16. This Code sets out procedures for handling matters between the public sector organisation and a primary service provider. Where the primary service provider transfers staff originally in the employ of the public sector organisation to a sub-contractor in consequence of the terms of the primary service provider's obligations to the public sector organisation, the primary service provider will be responsible for the observance of this Code by the sub-contractor.

Operation of the Code

17. Government departments will monitor the operation of the Code, following consultation with relevant employers and trade unions.

Cabinet Office
March 2005

ANNEX A

CODE OF PRACTICE ON WORKFORCE MATTERS: ALTERNATIVE DISPUTE RESOLUTION PROCEDURE

1 Introduction

This sets out a procedure for resolving disputes arising from the application of the Code of Practice on Workforce Matters. The procedure should be a last resort and all parties will make their best efforts to resolve problems by agreement. The ADR should be fast, efficient and cost-effective.

2 The need to exhaust local procedures

The parties must exhaust all normal local procedures as required by paragraph 9 and paragraph 13 of the Code before invoking the Alternative Dispute Resolution procedure (ADR) provided for in paragraph 14.

3 Who is responsible for resolving disputes?

The ADR procedure will be under the supervision of an independent person appointed from an approved list supplied by ACAS. If the parties so agree, they may appoint two "wing members" with an employer and trade union background to assist the independent person.

4   The dispute resolution process

Disputes will be resolved using the following three-stage procedure.

Stage 1: Initial reference to the independent person.

The independent person will be invited to answer three questions:
  (i)   Is this a dispute about the application of the Code?

If the answer is no, the matter can proceed no further. If yes, then the independent person will move to question (ii).
  (ii)   Have the parties exhausted local procedures?

If the answer is no, then the parties will be invited to make further local efforts to resolve the dispute. If yes, then the independent person will conduct an independent assessment, by answering question (iii) and giving reasons for the answer.
  (iii)   Do the terms and conditions of employment on offer to new employees comply with the Code?

If the answer is yes, then the matter is deemed to be concluded and the contractor can continue to offer the same package of conditions to new employees. If the answer is no, then the dispute will proceed to Stage 2.

Time limit: Twenty working days.

Stage 2: Discussions with a view to reaching an agreement on compliant terms and conditions

Stage 2 begins with the parties being invited to seek to resolve the matter through further discussions.

The independent person will make themselves available to the parties to facilitate the process. The parties also have the option of establishing other arrangements for mediation.

If the parties can reach an agreement consistent with the Code then the matter is closed and the new package of conditions of employment will be applied both to new starters and to those employed during the dispute.

If no agreement can be reached within the allotted time then the dispute will proceed to Stage 3.

Time limit: Ten working days, with the possibility that this might be extended by the agreement of the parties and with the consent of the independent person.

Stage 3: Final Reference to the Independent Person

The independent person invites the parties to make final submissions. If the independent person then believes it would be worthwhile, the parties may be given a short period of further discussion.

If there is no value in giving the parties more time – or if during any discussion the parties were unable to agree on how to bring the matter to a successful conclusion – then the independent person will proceed to a final binding arbitration. Having heard the evidence and reached a conclusion the independent person will impose a revised package of terms and conditions applicable to each of the affected employees.

Time limit: Ten working days.

PRECEDENTS, ETC

PRECIPITATE, ETC

Appendix 13

CHECKLIST – INFORMATION AND CONSULTATION REQUIREMENTS

CHECKLIST OF RESPONSIBILITIES UNDER THE TRANSFER OF UNDERTAKINGS (PROTECTION OF EMPLOYMENT) REGULATIONS 2006, SI 2006/246, REGS 13–16[1]

1. Identify which of the transferor's employees are 'affected employees'. These are employees who – regardless of whether they are likely to transfer or not – may be affected by the transfer or may be affected by measures taken in connection with the transfer. Consider whether this is merely limited to the transferring function/entity or to a wider part of the transferor's business.

2. Identify, in respect of each description of affected employee, who are the appropriate representatives of those affected employees. These may be:

    2.1 representatives of an independent trade union recognised by the transferor; or

    2.2 where there is no independent recognised trade union:

        2.2.1 representatives already appointed/elected by the affected employees for other purposes who have authority to act in this capacity, bearing in mind the purposes for which they were appointed/elected; or

        2.2.2 representatives elected by the employees for this purpose in an election which the transferor must facilitate.

3. The transferor has an obligation to inform – and maybe also to consult – the appropriate representatives of all affected employees employed by the transferor. Define the category of any affected employees who are represented by a recognised union. The union representatives will be the appropriate representatives for these purposes.

4. To the extent that the transferor does not recognise a trade union in respect of any given description of affected employees, identify whether there are any appointed/elected employee representatives already in place for other purposes who could be said to have authority from those

---

1   This checklist is written from the perspective of the purchaser of a business/incoming service provider in contemplation of a relevant transfer within the meaning of TUPE, reg 2 and is intended as a guide to the key responsibilities, set out in chronological order. The transferee will also have responsibilities – to deliver to the transferor information about measures and possibly to follow a like process of information and consultation where it has affected employees. For more detailed treatment of these issues see **chapter 5**.

employees to receive information and to be consulted for these purposes. If there are such representatives already in place, it is the transferor's choice whether the transferor deems them to be the appropriate representatives for the purposes of this TUPE information and consultation exercise or whether the transferor elects to inform/consult with alternative representatives.

5.   If the transferor would prefer to have new representatives elected (and assuming that the employees concerned are prepared to participate in electing new representatives) an election should be held for the specific purposes of appointing representatives for this TUPE exercise. The following steps should be taken:

- It is the transferor's responsibility to run the election. The transferor must make such arrangements as are 'reasonably practical' to ensure that the election is fair. Consider how this can best be achieved – make sure that every affected employee has written notice of how the election procedure is to be conducted; give clear instructions as to what candidates need to do to put themselves forward; ensure that the ballot is a secret ballot; take steps to ensure that employees are not concerned about being in any way open to a detriment by reason of participating.

- The transferor must determine how many representatives should be elected. There must be enough to represent all the affected employees. Ensure that there is at least one representative in respect of each class of employee. It is sensible to have enough representatives so that each constituency will always be represented notwithstanding occasional absences from meetings. Decide whether the consultation exercise can go ahead as one exercise or whether it is necessary to consult with different categories of employees separately.

- Determine the term of office of the representatives – ensure that it is long enough to last at least until the transfer has taken place.

- Candidates must be affected employees as at the date of the election. A candidate can be excluded – but not without good reason. Only affected employees can vote. An employee should have a number of votes equivalent to the number of representatives to be elected (or, where he or she is a member of a particular class, a number of votes equivalent to the number of representatives to be elected in respect of that particular class).

6.   If there is no recognised union, no representatives already in place and the employees do not respond to the prospect of an election, the transferor should issue the necessary information to the affected employees.

7.   When representatives have been identified, the necessary information should be given to them.[2] This is:

- the fact that the relevant transfer is to take place, the date when it is/is proposed to take place and the reasons for it; and

- the legal, economic and social implications of the transfer for the affected employees; and

---

2   See precedent letter at **appendix 17**.

- the measures which the transferor envisages it will, in connection with the transfer, take in relation to those employees or, if the transferor envisages that no measures will be taken, that fact; and
- the measures which the new employer envisages it will take in connection with the transfer in respect of transferring employees or, if none are envisaged, that fact.

8. The transferor should serve a formal request on the new employer asking it to let the transferor have the information necessary to enable compliance with the fourth bullet point in 7 above.[3] The new employer has a legal obligation to do so.

9. The information listed in paragraph 7 above must be given long enough before the transfer to enable consultation between the transferor and the appropriate representatives of the affected employees to take place. This requires a value judgement about how much time will be required. Unless constrained by other factors, the earlier the process begins, the more likely it is that these requirements will be fulfilled. Regard must be had to changes in the information, which will require the delivery of updated information and further consultation. Consultation is only necessary where measures are envisaged – in the event that no measures are envisaged in respect of affected employees of a particular description, there is no need to consult in relation to those employees and therefore the information may be conveyed only shortly prior to the transfer if the transferor chooses to delay. Only rarely will no measures be envisaged so as to dispense with the need to consult.

10. Information must be given in writing. It may be delivered to the representatives, sent by post to an address notified to the transferor by the representative or – in the case of union representatives – posted to the head/main office of the union.

11. Consultation must be entered into with a view to seeking the agreement of the representatives to the measures which are proposed. Representations of the representatives must be considered by the transferor and a reply must be given, with reasons where the representations are rejected.

12. The process of identifying the affected employees and the representatives should commence as early as possible. The results of this process should be kept under review as the transaction proceeds. Information should be gathered and imparted in good time for proper consultation. There is little point in running the risk of substantial penalties for non-compliance unless there are other valid reasons for delay. If there are special circumstances which render it impracticable to comply with these requirements, the transferor should take all practicable steps to comply in part. The legal timetable should be seen as a set of minimum requirements to be integrated into a wider programme of information and consultation designed to meet HR objectives such as motivating and reassuring staff.

---

3   See precedent letter at **appendix 10**.

Appendix 14

EMPLOYEE TRANSFER AGREEMENT

DATED

(1) [   ]

(2) [   ]

EMPLOYEE TRANSFER AGREEMENT[1]

THIS AGREEMENT is made the   day of   200[   ]

BETWEEN[2]

(1)   **[CLIENT]** whose registered office is at [   ] (the '**Client**');

and

(2)   **[SERVICE PROVIDER]** whose registered office is at [   ] (the '**Service Provider**')

WHEREAS

(A)   The Service Provider has agreed to provide the Client with the Services.

(B)   The parties acknowledge that there will be a transfer to the Service Provider of employees engaged wholly or mainly in the provision of services prior to the Transfer Date of a like nature to the Services.

(C)   This Agreement sets out the provisions agreed between the parties in relation to the transfer to the Service Provider of such employees.

---

1   Where employees move as a consequence of service provision changes, the documentation can take a number of forms (assuming that the parties wish to enter into an agreement regulating the employment law consequences of the transfer). A separate employment transfer agreement is sometimes prepared – this precedent is typical of the sort of document that would be prepared as a part of a suite of documents for an outsourcing transaction. Alternatively, similar provisions may be found as part of a more general document.

2   The contract is entered into between the client, to whom the service is provided, and the incoming service provider. If the services in question are already being carried out by a third party, the transfer of employees will not take place between the parties to the employee transfer agreement, but from the outgoing contractor to the incoming contractor, between whom there will ordinarily not be a contract. Hence the employee transfer agreement must be seen as one element of a 'triangle' of relationships. The client can regulate the transfer by means of the exit provisions in his contract with the incumbent and by entering into an employee transfer agreement with the incoming contractor.

IT IS AGREED as follows:

1.   **DEFINITIONS AND INTERPRETATION**

1.1   **Definitions**

In this Agreement (except where the context otherwise requires) the following words and expressions will have the following meanings:

'Disclosure Letter'	means the disclosure letter annexed to [this Agreement]
'Employee Liability Information'	means the information which a transferor is obliged to notify to a transferee pursuant to Regulation 11(2) of the Regulations regarding any person employed by him who is assigned to the organised grouping of resources or employees which is the subject of the Relevant Transfer
'Employees'	means all those employees of the Client and/or the Outgoing Contractor[3] wholly and/or mainly engaged in the Services[4] immediately before the Transfer Date whose names are listed in Schedule [ ], save for those who object to their transfer pursuant to Regulation 4(7) of the Regulations or otherwise resign or treat their employment as terminated
'Outgoing Contractor'[5]	means [ ]
'Personnel Information'	means all contracts of employment, policies, documents, files, details, records or information (whether stored electronically or otherwise) in [the Client's] possession that relate to the Employees or the Employees' terms and conditions of employment

---

3   The client may be reluctant to vouch for employees who are not its own employees. However, a properly drafted contract with the outgoing contractor will provide protections which can be passed on for the benefit of the incoming contractor.

4   The test in the *Botzen* case (*Botzen v Rotterdamische Droogdok Maatschappij BV* [1985] ECR 519, Case No 186/83) is who is 'assigned' to the transferring entity. The 'wholly or mainly engaged' wording is typically used in such clauses as it is felt to be a more meaningful and readily applied test for these purposes.

5   An incoming service provider will not draw a significant distinction between the employees transferring from the client and those transferring from a third party such as an outgoing service provider or a subcontractor. Liabilities transfer in either case; pricing assumptions are affected likewise. Hence the need for the client to foresee these issues and to ensure that suitable exit provisions are in place with contractors so as to be able to offer the necessary protections to the incoming contractor.

'Potential Returning Employees'	those personnel who are employees of the Service Provider or any Sub-Contractor and who are assigned to the provision of the Services or a relevant part of the Services for the purposes of the Regulations
'Regulations'	means the Transfer of Undertakings (Protection of Employment) Regulations 2006 (SI 246/2006) and/or any other regulations enacted for the purpose of implementing the Acquired Rights Directive (Council Directive 77/187/EEC, as amended by Council Directive 98/50 EEC and consolidated in Council Directive 2001/23/EC) into English law
'Replacement Service Provider'	means any alternative service provider appointed by the Client to perform the Services or any part of the Services after the Subsequent Transfer Date
'Relevant Transfer'	means a relevant transfer of an undertaking for the purposes of the Regulations
'Returning Employees'	means those persons listed in a Schedule to be agreed by the parties prior to the Subsequent Transfer Date who it is agreed were employed by the Service Provider (and/or any Sub-Contractor) wholly and/or mainly in the Services immediately before the Subsequent Transfer Date
'Services'	means the provision of [ ] services as more particularly described in the [Services Agreement]
'Sub-Contractor'	means any sub-contractor of the Service Provider appointed to perform the whole or any part of the Services
'Subsequent Transfer Date'	means the date or dates on which there is a transfer of responsibility for the provision of the Services or part of the Services between the Service Provider and the Client and/or a Replacement Service Provider (as the case may be) pursuant to the terms of the Services Agreement
'Transfer Date'	means [ ]
'Transferee'	means the person (being either or both of the Client or Replacement Service Provider) which takes on responsibility for the provision of the Services or part of the Services from the Service Provider on the Subsequent Transfer Date

1.2   Interpretation

In this Agreement (except where the context otherwise requires):

1.2.1 the clause headings are included for convenience only and will not affect the construction or interpretation of this Agreement;

1.2.2 the Schedules form part of this Agreement and will have effect as if set out in full in the body of this Agreement;

1.2.3 any reference to a Recital, Clause or Schedule is to the relevant recital, clause or schedule of this Agreement;

1.2.4 use of the singular includes the plural and vice versa;

1.2.5 words importing a particular gender do not exclude other genders;

1.2.6 any reference to a statute, statutory provision or statutory instrument includes a reference to that statute, statutory provision or statutory instrument together with all rules and regulations made under it as from time to time amended, consolidated or re-enacted; and

1.2.7 words which are defined in the [Services Agreement] shall have the same meaning in this Agreement.

2. INITIAL TRANSFER OF EMPLOYEES

2.1 Transferring Employees

2.1.1 The Client and the Service Provider intend and acknowledge[6] that the commencement of the Services on the Transfer Date by the Service Provider shall, with respect to the Employees, constitute a Relevant Transfer and agree that as a consequence of that Relevant Transfer the contracts of employment made between the Client (or, as the case may be, any Outgoing Contractor) and the Employees [and the collective agreements listed in the Disclosure Letter] (save insofar as such contracts [and such agreements] relate to benefits for old age, invalidity or survivors under any occupational pension scheme)[7] shall have effect from and after the Transfer Date as if originally made between the Service Provider and the Employees [(or between the Service Provider and the relevant trade union as the case may be)].

2.1.2 Notwithstanding the acknowledgement and agreement in clause 2.1.1 above and in recognition of the possibility that the transaction contemplated by this Agreement may be determined not to be a Relevant Transfer by a court or tribunal, the Service Provider shall with effect from the Transfer Date offer employment to each Employee on like terms to the terms on which they would have become employed by the Service Provider had there been a Relevant Transfer or, to the extent that it is not reasonably practicable to do so in respect of any such term, on terms which are not in such respect materially to the detriment of the Employee.[8]

---

6 See fn 9 at p 387.

7 From 6 April 2005, service providers have been obliged to establish a minimum level of pension provision for transferred employees, where such employees were entitled to participate in an occupational pension scheme prior to the transfer. This minimum 'safety net' requires the transferee to match employee contributions, up to 6% of salary, into a stakeholder pension, or offer an equivalent alternative (see **chapter 3**, at **3.115**, p 111). Hence this obligation is carved out of the general acknowledgement of the transfer of contractual terms.

8 See fn 9 at p 387. This clause provides certainty for both parties as to who will transfer and is likely to be particularly important in the context of contracts for the

2.1.3 The Service Provider shall (and shall procure that any Sub-Contractor shall) treat the period of continuous service of each Employee with the Client [and/or any Outgoing Contractor] up to the Transfer Date as continuous with such Employee's service with the Service Provider (or, where applicable, the Sub-Contractor).[9]

2.2 Information and Consultation

2.2.1 The Service Provider shall comply (and shall procure that any Sub-Contractor complies) with its obligations under Regulation 13 of the Regulations during the period prior to the Transfer Date.

2.2.2 The Client shall comply [and shall use reasonable endeavours to procure that any Outgoing Contractor complies] with its obligations under Regulations 13 and 14 of the Regulations during the period prior to the Transfer Date, save where the Client [and/or any Outgoing Contractor] is unable to do so as a result of the failure of the Service Provider and/or any Sub-Contractor to comply with their duties under Regulation 13 of the Regulations.

2.3 Indemnities

2.3.1 The Client[10] shall indemnify the Service Provider against all costs, claims, liabilities and expenses (including reasonable legal expenses) incurred by the Service Provider in connection with or as a result of:

(a) any claim or demand by any Employee (whether in contract, tort, under statute, pursuant to European law or otherwise) including, without limitation, any claim for unfair dismissal, wrongful dismissal, a redundancy payment, breach of contract, unlawful deduction from wages, discrimination on the grounds of sex, race, age, disability, sexual orientation, religion or religious belief, a protective award or a claim or demand of any other nature, in each case arising directly or indirectly from any act, fault or omission of the Client [or Outgoing Contractor] in respect of any Employee in the period on and before the Transfer Date;

(b) any failure by the Client [or the Outgoing Contractor] to comply with its [or their] obligations under Regulations 13 and 14 of the Regulations, or any award of compensation under Regulation 15 of the Regulations, save where such failure arises from the failure of the Service Provider and any Sub-Contractor to comply with its or their duties under Regulation 13 of the Regulations;

(c) any claim (including any individual employee entitlement

---

provision of services, where there is a need to price accurately the payroll cost of the workforce which will be deployed in the provision of the services.

9   The issue of continuity cannot be solved completely by the contract, where there is not a transfer pursuant to the provisions of TUPE. Continuity is a statutory concept and cannot be transferred by contract: see *Secretary of State for Employment v Globel Elastic Thread* [1979] IRLR 327, **chapter 3**, at **3.130**, note 147.

10 The ability of the client to give these indemnities without exposure will depend on the exit provisions in the contract with the incumbent contractor – ideally these indemnities will be tailored to match.

under or consequent on such a claim) by any trade union or other body or person representing the Employees (or other employees of the Client [or any Outgoing Contractor]) arising from or connected with any failure by the Client [or the Outgoing Contractor] to comply with any legal obligation to such trade union, body or person; and

(d)   [any claim made by a third party in connection with the contract of employment of an Employee pursuant to sections 1 or 2 of the Contracts (Rights of Third Parties) Act 1999 where such a claim arises as a result of any act, fault or omission of the Client [or the Outgoing Contractor] before, on or after Completion].[11]

2.3.2   The Service Provider shall indemnify the Client [(for itself and the Outgoing Contractor)] against all costs, claims, liabilities and expenses (including reasonable legal expenses) incurred by the Client [or the Outgoing Contractor] in connection with or as a result of:

(a)   any claim or demand by any Employee (whether in contract, tort, under statute, pursuant to European law or otherwise) including, without limitation, any claim for unfair dismissal, wrongful dismissal, a redundancy payment, breach of contract, unlawful deduction from wages, discrimination on the grounds of sex, race, age, disability, sexual orientation, religion or religious belief, a protective award or a claim or demand of any other nature, in each case arising directly or indirectly from any act, fault or omission of the Service Provider or any Sub-Contractor in respect of any Employee on or after the Transfer Date;

(b)   any failure by the Service Provider or any Sub-Contractor to comply with its obligations under Regulation 13 of the Regulations;

(c)   any claim (including any individual entitlement of an Employee under or consequent on such claim) by any trade union or other body or person representing the Employees arising from or connected with any failure by the Service Provider or any Sub-Contractor to comply with any legal obligation to such trade union, body or person;

(d)   any change or proposed change in the terms and conditions of employment or working conditions of the Employees on or after their transfer to the Service Provider on the Transfer Date, or to the terms and conditions of employment or working conditions of any person who would have been an Employee but for their resignation or decision to treat their

---

11   This clause seeks to protect the service provider where a third party seeks to claim rights under an employee's contract of employment. The likelihood of such claims is remote. An example would be the spouse of an employee who might bring a claim for loss of private medical insurance if the service provider does not provide this benefit.

employment as terminated under Regulation 4(9) of the Regulations on or before the Transfer Date as a result of any such changes;[12]

(e) the change of identity of employer occurring by virtue of the Regulations and/or this Agreement being significant and detrimental to any of the Employees, or to any person who would have been an Employee but for their resignation or decision to treat their employment as terminated under Regulation 4(9) of the Regulations on or before the Transfer Date as a result of the change in employer;

(f) [any claim made by a third party in connection with the contract of employment of an Employee pursuant to sections 1 or 2 of the Contracts (Rights of Third Parties) Act 1999 (including the rescission or variation of such a contract) where such a claim arises as a result of any actual or alleged act, fault or omission of the Service Provider or any Sub-Contractor on or after the Transfer Date].

2.4 **Employees Remaining Employed by the Client[/Outgoing Contractor]**

2.4.1 If as a result of the transaction contemplated by this Agreement it is found or alleged that any of the Employees remains an employee of the Client [or the Outgoing Contractor] after the Transfer Date:

(a) the Client shall notify the Service Provider, [and shall use reasonable endeavours to procure that the Outgoing Contractor shall notify the Service Provider], of that finding or allegation as soon as reasonably practicable after becoming aware of it;

(b) in consultation with the Client, the Service Provider shall within [7] days of becoming aware of the finding or allegation make that person a written offer of employment to commence immediately on the same terms and conditions as the Service Provider would be obliged to provide to that person if his employment had transferred pursuant to the Regulations and under which the Service Provider agrees to recognise that person's period of service with the Client [or the Outgoing Contractor], and the Client shall give all reasonable assistance requested by the Service Provider to persuade that employee to accept the offer;

(c) if the offer of employment made by the Service Provider is accepted by that person, the Client agrees to permit that person [(and to procure that the Outgoing Contractor permits that person)] to leave the Client's employment without having worked his full notice period, if that person so requests;

---

12 The dangers which can arise from the acts of an incoming contractor were highlighted in the case of *Oxford University v Humphries* [2000] IRLR 183, **chapter 5**, at **5.42**. See TUPE, reg 4(7) – whereby a person who objects to their transfer will not transfer under TUPE and reg 4(9), whereby an employee may treat his or her employment as having been terminated where a relevant transfer involves a substantial change in working conditions to the employee's material detriment. See also reg 4(11), which provides than an employee may terminate his or her contract without notice if the employer commits a repudiatory breach.

(d)   the Client [(or, where applicable, the Outgoing Contractor)] may within 28 days after becoming aware of that allegation or finding, if that person is still or still claims to be an employee of the Client (or Outgoing Contractor) and has not accepted an offer of employment with the Service Provider, dismiss the employee with immediate effect; and

(e)   the Service Provider shall indemnify and keep indemnified the Client against all costs, liabilities and expenses (including reasonable legal expenses) which the Client [(or, where applicable, the Outgoing Contractor)] may suffer or incur in respect of that dismissal in each case provided that the Client (or, where applicable, the Outgoing Contractor) takes all reasonable steps to minimise such costs, liabilities and expenses (including, for the avoidance of doubt, by following the statutory dispute resolution procedures where applicable).

2.5   Other Transferring Employees

2.5.1   If as a result of the transaction contemplated by this Agreement it is found or alleged that the employment of any person other than the Employees has transferred to the Service Provider or any Sub-Contractor on or after the Transfer Date pursuant to the Regulations:

(a)   the Service Provider shall notify the Client, or shall procure that the Sub-Contractor shall notify the Client, of that finding or allegation as soon as reasonably practicable after becoming aware of it;

(b)   in consultation with the Service Provider, the Client shall [(or shall use reasonable endeavours to procure that the Outgoing Contractor shall)] within [7] days of becoming aware of that allegation or finding make that person a written offer of employment to commence immediately on the same terms and conditions as that person was employed prior to the transfer (actual or alleged), and under which the Client [(or, where applicable, the Outgoing Contractor)] agrees to recognise that person's prior service with the Client [(or, where applicable, the Outgoing Contractor)], and the Service Provider shall give all reasonable assistance requested by the Client [(or, where applicable, the Outgoing Contractor)] to persuade that person to accept the offer;

(c)   the Service Provider (or, where applicable, the Sub-Contractor) may within 28 days after becoming aware of that allegation or finding, if that person is still or still claims to be an employee of the Service Provider (or, where applicable, the Sub-Contractor) and has not accepted an offer of employment with the Client, dismiss the employee with immediate effect; and

(d)   the Client shall indemnify and keep indemnified the Service Provider (both for itself and any Sub-Contractor) against all costs, liabilities and expenses (including reasonable legal expenses) which the Service Provider (or, where applicable, the Sub-Contractor) may suffer or incur in respect of that dismissal and the employment of that person up to the date of the dismissal and any other claim brought by that person, in each case provided that the Service Provider (or, where applicable, the Sub-Contractor) takes all reasonable steps to minimise such costs, liabilities and expenses (including, for the avoidance of doubt, by following the statutory dispute resolution procedures where applicable).

2.6 **Apportionments and Payments**[13]

2.6.1 The Client shall be responsible for all emoluments and outgoings in respect of the Employees (including, without limitation, all wages, bonuses, commission, PAYE and national insurance contributions and pension contributions) which are attributable to the period up to and including the Transfer Date (including bonuses or commission which are payable after the Transfer Date but attributable to the period on or before the Transfer Date), and will indemnify the Service Provider (both for itself and any Sub-Contractor) against all costs, claims, liabilities and expenses (including reasonable legal expenses) incurred by the Service Provider or any Sub-Contractor in respect of the same.

2.6.2 The Service Provider shall be responsible for all emoluments and outgoings in respect of the Employees (including, without limitation, all wages, bonuses, commission, PAYE and national insurance contributions and pension contributions) which are attributable to the period after the Transfer Date (including any bonuses or commission which are payable before the Transfer Date but which are attributable to the period after the Transfer Date), and will indemnify the Client [(both for itself and any Outgoing Contractor)] against all costs, claims, liabilities and expenses (including reasonable legal expenses) in respect of the same.

2.6.3 If any Employee has taken holiday in excess of holiday entitlement which has accrued in respect of that Employee at the Transfer Date, the Service Provider shall pay to the Client within one (1) month of the Transfer Date a sum equivalent to pay in lieu of such excess holiday. If any Employee has not taken all holiday which has accrued to that employee at the Transfer Date, the Client [will pay][will use reasonable efforts to ensure that the Outgoing Contractor will pay] to the Service Provider a sum equivalent to pay in lieu of such accrued but untaken holiday.

2.6.4 Within one (1) month of the Transfer Date, the Service Provider shall pay to the Client a sum equal to the outstanding balance on the Transfer Date of any loan, salary, advance or other agreed indebtedness of any Employee due to the Client [or Outgoing Contractor] immediately prior to the Transfer Date.

---

13 A number of practical issues surround the issue of prepayments. Whilst TUPE provides for the continuity of the relationship, there is a break from an accounting perspective. The employees will remain within their holiday entitlements, still have the right to benefits such as cars and insurance policies, but practical steps will need to be taken by the transferee employer to provide these. At the same time, the transferor may seek credit from the transferee in respect of advance payments made in respect of the employees, the benefit of which will be received by the transferee.

3. **WARRANTIES**[14]

3.1 The Client warrants that the Employee Liability Information:[15]

   3.1.1 [has been][will be] provided to the Service Provider at such time or times as are required by the Regulations;

   3.1.2 [was][will be] complete and accurate at the time it [was][is] provided to the Service Provider;

   3.1.3 [has been][will be] updated to take account of any changes to such information, as required by the Regulations.

3.2 The Client warrants that the Employees Schedule contains the name, date of birth, gender, date of commencement of employment, period of continuous employment, job title, salary and other benefits, notice period and holiday entitlement of each of the Employees.

3.3 The Client warrants that there are no employees other than the Employees who are wholly and/or mainly engaged in the Services at the Transfer Date.[16]

3.4 The Client warrants that the Personnel Information Schedule contains complete and accurate details of the Personnel Information and that there are no material terms and conditions of employment relating to any Employee which are not set out in the Personnel Information Schedule.

3.5 The Client warrants that it has not agreed to vary any of the terms and conditions of any of the Employees, and it has not made any changes to the terms and conditions of employment of any of the Employees in connection with the transfer of their employment to the Service Provider. For the avoidance of doubt, the reference to terms and conditions includes pay.

3.6 The Client warrants that no Employee is currently in receipt of benefits under a long-term disability insurance policy or similar scheme or arrangement.

3.7 The Client warrants that there have been no transfers of employees into the Services within the period of [six] months prior to the date of this Agreement or changes of job title or role amongst the Employees within such period.[17]

3.8 The Client warrants that no employees employed in the Services have been dismissed or have resigned within the period of [six] months prior to the date of this Agreement.

3.9 The Client warrants that there are no current claims, disputes, trade

---

14 Extensive warranties of the type found in the sale and purchase of a business are unusual in service change documentation. They are normally restricted to the accuracy of the details regarding the transferring staff. The impact of a breach is ordinarily felt in the price for the service and hence a price adjustment clause can be an effective way of providing a remedy.

15 Although TUPE requires the transferor to provide certain information to the transferee regarding staff assigned to the transferring undertaking, the scope of this duty is not as wide as the obligation which the transferee employer will want to impose. Moreover, the transferee employer will want to adjust the price for delivering the services, rather than seeking compensation in the tribunal.

16 Not required if 2.5.1(d) is included.

17 This clause is designed to give some protection against 'dumping', the transfer of surplus or substandard staff. The incoming employer must also be alert to the risk of the outgoing employer 'cherry picking' staff who would otherwise transfer (and who may have key skills or knowledge) so as to take them out of the scope of the transfer.

disputes, or industrial action of any type against the Client by any Employee or any representative of any Employee and the Client has not received any notification (whether verbal or written) threatening any such claims, disputes, trade disputes or industrial action.

4. **PRICE ADJUSTMENT**

4.1 If the cost to the Service Provider of employing personnel in the provision of the Services is greater than that which is set out in the [Employee Costs Schedule][18] as a result of:

4.1.1 the costs in the Employee Costs Schedule having been determined by the Service Provider on the basis of information set out in the Employees Schedule or Personnel Information Schedule which was, at the time at which it was delivered, erroneous or incomplete; and/or

4.1.2 any change in the terms and conditions of any of the Employees between the date of this Agreement and the Transfer Date [only to the extent that such costs exceed the percentage change in the Retail Price Index in respect of such period];[19] and/or

4.1.3 any pay award being made in respect of the salary and allowances of any Employee in the period between the date of this Agreement and the relevant Transfer Date [but only to the extent that such pay award exceeds the percentage change in the Retail Price Index in respect of such period]; and/or

4.1.4 any increase in the number of employees specified in the Employees Schedule who transfer to the Service Provider;[20] and/or

4.1.5 any increase arising from a variation in job title, role or function or any material change in the skill sets of the Employees or any other difference in employee information and specifications that at the relevant Transfer Date is not reflected in the Employees Schedule or Personnel Information Schedule,

then there shall be a price adjustment. The price adjustment shall operate as follows:[21]

5. **POST TRANSFER REPORTING**[22]

---

18 This will be some point of reference whereby it is clear that the actual cost of employing transferees exceeds the budgeted cost by reason of inaccurate/incomplete information having been delivered.

19 The position is complicated where there is a delay between the date on which the contract is signed and the date upon which the workforce transfers. Some element of movement in the employee data may have been anticipated within the pricing model.

20 There is already protection (at clause 2.4.1(e) – indemnity – and clause 3.3 – warranty) to cover the possibility of further employees transferring; however, the price adjustment is a more satisfactory way of addressing any such discrepancies and leaves the other clauses as a fall back.

21 Detail will need to be inserted at this stage, depending on how the services have been priced in the first place.

22 This will only be appropriate in certain cases. Reporting of this nature is common in public sector outsourcing and may be appropriate in a private sector context. Given that many service contracts will be short term and that the workforce will in all likelihood return to the client or transfer to a new service provider on exit, it is legitimate for the client to retain an interest in the HR management of the workforce.

5.1 The Service Provider shall provide the Client with the following information as part of the normal reporting regime of the contract on a monthly basis:

    5.1.1 Proposed, agreed or imposed changes to terms and conditions of employment in respect of Potential Returning Employees;

    5.1.2 Disputes relating to compliance with the Regulations which are regarded as unresolved by any recognised trade unions;

    5.1.3 Any court action or tribunal proceedings relating to compliance with the Regulations;

    5.1.4 Completed court action or tribunal proceedings relating to compliance with the Regulations;

    5.1.5 'Out of court' settlements relating to compliance with the Regulations.

Such reports submitted shall also include information relating to Potential Returning Employees employed by any Sub-Contractor.

6. **EXIT MANAGEMENT**[23]

6.1 **Transfer of Returning Employees**

    6.1.1 The parties acknowledge and agree that where all or part of the Services cease to be provided by the Service Provider (or by a Sub-Contractor) for any reason and/or where all or part of the Services continue to be provided by the Client or by a Replacement Service Provider it is desirable that there should be a transfer of the Returning Employees to the Client or to the Replacement Service Provider on the terms set out in this clause 6.[24]

    6.1.2 In the event that the Regulations do not apply so as to effect a Relevant Transfer of the Returning Employees as envisaged in clause 6.1.1 above the Client agrees that it shall and shall procure that any Replacement Service Provider shall offer employment to each Returning Employee on like terms to the terms on which they would have been employed had the Regulations applied or, to the extent that it is not reasonably practicable to honour any such term, on terms which are not in such respect materially to the detriment of the Potential Returning Employees.

    6.1.3 Save where the parties reasonably believe that there will be no relevant transfer for the purpose of the Regulations, the parties shall co-operate in agreeing a list of Returning Employees prior to the Subsequent Transfer Date, and shall co-operate in seeking to ensure the orderly transfer of the Returning Employees to the Client and/or the Replacement Service Provider.

---

23 On a retender of the services, the potential transferee employer will seek protection against transferring liabilities. If the client has anticipated this requirement in the shape of robust exit provisions, he or she will be able to offer such protection. If not, the liabilities will find their way into the price or may have to be underwritten by the client.

24 The concern here is that if the client does not give an assurance of this nature, the risk of redundancies on exit if TUPE were not to apply will be incorporated into the service provider's price. Given that there is likely to be a TUPE transfer in the vast majority of cases, it makes sense for this risk to be removed and hence to be excluded from the price. The service provider will need to consider to what extent there remains a residual risk of redundancy liabilities.

6.1.4 Regardless of whether the Regulations apply to the transfer of the Returning Employees, the parties acknowledge and agree that the Client and/or any Replacement Service Provider may make an offer of employment to any of the Potential Returning Employees, and where such offers are accepted, the Service Provider undertakes that it shall waive (and shall procure that any Sub-Contractor shall waive) any notice of termination of employment required to be given by the relevant Potential Returning Employees, and shall not (and shall procure that any Sub-Contractor shall not) restrict, prevent or delay any such Potential Returning Employees from taking up or commencing (or agreeing to take up or commence) employment or engagement with the Client and/or any Replacement Service Provider on the date of termination of the Agreement, or where relevant, the termination of that part of the Services in which such Potential Returning Employees are engaged.

6.2 **Provision of Information and Warranties**

6.2.1 The Service Provider shall not later than [twelve][25] months prior to the expiry of [the Services Agreement] (or, if earlier, within twenty eight days of notice being given of termination of the Services Agreement), [or at any other time reasonably directed by the Client] to the extent lawfully permitted provide the Client with:

   (a) a list of the Potential Returning Employees, including details of their job titles, age, length of continuous service, current remuneration, benefits and notice;

   (b) details of any Potential Returning Employees who might reasonably be regarded as a key employee in the context of the maintenance of the Services after the Subsequent Transfer Date;

   (c) a list of agency workers, agents and independent contractors engaged by the Service Provider and any Sub-Contractor;

   (d) the total payroll bill of the Potential Returning Employees;

   (e) the terms and conditions of the Potential Returning Employees;

   (f) details of any current disciplinary or grievance proceedings ongoing or circumstances likely to give rise to such proceedings in respect of the Potential Returning Employees;

   (g) details of any claims, current or threatened, brought by the Potential Returning Employees or their representatives;

   (h) details of all death, disability benefit or permanent health insurance schemes and other similar arrangements with or in respect of the Potential Returning Employees including the identities of any such employees in receipt of benefits under any such scheme;

   (i) details of all collective agreements relating to or affecting

---

25 The provisions in reg 11 of TUPE are of no assistance in the tendering process. The information is deliverable far too late. Hence the need for this to be deliverable as a matter of contract – the date on which it should be made available will depend on the client's procurement processes.

the Potential Returning Employees, with a brief summary of the current state of negotiations with such bodies and with details of any current industrial disputes or claims for recognition by any trade union.

The Client shall keep such information confidential and shall use it for the sole purpose of a tender exercise for a continuation of the Services, in which case the information may be disclosed to a prospective tenderer.[26]

6.2.2 At intervals to be stipulated by the Client (which shall not be more frequent than every [30] days) and immediately prior to the Subsequent Transfer Date, the Service Provider shall deliver to the Client a complete update of all such information as shall have been deliverable pursuant to clause 6.2.1 and the Service Provider shall meet with the Client to discuss the information disclosed.

6.2.3 At the time of providing the information to the Client pursuant to clauses 6.2.1 and 6.2.2, the Service Provider shall warrant the completeness and accuracy of all such information and the Client may assign the benefit of this warranty to the Replacement Service Provider.

6.3 Meeting with Employee Representatives[27]

During the period of [twelve] months preceding the expiry of the Services Agreement [or at any other time reasonably directed by the Client] or after the Client has given notice to terminate the Services Agreement, the Service Provider shall enable and assist the Client and such other persons as the Client may determine to communicate with and meet the Potential Returning Employees and their trade union or other employee representatives.

6.4 Maintenance of Records[28]

The Service Provider shall (and shall procure that any Sub-Contractor shall) maintain current adequate and suitable records regarding the service of each of the Potential Returning Employees including without limitation details of terms of employment, payments of statutory sick pay and statutory and non-statutory maternity pay, disciplinary, grievance and health and safety matters, income tax and social security contributions and any enhanced redundancy entitlement in excess of statutory redundancy pay and (save to the extent prohibited by law) shall transfer the same or a complete copy of the same to the Client or any Replacement Service Provider within 14 days of [the transfer of each Potential Returning Employee to whom the records refer by operation of the Transfer Regulations or pursuant to clause 6.1.2 above].

---

26   Data protection laws mean that the information will be anonymised at this stage.
27   This may be a sensitive issue, but TUPE does not provide for access to employee representatives on the part of the client or prospective employers of the workforce.
28   The maintenance of appropriate records will be necessary for proper HR management of the workforce. This provision is inserted for the benefit of the prospective employer. Nothing in TUPE requires the maintenance or transfer of such records, save for the delivery of certain employee liability information under reg 11. This is generally considered to be too narrow to satisfy the requirements of the incoming employer.

6.5 **Financial Information**

Within twenty-eight (28) days after the Subsequent Transfer Date, the Service Provider shall, on request by the Client, provide to the Client and/or any Replacement Service Provider updated financial details for the relevant Returning Employees. Such financial details shall include sums payable in respect of each Returning Employee relating to the following:

6.5.1 Salary and benefits;

6.5.2 PAYE and national insurance contributions; and

6.5.3 Miscellaneous costs (for example, training grants and staff loans).

6.6 **Restrictions**[29]

The Service Provider undertakes to the Client that, during the [twelve] months prior to the expiry of the [Services Agreement] or, if earlier, at any time after notice has been served to terminate the [Services Agreement] and in respect of that part of the Services which will cease to be provided by the Service Provider (or any Sub-Contractor) at the Subsequent Transfer Date (the '**Affected Services**' for the purposes of this clause), the Service Provider shall not (and shall procure that any Sub-Contractor shall not) other than in the ordinary course of business and without the prior written consent of the Client (such consent not to be unreasonably withheld or delayed):

6.6.1 amend or vary (or purport or promise to amend or vary) the terms and conditions of employment or engagement) (including, for the avoidance of doubt, pay) of any Potential Returning Employees (other than where such amendment or variation has previously been agreed between the Service Provider and the Potential Returning Employees in the normal course of business, and where any such amendment or variation is not in any way related to the transfer of the Services);

6.6.2 terminate or give notice to terminate the employment or engagement of any Potential Returning Employees (other than in circumstances in which the termination is for reasons of misconduct or lack of capability);

6.6.3 transfer away, remove, reduce or vary the involvement of any of the Potential Returning Employees from or in the provision of the Affected Services (other than where such transfer or removal was planned as part of the individual's career development and will not have any adverse impact upon the delivery of the Services by the Service Provider, (PROVIDED THAT any such transfer, removal, reduction or variation is not in anyway related to the transfer of the Services));

---

29 There is a tension between the need to protect the incoming employer and the requirement that the service provider be free to deliver the service to specification without undue encumbrance. This clause is designed to leave the service provider free to deliver the service in the ordinary course of business, whilst at the same time preventing anti-competitive practices in the period prior to the end of the agreement whereby an unconscionable existing service provider might either 'dump' unwanted staff onto contracts or hold back staff it particularly wishes to keep. The service provider might also seek to inflate wages artificially (and thereby the liabilities the new service provider might take on following a TUPE transfer) to dissuade competitors from bidding.

6.6.4   recruit or bring in any new or additional individuals to provide the Affected Services who were not already involved in providing the Affected Services prior to the relevant period.

6.7   **Apportionments and Payments**

6.7.1   The Service Provider shall be responsible for all emoluments and outgoings in respect of the Returning Employees (including without limitation all wages, bonuses, commission, PAYE and national insurance contributions and pension contributions) which are attributable to the period up to, and including, the Subsequent Transfer Date (including any bonuses or commission which are payable after the Subsequent Transfer Date but attributable to the period on or before the Subsequent Transfer Date) and the Service Provider will indemnify the Client (both for itself and any Replacement Service Provider) against any costs, claims, liabilities and expenses (including reasonable legal expenses) incurred or suffered by the Client or any Replacement Service Provider in respect of the same.

6.7.2   The Client will be responsible for all emoluments and outgoings in respect of the Returning Employees (including all wages, bonuses, commission, PAYE and national insurance contributions and pension contributions) which are attributable to the period after the Subsequent Transfer Date (including any bonuses or commission which are payable on or before the Subsequent Transfer Date but which are attributable to the period after the Subsequent Transfer Date), and will indemnify the Service Provider (both for itself and any Sub-Contractor) against any costs, claims, liabilities and expenses (including reasonable legal expenses) incurred or suffered by the Service Provider or any Sub-Contractor in respect of the same.

6.8   **Non-Solicitation**

The Service Provider undertakes to the Client that, in the period of six (6) months after the relevant Subsequent Transfer Date (or such other period as the parties may agree in writing), it shall not (and shall procure that any Sub-Contractor shall not) employ or solicit (or procure that any other employer employs or solicits) any individuals who were Returning Employees from the Client or from any Replacement Service Provider without the Client's or any new Replacement Service Provider's prior written consent. This provision shall not prevent the Service Provider or any Sub-Contractor from employing any Client or Replacement Service Provider personnel who have made an unsolicited response to a general recruitment advertisement published by or on behalf of the Service Provider or any Sub-Contractor.

6.9   **Indemnities**

6.9.1   The Service Provider shall indemnify the Client (both for itself and a Replacement Service Provider) against all costs, claims, liabilities and expenses (including reasonable legal expenses) incurred by the Client and a Replacement Service Provider in connection with or as a result of:

(a)   any claim or demand by any Potential Returning Employee (whether in contract, tort, under statute, pursuant to European law or otherwise) including, without limitation, any claim for unfair dismissal, wrongful dismissal, a redundancy payment, breach of contract, unlawful deduction from wages, discrimination on the grounds of sex, race, age, disability, sexual orientation, religion or religious belief, a protective award or a claim or demand of any other nature, in each case arising directly or indirectly from any act, fault or omission of the Service Provider or any Sub-Contractor in respect of any Potential Returning Employee on or before the Subsequent Transfer Date;

(b)   any failure by the Service Provider or any Sub-Contractor to comply with its or their obligations under Regulations 13 and 14 of the Regulations, or any award of compensation under Regulation 15 of the Regulations, save where such failure arises from the failure of the Client or a Replacement Service Provider to comply with its or their duties under Regulation 13 of the Regulations;

(c)   any claim (including any individual employee entitlement under or consequent on such a claim) by any trade union or other body or person representing the Potential Returning Employees arising from or connected with any failure by the Service Provider or any Sub-Contractor to comply with any legal obligation to such trade union, body or person;

(d)   any claim made by a third party in connection with the contract of employment of a Returning Employee pursuant to sections 1 or 2 of the Contracts (Rights of Third Parties) Act 1999 where such a claim arises as a result of any act, fault or omission of the Service Provider or any Sub-Contractor before or on the Subsequent Transfer Date;

(e)   the provision of inaccurate or incomplete information pursuant to clauses 6.2.1 and 6.2.4;

(f)   any claim by any person who is transferred by the Service Provider to the Client and/or a Replacement Service Provider or whose name is included in the list of Returning Employees where such person was not engaged wholly or substantially in providing the Services prior to the Subsequent Transfer Date; and

(g)   any sub-contract which it enters into with a Sub-Contractor.

6.9.2   The Client shall indemnify the Service Provider (both for itself and for any Sub-Contractor) against all costs, claims, liabilities and expenses (including reasonable legal expenses) incurred in connection with or as a result of:

(a)   any claim or demand by any Returning Employee (whether in contract, tort, under statute, pursuant to European law or otherwise) including, without limitation, any claim for unfair dismissal, wrongful dismissal, a redundancy payment, breach of contract, unlawful deduction from wages, discrimination on the grounds of sex, race, age, disability, sexual orientation, religion or religious belief, a protective award or a claim or demand of any other nature, in each case arising directly or indirectly from any act, fault or omission of the Client or a Replacement Service Provider in respect of any Returning Employee on or after the Subsequent Transfer Date;

(b) any failure by the Client or a Replacement Service Provider to comply with its obligations under Regulation 13 of the Regulations;

(c) any claim (including any individual entitlement of a Returning Employee under or consequent on such claim) by any trade union or other body or person representing the Returning Employees arising from or connected with any failure by the Client or a Replacement Service Provider to comply with any legal obligation to such trade union, body or person;

(d) any change or proposed change to the terms and conditions of employment or working conditions of the Potential Returning Employees on or after their transfer to the Client or a Replacement Service Provider on the Subsequent Transfer Date;

(e) any change of identity of employer occurring by virtue of the Regulations and/or this Agreement being significant and detrimental to any of the Potential Returning Employees; and

(f) any claim made by a third party in connection with the contract of employment of a Returning Employee pursuant to sections 1 or 2 of the Contracts (Rights of Third Parties) Act 1999 (including the rescission or variation of such a contract) where such a claim arises as a result of any actual or alleged act, fault or omission of the Client or a Replacement Service Provider on or after the Subsequent Transfer Date.

6.9.3 The Client may in its discretion assign the benefit of the indemnities set out in this clause 6 to the Replacement Service Provider.

6.10 Returning Employees Remaining Employed by the Service Provider/Sub-Contractor

6.10.1 If as a result of the cessation of all or part of the Services by the Service Provider it is found or alleged that any of the Returning Employees remains an employee of the Service Provider and/or any Sub-Contractor after the Subsequent Transfer Date:

(a) the Service Provider shall notify the Client, [and shall procure that any Sub-Contractor shall notify the Client], of that finding or allegation as soon as reasonably practicable after becoming aware of it;

(b) in consultation with the Service Provider, the Client shall within [7] days of becoming aware of the finding or allegation make that person a written offer of employment to commence immediately on the same terms and conditions as the Client would be obliged to provide to that person if his employment had transferred pursuant to the Regulations and under which the Client agrees to recognise that person's period of service with the Service Provider or any

Sub-Contractor (as applicable) and the Service Provider shall give all reasonable assistance requested by the Client to persuade that person to accept the offer;

(c)   if the offer of employment made by the Client is accepted by that person, the Service Provider agrees to permit (and to procure that any Sub-Contractor permits) that person to leave the Service Provider's (or, where applicable, the Sub-Contractor's) employment without having worked his full notice period, if that person so requests;

(d)   the Service Provider (or, where applicable, the Sub-Contractor) may within 28 days after becoming aware of that allegation or finding, if that person is still or still claims to be an employee of the Service Provider (or Sub-Contractor) and has not accepted an offer of employment with the Client, dismiss the employee with immediate effect; and

(e)   the Client shall indemnify and keep indemnified the Service Provider against all costs, liabilities and expenses (including reasonable legal expenses) which the Service Provider (or, where applicable, the Sub-Contractor) may suffer or incur in respect of that dismissal in each case provided that the Service Provider (or, where applicable, the Sub-Contractor) takes all reasonable steps to minimise such costs, liabilities and expenses (including, for the avoidance of doubt, by following the statutory dispute resolution procedures where applicable).

6.11 Other Transferring Employees

6.11.1 If it is found or alleged that the employment of any person other than the Returning Employees transfers to the Client or a Replacement Service Provider on or after the Subsequent Transfer Date pursuant to the Regulations:

(a)   the Client shall notify the Service Provider, or shall procure that the Replacement Service Provider notifies the Service Provider of that finding or allegation as soon as reasonably practicable after becoming aware of it;

(b)   in consultation with the Client, the Service Provider shall within [7] days of becoming aware of that allegation or finding make that person a written offer of employment to commence immediately on the same terms and conditions as that person was employed prior to the transfer (actual or alleged), and under which the Service Provider agrees to recognise that employee's prior service with the Service Provider (or, where applicable, the Sub-Contractor) and the Client shall give all reasonable assistance requested by the Service Provider to persuade that person to accept the offer;

(c)   the Client or Replacement Service Provider may, within 28 days after becoming aware of that finding or allegation, if that person is still an employee of the Client or the Replacement Service Provider and has not accepted an offer of employment with the Service Provider dismiss that person; and

(d)   the Service Provider shall indemnify and keep indemnified the Client against costs, liabilities and expenses (including reasonable legal expenses) which the Client and the Replacement Service Provider may suffer or incur in relation to that dismissal and the employment of that person up to the date of that dismissal and any other claim brought by that person in each case provided the Client and the Replacement Service Provider take all reasonable steps to minimise such costs, liabilities and expenses (including, for the avoidance of doubt, by following the statutory dispute resolution procedures where applicable).

6.12   Redundancy Costs[30]

6.12.1 Where all or part of the Services cease to be provided by the Service Provider the Client shall indemnify the Service Provider in respect of any statutory or contractual (save to the extent that such contractual entitlements have been enhanced by the Service Provider) redundancy payment (excluding, for the avoidance of doubt, any sum for unfair dismissal, damages, pensions, interest or costs) which shall be payable to any of the Returning Employees provided that the dismissal by reason of redundancy arises from either:

(a)   the termination of the Services Agreement by effluxion of time; or

(b)   any material variation or amendment of the Services Agreement made at the behest of the Client;[31] or

(c)   the termination of the Services Agreement by the Client for reasons which are not due to breach by the Service Provider.

6.12.2 The Service Provider warrants that it shall and shall procure that any Sub-Contractor shall:

(a)   use all reasonable endeavours to avoid declaring any Returning Employee redundant including but not limited to seeking alternative employment within the Service Provider and its associated companies;

(b)   seek to effect the dismissal on grounds of redundancy of any Returning Employee in accordance with the terms and conditions of employment of the Returning Employee and in accordance with any applicable collective agreements; and

(c)   comply with all relevant statutory obligations which are imposed on an employer (including, for the avoidance of doubt, the statutory dispute resolution procedures); and

(d)   use its reasonable endeavours to effect any dismissal on grounds of redundancy fairly.

---

30   Assuming that the client is prepared to offer an indemnity in respect of redundancy costs. There will be many cases where this is not the case, in which case the document may remain silent on the point.

31   A further circumstance which the service provider may want to cover is where the contract does not deliver a guaranteed volume of work. It may be, for example, that a workforce transfers consistent with a given level of work which occupies that size of workforce; however, volume drops (without that being a breach of contract) such that the service provider is forced to make a part of the workforce redundant.

6.12.3 For the purposes of this clause, it will be for the Service Provider if so requested to demonstrate to the reasonable satisfaction of the Client that in any particular case:

(a) redundancy is or was the genuine reason for the dismissal; and

(b) the Service Provider or any Sub-Contractor has followed a fair procedure in effecting the dismissal.

6.13 **Information and Consultation**

6.13.1 The Service Provider shall comply (and shall procure that any Sub-Contractor shall comply) with its duties under Regulations 13 and 14 of the Regulations in relation to any Relevant Transfer, save where it is unable to do so as a result of the failure of the Client and/or a Replacement Service Provider to comply with their obligations under Regulation 13 of the Regulations.

6.13.2 The Client shall and shall procure that any Replacement Service Provider shall comply with its/their duties under Regulation 13 of the Regulations in relation to any Relevant Transfer.

7. **CONDUCT OF CLAIMS**

7.1 In respect of the indemnities given in this Agreement:

7.1.1 The indemnified party shall give written notice to the indemnifying party as soon as is practicable of the details of any claim or proceedings brought or threatened against it by a third party in respect of which a claim will or may be made under the relevant indemnity;

7.1.2 The indemnifying party shall at its own expense have the exclusive right to defend, conduct and/or settle all claims and proceedings which may be brought by a third party to the extent that such claims or proceedings may be covered by the relevant indemnity provided that where there is an impact on the indemnified party, the indemnifying party shall consult with the indemnified party and shall at all times keep the indemnified party informed of all material matters; and

7.1.3 The indemnified party shall, at the indemnifying party's expense, provide all reasonable assistance and documentation required by the indemnifying party in connection with, and act as or be joined as a defendant in, any claim or proceedings brought by a third party. The indemnifying party shall reimburse the indemnified party for all reasonable costs and expenses (including but not limited to legal costs and disbursements) incurred in providing such cooperation and/or arising as a result of the indemnifying party's failure to defend, conduct and/or settle such claims and proceedings.

8. **DATA PROTECTION**

The Service Provider shall use its best endeavours to ensure (and shall ensure that any Sub-Contractor uses its best endeavours to ensure), in time for the Client to be able to meet its obligations under this Agreement, that it is lawfully permitted to disclose the information required to be disclosed under this Agreement, which will include the Service Provider using all reasonable endeavours to secure the consent of the Potential Returning Employees to such disclosure of information relating to them where consent is necessary for the disclosure.[32]

9. **ENTIRE AGREEMENT**

This Agreement together with the [Services Agreement] [list others] constitutes the entire agreement and understanding between the Parties in respect of the matters dealt with in them and supersedes, cancels and nullifies any previous agreement between the Parties relating to such matters notwithstanding the terms of any previous agreement or arrangement expressed to survive termination.

10. **GOVERNING LAW AND JURISDICTION**

This Agreement shall be governed by and construed in accordance with English law and each party hereby submits to the exclusive jurisdiction of the courts of England and Wales.

SCHEDULE 1: EMPLOYEES' SCHEDULE

SCHEDULE 2: PERSONNEL INFORMATION SCHEDULE

SCHEDULE 3: EMPLOYEE COSTS SCHEDULE

SIGNED by or on behalf of the parties on the date which first appears in this Agreement

....

for and on behalf of **[CLIENT]**

Dated ....

....

for and on behalf of **[SERVICE PROVIDER]**

Dated ....

---

32 A helpful summary of the duties imposed on the parties by data protection laws with regard to employee information may be found in The Employment Practices Code published by the Information Commissioner, particularly at section 2.12. See www.ico.gov.uk.

Appendix 15

SALE OF BUSINESS – TUPE[1] WARRANTIES AND INDEMNITIES

WARRANTIES

Sample employee warranties for use in a business sale agreement

The very suggestion that there is a set of draft warranties that may have general use can be dangerous. The clauses set out here will deal with many of the frequently encountered concerns. However, the success of the warranties as a protective mechanism will depend to a large extent on the skill of the purchaser and his/her advisors in moulding the warranties to the specific concerns which arise from an examination of the target.Given that the warranties are sought by the purchaser as a response to the principle of caveat emptor, this set of draft warranties is prepared from the standpoint of the purchaser. The vendor will, of course, wish to limit them in scope and to disclose against them.

Employee Liability Information[2]

1.1 The Employee Liability Information:

    1.1.1 has been provided to the Purchaser at such time or times as are required by the Regulations;

    1.1.2 was complete and accurate at the time it was provided to the Purchaser;

    1.1.3 has been updated to take account of any changes to such information, as required by the Regulations.

Particulars of Employees

1.2 There are no employees other than the Employees employed in the Business, and the Vendor has not offered employment in the Business to any other person.

1.3 Schedule [ ] contains true, complete and accurate particulars for each Employee[3] in respect of the following:

    1.3.1 Name;

---

1   Transfer of Undertakings (Protection of Employment) Regulations 2006, SI 2006/246.

2   This warranty provides a contractual remedy for failure to supply the information in relation to employee liability which is required under TUPE. The existence of the contractual remedy will be taken into account when considering any statutory remedy.

3   This will frequently be a very important warranty in the context of the employment aspects of the deal, as it relates to data which reveal the cost of employing the workforce, the cost of making employees redundant etc.

1.3.2   Age and date of birth;

1.3.3   Sex;

1.3.4   Date of commencement of employment and date of commencement of continuous employment;

1.3.5   Any terms and conditions relating to:

    (a)   hours of work (including any terms and conditions relating to normal working hours);

    (b)   entitlement to holidays, including public holidays, and holiday pay (including details of holiday pay payable on termination);

    (c)   incapacity for work due to sickness or injury, including any provision for sick pay.

1.3.6   Notice period (to be given and received by each Employee);

1.3.7   The title of the job which each Employee is employed to do or a brief description of the work for which he/she is employed;

1.3.8   Where the employment is not expected to be permanent, the period for which it is expected to continue or, if it is for a fixed term, the date when it is to end;

1.3.9   Either the place of work or, where the Employee is required or permitted to work at various places, details of such places;

1.3.10 Where any Employee is required to work outside the United Kingdom for a period of more than one month:

    (a)   The period for which he/she is to work outside the United Kingdom;

    (b)   The currency in which remuneration is to be paid while he/she is working outside the United Kingdom;

    (c)   Any additional remuneration payable to him/her, and any benefits to be provided to or in respect of him/her, by reason of his/her being required to work outside the United Kingdom; and

    (d)   Any terms and conditions relating to his/her return to the United Kingdom;

1.3.11 Pay review date;

1.3.12 Normal retirement age;

1.3.13 Disciplinary rules or disciplinary or dismissal procedures;

1.3.14 Name or description of a person to whom an Employee can apply if dissatisfied with any disciplinary or dismissal decision taken relating to him/her, and the manner in which any such application should be made;

1.3.15 Name or description of a person to whom an Employee can apply for the purpose of seeking redress of any grievance relating to his/her employment, and the manner in which any such application should be made;

1.3.16 all remuneration and benefits actually provided or which the Seller is bound to provide (whether now or in the future) including, but not limited to, details of the following (which shall include details of the scale or rate of such remuneration or the method of calculating such remuneration and the intervals at which such remuneration is paid):

    (a)   wages or salary;

    (b)   overtime pay;

(c)   commission;

(d)   allowances;

(e)   bonus or other profit-sharing or incentive arrangements (whether contractual or not);

(f)   enhanced redundancy pay;

(g)   payments or benefits payable on termination, breach, suspension or variation of the contract of employment;

(h)   payments or allowances, lump sums or other benefits on death or during any periods of sickness or disablement for the benefit of any of the Employees or their dependants;

(i)   motor vehicle;

(j)   any benefit schemes, arrangements or understandings operated.

1.4   Each Employee is employed solely by the Vendor and not by any other person or jointly with any other person. Each Employee has been employed exclusively in the Business since the start of their employment with the Vendor.

1.5   All the Employees work on a full-time basis in the Business.

1.6   So far as the Vendor is aware, no Employee objects to the transfer of their employment to the Buyer for the purposes of Regulation 4(7) of the Regulations.

Terms and Conditions

1.7   Copies of the following are attached to the Disclosure Letter:

1.7.1   all standard terms and conditions of employment between the Vendor and the Employees and details of which terms and conditions apply to each Employee;

1.7.2   the terms and conditions of employment between the Vendor and any Employee earning in excess of [£   ];

1.7.3   all staff handbooks, policies and procedures (including, without limitation, any disciplinary or grievance policy and procedure and any equal opportunities policies and procedures) which apply to the Employees; and

1.7.4   any other written agreement or details of any verbal agreement or arrangement relevant to the Employees (including, for the avoidance of doubt, any collective agreement).

Workers

1.8   There are no workers (not being Employees), self-employed consultants or secondees engaged in the Business.

Termination

1.9   The contract of employment of each of the Employees can be terminated without the payment of damages or compensation (other than that payable under statute) by giving three months' notice or less.

1.10   The Vendor has not within the last [12] months given or received notice of resignation from any of the Employees and the Vendor is not aware of any Employee who intends to give notice of resignation.

1.11   No Employee will be entitled as a result of or in connection with this Agreement or the transfer of the Business pursuant to this Agreement:

1.11.1 to terminate his/her employment with the Vendor;

1.11.2 to receive any payment, reward or benefit of any kind;

1.11.3 to receive any enhancement in or improvement to his/her remuneration, benefits or terms and conditions of employment; or

1.11.4 to treat him/herself as being dismissed on the ground of redundancy or otherwise released from any obligation to the Vendor.

1.12 There has been no change in the numbers or identities of the individuals employed by the Vendor in the Business during the 12 months preceding this Agreement and each Employee has held his/her current post during the 6 months preceding this Agreement.

Changes in Remuneration

1.13 The aggregate level of remuneration payable to Employees has not increased by more than [3] per cent within the last 12 months.

1.14 It is not the common practice of the Vendor to increase remuneration payable to any Employee on an annual basis and there is no contractual or other obligation to increase or otherwise vary the remuneration payable to any Employee.

1.15 The Vendor has not within the last [12] months:

1.15.1 increased or offered or agreed to increase the remuneration of, or

1.15.2 altered or offered or sought to alter any of the terms and conditions of employment of

any Employee, nor are any negotiations for any such increase or alterations expected or likely to take place within the next 6 months.

Accrued and Potential Liabilities

1.16 There is no liability, outstanding or contingent or anticipated, to any present or former Employee other than remuneration accrued for the current wage or salary period or for reimbursement of normal business expenses.

1.17 No present or former Employee or any applicant for any role in the Business has any:

1.17.1 claim, outstanding or contingent or anticipated, against or

1.17.2 right to be indemnified by

the Vendor arising out of an act or omission by the Vendor on or before the date of this Agreement and [so far as the Vendor is aware] there are no facts or circumstances that might give rise to the same.

1.18 So far as the Vendor is aware, none of the Employees is in breach of his/her contract of employment or any other obligation or duty he/she owes to the Vendor.

1.19 No Employee has any current disciplinary sanction in force against him/her or is currently or has been within the last [2] years the subject of any current disciplinary investigation or procedure (whether under the Vendor's disciplinary policy, the Employment Act 2002 (Dispute Resolution) Regulations 2004 or otherwise), and no Employee has within the last [2] years brought a grievance or otherwise raised a complaint against the Vendor or any of its employees, officers or workers (whether under the Vendor's grievance policy, the Employment Act 2002 (Dispute Resolution) Regulations 2004 or otherwise).

1.20 The Vendor is not and has not within the last [2] years been engaged in any dispute, claim or legal proceedings whether arising under common law, contract, statute, pursuant to European Community law or otherwise with or in relation to any of the Employees and there is no fact or matter in existence which can reasonably be foreseen as likely to give rise to any such dispute, claim or legal proceedings.

1.21 None of the Employees has at the date of this Agreement any:

1.21.1 accrued rights to holiday pay or to pay in lieu of holidays [which have not been provided for in full in the Management Accounts];

1.21.2 loan or advance or has received any financial assistance from the Vendor;

1.21.3 outstanding claim under any PHI or medical expenses insurance scheme provided by the Vendor;

1.21.4 right now or in the future:

(a) to return to work (whether for reasons connected with maternity, paternity, adoption or parental leave or absence by reason of illness or incapacity, secondment or otherwise);

(b) to be reinstated or re-engaged by the Seller; or

(c) to any other compensation.

1.22 None of the Employees is suffering from or has suffered from within the last 12 months any medical or other condition which impairs or might impair his/her ability to continue to perform their employment duties and/or which require or might require any arrangement or adjustment within the workplace.

1.23 No arrangements or adjustments have been made, nor so far as the Vendor is aware, need or will need to be made by the Vendor by virtue of the provisions of the Disability Discrimination Act 1995 to any of the Employees.

1.24 No Employee has at any time in the last six months exercised a right to request a contract variation under section 80F of the Employment Rights Act 1996.

1.25 No Employee has made a protected disclosure for the purposes of the Employment Rights Act 1996 at any time during the last 12 months.

Restrictive Covenants

1.26 No Employee is currently bound by a restrictive covenant entered into with a former employer or any other business or undertaking.

Trade Unions, representation, collective issues and disputes

1.27 The Vendor does not have any agreement or other arrangement, whether oral or written, formal or informal (and whether legally binding or not) with any trade union or works council or other body representing the Employees or any of them, and the standard information and consultation provisions set out in the Information and Consultation of Employees Regulations 2004[4] do not apply in respect of the Employees.

1.28 The Vendor does not recognise any trade union or works council or other body representing the Employees or any of them.

1.29 The Vendor has not done any act or thing that may be construed as recognition of any trade union or works council or other body representing the Employees or any of them.

1.30 No requests for recognition pursuant to Schedule A1 to the Trade Union and Labour Relations (Consolidation) Act 1992 (as amended) have been

---

4 SI 2004/3426.

received by the Vendor in respect of the Employees or any of them, and no requests to commence negotiations to reach an agreement have been made pursuant to the Information and Consultation of Employees Regulations 2004 in respect of the Employees or any of them.

1.31 The Vendor is not in respect of the Employees or any of them involved in any industrial or trade dispute or any dispute or negotiation with any trade union or association of trade unions or works council or body of Employees, and there are no circumstances likely to give rise to any such dispute.

1.32 There has been no strike, work to rule or industrial action (official or unofficial) by any Employee and the Vendor has not conducted a lock-out within the last five years and [so far as the Vendor is aware] there are no current facts which might give rise to the same.

1.33 The Vendor has not within the period of 12 months preceding the date of this Agreement:

1.33.1 given notice of any redundancies to the Secretary of State or

1.33.2 started consultations with any appropriate representative

under the provisions of Part IV of the Trade Union and Labour Relations (Consolidation) Act 1992, nor has the Vendor failed to comply with such obligation under that Part.

1.34 The Vendor has not within the period of 12 months preceding the date of this Agreement:

1.34.1 been a party to any Relevant Transfer for the purpose of any transfer or service provision change taking place on or after 6 April 2006, or any relevant transfer as defined in the Transfer of Undertakings (Protection of Employment) Regulations 1981[5] for the purpose of any transfers of undertakings taking place before 6 April 2006; or

1.34.2 failed to comply with any duty to inform and consult any appropriate representative arising under the Regulations or the Transfer of Undertakings (Protection of Employment) Regulations 1981.

Compliance

1.35 The Vendor has, in relation to each of the Employees:

1.35.1 complied and continues to comply [in all material respects] with all obligations, awards, orders and recommendations imposed on it or made by or under statute, statutory instrument, European Union law, common law, contract, any collective agreement, the terms and conditions of employment, staff handbook, company policy, any customs and practice and any codes of conduct and practice;

1.35.2 complied and continues to comply with any recommendations made by the Advisory Conciliation and Arbitration Service, the Equal Opportunities Commission, the Commission for Racial Equality, the Disability Rights Commission, the Central Arbitration Committee or any other bodies with similar functions or powers in relation to employees, and with any arbitration awards and declarations; and

---

5   SI 1981/1794.

1.35.3 maintained and continues to maintain adequate and suitable personnel records (including records of working time) which are up to date, complete and accurate.

1.36 The Vendor is not and has not been the subject of any enquiry or investigation by the Commission for Racial Equality, the Equal Opportunities Commission, the Disability Rights Commission, any health and safety enforcement body or any other statutory or regulatory body in respect of any act, event, omission or other matter relating to any Employee and there are no facts which might give rise to the same.

1.37 All Employees have leave to enter and remain in the United Kingdom and are entitled to work in the United Kingdom under the Asylum and Immigration Act 1996.

Training

1.38 There is and has never been any training scheme, arrangement or proposal in relation to the Business in respect of which a levy is currently or may in the future become payable by the Vendor under the Industrial Training Act 1982.

INDEMNITIES

Operative clauses for inclusion in the sale and purchase agreement

Transfer of Employees[6]

X.1 The Vendor and the Purchaser intend and acknowledge that the transfer of the Business to the Purchaser on Completion shall, with respect to the Employees,[7] constitute a Relevant Transfer,[8] and agree[9] that as a consequence of that Relevant Transfer, the contracts of employment made between the Vendor and the Purchaser [and the collective agreements listed in the Disclosure Letter] (save insofar as such contracts [and such agreements] relate to benefits for old age, invalidity or survivors under any occupational pension scheme) will have effect from and after

---

6   This set of clauses contemplates an orthodox transfer of the employees of the target business to the purchaser. It is not a stand-alone set of clauses: it fits within the body of the agreement and must be drafted in that context. It is drafted from the perspective of the purchaser; conventionally, the purchaser will prepare the initial draft of the agreement. The vendor then seeks to negotiate the sale on the basis of less onerous provisions.

7   This defined term is important. It should refer to employees who will transfer by operation of TUPE *and* who will be listed on a list of transferring employees which the purchaser will have vetted in advance.

8   Defined as a relevant transfer for the purposes of TUPE.

9   Of course, this is not a matter which can be determined by the parties. Whether there is a TUPE transfer is something which only a tribunal can determine conclusively. However, the fact that the parties have reached this agreement will have some weight in the mind of the tribunal when considering this point and the act of the purchaser in taking the employees into its employment will also be of consequence. Above all, this agreement determines the practical consequences for the employees – the purchaser will henceforth act as the employer, and that situation will prevail unless and until an employee seeks to question this and is able to establish that there was no transfer as a matter of law.

Completion as if originally made between the Purchaser and the Employees [(or between the Purchaser and the relevant trade union as the case may be)].

Employee Tax arising on Share Options/Share Acquisitions

X.2	The Vendor covenants to pay to the Purchaser an amount equal to any liability of the Purchaser or any member of the Purchaser's group to account for income tax under the PAYE system or national insurance contributions which arises after Completion in respect of an option or other right to acquire shares granted prior to Completion by the Vendor or any other person to any of the Employees or which arises in respect of the shares acquired as a result of the exercise of any subscription or right, together with any interest and penalties arising in respect of such a liability.

X.3	If any payment made pursuant to Clause X.2 is chargeable or assessable to Tax in the hands of the Purchaser or any member of the Purchaser's group, the Vendor shall pay such additional amounts as shall be required to ensure that the net amount received and retained by the Purchaser (after Tax) will equal the full amount which would have been received and retained by it had no such liability to Tax been incurred, and in applying this Clause X.3, the availability to the Purchaser of any relief from or credit against such Tax shall be ignored.

Indemnities

X.4	The Vendor shall indemnify[10] the Purchaser against all costs, claims, liabilities and expenses (including legal expenses on an indemnity basis) incurred in connection with or as a result of:

    X.4.1	any claim or demand by any Employee (whether in contract, tort, under statute, pursuant to European law or otherwise) including, without limitation, any claim for unfair dismissal, wrongful dismissal, a redundancy payment, breach of contract, unlawful deduction from wages, discrimination on the grounds of sex, race, age, disability, sexual orientation, religion or religious belief, a protective award or a claim or demand of any other nature in each case arising directly or indirectly from any act, fault or omission (or any alleged act, fault or omission) of the Vendor in respect of any Employee and whether arising before, on or after Completion;

    X.4.2	any failure by the Vendor to comply with its obligations under Regulations 13 and 14 of the Regulations, or any award of compensation under Regulation 15;

    X.4.3	any claim (including any individual employee entitlement under or consequent on such a claim) by any trade union or other body or person representing the Employees arising from or connected with any failure by the Vendor to comply with any legal obligation to such trade union, body or person whether any such claim arises before, on or after Completion;

    X.4.4	any claim made by a third party in connection with the contract of

---

10	Regardless of whether the purchaser has generally been able to secure indemnity protection within the agreement, specific employment indemnities will always be in order by reason of the impact of TUPE.

employment of an Employee pursuant to sections 1 or 2 of the Contracts (Rights of Third Parties) Act 1999 where such a claim arises as a result of any actual or alleged act, fault or omission of the Vendor before, on or after Completion; and

X.4.5 any error in or omission from Schedule [ ],[11] whether such extra costs, claims, liabilities and expenses arise before, on or after Completion.

Other Transferring Employees

X.5 If as a result of the sale of the Business and/or the application of the Regulations and/or the Directive it is found or alleged that the employment of any person other than the Employees has transferred to the Purchaser on or after Completion pursuant to the Regulations:[12]

X.5.1 the Purchaser shall notify the Vendor of that fact or allegation as soon as reasonably practicable after becoming aware of it;

X.5.2 in consultation with the Purchaser, the Vendor shall within [7] days of becoming aware of that allegation or finding make that person a written offer of employment to commence immediately on the same terms and conditions as that person was employed prior to the transfer (actual or alleged), and under which the Vendor agrees to recognise that person's prior service with the Vendor;

X.5.3 upon the offer being made as referred to in Clause X.5.2 (or at any time after the expiry of the [7] days if the offer is not made as requested), the Purchaser may dismiss the person concerned with immediate effect;

X.5.3 the Vendor shall indemnify the Purchaser against all costs, claims, liabilities and expenses (including legal expenses on an indemnity basis) in connection with or as a result of:

(a) any claim or demand by that person (whether in contract, tort, under statute, pursuant to European law or otherwise) including, without limitation, any claim for unfair dismissal, wrongful dismissal, a redundancy payment, breach of contract, unlawful deduction from wages, discrimination on the grounds of sex, race, age, disability, sexual orientation, religion or religious belief, a protective award or a claim or demand of any other nature and whether arising before, on or after Completion;

(b) any failure by the Vendor to comply with its obligations under Regulations 13 and 14 of the Regulations, or any award of compensation under Regulation 15 of the Regulations;

(c) any claim (including any individual employee entitlement under or consequent on such a claim) by any trade union or other body or person representing that person arising from or connected with any failure by the Vendor to comply with

---

11   The details of the transferring employees and associated information.

12   Colloquially known as a 'woodwork clause', this clause speaks to the concern that there may be transferring staff who the purchaser was not expecting. The clause contains a mitigation mechanism that is far from ideal as a matter of law by reason of breaking continuity of employment, though this problem is solved in part in X.5.2, but is nevertheless conventional.

any legal obligation to such trade union, body or person whether any such claim arises before, on or after Completion;

(d)   any claim made by a third party in connection with the contract of employment of that person pursuant to sections 1 or 2 of the Contracts (Rights of Third Parties) Act 1999 where such a claim arises as a result of any actual or alleged act, fault or omission of the Vendor before, on or after Completion.

Discrimination and Equal Pay Claims

X.6   If any employee of the Purchaser claims that he or she has been unlawfully discriminated against by reason of sex, marital status, gender reassignment, race, age, disability, sexual orientation, religion or religious belief (whether in breach of the provisions of the Treaty of Rome, the Equal Pay Directive,[13] the Equal Treatment Directive,[14] the Equal Pay Act 1970, the Sex Discrimination Act 1975, the Race Relations Act 1976, the Disability Discrimination Act 1995, the Employment Equality (Sexual Orientation) Regulations 2003,[15] the Employment Equality (Religion or Belief) Regulations 2003[16] or otherwise) and such claim relates to a term, benefit or other thing (whether under contract or otherwise) provided by the Vendor to any employee who transfers or is transferred to or accepts employment with the Purchaser whether pursuant to this Agreement or as a result of the provisions of the Regulations and/or the Directive (the 'Comparator') and such term, benefit or thing was provided by the Purchaser to the Comparator because of its obligations under the Regulations and/or the Directive to provide that term, benefit or other thing the Vendor shall indemnify the Purchaser against any costs, claims, liabilities and expenses (including legal expenses on an indemnity basis) arising from or in connection with any such claim.

Conduct of Claims

X.7   Where the Purchaser is entitled to an indemnity from the Vendor pursuant to this clause X.7, the Purchaser may in its absolute discretion defend, settle or compromise any claim referred to within the said indemnity and the Vendor will on demand indemnify the Purchaser against all costs, claims, liabilities and expenses (including legal expenses on an indemnity basis) arising out of, or in connection with, the Purchaser so doing.

Apportionments and Payments

X.8   Clauses [   ] (Apportionments) shall not apply in relation to emoluments and outgoings arising in respect of the Employees.[17]

X.9   The Vendor shall be responsible for all emoluments and outgoings in respect of the Employees (including without limitation all wages, bonuses,

---

13   Council Directive 75/117/EC.
14   Council Directive 2000/43/EC.
15   SI 2003/1661.
16   SI 2003/1660.
17   Because of the specific issues that arise under TUPE, it is usual for the agreement to contain

commissions, PAYE, national insurance contributions and pension contributions) which are attributable to the period up to, and including Completion (including any bonuses or commission which are payable after Completion but attributable to the period before Completion) and the Vendor shall indemnify the Purchaser against all costs, claims, liabilities and expenses (including legal expenses on an indemnity basis) in respect of the same.

X.10 The Purchaser shall be responsible for all emoluments and outgoings in respect of the Employees (including without limitation all wages, bonuses, commissions, PAYE, national insurance contributions and pension contributions) which are attributable to the period after Completion.

X.11 The Purchaser will assume the outstanding obligations of the Vendor in respect of any accrued holiday entitlements and accrued holiday remuneration of the Employees at Completion and, in consideration, the Vendor will pay the Purchaser within 14 days of Completion the full amount necessary to enable the Purchaser to meet the cost of providing such holiday entitlements and remuneration as at Completion.[18]

[Redundancy Payments][19]

X.12 [In consideration of the Purchaser assuming the accrued prospective liability of the Vendor at Completion in respect of redundancy payments which might become payable to the Employees upon their being made redundant after Completion, the Vendor will pay to the Purchaser on or before [insert date] a sum equal to the total sum which the Vendor would have paid as redundancy compensation (whether by virtue of a legal obligation or otherwise but after deduction of any tax due) if all of them had been made redundant on the date of Completion. Redundancy compensation for these purposes includes both statutory and other redundancy payments, but excludes any notice pay.]

Clauses for insertion by the vendor on review

1.   [Notwithstanding the acknowledgement and agreement in Clause X.1 above, and in recognition of the possibility that the transfer of the Business may be determined not to be a Relevant Transfer by a court or tribunal, the Purchaser shall, with effect from Completion, offer employment to each Employee on like terms to the terms on which they would have become employed by the Purchaser had there been a Relevant Transfer, or, to the extent that it is not reasonably practicable to do so in

---

specific employment-related apportionment provisions. Apportionment generally will typically be the subject of clauses of general application, which will have to be disapplied for these purposes.

18 Holiday pay can be a substantial sum. Much will depend on when in the holiday year the transaction completes. The apportionment provisions will have to be considered in this light and adjusted accordingly.

19 If redundancies are an inevitable consequence of the transaction, there are a number of ways for this to be handled. A straight financial provision is one option. A presumption is raised under TUPE that the dismissals by reason of redundancy will be automatically unfair, so consideration will need to be given to how best to rebut this presumption by demonstrating an economic, technical or organisational reason.

respect of any such term, on terms which are not in such respect
materially to the detriment of the Employee.][20]

2.   The Purchaser shall indemnify the Vendor against all costs, claims,
      liabilities and expenses (including legal expenses on an indemnity basis)
      incurred in connection with or as a result of:

      2.1   any claim or demand by any Employee (whether in contract, tort,
             under statute, pursuant to European law or otherwise) including,
             without limitation, any claim for unfair dismissal, wrongful
             dismissal, a redundancy payment, breach of contract, unlawful
             deduction from wages, discrimination on the grounds of sex, race,
             age, disability, sexual orientation, religion or religious belief, a
             protective award or a claim or demand of any other nature in each
             case arising directly or indirectly from any act, fault or omission
             (or any alleged act, fault or omission) of the Purchaser in respect
             of any Employee and whether arising before, on or after
             Completion;

      2.2   any failure by the Purchaser to comply with its obligations under
             Regulation 13 of the Regulations;

      2.3   any claim (including any individual employee entitlement under or
             consequent on such claim) by any trade union or other body or
             person representing the Employees arising from or connected with
             any failure by the Purchaser to comply with any legal obligation to
             such trade union, body or person whether any such claim arises
             before, on or after Completion;

      2.4   any change or proposed change in the terms and conditions of
             employment or working conditions of the Employees on or after
             their transfer to the Purchaser on Completion, or to the terms and
             conditions of employment or working conditions of any person
             who would have been an Employee but for their resignation (or
             decision to treat their employment as terminated under
             Regulation 4(9) of the Regulations) on or before Completion as a
             result of any such proposed changes;

      2.5   the change of identity of employer occurring by virtue of the
             Regulations and/or this Agreement being significant and
             detrimental to any of the Employees, or to any person who would
             have been an Employee but for their resignation (or decision to
             treat their employment as terminated under Regulation 4(9) of the
             Regulations) on or before Completion as a result of the change in
             employer;

      2.6   any claim made by a third party in connection with the contract of
             employment of an Employee pursuant to sections 1 or 2 of the
             Contracts (Rights of Third Parties) Act 1999 (including the
             rescission or variation of such a contract) where such a claim arises

---

20   This clause would be inserted after Clause X.1 and seeks to limit any risk of employees not
     transferring. If TUPE did not apply to the transaction and the vendor is left with surplus
     labour, there could be a substantial redundancy cost. Hence the fall-back of the purchaser
     being required to make offers of employment, replicating TUPE by contract. There are two
     shortcomings: continuity of employment cannot be fully replicated by contract; furthermore
     the offer of employment may not be accepted.

as a result of any actual or alleged act, fault or omission of the Purchaser on or after Completion.

Clauses where TUPE is not expected to apply[21]

VARIANT ONE

The Vendor and the Purchaser believe that the sale of the Business does not amount to the transfer of an undertaking for the purposes of the Regulations and/or the Directive and no person employed in the Business will be employed by the Purchaser following the transfer of the Business.

VARIANT TWO

1. It is not the intention of the parties that any past or present employees of the Vendor will be employed by the Purchaser following the transfer of the Business.

2. If as a result of the sale of the Business and/or the application of the Regulations and/or the Directive any past or present employee of the Vendor shall become, or otherwise be deemed to be, or shall claim or is alleged to have become, an employee of the Purchaser:

    2.1   the Purchaser shall notify the Vendor of that fact or allegation as soon as reasonably practicable after becoming aware of it;[22]

    2.2   in consultation with the Purchaser, the Vendor shall within [7] days of becoming aware of that fact or allegation make that person a written offer of employment to commence immediately on the same terms and conditions as that person was employed immediately prior to the transfer (actual or alleged), and under which the Vendor agrees to recognise that person's prior service with the Vendor;

    2.3   upon the offer being made as referred to in Clause 2.2 (or at any time after the expiry of the [7] days if the offer is not made as requested), the Purchaser may dismiss that person concerned with immediate effect;

    2.4   the Vendor shall indemnify the Purchaser against all costs, claims, liabilities and expenses (including legal expenses on an indemnity basis) in connection with or as a result of:

        (a)   any claim or demand by that person (whether in contract, tort, under statute, pursuant to European law or otherwise) including, without limitation, any claim for unfair dismissal, wrongful dismissal, a redundancy payment, breach of contract, unlawful deduction from wages, discrimination on the grounds of sex, race, age or disability, sexual orientation, religion or religious belief, a protective award or a claim or demand of any other nature and whether arising before, on or after Completion;

        (b)   any failure by the Vendor to comply with its obligations

---

21   Admittedly, not a common occurrence. Generally, the fact that the purchaser seeks to acquire the business as a going concern will mean that there is a clear transfer of an 'economic entity'.

22   This is the 'woodwork' model described above.

under Regulations 13 and 14 of the Regulations, save where occasioned by the default of the Purchaser, or any award of compensation under Regulation 15 of the Regulations, save to the extent that the same was awarded by reason of the default of the Purchaser;

(c)   any claim (including any individual employee entitlement under or consequent on such a claim) by any trade union or other body or person arising from or connected with any failure by the Vendor to comply with any legal obligation to such trade union, body or person whether any such claim arises before, on or after Completion; and

(d)   any claim made by a third party in connection with the contract of employment of an Employee pursuant to sections 1 or 2 of the Contracts (Rights of Third Parties) Act 1999 where such a claim arises as a result of any actual or alleged act, fault or omission of the Vendor before, on or after Completion.

3.   Where the Purchaser is entitled to an indemnity from the Vendor pursuant to this clause, the Purchaser may in its absolute discretion defend, settle or compromise any claim referred to within the said indemnity and the Vendor will on demand indemnify the Purchaser against all costs, claims, liabilities and expenses (including legal expenses on an indemnity basis) arising out of, or in connection with the Purchaser so doing.

4.   If, contrary to the expectation of the parties, the Regulations apply so as to transfer the contracts of employment of any persons employed in the Business to the Purchaser, the Purchaser shall indemnify the Vendor against any costs, claims, liabilities and expenses (including legal expenses on an indemnity basis) in connection with or as a result of:

4.1   any claim or demand by such persons (whether in contract, tort, under statute, pursuant to European law or otherwise) including, without limitation, any claim for unfair dismissal, wrongful dismissal, a redundancy payment, breach of contract, unlawful deduction from wages, discrimination on the grounds of sex, race, age, disability, sexual orientation, religion or religious belief, a protective award or a claim or demand of any other nature arising directly or indirectly from any act, fault or omission (or any alleged act, fault or omission) of the Purchaser in respect of any Employee and whether arising before, on or after Completion;

4.2   any failure by the Purchaser to comply with its obligations under Regulation 13 of the Regulations;

4.3   any claim (including any individual entitlement of such a person under or consequent on such claim) by any trade union or other body or person representing such persons arising from or connected with any failure by the Purchaser to comply with any legal obligation to such trade union, body or person whether any such claim arises or has its origin before or after Completion;

4.4   any change or proposed change in the terms and conditions of employment or working conditions of such persons on or after their transfer to the Purchaser on Completion;

4.5 the change of identity of employer occurring by virtue of the Regulations and/or this Agreement being significant and detrimental to such persons;

4.6 any claim made by a third party in connection with the contract of employment of such persons pursuant to sections 1 or 2 of the Contracts (Rights of Third Parties) Act 1999 (including the rescission or variation of such a contract) where such a claim arises as a result of any actual or alleged act, fault or omission of the Purchaser before, on or after Completion.

5. Where the Vendor is entitled to an indemnity from the Purchaser pursuant to Clause 4 the Vendor may at its entire discretion defend, settle or compromise any claim referred to within the said indemnity and the Purchaser shall on demand indemnify and hold harmless the Vendor against all claims, costs, demands, liabilities and expenses (including legal expenses on a full indemnity basis) arising out of or in connection with so doing.

Appendix 16

LETTER REQUESTING
MEASURES INFORMATION

[TO BE TYPED ON THE HEADED NOTEPAPER OF TRANSFEROR[1]]

[Name and address of transferee employer]

[Date]

Dear [Name]

PROPOSED SALE OF [   ]

I am the HR manager of [the Vendor] assigned to the project team working on the proposed sale of [   ]. I shall be dealing with the employment aspects of the proposed sale.

We are aware that we are required under the Transfer of Undertakings (Protection of Employment) Regulations 2006[2] ('TUPE') to pass on to the trade union representatives of our affected employees the information set out in Regulation 13(2) of TUPE, which includes information about the 'measures' to be taken by you in connection with the proposed sale.

As you may be aware, under Regulation 13(4) of TUPE, you – as the transferee – are obliged to give us as the transferor information about the 'measures' you intend to take in sufficient time to enable us to comply with our duty to pass on that information to trade union representatives and to allow time for proper consultation.

I should therefore be grateful if you would let me have in writing full details of the 'measures' you intend to take in relation to any of our current employees following the transfer, as soon as possible.

Yours etc.

---

1   The duty on the transferee employer to disclose to the transferor the proposed measures arises without the need for formal request. However, a letter in a form such as that above may be used to move the process forward. The form and substance of the measures information which will be disclosed may vary significantly from transaction to transaction.

2   SI 2006/246.

Appendix 17

LETTER TO EMPLOYEE REPRESENTATIVES

[TO BE TYPED ON THE HEADED NOTEPAPER OF THE TRANSFEROR]

[By Hand] or [By Post]

[Name and address of representative] or [Name of Trade Union and address of Head or Main Office]

[Date]

Dear [Name(s)]

Proposed Sale of the [   ] Division of [   ] to [   ]

The purpose of this letter is to advise you that we propose to sell our [   ] Division to [   ]. The sale would affect [description of affected employees] (the 'Affected Employees') and we are writing to you in the context of your role as a representative of [some or all of] those employees.

We believe that the Transfer of Undertakings (Protection of Employment) Regulations 2006[1] ('TUPE') will apply to the proposed transfer. As you will be aware, under Regulation 13 of TUPE we are obliged to provide certain information to appropriate representatives of any employees who may be affected by the proposed transfer or by measures taken in connection with it. In addition, in certain circumstances there is an obligation to consult with those representatives. The purpose of this letter is to provide the information which we are obliged to deliver to you.

Proposed Date and Reason for Transfer

- we propose to sell the [   ] Division to [   ].
- it is currently planned that the sale will be completed on [or about] [date].
- the reason for the sale is that we are seeking to channel our resources into our core businesses. The [   ] Division is not seen as one of our core businesses and it requires investment to develop the business which are not available to it within our current budget.

Legal, Economic and Social Implications

The proposed sale would affect [number and description of Affected Employees of the transferor] who are currently employed in the Division. It is anticipated that their employment will transfer to [the purchaser] under TUPE

---

1   SI 2006/246.

on their current terms of employment, save in respect of certain pension entitlements. Their period of continuous employment would be preserved. [Give details of any other legal implications for the transferor's affected employees.]

- The only economic implication of the proposed transfer which we envisage relates to the affected employees' membership of an occupational pension scheme. The affected employees will cease to be active members of the [   ] Pension Scheme at the date of transfer.
- [We do not envisage any social implications of the proposed transfer] OR [Give details of any social implications].

Measures Envisaged

- [We envisage taking the measures specified below] OR [We do not envisage taking any measures] in relation to the Affected Employees in connection with the proposed transfer.
- [Name of purchaser] has informed us that it [envisages taking the measures specified below] OR [does not envisage taking any measures in relation to the transferring employees in connection with the transfer].

[Insert details of the measures.]

[As no measures are envisaged in relation to the proposed sale, no consultation is required under TUPE. If that position changes, we shall let you know with a view to entering into consultations in relation to the same.] OR [We will be arranging to meet with all the appropriate representatives at the earliest opportunity to discuss the proposed transfer and to consult about the measures which we envisage taking in relation to our employees in connection with the proposed sale. The aim of this consultation will be to seek your agreement to those measures. I have arranged a meeting with all of the representatives for [Date, Time and Location], at which we will explain the proposals to you in more detail, outline our suggestions for the consultation programme and consider any initial representations that you wish to make on the proposed measures].

Please let me know if you have any queries.

Yours etc

Appendix 18

LETTER TO EMPLOYEE RE CONSULTATION PROCESS

[TO BE TYPED ON THE HEADED NOTEPAPER OF THE TRANSFEROR[1]]

[Name]

[Address of employee]

[Date]

Dear [Name of employee]

TRANSFER OF UNDERTAKINGS (PROTECTION OF EMPLOYMENT) REGULATIONS 2006[2] ('TUPE')

I am writing further to the meeting which took place on [date] to confirm the [Transferor]'s proposals in relation to the transfer of the service currently provided by the [Name of department] to [Name of new service provider].

We have been undertaking an analysis of our current operations and your role is one which has been identified as an in scope role and therefore one which will transfer across to [Name of new service provider].

The reason that your employment will transfer to [Name of new service provider] is that this transaction is covered by TUPE. It is proposed that this transfer will take place on or about [date].

In addition to ensuring that your contract of employment is transferred to [Name of new service provider] on completion, TUPE also provides that the representatives of all employees who may be affected by the transfer have the right to receive certain information and in many cases – of which this is one – there is also a requirement that consultation takes place with representatives.

Your representatives for this purpose are [Name of representatives] of the [Name of Union]. Their aim is to:

- meet with representatives of our management team;
- receive the information required by TUPE;

---

1   The information and consultation provisions of TUPE contemplate a collective process with the representatives of the employees rather than with the employees themselves. However, the employer may wish to produce information for the employees generally – this could be by letter similar to the draft set out above, by presentations, by bulletins or by an intranet site.

2   SI 2006/246.

- receive questions/comments regarding the proposals from you or the other employees; and
- answer questions if possible or to put them to us at the next consultation meeting.

Your continuity of employment will be preserved and it is not envisaged that there will be any changes to your terms of employment, save for changes specifically negotiated by [Name of new service provider] with [Name of Union].

Consultation will be on an ongoing process over the next [   ] weeks and we have put together a timetable which is being communicated to your representatives.

Of course, if you have any questions then you should not hesitate to contact [name] or alternatively you may wish to put them to your representative who will then feed them back to us during the information and consultation process.

Yours etc.

INDEX

References are to paragraph numbers and Appendices.